Dr Seán Patrick Donlan is currently
a Lecturer at the University of
Limerick. He has worked as a
contributor to the Dictionary of
Irish Biography project and has
written numerous articles on
Edmund Burke.

EDMUND BURKE'S IRISH IDENTITIES

EDMUND BURKE'S
IRISH IDENTITIES

Editor
SEÁN PATRICK DONLAN
University of Limerick

IRISH ACADEMIC PRESS
DUBLIN • PORTLAND, OR

First published in 2007 by
IRISH ACADEMIC PRESS
44 Northumberland Road, Dublin 4, Ireland

and in the United States of America by
IRISH ACADEMIC PRESS
c/o ISBS, Suite 300
920 NE 58th Avenue
Portland, Oregon 97213-3786

***Website*: www.iap.ie**

Individual Contributors © 2006
This edition © Irish Academic Press

British Library Cataloguing in Publication Data
An entry can be found on request

ISBN 0 7165 3365 0 (cloth)
ISBN 978 0 7165 3365 8
ISBN 0 7165 3385 5 (paper)
ISBN 978 0 7165 3385 6

Library of Congress Cataloging-in-Publication Data
An entry can be found on request

Printed by Biddles Ltd., King's Lynn, Norfolk

Contents

Notes on Contributors

Michael Brown is a Research Fellow at the Centre for Irish-Scottish Studies, Trinity College, Dublin. He is the author of *Francis Hutcheson in Dublin* (2002) and the current general editor of *Eighteenth-Century Ireland*, co-editor of *The Irish Act of Union: Bicentennial Essays* (2003) and *Converts and Conversion in Ireland, 1650–1850* (2005). He is currently writing a study of the Irish Enlightenment.

Helen Burke is an Associate Professor of English at Florida State University. She has published articles on eighteenth-century Irish and British drama and literature, and is the author of *Riotous Performances: The Struggle for Hegemony in the Irish Theatre, 1712–1784* (2003). She is currently working on a book manuscript that looks at the eighteenth-century Irish emigrant playwright in the context of the broader Irish diaspora.

L.M. Cullen is professor emeritus of modern Irish history, Trinity College, Dublin and visiting scholar, International Research Center for Japanese Studies, Kyoto, 2002–03. His research interests are in Irish and French, and more recently, Japanese history. His latest books are *The Brandy Trade of the Ancien Regime: Regional Specialisation in the Charente* (1998; French translation 2000); *The Irish Brandy Houses of Eighteenth-century France* (2000, French translation 2006), and *A History of Japan 1582–1941: Internal and External Worlds* (2003).

Seán Patrick Donlan lectures in law at the University of Limerick. He has edited a reprint of Francis Stoughton Sullivan, *Lectures on the Constitution and Laws of England* (2nd edn, 1776) and has published numerous articles on law, history and on Burke. He is currently researching the study of law in the late eighteenth century.

Michael J. Griffin teaches English literature at the University of Limerick. He has recently completed a book on Oliver Goldsmith, due for publication in 2007, and has also commenced work on an edition of late eighteenth-century Clare poet Thomas Dermody.

Dáire Keogh lectures in History at St Patrick's College, Drumcondra. He is currently researching a history of Edmund Rice (1762–1844) and the Irish Christian Brothers.

Elizabeth Lambert is Professor of English and holder of the Johnson Distinguished Teaching Chair in the Humanities at Gettysburg College (US). She is author of *Edmund Burke of Beaconsfield* and has published articles on various aspects of Burke's life and thought, including his religion, his friendship with Samuel Johnson, and the ways James Boswell's portrayal of Burke in the *Life of Johnson* was influenced by their personal relationship. Her future projects include biographical work on Gilbert Elliot and continued work on Burke's Nagle relatives.

F.P. Lock is Professor of English at Queen's University, Kingston, Canada. He is the editor of *Burke's Reflections on the Revolution in France* (1985) and has edited three collections of unpublished Burke letters for the English Historical Review (1997, 1999 and 2003). The first volume of his biography, *Edmund Burke*, covering 1730–84, appeared in 1999; the second, covering 1784–97, in 2006.

W. J. Mc Cormack is Librarian in Charge at the Edward Worth Library (1733), Dublin. He was formerly Professor of Literary History at Goldsmiths College, University of London, and head of the English department there. His most recent publication of eighteenth-century interest is *The Silence of Barbara Synge* (2003). *Blood Kindred; W.B. Yeats, His Politics and Death* appeared in 2005.

Katherine O'Donnell is Head of Women's Studies in the School of Social Justice at University College Dublin. Her publications include articles on the politics and speeches of Edmund Burke and co-editing (with Michael O'Rourke) *Love, Sex, Intimacy and Friendship Between Men, 1550–1800* (Palgrave, 2003) and *Queer Masculinities, 1550–1800* (Palgrave, 2005).

Eamon O'Flaherty lectures in History at University College, Dublin.

Tadgh O'Sullivan is currently Lecturer in Modern History at St Hugh's College, Oxford, and works on ideologies of improvement in late-eighteenth and early-nineteenth-century Ireland.

Nathan Wallace is Visiting Assistant Professor in the English Department of Union College, Schenectady, New York.

Acknowledgements

My thanks to all of those participating, but especially to Michael Brown and Michael Griffin for their advice, if not always consent. Thanks also to those unable to participate in the book, especially Richard Bourke, Seamus Deane, Michel Fuchs, Luke Gibbons, Seán Moore, Sean Murphy, Conor Cruise O'Brien and Kevin O'Neill. I am also grateful to the patience of Professor Paul McCutcheon and the School of Law at the University of Limerick and to the support of those involved in the *Burke Society of America/Newington-Cropsey Foundation* conference (Washington, DC: 21–22 November 2003) and the *American Conference for Irish Studies* (Notre Dame, IN – 13–18 April 2005). I wish to thank Lisa Hyde of Irish Academic Press for numerous kind and calming conversations.

Finally, I also want to thank my lovely wife Jenny: *Who can see and know such a creature, & not love to Distraction?*

Seán Patrick Donlan
August 2006

Abbreviations

Correspondence   T.W. Copeland (ed.), *The Correspondence of Edmund Burke* (Cambridge: Cambridge University Press, 1958–78, 10 vols).

Writings and speeches P. Langford (ed.), *The Writings and Speeches of Edmund Burke* (Oxford: Clarendon Press, 1981–, 9 vols).

1

Introduction

SEÁN PATRICK DONLAN

'Being born in a stable does not make one a horse.'
Arthur Wellesley (1769–1852), the first duke of Wellington,
on being called Irish.

THE PLACE OF HIS NATIVITY

For two centuries, the legacy of Edmund Burke has been hotly contested
and arguably distorted by opponents and apologists alike. The former incline to
caricature; the latter to hagiography. His writings and speeches appear almost
to demand that readers – as well as those who have never read him – adjudicate
on his views and values. Indeed, whether arguing against the age through Burke
or recruiting him to present causes, scholars have often infused interpretations
with their own personalities and prejudices. Perhaps such diverse readings
should not be surprising. Burke was, after all, an Irish-born British statesman,
a protestant of the established church with extensive links and sympathy to
Catholicism, a 'new man' (*novus homo*) who defended the modernity of
the British *ancien régime*, and a reforming Whig who vehemently opposed the
revolution in France and was adopted by latter-day political conservatives as a
result. There also exist over twenty modern volumes of Burke's collected writings, speeches and correspondence. But these numerous and varied texts were
written in complex, rapidly changing contexts and instead of proscribing our
interpretations to narrow limits, they invite all manner of special pleading.
While this complexity may not absolve commentators from reasonable eviden-
tiary demands and coherence, considerable interpretive liberties are predictable.

My intention in editing this volume was not to impose consensus on its
contributors, but simply to invite discussion of Burke's relationship to Ireland.
Those participating were intentionally drawn from numerous disciplines
and diverse viewpoints. In the pages that follow, there remain numerous 'Irish'
disagreements about: Burke's birthplace, his facility (if any) with the Irish
language, his (alleged) Jacobite sympathies, et cetera. At the core of these
differences is the character and importance of Burke's Irish inheritance. In a

speech on Irish commercial propositions, Burke's response to William Pitt was recorded:

> The Right Hon. Gentleman had thought proper to remind him, that he was a native of Ireland; it was true; and he conceived that much was due by every man to the place of his nativity, but this duty ought not to absorb every other; when another country was generous enough to receive a man into her bosom, and raise him from nothing, as this great country had raised him, to stations of the greatest honor and trust, and conferred on him the power of doing good to millions, – such a country had claims upon him not inferior to those of that which had given him birth; it was the duty of such a man to reconcile, if possible, the two duties; however should they unfortunately point different ways, it was his bounden duty, either to return the trust reposed to him by the adopting country, or else consider its interests as paramount to every other upon earth. – To consult the interests of England and Ireland, to unite and consolidate them in one, was a task which he would undertake, as that by which he could best discharge the duties he owed to both.[1]

Burke's reconciliation, both personal and political, of the duties to Ireland and Britain is at the centre of the articles that make up this collection.

Answering these questions is complicated by the unreliability of much of the information we have on both Burke and Ireland. Writing as a jurist and historian, I am acutely aware that the weighting of evidence is no simple process. Burke's texts, whether private correspondence or public commentary, require difficult choices to be made between literal and liberal interpretations and there are inevitably lacunae to be filled. And 'prejudice', as any student of Burke knows, is not inherently pejorative. Similarly, many contemporary approaches to the interpretation of texts stress the importance of 'constructive' prejudices and the impossibility of inquisitorial disengagement. In the Anglo-American legal world, justice, if not truth, is generally believed best secured by an adversarial process. In the articles collected here, the advocates of numerous positions on Burke and Ireland are given the opportunity to plead their causes. In discussing Irish history, Burke wrote that 'rational conjectures are more to be relied on than improbable relations'.[2] Judgement as to where we have gone beyond the pale of 'rational conjecture' is unavoidably left to the reader. If Burke's ideas on monarchy or custom do not *require* Irish sources, do the interpretations presented here make better sense of his life and thought? '*Affirmanti non neganti incumbit probatio*', as the lawyer might say: 'the burden of proof is upon him who affirms, not upon him who denies'.

THE HOLY WELL OF HIS INSPIRATION

No less than our own time, nineteenth-century writing on Burke and on Ireland reflected the conventions and interests of the period. There was, perhaps surprisingly, little specifically Irish about commentary on Burke for most of the century.[3] Matthew Arnold's publication of Burke's *Letters, Speeches and Tracts on Irish Affairs* (1881) was intended, in part, to consolidate English and Irish interests:

> Arnold managed to persuade himself and a considerable number of his readers that the dull and hard English could not, by virtue of the blighted middle-class nature, legislate effectively for the sanguine, vivacious and overly imaginative Irish. Although the argument for a separation between the two countries was implicit, Arnold refused it as vigorously as Burke would have done. Instead, he pleaded for a change in the English middle classes which would enable them to win over the Irish.[4]

Aside from political complications, Arnold's essentialist distinction between 'Teuton' and 'Celt' was but a variation on ancient themes. It was, and is, as often embraced by many Irish nationalists. But given editor and subject, Arnold's unproblematic use of 'English' for one 'by birth an Irishman' in the introduction of Burke's Irish writings is at least curious.[5] The complex, composite states of the old regimes allowed, arguably without modern anxieties about authenticity and alienation, nested identities and loyalties. Burke, of course, made a similar use of 'English' or 'Englishman'. As Jonathan Clark has recently written, 'a loyal Irishman', Burke 'could write of himself as " an Englishman" to indicate his second identity as a member of a larger polity where one might now expect him to use "British": nineteenth-century nationalism had not yet created its antagonisms.'[6]

Burke also played a small but not unimportant role in historical debates late in the century between J.A. Froude and W.E.H. Lecky. The work of both historians was presented in terms little different from earlier histories. Froude's *English in Ireland in the Eighteenth-century* (1872–74) was deeply critical of Ireland, especially its Catholicism, throughout suggesting the futility of conciliation with the Irish. Threatened with insult, the Anglo-Irish Lecky leaped to her defence. Contemporary concerns about the constitutional relationship between Britain and Ireland, about devolution and 'Home Rule', were no less present than in Arnold. A liberal Unionist and absentee landlord, Lecky's analysis (1892–96) owed much of its substance and spirit to Burke. For him, Burke

> urged the absolute necessity of blending the two great sections of the Irish people, the extreme danger as well as the extreme injustice of maintaining a system of permanent political monopoly, the certainty that such a system must one day break down, the danger of persuading the Catholics that their only hope of entering the Constitution was by the assistance of democratic dissenters.[7]

As he had for Arnold, Burke suggested for Lecky the necessity of repentance – though largely on England's part – and the possibility of reconciliation. The historian, perhaps confident in his own Irish protestant identity, would have had little difficulty comprehending Burke's complex relationship to faith and fatherland. And if Burke always saw Ireland joined to Britain, his views on political union are far from clear.

The diversity of 'Irish' interpretations was complicated still further by political developments early in the last century. Shortly after the creation of the Irish Free State, A.P.I. Samuels' *The Early Life Correspondence and Writings of the Rt. Hon. Edmund Burke* (1923) was published posthumously. Samuels was one of thousands of Irishmen of all backgrounds killed in the First World War fighting as members of British forces. The same period also saw the Easter Rising in Dublin and, through a sequence of events too complex to detail here, steps towards Irish independence. The work was introduced and supplemented by Samuels' father, a member of parliament and judge of the High Court of Justice in Ireland. In a paragraph that echoes Edmund Burke's loss of his own son, the elder Samuels wrote:

> The devoted generation of young Irishman, such as he, trained and educated like him, and with aspirations such as his, has been almost exterminated. Whether there was to be left any longer a place for such as they in their native land – is a question they have not had to solve. Perhaps this volume may be taken as some surviving service to his Country by one of them, who had tried in his time to serve her, and had hoped to serve her more.[8]

The work of the Samuels was a significant contribution to understanding Burke's early life in Ireland. More problematic was the contribution to the long-running debate on Burke's relationship to the Dublin politician, Charles Lucas (1713–71). Burke, the Samuels argued, 'was not the opponent but the supporter of the views advocated by Lucas'.[9] Given that Lucas' confrontational brand of patriotism has often been seen as anti-Catholic, this was not unimportant.

Very different views were expressed in the following years by the very different nationalisms of William O'Brien and William Butler Yeats. In *Edmund Burke as an Irishman* (1924), O'Brien enthusiastically claimed Burke to be 'the greatest Irish name in the history of Civilization'.[10] Nor was he simply, as for Arnold and many others, 'by birth an Irishman':

> English writers have accustomed even Irishmen to look upon Burke's native land as an unregarded corner of the stupendous prospect of world-wide realms, sun-kissed Alps and thunderous torrents over which his greatness range. It will be found quite otherwise, that in his own eyes Ireland was the spiritual home of one for whom associations of home constituted the bliss and the heaven of his life, that she was the Holy Well of his inspiration, the mother from whose veins he drew the special virtues

and blemishes of his Irish origin, whose charms enchanted him in childhood, and whose sufferings occupied his last thoughts and his last words
on the day on which he died.[11]

O'Brien's biography thus served, as he acknowledged, as a '*Mémoire pour
server*', placing Burke in the pantheon of nationalist or proto-nationalist heroes
of a politically and culturally independent Ireland.[12] But the author's uncritical
acceptance of oral history, early biographers, and ambiguous genealogical work
undermined his critique of England's claim on Burke. More superficially, Yeats
claimed Burke, without qualification, as one of the Ascendancy. Given Burke's
caustic critique of that phrase and the protestant interest, this was not a little surprising.[13]

Edmund Burke as an Irishman was the sort of history that soon became
unfashionable among the ranks of Ireland's professional historians. Historical
'revisionism' in British and Irish historiography reacted against teleological
English 'Whig' and Irish nationalist histories respectively. Thomas H.D.
Mahoney's *Edmund Burke and Ireland* (1960) was a far more critical work than
those of his predecessors. The American historian noted Burke's sympathy with,
and understanding of, Catholicism and Irish Catholics, but also underscored the
Irishman's 'great devotion to the British Empire'.[14] He also stressed Burke's
insistence on Catholic loyalty to the crown. Mahoney summarized by noting

> The persistency with which [Burke] hammered away over the years on
> such points as the following was as admirable as it was true: (1) the
> Catholics of Ireland were firmly attached to the monarchy; (2) there had
> always been an inequitable tendency to exaggerate Catholic participation
> in popular disturbances while neglecting at the same time mention of the
> fact that among the lower classes the Catholics formed an overwhelming
> majority; (3) the tendency to ascribe falsely to the Catholics the motive of
> zeal for their religion as the cause of their involvement in disorders rather
> than the true motivating force which was economic; (4) the palpable fal-
> sity of the charge that the Catholics were in league with foreign powers;
> (5) the baselessness of fear of the pope should the Catholics receive eman-
> cipation; and (6) the responsibility of the Ascendancy for the plight of the
> Catholics.[15]

With *Edmund Burke and Ireland*, it appeared possible to suggest that '[f]rom
the standpoint of information, there is no need for any more monographs'.[16]
Indeed, even with the publication of critical editions of Burke's correspondence
and writings and speeches, there has been little new information in the forty
years since Mahoney published.

Mahoney's recognition of Burke's Catholic sympathies and integration within empire remains the general consensus. Many allied with Irish 'revisionism'
have also emphasized the degree to which the intellectual, if not emotional,

context within which Burke worked was in significant respects 'English' or 'British'. Although Burke 'continued throughout life to take an active interest in the affairs of his native country', J.C. Beckett suggested:

> there is nothing national, let alone nationalist about the policies he advocated for Ireland. Indeed, if we are to describe Burke as in any sense a 'nationalist' than he was an English (or perhaps one should say British), rather than an Irish nationalist. Again, though it may be possible to find in his views on politics and society some elements that may reasonably be traced to his Irish background, his writings, taken as a whole, cannot be regarded as the product of a distinctly Irish culture.[17]

Without denying Irish influences and concerns, R.B. McDowell has presented a similar picture. While Burke's 'contact with the Irish Gaelic world may help to explain some of the distinctive features of his prose', he wrote, 'temperament rather than nationality may account for these qualities'.[18] With the notable exception of Louis Cullen, whose relationship to revisionism is particularly complex, few Irish historians have spent much time analysing Burke's Irish experiences and influences. 'Our understanding of Burke's writings', Cullen has written, 'suffers from the tendency of commentators – even recent Irish ones such as [Roy] Foster and Beckett – to consider him as Anglo-Irish or even virtually an Englishman'.[19]

Irish revisionism did not, however, go unchallenged.[20] Many were critical of the ostensibly neutral scholarship, untainted by contemporaneous issues and ideologies, that it seemed to suggest. Indeed, revisionism was criticized for being Anglocentric and conservative, simply mimicking British historiographical trends. But these and other contemporary Irish historiographical debates seem essential to the interpretation of Burke. Whether eighteenth-century Ireland is, for example, more accurately and usefully seen as an 'ancien régime' society on a common corporate and confessional European model, or as a 'colony', is perhaps of obvious relevance.[21] To these could be added a wide range of work on 'Britishness' and national identity in the eighteenth century. Historians have also continued to assess the proper balance of engagement and detachment in scholarship. Recently, bicentennial celebrations of the Irish rebellion of 1798 revived questions about the relationship of presentism, politics and scholarship to what was labelled 'commemorative' or 'commemorationist' history. '[W]hat gives one pause for thought', Roy Foster wrote:

> is the extent to which professional historians were involved in the repacking and alterations of emphasis. There seemed, in some quarters at least, to be an agreed agenda, which owed more to perceived late-twentieth-century needs than to a close reading of events and attitudes two hundred years ago.[22]

Even if one disagrees – and many do – with Foster's assessment in relation to 1798/1998, historians were again confronted with the apparent reclamation of the past for political purposes.

As Seán Connolly has written, the alternative to the view that 'Burke was a metropolitan author whose concern for Ireland faded once he had moved to England', was that of the politician and historian Conor Cruise O'Brien's *Great Melody* (1992).[23] Taking his title from Yeats, this 'great melody' was 'a profound inner harmony within Burke's writings and speeches on the four themes' of Ireland, America, India and France.[24] This was an Irish air and O'Brien laid great stress, as he had in an earlier introduction to the *Reflections*, on Burke's Irish identity and experiences. A robust and challenging work, it offers much of value to any student of Burke. The response to *The Great Melody* was, however, complicated in Ireland by O'Brien's own role in Irish public life. Much of the criticism of the work, both in Ireland and abroad, centred on questions of interpretive inference, most notably the insistence on the anxiety generated by Burke's Catholic inheritance.[25] O'Brien acknowledged

> In studying Burke, I have often found that, whenever there is an unexpected silence, a failure to refer to something obviously relevant, or a cryptically guarded formulation, the probable explanation is usually to be found at the 'Irish layer', the suspect and subterranean area of emotional access to the forbidden world of Catholicism.[26]

For some, this discovery of a 'hidden Burke' undermined O'Brien's other observations.[27] It should not, however, have surprised those familiar with Burke scholarship. As Colin Kidd has recently noted more generally, arguments from secret or concealed motives remain the stock-in-trade of Burke commentary. His influence is frequently 'approached … via spectral presences and post-Burkean silences'.[28]

Much modern commentary on both Burke and the Irish past comes from beyond the discipline of history. A dominant presence in the contemporary study of Burke and Ireland is the writer and critic Seamus Deane.[29] In a number of works, he has elaborated on Burke's Irish experiences and his defence of traditional authority and particularism. This defence was not simply an anachronistically 'conservative' or 'Counter-Enlightenment' reaction. Instead:

> Abstraction is the product of an extraordinary and perverted energy that manifests itself in symmetrically organised systems of power that are hostile to the native disorderliness and intricacies of human communities and their histories. This energy is encouraged in situations in which a monopoly of power is concentrated in the hands of a faction, sect, or cabal. Politically, such energy tends to characterise a new *arriveste* class, since established societies have an inertial force that gives them durability and checks or even stifles volatile and subversive movements. Obvious examples of such an

aspirant and urgent class would be the French Jacobins, Irish Protestants, and East India Company men in India.[30]

As this suggests for the Irish context, Burke's hostility was less directed at England than towards the Anglo-Irish – at least as Ascendancy – to which he also in some sense belonged. The complexity of Burke's national identity, especially in respect to the colonizing universalism of the Enlightenment and the revolution in France, is central to Deane's work. As he has recently written, 'Burke sought to reinforce ... national specificities without making a fetish of their provincial nature'.[31]

Deane is in the first rank of the wide variety of modern schools of thought that are engaged in the study of Burke from an Irish perspective. In the context of Irish history generally, Connolly has suggested that

> an emphasis on the divided character of Irish society is more marked among historians concerned with cultural and intellectual development than among those concerned with the practical workings of the economy, the land system or the criminal law. This could be taken as further evidence of the dangers of too heavy a reliance on the literary imagination; alternatively it reveals the ability of cultural studies to expose the tensions hidden beneath a superficially placid surface.[32]

A similar division may be evident in Burke scholarship between historians by discipline and those exploring the 'tensions hidden beneath' the public Burke. These post-moderns, literary theorists, post-colonial or 'post-nationalist' writers, and those engaged in 'Irish Studies' highlight – at least from the perspective of more traditional historiography – the promise and problem of interpretive inference. But if there must be some ground between an anxious empiricism and imaginative speculation, different standards may reasonably exist for different disciplines and traditions.

Although generally proponents of an 'Irish' Burke, such theorists are not of one mind either in their methods or conclusions. Terry Eagleton's commentary on Burke is perhaps the most overtly politicized and aestheticized. In this reading, Burke contrasts, not unproblematically, with the Enlightenment reification of human nature and culture. Others have emphasized Gaelic sources for Burke's thought and works. Declan Kiberd suggests that in response to British activities in India, 'Burke offered his plangent *caoineadh ar chéim síos na nuasal* (lament for fallen nobility)' and that in his literary portrait of Marie Antoinette, Burke 'cast himself in the role made familiar by a hundred *aisling* (vision) poems' of Gaelic tradition.[33] 'Colonial' and 'post-colonial' readings, often intersecting with these others, have become increasingly common. Among the best of these is Michel Fuchs' *Edmund Burke, Ireland, and the Fashioning of Self*. Fuchs concludes that Burke 'was a cultural cross-breed, and as such was rejected by both sides'.[34] T.O. McLoughlin's Burke is similarly divided. He has published a number of articles on Burke, especially on his early life. Collectively, these analyses have significantly expanded the avenues of inquiry available to Burke scholars.

Recently, Luke Gibbons' *Edmund Burke and Ireland: Aesthetics, Politics, and the Colonial Sublime* (2003) brought together a number of these ideas. But his work is perhaps the most radical reading of Burke's relationship to Ireland. '[N]ot the least of the ironies of Burke's colonial sublime', Gibbons writes

> is that, in an Irish context, its cultural logic led ultimately to the political project of the United Irishmen, the radical movement which sought to bring the revolutionary energies of America to bear on the political upheavals in Ireland in the 1790s. Transplanted from the venerable oak of the ancient constitution in Britain onto the tree of liberty in late eighteenth-century Ireland, Burke's concept of tradition – in this case, the subaltern culture of his Gaelic, Catholic background – bore fruit in a grafting of a radical strain of Romanticism onto Enlightenment thought.[35]

A stimulating collection of reflections on Burke and Ireland, the work has not gone uncriticized. Fred Lock wrote that the 'book is best understood as an attempt to re-conquer Burke for Ireland' and 'to capture Burke for post-colonialism'.[36] Gibbons' insistence that Burke advocated 'an aesthetics of intervention rather than of detachment' unnervingly mirrors his own historiographical method.[37]

BURKE'S IRISH IDENTITIES

As noted, many of the details of Burke's life remain disputed. This is especially true of his early years, the most difficult to document and the most critical for tracing Irish influences. His father was an attorney and belonged to the established church. Conor Cruise O'Brien and others have placed great emphasis on the possibility of his having only recently converted before Edmund's birth. It is agreed that Burke's mother remained a Catholic and raised her surviving daughter in that faith. The young Burke spent a significant amount of time with his maternal relatives of County Cork. With links to the old religion of the country, his experiences and education there have often been seen as important. Katherine O'Donnell, here and elsewhere, has argued that elements of Catholic and Gaelic royalist culture lie behind the political style and obsessions of the mature British statesman. In '"To Love the little Platoon": Edmund Burke's Jacobite Heritage', she argues that this heritage was

> the motivation for his political career which was fuelled by a desire to protect the riches of traditional culture and societies from the arrogance of greed and from persecution based on a hatred fuelled by myths, savage caricatures and colonial stereotypes.

Burke's experiences in Cork and, subsequently, in a Quaker preparatory school in Kildare certainly ensured that he was well-schooled in the confessional intricacies of Irish life.

Burke's education at Dublin's Trinity College and involvement in the Trinity 'Club' were also important. He appears to have been the driving force behind *The Reformer*, a successful, but short-lived, Dublin periodical. On the surface, the journal addressed questions of Irish trade, landlord absenteeism, and the contemporary Jacobite rising in Scotland. In 'Speaking from Behind the Scenes: Edmund Burke and the Lucasians, 1748–49', Helen Burke suggests that it was also part of a wider debate. Her namesake was engaged 'behind the scenes' in a complex campaign between the disposed and marginalized native gentry and the political ascendancy of protestant newcomers. Interceding in the continuing dispute about his relationship to Charles Lucas, she writes: '[i]n issues four through nine of *The Reformer*, Burke also articulated the gentry alternative to Lucas's populist patriotism'. Burke's connections to Trinity and Dublin did not end with his departure for London. In what was originally delivered as a speech at Trinity on the bicentenary of Burke's death, L.M. Cullen's 'Edmund Burke and Trinity College: Lifetime Ties and later College Commemoration' follows his continuing links with his Trinity contemporaries, the university itself, its academics and administrators. Most notably, he maintained long friendships and correspondence with John Hely-Hutchinson, Thomas Leland and John Monck Mason. 'The College', Cullen writes, 'was never far from Burke's thoughts'.

After his arrival in England, Burke seldom returned to Ireland. This is not to say he left the Irish behind. Elizabeth Lambert's 'Burke's Irish Connections in England' emphasizes both the importance of his tender years in Ireland, and the Irish associates in his adopted country. 'Like many of his fellow countrymen', she writes, '...Burke arrived in England wearing his Irish nationality as an unambiguous form of identity. Unlike many of them he did not play down his Irishness by taking elocution lessons to get rid of his brogue or strive to keep his relatives in a "decent obscurity"'. His acceptance of a position as personal secretary to William Hamilton, soon after Irish Chief Secretary, is noted by Lambert and several other contributors. The position involved him in the furore surrounding the 'Whiteboy' disturbances of rural Munster. During these years, Burke wrote or commenced numerous pieces. Most important for his subsequent reputation, and Irish historiography, was the 'Tracts relating to popery laws (c.1765)'. Though unpublished, different versions of the work circulated among the more progressive elements of Irish and British opinion. In 'The "genuine voice of its records and monuments"?: Edmund Burke's "interior history of Ireland"', Seán Patrick Donlan documents Burke's relationships with Irish historians and his engagement with contemporary Irish historiographical debates. If this 'interior history' 'was neither especially novel nor always accurate', he argues, 'concepts critical to Burke scholarship ... take on added significance in light of his Irish experiences and his views on its past'. Indeed, 'contextualizing him in this way may also assist in understanding the complex varieties of Irish and British identities in the eighteenth century'.

Having fallen out with Hamilton, Burke soon found himself working as personal secretary for Charles Watson Wentworth, Lord Rockingham, an important Whig politician. Shortly afterwards, he entered Parliament himself. Eamon O'Flaherty examines the degree to which Burke's views on the Irish constitution, on justice and sovereignty, were at odds with Irish protestant patriotism. This is especially true in his 'metropolitan, imperial perspective and a concern for Catholic rights rooted in his own personal experience and family connections'. Even in his most critical comments on Ascendancy, he wrote 'as an Anglican and a defender of the transcendent virtues of the British constitution which he saw as a universal benefit in his idea of empire'. Given Ascendancy dominance, the Westminister Parliament was perhaps the best place from which to exert pressure for Irish reforms. In 'Burke, Goldsmith, and the Irish Absentees', Michael Griffin explores the personal and political relationship between the two Irishmen. This is in many respects a study of their differences. Goldsmith's Jacobite-patriotism contrasts with the 'necessary compromises' of Burke's English politics. 'Goldsmith's major poems', Griffin argues, 'were consistently anti-imperial ... ideologically closer to the Burke of the *Reformer* than the Rockingham Burke'. In contrast, the judgement of Goldsmith was that Burke 'narrow'd his mind'.

For nearly twenty years, Burke was the chief ideological spokesman of the Rockingham Whigs. In 'Edmund Burke's Anglo-Irish Double Vision in *Thoughts on the Cause of the Present Discontents*', Nathan Wallace suggests that the work (1770) functioned beyond the public and political level for which it is generally recognized. The *Thoughts* also worked on a 'private level ... as a justification of and guide to ... Burke's own assimilation as an Irish new man, to the English imperial system'. This assimilation and rhetoric, Ciceronian with an Irish accent, 'does not mean denying the Englishness he so frequently claimed for himself'. Burke's involvement in Indian affairs, most notably in the Impeachment of Warren Hastings over the latter's actions as Governor-General of India, are often interpreted as drawing emotionally and intellectually from his Irish experiences. In 'Burke, Ireland and India: Reason, Rhetoric and Empire', Fred Lock argues that instead of seeing Burkean rhetoric as expressing 'emotional identification or submerged loyalties', his responses were essentially a 'rationally sustained distinction between the theory and practice of empire'. This is not, however, to deny the complexity of his identity:

A firm believer in monarchy, Burke could be highly critical of kings; an ardent supporter of aristocracy, he could satirize rogue aristocrats so mordantly as to be accused of Jacobinism; he was no less convinced an imperialist, though no one more savagely or persistently exposed the dismal actualities of empire.

The intellectual acknowledgment that imperialism carried moral obligations does not, however, make Burke anti-colonial.

The 1780s also exposed the internal Whig divisions between reformers and radicals that were to be exacerbated by the 'revolution in France'. The revolution, and Burke's response to it, were complex acts. The implications of both to Ireland were no less complicated. In 'Burke, Ireland and the Counter-revolution, 1791–1801', Tadhg O'Sullivan discusses 'Burkean' positions in Irish print culture that sought 'to defend legal, social and political proprieties against the Jacobin challenge, while also displaying a reluctance to identity with the Anglican *ancien régime*'. He argues that understanding these responses will begin to fill in significant historiographical gaps about the period in Ireland. That fact that 'Catholic and liberal anti-radical stances had a greater claim on Burkean authority than that available to Ascendancy loyalism' is no doubt also relevant to comprehending the English responses to Burke and revolution. Burke's counter-revolutionary activities did not, of course, detract from a continuing preoccupation with Irish affairs. This included correspondence with the Reverend Thomas Hussey, president of the Catholic seminary at Maynooth. Dáire Keogh's 'Thomas Hussey, Edmund Burke and the Irish Directory' traces their connection, primarily focusing on Burke's letter of 9 December 1796 to Hussey. As Keogh notes, Burke believed that the real threat to Ireland 'came not from the United Irishmen or the Defenders, but from this junto *within* the Castle'. It was this 'cabal' that 'were the real Jacobins of Ireland'. More generally, we are again faced with the apparent 'paradox of Burke: his opposition to reform in England, while advocating a radical reordering of society in Ireland'.

The complexity, if not paradox, of 'The National Identity of Edmund Burke' is the focus of Michael Brown's contribution. He argues for a middle ground between the inattention of many outside Ireland to Burke's Irish origins and contemporary Irish approaches. After examining what he refers to as the 'Gaelic', 'Catholic' and 'Post-colonial' theses and the multi-layer nature of identity in eighteenth-century Britain and Ireland, Brown writes that Burke is Irish 'but only in a limited and highly specific sense. To focus attention on this component of his identity can be rewarding, and informative, but care must always be taken to evade the temptress of reduction. Burke's national identity was multiple, polyphonic and integrative.' As has been seen throughout this introduction, Burke's Irish identity has been, and will likely remain, contested. The book's concluding essay, Bill Mc Cormack's 'Edmund Burke, Yeats and Leo Frobenius: "The State a tree"?' explores one of the more famous of Irish responses to, and appropriations of, Burke. Yeats' use of Burke, along with others like Jonathon Swift and Henry Grattan, '[t]o some extent ... signified the difficulties inherent in any conception of "protestant Ireland" for the eighteenth century'. Yeats' use or abuse of Burke was the invocation of this complex legacy. But, as Mc Cormack notes, '[t]he tendency to substitute a familiar code, where a different one is either present or required, could be taken as exemplary for readers of Edmund Burke. Too often he is pronounced one of *us*, and hence not one of *you*.'

IMAGINATION AND EMPATHY

While each of the contributors sees Burke's Irish inheritance as meaningful, there is a wide diversity of opinion on the precise borders of his identity.[38] This diversity of interpretation – Anglo-Irish, British, Catholic, Gaelic, Irish, Jacobite, Protestant – ought perhaps to be welcomed. Our apparently anglicized Irishman problematizes any simplifications of eighteenth-century *mentalités* in Britain and Ireland. It is precisely the difficulty in answering how Ireland matters to Burke that suggests that he must matter to the study of Ireland. That said, it is important that we be cautious in our use (or abuse) of Burke. A decade ago in the debates over Irish revisionism, Ciaran Brady suggested that

> the recognition that historians can never fully apprehend but must always imagine the very processes that give value to their work should not be disabling. Rather the acceptance that the assertions, dissensions and reappraisals that constitute historical discourse are necessarily incomplete and conditional validates an attitude toward the investigation of the fragments of the past that is at once critical, self-critical and available to endless modulation and qualification. Thus the most important demand to be made of historians as they undertake the representation of their research is not that they be a little more imaginative or emphatic – subjective and immeasurable desiderata which they have always attempted, with varying degrees of success, to satisfy. It is rather that they should be more humble.[39]

The variety of Burke commemoration and condemnation, both in Ireland and abroad, suggests that we be wary of excessive imagination and empathy. To reclaim Burke for Ireland, at least in any vulgar way, simplifies both. The failure to acknowledge our limitations may also mean that Burke continues to be held, as he has been so often by so many, a hostage to fashion.

NOTES

An earlier, condensed version of this introduction was read at the *American Conference for Irish Studies* (Notre Dame, IN: 13–18 April 2005). I am grateful to Michael Brown, Helen Burke, Luke Gibbons, Michael Griffin, Katherine O'Donnell and Nathan Wallace for their comments on the drafts or presentation of that paper. I remain responsible for all errors made and prejudices displayed.

1. E. Burke, *Writings and speeches*, vol.ix, p.590.
2. Ibid., vol.i, p.510.
3. But see C. McCormick, *Memoirs of the Right Honourable Edmund Burke* (London, printed by the author, 1797); J. Prior, *Memoir of the Life and Characters of Edmund Burke* (London, Baldwin, Cradock and Joy, 1824); J. Burke, *Speeches of the Rt. Hon. Edmund Burke with Memoirs and Historical Introduction* (Dublin: Duffy, 1853); T. MacKnight, *History of the Life and Times of Edmund Burke*, 3 vols (London: Chapman and Hall, 1858–60); J.B. Robertson, *Lectures on the Life, Writings, and Times of Edmund Burke* (London: John Philip, 1869).
4. S. Deane, 'Arnold, Burke and the Celts', in S. Deane, *Celtic Revivals: Essays in Modern Irish Literature 1880–1980* (London: Faber, 1985b), p.22. See also Deane's 'An example of tradition', *Crane Bag*, 3 (1979), pp.41–47.
5. M. Arnold, *Letters, Speeches and Tracts on Irish Affairs* (London: Macmillan, 1881), p.v.
6. J.C.D. Clark, 'Protestantism, Nationalism, and National Identity, 1660–1832', *The Historical*

Journal, 43 (2000), pp.249–76 at p.274. On Clark and Burke, see M. Brown, 'J.C.D. Clark's *Reflections* and Edmund Burke's Irish society', *20 Studies in Burke and His Time* (2005) (n.s.) pp.127–44.

7. W.E.H. Lecky, *A History of Ireland in the Eighteenth century* (London: Longmans, Green, and Co., 1913), vol.iii, pp.31–2.

8. A.P.I. Samuels, *The Early Life Correspondence and Writings of the Rt. Hon. Edmund Burke: with a transcript of the minute book of the debating 'Club' founded by him in the Trinity College, Dublin* (with an introduction and supplementary chapters on Burke's contributions to the *Reformer* and his part in the Lucas controversy, by the Rt. Hon. Arthur Warren Samuels) (Cambridge: Cambridge University Press, 1923), p.xi. Cf. the comments of Wolfe Tone to Tom Paine on Burke and the loss of his son cited in C.C. O'Brien, *The Great Melody: A Thematic Biography and Comment Anthology of Edmund Burke* (London: Sinclair-Stevenson, 1992), p.571, n.1, and subsequently in L. Gibbons, *Edmund Burke and Ireland: Aesthetics, Politics, and the Colonial Sublime* (Cambridge: Cambridge University Press, 2003), pp.237–8.

9. Ibid. For a similar modern view, see S. Murphy, 'Burke and Lucas: An Authorship Problem Re-examined', *Eighteenth-Century Ireland/Iris an dá chultúr*, 1 (1986), pp.143–56.

10. W. O'Brien, *Edmund Burke as an Irishman* (Dublin: M.H. Gill and Son, Ltd., 1924), p.vii.

11. Ibid., pp.ix–x.

12. Ibid., p.xiii.

13. W.J. McCormack, 'Edmund Burke and the Imagination of History', in W.J. McCormack, *From Burke to Beckett: Ascendancy, Tradition and Betrayal in Literary History* (Cork: Cork University Press, 1996), Chapter 2. pp.49–93. On the origins of the term, cf. J. Kelly, 'The Genesis of the Protestant Ascendancy', in G. O'Brien (ed.), *Parliament, Politics, and People: Essays in Eighteenth-century Irish History* (Dublin: Four Courts Press, 1989), pp.93–128 and 'Eighteenth-century Ascendancy: A Commentary', *Eighteenth-Century Ireland/Iris an dá chultúr*, 5 (1990), pp.173–88.

14. T.H.D. Mahoney, *Edmund Burke and Ireland* (Cambridge, MA: Harvard University Press, 1960), p.310.

15. Ibid.

16. C.B. Cone, 'Review of T.H.D. Mahoney, *Edmund Burke and Ireland*', *The William and Mary Quarterly* (3rd Ser.), 17, 4 (Oct 1960), pp.539–41 at p.541. Cone added that 'because some aspects of the Irish problem are controversial, there will doubtless continue to be disagreement about inter-pretations'. Ibid. A number of other Americans – James Conniff, Walter Love, John Weston – have made important contributions to the subject.

17. J.C. Beckett, 'Burke, Ireland and the Empire', in O. MacDonagh, W.F. Mandle and P. Travers (eds), *Irish Culture and Nationalism, 1750–1950* (London: Macmillan Press, 1983), pp.1–13, at p.1.

18. R.B. McDowell (ed.), 'Introduction' to Part II of E. Burke, *Writings and speeches*, vol.ix, p.391. Cf. Yeats' biographer and historian Roy Foster's Yeatsian claim that Burke 'forms with Swift and Berkeley the great intellectual triumvirate of Ascendancy culture'. Roy Foster, *Modern Ireland 1600–1972* (London: The Penguin Press, 1988), pp.174–5.

19. L.M. Cullen, 'Burke's Irish Views and Writings', in I. Crowe, *Edmund Burke: his Life and Legacy* (Dublin: Four Courts Press, 1997), pp.62–75, at p.62.

20. See C. Brady (ed.), *Interpreting Irish History: The Debate on Historical Revisionism 1938–1994* (Dublin: Irish Academic Press, 1994). See also D.G. Boyce and A. O'Day (eds), *The Making of Modern Irish History: Revisionism and the Revisionist Controversy* (London: Routledge, 1996) and K. Whelan, 'The Revisionist Debate in Ireland', *boundary* 2, 31 (2004), pp.179–205.

21. See Connolly, *Religion, Law and Power: The Making of Protestant Ireland* (Oxford: Clarendon Press, 1992); C.D.A. Leighton, *Catholicism in a Protestant Kingdom: A Study of the Ancien Régime* (New York: St Martin's Press, 1994); J. Hill, *Dublin Civic Politics and Irish Protestant Patriotism, 1660–1840* (Oxford: Clarendon Press, 1997).

22. R.F. Foster, 'Remembering 1798', in *The Irish Story: Telling Tales and Making it up in Ireland* (Oxford: Oxford University Press, 2002), p.228. Cf. T. Bartlett, 'Review of R.F. Foster, *The Irish Story*', *T.L.S.* (25 Jan. 2002). See also T. Dunne, 'Commemorationist History?', in *Rebellions: mem-oir, memory and 1798* (Dublin: The Lilliput Press, 2003) and the exchange between Dunne and K. Whelan in Whelan, 'Review of T. Dunne, *Rebellions*', *The Irish Times* (6 March 2004) and Dunne, Letter to the editors, *The Irish Times* (18 March 2004).

23. Connolly, 'Introduction: Varieties of Irish Political Thought', in Connolly (ed.), *Political Ideas in Eighteenth-century Ireland* (Dublin: Four Courts Press, 2000), p.11, n.2.

24. O'Brien, *The Great Melody*, p.xxv. The work was subsequently abridged by J. McCue as *Edmund Burke* (London: Sinclair-Stevenson, 1997a).

25. In an elaborate gloss on his text, O'Brien defended the use of 'fantasia'. 'We call great historians', he wrote, 'only those who not only are in full control of the factual evidence obtained by the use of the best critical methods available to them, but also possess the depth of imaginative insight that characterises great novelists.' O'Brien, *The Great Melody*, p.xxxi (citing a discussion of Giambattista Vico in Isaiah Berlin's *The Crooked Timber of Humanity: Chapters in the History of Ideas*). This may be about history *writing* rather than historiography. See L.M. Cullen, 'Review of C.C. O'Brien, *The Great Melody*', *Eighteenth-Century Ireland/Iris an dá chultúr*, 8 (1993a), p.152. Cf. T. Dunne, 'Unchained Melody', *Irish Review*, 13 (1992/93), pp.165–9.

26. O'Brien, *The Great Melody*, p.450.

27. The thinly veiled reference is to Daniel Corkery's influential *The Hidden Ireland: A Study of Gaelic Munster in the Eighteenth Century* (1927). The classic, still valuable, riposte of L.M. Cullen was republished with additional remarks as *The Hidden Ireland: Reassessment of a Concept* (Dublin: Lilliput Press, 1988) (originally published in *Studia Hibernica*, 9 [1968] pp.7–47).

28. C. Kidd, '"Beyond the Canon", Review of Connolly (ed.), *Political Ideas in Eighteenth-century Ireland* and J. Whale (ed.), *Edmund Burke's Reflections on the Revolution in France: New Interdisciplinary Essays* (Manchester: Manchester University Press, 2000)', in *Irish Review*, 28 (2001), pp.178–83, at p.179.

29. For brief comments on Conor Cruise O'Brien and Deane, Burke's 'protean availability' and the importance of 'linguistic issues' to Burke studies, see W.J. McCormack, 'Edmund Burke', in W.J. McCormack, *The Blackwell Companion to Modern Irish Culture* (Oxford: Blackwell, 1999), pp.86–9. See also R. Haslam, 'Ghost-colonial Ireland', *Bullán*, 5 (2000), pp.63–80.

30. S. Deane, 'Factions and Fictions: Burke, Colonialism and Revolution', *Bullán*, 4 (2000), pp.1–26.

31. S. Deane, *Foreign Affections: Essays on Edmund Burke* (Cork: 2005), p.2.

32. Connolly, 'Eighteenth-century Ireland: Colony or *ancien regime?*' in Boyce and O'Day, *The Making of Modern Irish History*, pp.15–33, at p.27.

33. D. Kiberd, *Inventing Ireland* (London: Jonathon Cape, 1995), p.18.

34. M. Fuchs, *Edmund Burke, Ireland, and the Fashioning of Self* (Oxford: Voltaire Foundation, 1996), p.311.

35. L. Gibbons, *Edmund Burke and Ireland*, p.xiii. '[T]he trope', Gibbons writes, 'of the injured body recurs as a national allegory of the plight of colonial Ireland in the eighteenth century'. Ibid., p.xii.

36. F.P. Lock, 'Review of Gibbons, *Edmund Burke and Ireland*', *Eighteenth-Century Ireland/Iris an dá chultúr*, 19 (2004), pp.211–16, at p.211. Cf. T. Bartlett, 'Brought to Burke: The Irish Experience of Colonialism Lies at the Heart of Edmund Burke's Thought', *Irish Times* (24 Jan. 2004).

37. Gibbons, *Edmund Burke and Ireland*, p.110.

38. There remain numerous topics not addressed here or only very lightly touched on, for example, the possible influence of Francis Hutcheson; the complex relationship of Burke's faith and fatherland; his Irish correspondence, perhaps especially Richard Shackleton and Charles O'Hara; his connections with Irish politicians, perhaps especially Henry Flood and Henry Grattan; his involvement (if any) in the writing of *Account of the European Settlements in America* (1758) and the implications of such involvement; Arthur Young's visits to Ireland; his views of political union. Readers may also be interested in reading C. Fabricant, 'Colonial Sublimities and Sublimations: Swift, Burke, and Ireland', *English Literary History*, 72 (2005), pp.309–37.

39. C. Brady, '"Constructive and Instrumental": The Dilemma of Ireland's first "New Historians"', in Brady (ed.), *Interpreting Irish History*, p.29.

2

'To Love the little Platoon': Edmund Burke's Jacobite Heritage

KATHERINE O'DONNELL

> To be attached to the subdivision, to love the little platoon we belong to in society, is the first principle (the germ as it were) of public affections. It is the first link in the series by which we proceed towards a love to our country, and to mankind.
>
> Edmund Burke, *Reflections on the Revolution in France*

It is one of the ironies of eighteenth-century studies that the marginal political figure of Edmund Burke (1730–97) holds such a central position.[1] Most of Burke's political career was spent in opposition, and even when the Whigs enjoyed a brief period in power, he never held a cabinet position. Moreover, he seemed to consistently support the least successful causes: at the beginning of his political career he advised the British Government to conciliate with the American Revolutionaries and argued for fair trade between Britain and Ireland. For some fourteen years Burke investigated the colonial crimes of the East India Tea Company, and he was the foremost prosecutor in the impeachment of Warren Hastings, the Governor General of India. He insisted that 'I know what I am doing, whether the white people like it or not', but prosecuting the man who had won India for the British doomed him to public odium.[2] Then, when 'Bliss it was in that dawn to be alive', he led the charge in denouncing the Revolution which proclaimed Equality, Freedom and Brotherhood to the world. However, Burke remains the focus of academic attention and one of the primary reasons why so many monographs and biographies continue to be written on him is that the potency of his speeches still arrests the emotions and attracts the intellect.[3]

Burke's speeches are wonderfully composed, but they are also deemed to be strange and curious, not only without precedent in British literature but also having a prophetic, prescient quality in describing events and realities which only later came to pass. Contemporary opinions on his speeches also register recognition of the strangeness of his compositions. He is credited with being one of the foremost orators in the history of the British Parliament, and yet, according to his first biographer, Bisset, 'the uncommon genius and eloquence of Burke' was often treated most disrespectfully by the members of the House of Commons who expressed loud disdain for what Bisset admits were his 'most violent expressions' in his crusading speeches against the East India Company. Matthew Arnold complains of his 'Asiatic style ... barbarously rich and over-loaded', and Sir Philip Magnus explains that Burke's Irishness allowed for an added impetus to the hooting and jeering which accompanied many of his speeches towards the end of his career: 'Burke spoke always with a pronounced brogue, which helped to emphasise his strangeness, and his gestures when he was on his feet were ungainly'.[4]

In his annotated bibliography of works on Burke, Conor Cruise O'Brien gives an example of one of the more gratuitously offensive depictions of the Irish Burke which were common currency until the publication of his cor-respondence, and echoes of which still survive today: 'If we regard his social origins, we can only classify as an Irish adventurer the great Edmund Burke, the theorist and the high priest of snobbery.'[5] There are many examples, even in his own lifetime, where he is depicted as the eighteenth-century theatrical stereo-type: the Irishman-on-the-make. The successful tagging of him as an 'Irish Adventurer' by those who wished to belittle or dismiss his achievements has perhaps led to the situation where many academics who found much to value in him chose to ignore his Irish nationality.

This troublesome Irish dimension of Burke, which Magnus says accentuated his 'strangeness', has only recently been used to provide a perspective on the apparent contradictions of his life and work. Cruise O'Brien reads his speech-es on America, India and France to show how his private preoccupation with Ireland ghosts those great public crusades, particularly his campaign to impeach Hastings. Seamus Deane argues that Burke's *Reflections on the Revolution in France* is a 'foundational text' in the canon of Anglo-Irish literature and can be read as 'generating the possibility' for a narrative of that great body of work which is Irish writing in English.[6] Most recently, Luke Gibbons shows how Burke's early aesthetic writings which are concerned with the dynamics of vio-lence, sympathy and pain, haunt the speeches of his political career.[7] Gibbons demonstrates that Burke's career is preoccupied with political terror, a terror of a kind witnessed by Burke first hand in the persecution of his extended family and other Irish Catholics by that 'Junto of Jobbers ... this new Idea of *Protestant* ascendancy'.[8] W.J. McCormack illustrates how Burke, claimed by Yeats to be one of the Protestant ascendancy, was in fact scathing of the self-styled Ascendancy.[9] While the *Reflections* gained international currency and Burke was publicly engaged in his crusade against the French Revolution, his letters to his son Richard and to Hercules Langrishe show him to be also committed to the liberation of the Irish Catholics from the oppressive rule of the Protestant interest, a commitment that complicates any simple depiction of him as a reactionary conservative.[10] The result of reading Burke's politics as those of a 'crypto-catholic' Irishman and reading his *Reflections* within the context of the Irish literary tradition is that he no longer is an 'ungainly', strange, confusing or confused British statesman, nor an Irish adventurer replete with violent oratory, but he is clearly a brilliant and unique eighteenth-century Irish orator, a product of his Gaelic Jacobite upbringing and his patriotic Irish education at Trinity College Dublin. An investigation of Burke's 'social origins' provides a backdrop that brings his political performance into sharp relief.

Burke's maternal family, the Nagles, was one of the greatest surviving Catholic families in eighteenth-century Ireland, having managed to escape the confiscation of property after the fall of the Stuarts at the Battle of the Boyne. Four branches of Nagles were settled in the Blackwater Valley of North Cork, an area still known as 'Nagle Country', and the leadership of the region's Gaelic Catholic interest remained in their hands for the first half of the eighteenth century. The survival, indeed the prosperity of minor Catholic families in the area, such as the Hennessys, depended on the security of the Nagles, who leased land to them on advantageous terms. The security of this Catholic enclave was strengthened by marriages to the Tipperary Catholic gentry. There was no other region in Munster or Leinster that had a comparable network of Catholic and nominally apostate, crypto-Catholic landowners. The affluent Catholic landowners of Galway are the only other group anywhere in Ireland to succeed in protecting the old Gaelic Catholic landed class under the restrictions of the Penal Laws and the encroachment of increasingly thriving middle-class interests. In the 1750s the Nagles married into this affluent Galway society and into the Catholic gentry of the Pale, achieving a position of influence and connection unequalled by any other Catholic family in Ireland.[11]

Paradoxically, the Nagles were surrounded by the largest Protestant gentry presence in the country. Breandán Ó Buachalla aptly describes the extended Nagle stronghold in the Blackwater as 'an island of Catholic hegemony in a sea of Protestant ascendancy'.[12] The heart of the Blackwater Valley is about six miles from Mallow, which was a large centre of English settlement in the eighteenth century, with sporting attractions and spa waters that drew many visitors. Within five miles of Mallow there were some fifty seats, including the large estates of the Brodericks and the Kings. Perhaps inevitably, the Nagles attracted the wrath of the ruling Protestants of the area and the bitter sectarian politics of Cork, which flared in the 1730s, 1750s and 1760s, were focused on the Nagles and their dependents. Joseph Nagle, who had been a lawyer before the 1704 proscription on Catholics entering the profession, was most astute in defending and maintaining both the local hegemony of the Nagle family and even in making interventions on behalf of the landed Catholic interest on a national scale. Burke's kinswoman, Nano Nagle, founder of the teaching order of Presentation Nuns (in flagrant disregard of the Penal Laws), wrote that her uncle Joseph was 'the most disliked by the Protestants of any Catholic in the kingdom'.[13]

Conversion to the Protestant religion and subsequent 'discoveries' by these converts of land illegally held by Catholics, became a routine part of conveyancing in eighteenth-century Ireland. It was in this context, Basil O'Connell argues, that Burke's father conformed to the state church in 1722, when he was named executor to the estates of two uncles, and because his father had converted before his sons were born, the young Burkes were considered Protestant. His mother remained a Catholic and, as was the custom at the time, his sister, Juliana, followed her mother's religion.[14] Kevin Whelan argues that these 'conversions' strengthened rather than weakened the Catholic position: prominent converts such as Anthony Malone, Lucius O'Brien and John Hely-Hutchinson could express their sympathy for Catholics in Parliament, and Edmund Burke must be understood in this tradition.[15]

F.P. Lock argues against thinking of Richard Burke as a convert but his arguments are not convincing. He claims that, 'At some point in Burke's public career, his enemies would have discovered [his father's conversion]. Instead of relying on gossip and innuendo about his Catholic background, they would gleefully have trumpeted such an authenticated matter of record.'[16] Burke's enemies did not need to authenticate Burke's Catholicism, they did not seek out proof of his parents' religion: the gossip and innuendo were lively enough to do sufficient damage to his status and credibility. According to Lock the strongest evidence for discounting Richard Burke's conversion comes from a statement by one of Burke's oldest friends, the Quaker Richard Shackleton, who describes Burke's father as 'a protestant ... more concerned to promote his Children's Interest in the world, than to trouble himself about controverted points of Religion; therefore brought his Sons up in the Profession of that which he thought the most publick road to preferment, the religion of the Country established by Law'. Lock's assertion that, 'From such a scrupulous witness, Shackleton's statement that "Richard was a protestant" must mean that he was born and brought up as one.'[17] Surely Shackleton's description of Burke's father describes more the pragmatic mentality of a convert faced with Penal Laws curtailing a myriad of opportunities: one who is untroubled by 'controverted points of Religion' and who '*therefore* brought his Sons up in the Profession of that which he thought the most publick road to preferment'.

Whatever about his father, Burke's association with Catholic Ireland ran deep: O'Connell argues that it is likely that he was born in his uncle James' house in the Nagle country at Shanballymore, in the townland of Ballywalter. James Nagle was married to a cousin of Burke's father.[18] When he was six the young Edmund went to live in the house where his mother grew up with the family of his uncle Patrick Nagle. The house in Shanballyduff was in the parish of Monanimy, near the village of Killavullen in the townland of Ballymacmoy, in the last region of Co. Cork in which a group of comfortable, propertied Catholics survived in the eighteenth century. He lived with his uncle until he was eleven, and, in one of those rare personal letters that have survived, remembered him with affection and respect:

> One of the very best men, I believe, that ever lived, of the clearest integrity, the most genuine principles of religion and virtue, the most cordial good-nature and benevolence that I ever knew or, I think, ever shall know

... for all the men I have seen in any situation I really think he is the person I should wish myself, or anyone I dearly loved, the most to resemble.[19]

Burke attended a hedge-school (an unlicensed academy that provided education for Gaelic Catholics in contravention of the Penal Laws) in Monanimy in the ruins of the great Nagle castle, where Edmund Spenser's son, Sylvanus, once married Eileen Nagle, one of the seven daughters of Burke's great-grandfather, David Nagle.[20] The hedge-school master was a Mr O'Halloran: Richard Hennessy, a year older than Edmund and later to establish the renowned Cognac house, was a classmate. Further instruction seems to have been supplied by the Jacobite poet Liam Inglis/English, who was the hedge-school master at nearby Castletownroche before he became an Augustinian friar in Cork city.[21]

The Nagle house at Ballyduff is still standing, situated high on a recessed slope of the Nagle Mountains. It is a typical seventeenth-century Gaelic style building: two storeys high, enclosing a cobbled courtyard, or Bawn, on three sides, with large buttresses and just a few narrow windows.[22] It is likely that Burke's own marriage came about through his association with the Blackwater Valley. He spent his early 20s based in England and did not complete his studies at the Middle Temple but spent about five years leading a dissolute life in the disreputable company of William Burke. William Burke was no immediate blood relation of Edmund's, though they both claimed they were kinsmen and they shared a common purse and home all their lives. Following a severe physical and psychological breakdown, Burke recovered at the home of Dr Nugent, an Irish Catholic physician, and subsequently married his daughter, Jane, in 1757. A few years later, Dr Nugent's son, John, married cousin Garret's daughter, Lucinda. Nagles and Nugents had been connected through marriage at least since the seventeenth century, when James Nagle of Annakissy married Honora Nugent of Aghanagh.[23]

The Nagles' Jacobite credentials were impeccable; Richard Nagle, head of the family in the 1680s, was advisor to King James in the War of the Two Kings; James had stayed at the Nagle castle while on his way to Dublin. (Burke could see the tops of the towers of this great Nagle house from the hedge-school at Monanimy.) Richard Nagle became the attorney general for the Jacobite government in Ireland, Speaker of the House in the Jacobite Parliament, and reputed author in 1689 of the famous act that sought to return to the original owners the lands confiscated and settled in the seventeenth century plantations. He followed James to France where he was Chief Secretary for Ireland at the court in St Germain.[24]

There is evidence that the Burke's paternal forebears were also at the centre of national political movements and were also supporters of the Stuarts. Burke's first biographer, Dr Robert Bisset quotes Burke's executor, French Laurence, as relating that Burke's ancestor's substantial estate in Limerick was confiscated during the Cromwellian period.[25] Another early biographer, Sir James Prior, also repeats the story about the confiscation of a large estate, and states that Burke's great-grandfather, John Burke, was Mayor of Limerick in 1646.[26] John Burke tried to garner support for Ormonde's attempt to make an alliance between the Gaelic forces inspired by Owen Roe O'Neill and the Old-English Royalists who supported the Stuarts. He followed Ormonde in believing that such an alliance was the only combination capable of overthrowing Cromwell and his Parliamentary Army. Mayor Burke read a proclamation from the Lord Lieutenant announcing friendship and toleration for Irish Catholics in the hope of rallying them to support King James. The Limerick citizens who supported O'Neill rose in fury at the suggestion of an alliance; they tore up the cobble stones and flung them at the city magistrates; the ensuing riot is still remembered in Limerick as 'Stony Thursday'.[27]

Burke's own father, Richard, is reported to have lived just over the county line in Bruff, Co. Limerick, though his marriage licence bond described him as 'of Shanballyduff', though this might imply a residency rather than birthplace.[28] He represented James Cotter, the son of the Jacobite commander, Sir James Cotter, at his trial.[29] L.M. Cullen describes Cotter's trial and subsequent hanging in 1720 as 'easily the most traumatic political event of the first half of the century in Ireland, having no parallel in the rest of Ireland'.[30] It is likely that Richard Burke got the task of providing counsel to Cotter through the connection of his wife's family to Cotter. Besides being a neighbour of the Nagles in the Blackwater Valley, Cotter was married to a sister of Garrett Nagle's wife; Garrett Nagle being brother to that 'most disliked' attorney Joseph Nagle. Lock states that: 'In 1719... a wave of anti-Jacobite hysteria had been prompted by a threatened invasion of England to restore the Pretender. To have worked for Cotter at such a time implies a degree of personal commitment to, or at least sympathy for, the Jacobite cause.'[31] Lock warns that we cannot be certain that the Richard Burke who was Cotter's agent was Edmund's father, but Gibbons has recently produced evidence of a notice in the *Corke Journal* of 30 May 1757 which shows Burke's father dealing with the estate of the recently deceased Joseph Nagle, thus definitively linking Burke's father to the Cotter circle.[32] After Cotter's execution the Nagles and their dependents came under enormous pressure from the politicised Protestants of North Cork: Joseph had to battle with the Penal laws to retain his estates and alleged Jacobite conspiracies were again used to terrorise the Nagles and Hennessys in 1731–32 and 1733.[33]

Cullen states that it was the haunting memory of the trial and execution of Cotter, recollected by both Protestants and Catholics, that was 'the spark which set alight the sectarian tensions in Munster in the early 1760s.'[34] Cullen provides fascinating detail of Edmund Burke's crucial work on behalf of his relatives and other Munster Gaelic Catholics who were being prosecuted as Whiteboys in the 1760s.[35] Burke's political manoeuvring and legal intervention was too late to save his distant relatives, Fr Nicholas Sheehy and Edmund Sheehy, from being hanged but he managed to save many other lives.[36] Whelan finds it remarkable that political involvement of the old Gaelic and Anglo-Norman families such as the Nagles and Burkes can be traced, almost as an inheritance, through so many movements: from Jacobite to Catholic Committee to the United Irishmen, to the O'Connell and the Tithe agitations and on to the Young Irelanders.[37] In the words of Roy Foster: 'Family alliances from the early eighteenth century often provide the subtext to political associations in later generations.'[38] We can see Edmund and his own son Richard, who worked on behalf of the Catholic Committee, continuing this family tradition of political involvement.[39]

Whelan describes how the old Catholic gentry families such as the Nagles 'enjoyed immense social prestige, especially in areas distant from Dublin, where the tendency persisted to regard personal and territorial claims as more legitimate than impersonal state ones'.[40] According to Foster, 'deference was as influential as dependence', and 'geography, tradition, kinship, [and] gratitude' were instrumental in establishing and maintaining gentry status and power in eighteenth-century Ireland.[41] Burke's own correspondence reveals his deferential attitude to the Catholic nobleman, Lord Kenmare, owner of a vast estate in Kerry, in his efforts to secure the social and political position of the Nagles. He is constantly recommending his Nagle cousins to the protection of Lord Kenmare and thanking him for favours shown to the Nagles.

While Burke lived in North Cork the Nagles performed their role as Gaelic gentry, sponsoring music and poetry, dispensing profuse hospitality, and patronizing popular sports such as hunting, horse-racing, hurling and cock-fighting. In the 1760s the last great Irish-language poet of eighteenth-century Ireland, Eoghan Rua Ó Suilleabháin, was tutor to the Annakissy Nagles. When Charles Fox visited Burke's cousin Garret at his lodge in Killarney in 1777, Burke teased Garret: 'You are now become a man of the Lough; and must be admitted to be the true *Garroit Iarla*, who is come at last.' The reference is to Garrett Fitzgerald, 3rd Earl of Desmond who according to legend was sleeping beneath Lough Gur and would one day rise. Burke was delighted when Fox reported that 'the old spirit and character of the country is fully kept up which rejoices me beyond measure'.[42] He was eager to assure Garret that Fox was one of the first men in England and even if he did not think much of Fox on first meeting him, he was sure he would like him very much on further acquaintance. Burke's assurances to this member of the obscure Gaelic Munster Catholic gentry might appear remarkable but it must be remembered that the Nagles were very conscious of their own aristocratic heritage and were also more accustomed to looking towards France rather than England for aristocratic counterparts.

A month previously, in another letter to Garret, which had been concerned mainly with farming matters, Burke expressed his grief 'that the old stock [of the Gaelic gentry] is wearing out. God send that their successors may be better.' He assures Garret 'that nothing can do you all so much good, as keeping up your old union and intercourse, and considering yourselves as one family. This is the old burthen of my song. It will answer infallibly, at one time, or in one way or

other.'[43] As the eighteenth century progressed, middlemen and mercantile interests increasingly undermined the status of the Gaelic gentry, and they slowly
withdrew from their role as patrons of Gaelic culture. Burke was acutely aware
of this phenomenon, and in a letter to his son Richard in 1792, he warns him that
the Blackwater Nagles who are still alive 'and not quite ruined there', must not
'show [him] any honours, in the way, which in old times was not unusual with
them, but which since are passed away'.[44] He is fearful that the 'mischievous'
newspapers would pick up on the traditional Gaelic celebrations which might be
occasioned by Richard's visit to the area. Being so clearly associated with such
old-style neo-Jacobite Catholics could unsettle the young man's position as
secretary for the Catholic Committee in delicate negotiations on repeal of the
Penal Laws. This particular letter to Richard is full of his memories of past
oppression and Protestant conspiracies. He urges Richard to collect more
evidence for discrediting the Protestant version of that 'pretended Massacre in
1641' and to inquire (discreetly, of course) into the 'shameful rage in Munster'
in the 1760s. He asks Richard to give money to two daughters of his beloved
uncle, Patrick Nagle, 'without any other reference to me, than that you know
how much I loved them'. He tells Richard that:

> I have long been uneasy in my Mind when I consider the early obliga-
> tions, strong as debts, and stronger than some Debts, to some of my own
> family – now advanced in Life, and fallen, I believe, into Great Penury.
> Mrs. Crotty is daughter of Patrick Nagle, to whom (the father) I cannot
> now tell you all I owe; she has had me a child in her arms.

The cryptic phrase 'I cannot now tell you all I owe', points to Burke's secret
debt to the once vibrant outpost of the Catholic gentry.

In tandem with the demise of the old-style Catholic gentry class which was
gradually submerged during the long eighteenth century by the interests of
middlemen farmers and the developing mercantile sector, Irish and the closely
related Scots Gaelic also declined as the languages spoken by the vast majority in Ireland and Scotland. However, in 1726, just three years before Burke was
born, there were at least twenty-six Irish language scholars and composers
working in Dublin, the most Anglicized part of Ireland.[45] In the Munster
province of his boyhood and the western province of Connaught where his
sister settled, Irish remained the dominant language throughout the eighteenth
century. In 1731, two-thirds of the entire population used Irish as their first language and two years after he died, in 1799, about half spoke Irish for everyday
use and conversation.[46] Over 90 per cent of the population still spoke Irish in
North Cork as late as 1781.[47] Even by the end of the century, Irish was still the
predominant language in that region. In his book, *Travels in Ireland*, Edward
Wakefield says that in 1812 'The Irish was so much spoken by the common
people of Cork city and its neighbourhood, that an Englishman was apt to
forget where he was; and to consider himself in a foreign city.' In his memoir,

Mo Scéal Féin, Fr O'Leary says that when he was curate in Bweeng, in the Ballyhouras, in 1868, Irish was still the spoken language of most of his parishioners and of the majority of the people in the townlands along the Blackwater. Even in the early twentieth century, in 1906, when a Gaelic League organiser visited the Mallow area he found that Irish had lingered on with a few of the older generation in remote places.[48]

According to Bisset, Burke was still fluent in Irish after many years of living in England. Bisset describes Burke's visit to the Scottish Highlands in 1785 and says that near Inverary Burke and his companion, William Windham, met with a local celebrity, Dr McIntyre: 'Burke who understood the Gaelic, spoke to Dr McIntyre in that tongue. He was answered in Erse; and they understood each other in many instances, from the similarity of these two dialects of the ancient Celtic.'[49] R.B. McDowell speculates that Burke knew Irish but cannot come to any definitive statement as to his fluency.[50] However, Burke's library provides us with the most direct evidence of his preoccupation with the Irish language: he had a copy of *The Catechism in Irish and English* published in Paris in 1742, *Tracts relative to the Celtic Language* by Cleland, and the *Irish-English, English-Irish Dictionary* published in Paris in 1768 (which was the work of Conor Begley and Hugh Mac Curtin). This dictionary is one of the very few books in which he made annotations. Burke collected Irish manuscripts and did much to encourage the use of Irish language sources in the writing of Irish history. He arranged that Charles O'Conor of Belanagare (the model for Lady Morgan's 'Prince of Coolavin' in *The Wild Irish Girl*) was granted access to Trinity College's library, he encouraged Vallency to publish Irish annals in the original and with translations, and he persuaded Sebright to donate the Irish manuscripts which he had bought from Lhuyd to the library at Trinity College. These invaluable texts became the basis of Trinity College's Irish manuscript collection.[51]

While at Trinity, Burke admitted to Dick Shackleton that he was gripped by a '*furor historicus*' and for the rest of his life he maintained a keen interest in Irish history and historiography. His library contained all the Irish histories written by those who supported the Gaelic cause, including O'Halloran, Vallency, Curry and O'Flaherty. He had Campbell's *Ecclesiastical and Literary History of Ireland*, a copy of Lhwyd's *Archaelogia Britannica*, and *Histoire Monastigue d'Irelande* published in Paris in 1690, as well as many other publications and manuscripts which were of direct Irish historical and topographical interest, including Beaufort's 1792 *Memoir of a Map of Ireland* with handwritten annotatations by Burke.[52] He had a number of famous Jacobite trails in his collection including the trail of Oliver Plunkett, but it was the rebellion of the Irish Jacobites in 1641 that was the prime focus of Burke's historical interest. He was adamant that the insurrection of 1641 was not a rebellion against government but was a display of loyalty to the Royal House of Stuart who were the rightful Kings of England but who had been temporarily deposed by the disloyal Puritans. Bisset gives a long and entertaining account of Burke's quarrel with Hume on this matter. Bisset is unsympathetic to Burke's position: 'The genius, wisdom and learning of Burke did not prevent him from entertaining some opinions totally unfounded ... He most strenuously denied the Irish massacre.' In arguing with Hume, Burke affirmed that on the banks of the Shannon, thousands of Irish people had witnessed the ghosts of numbers of Catholics who had been killed and thrown into the river. Bisset reports that Burke could not speak on 'the Irish massacre' without being 'transported into a rage'.[53]

The Catholic, Gaelic, Royalist gentry world of Burke's youth in North Cork was a vibrant culture of oral performance and scribal activity. Elsewhere I have examined at length this Gaelic cultural substratum to Burke's political positions and the style of his political interventions, making comparisons between eighteenth-century Cork and Kerry Irish compositions and some of his famous speeches to demonstrate how he shares in their political assumptions and stylistic traditions.[54] Burke's political career has been characterized as a long defence of traditional societies. He argued for conciliation with the Americans because Britain had broken the long established contract with the colonists. India, according to Burke, had a culture more ancient and venerable than anything in Britain and should be honoured as such, and he deplored the French revolutionists who were destroying their inheritance for the sake of ideals. In seeing Edmund Burke among the faded remnants of Catholic, Gaelic, Royalist gentry stock, we can see the motivation for his political career which was fuelled by a desire to protect the riches of traditional culture and societies from the arrogance of greed and from persecution based on a hatred fuelled by myths, savage caricatures and colonial stereotypes.

NOTES

1. I follow Burke's early biographers and in particular one of his most recent biographers, F.P. Lock, *Edmund Burke: Volume I, 1730–1784* (Oxford: Clarendon Press, 1998), pp.16–17 who persuasively argues that Burke was born on 12 January 1730 and not in the year 1729, the year that has been often ascribed as Burke's year of birth.
2. 19 January 1786 to Mary Palmer, niece and favourite of Sir Joshua Reynolds. *Correspondence*, vol.v, p.252.
3. Burke was the sixth most caricatured person in the Hanoverian era. Nicholas Robinson, *Burke: A Life in Caricature* (New Haven: Yale University Press, 1996).
4. Sir Philip Magnus, *Edmund Burke: A Prophet of the Eighteenth Century* (London: John Murray, 1939), p.77.
5. Quoted by Conor Cruise O'Brien, *The Great Melody* (London: Minerva, 1993), p.xlix.
6. Seamus Deane, *Strange Country: Modernity and Nationhood in Irish Writing since 1790* (Oxford: Clarendon Press, 1997), p.1.
7. Luke Gibbons, *Edmund Burke and Ireland* (Cambridge: Cambridge University Press, 2003).
8. *Correspondence,* vol.vii, pp.290–4.
9. W. J. McCormack, *From Burke to Beckett: Ascendancy, Tradition and Betrayal in Literary History* (Cork: Cork University Press, 1994).
10. Burke's candid, private letters to Richard were often sent care of Frank Kiernan in the Dublin Custom House. Burke feared interception by Dublin Castle. See, in particular, letters from Edmund to Richard: *Correspondence*, vol.vii (Jan.–March 1792), pp.8–12, 15–17, 29–31, 40–1, 48–50, 64–7, 80–4, 100–107, 118–20; (Nov. 1792), pp.280–8, 289–93, 298–301. See also *Writings and speeches*, vol.ix and Thomas H.D. Mahoney, *Edmund Burke and Ireland* (Cambridge MA: Harvard University Press, 1960).
11. Burke's sister Juliana (also Julia) married Pat French of Loughrea in 1766. L.M. Cullen, 'The

Blackwater Catholics and County Cork Society and Politics in the Eighteenth Century', in Patrick O'Flanagan and Cornelius G. Buttimer (eds), *Cork History and Society* (Dublin: Geography Publications, 1993b), p.541.

12. Breandán Ó Buachalla, 'A Cork Jacobite', in O'Flanagan and Buttimer (eds), *Cork History and Society*, p.472.
13. Quoted by Cullen, 'The Blackwater Catholics', p.559.
14. Basil O'Connell, *Edmund Burke (1729–1797): A Basis for a Pedigree*. Reprinted from *Journal of Cork Historical and Archaeological Society*, 61 (1956), pp.72–3.
15. Kevin Whelan, *The Tree of Liberty: Radicalism, Catholicism and the Construction of Irish Identity 1760–1830* (Cork: Cork University Press in association with Field Day, 1996), p.6.
16. Lock, *Edmund Burke*, p.5.
17. Ibid., p.6.
18. O'Connell, *Edmund Burke*, p.119.
19. *Correspondence*, vol.i, p.346. It is tempting to speculate that it was Patrick Nagle who inspired Burke's observation that: 'The authority of a father ... hinders us from having that entire love for him that we have for our mothers, where the parental authority is almost melted down into the mother's fondness and indulgence. But we generally have a great love for our grandfathers, in whom this authority is removed a degree from us, and where the weakness of age mellows it into something of a feminine partiality.' *A Philosophical Enquiry Into the Origin of Our Ideas of the Sublime And Beautiful*, III.x.
20. William O'Brien says he was better known as 'Sylvy': W. O'Brien, *Edmund Burke as an Irishman* (Dublin: M.H. Gill, 1924), pp.17ff.
21. See also: Eamon Ó Ciardha, 'A Voice from the Jacobite Underground: Liam Inglis (1709–1778)', in Gerard Moran (ed.), *Radical Irish Priests 1660–1970* (Dublin: Four Courts Press, 1998); Cornelius G. Buttimer, 'Gaelic Literature and Contemporary Life in Cork, 1700–1840,' in O'Flanagan and Buttimer (eds), *Cork History and Society*; and Risteárd O´Foghludha, *Cois na Bríde: Liam Inglis* (Baile Átha Cliath: Oifig Díolta Foillseacháin Rialtais, 1937).
22. Half of the house was still inhabited by a family named Barry until 1991. This information was provided by the farmer, Mrs Barry, who lives in Ballyduff Lodge. Conversation, July 1997.
23. Cullen, 'The Blackwater Catholics', p.553 and Basil O'Connell, *The Nagles of Annakissy*, Reprinted from *The Irish Genealogist*, 2, 11, p.1.
24. O'Brien, *Edmund Burke as an Irishman*, p.20.
25. Robert Bisset, *The Life of Edmund Burke, Comprehending an Impartial Account of his Literary and political Efforts and a Sketch of the Conduct and Character of his Associates, Coadjutors and Opponents* (London: George Cawthorn, 1798), p.39.
26. James Prior, *Memoir of the Life and Character of the Right Honourable Edmund Burke with Specimens of his Poetry and an estimate of His Genius and Talents Compared with Those of His Contemporaries* (London: Baldwin, Craddock & Joy, 2nd edition, 1826), pp.3–5. The second edition of 1826 is much more substantial than the first (1824) or revised fifth edition.
27. O'Brien, *Edmund Burke as an Irishman*, p.3.
28. O'Connell refers to a tradition that Richard Burke was born in Bruff, and Bisset, *The Life of Edmund Burke*, p.18 and Peter Burke, *The Public and Domestic Life of the Right Hon. Edmund Burke* (London : Ingram, Cooke, 1853 – The National Illustrated library, vol.31), p.3, both state that he lived, at least for a period of time, in Limerick.
29. W. Hogan and Seán Ó Buachalla, 'James Cotter's Papers', *Cork Historical and Archaeological Society Journal*, 68 (1963), pp.71–95. Among James Cotter's Papers we have a letter from him to a Nugent cousin, which might prove to be a further intriguing connection between Cotter and Burke if this Nugent should prove to be a forebear of Jane who married Burke.
30. L.M. Cullen, *Emergence of Modern Ireland*, p.199. See also F.J. Froude, *The English in Ireland* (London: 1881), pp.432–3.
31. Lock, *Edmund Burke*, p.7.
32. Gibbons, *Edmund Burke and Ireland*, p.24.
33. Cullen, 'The Blackwater Catholics', pp.535–48.
34. Cullen, *Emergence of Modern Ireland*, p.200.
35. Cullen, 'The Blackwater Catholics', pp.561–73.
36. See also Gibbons, *Edmund Burke and Ireland*, pp.21–3.
37. Whelan, *The Tree of Liberty*, p.18.
38. Roy Foster, *Modern Ireland: 1600–1972* (London: Penguin, 1988), p.232. See also Breandán Ó Buachalla, 'Irish Jacobite Poetry,' *The Irish Review*, 12 (Spring\Summer 1992), pp.40–9 for a discussion of how Gaelic Jacobite poetry employed the traditional literary mode of describing the king as spouse of Ireland to impart innovatory political messages.

39. Richard went to Ireland in 1791 to act as agent to the Committee which occasioned a series of let-ters from Burke remarkable for their testimony to Burke's loathing of the Protestant Ascendancy and sympathetic understanding of the attraction of the French Revolution for Irish Catholics. Burke's candid, passionate letters to Richard were often sent care of Frank Kiernan in the Dublin Custom House. Burke feared interception by Dublin Castle. See in particular, letters from Edmund to Richard: *Correspondence*, vol.vii (Jan.–March 1792), pp.8–12, 15–17, 29–31, 40–1, 48–50, 64–7, 80–4, 100–107, 118–20; (Nov. 1792), pp.280–8, 289–93, 298–301.

40. Whelan, *The Tree of Liberty*, p.15.

41. Foster, *Modern Ireland: 1600–1972*, p.236.

42. *Correspondence*, vol.iii, pp.391–2.

43. Ibid., pp.371–2.

44. Ibid., vol.vii, pp.102–6.

45. Breandán Ó Buachalla, 'Seacaibíteachas Thaidhg Uí Neachtain,' *Studia Hibernica*, 26 (1991–92).

46. That is 1,340,808 Gaelic speakers in 1731 from a population of 2,011,219 and 2,400,000 speakers in 1799 from a population of 4.75 million. See Brian Ó Cuív, 'Irish Language and Literature: 1691–1845', in T.W. Moody and W.E. Vaughan (eds), *A New History of Ireland* (Oxford: Clarendon Press, 1986), vol.4, p.383 and *Irish Dialects and Irish–Speaking Districts* (Dublin: Institute for Advanced Studies, 1951), p.19.

47. Garret Fitzgerald, 'The Decline of the Irish Language 1771–1871', in Daly and Dickson (eds), *Origins of Popular Literacy in Ireland* (Dublin: 1990), p.70.

48. Quoted by John J. Kavanagh, 'Kilshannig – The Changing Times', *Mallow Field Club Journal*, (1990), pp.89–90.

49. Bisset, *The Life of Edmund Burke*, pp.447–8.

50. *Writings and Speeches*, vol.ix, p.391.

51. William B. Todd, *Bibliography of Burke* (Godalming, Surrey: St Paul's Bibliographies, 1982), p.273 and William O'Sullivan, 'The Irish Manuscripts in Case H in TCD', *Celtica*, 11 (1976), pp.229–50.

52. Burke also had a two volume manuscript entitled *A List of Payments to be made for Civil Affairs, to begin from the first day of April, 1684*, tracts in reply to the treasury Pamphlet on Irish Trade; a *Letter from an Irishman on the proposed System of Commerce* 2 vol. in 1, with a few (rare for Burke) MS corrections; *Proceedings upon the Claims to the titles of Viscount Valentia* bound in red moroc-co, Dublin, 1773; the *Collection of Protests* from 1737, which are protests by the Protestant interest in Ireland against various measures proposed by the English administration, including the Drapier's letters and an intriguingly titled *Munsteri Cosmographia Universalis* with woodcuts published in Basil in 1559. Burke was also well versed in the work of Keating, see *Correspondence*, vol.v, pp.208–9.

53. Bisset also reports that Burke never forgave Hume for making it known that it was to Burke that he was alluding in his *History of England* when he wrote about the 'Irish Catholic, who denies the mas-sacre in 1641'. According to Hume, this Irish Catholic, was like the English Whig who believes in the Popish plot, and the Scots Jacobite who believes in the innocence of Queen Mary: they are all 'party men' and should be considered as 'men beyond the reach of argument, and must be left to their own prejudices'. Bisset, *The Life of Edmund Burke*, pp.195–7.

54. Katherine O'Donnell, 'Edmund Burke and the Heritage of Oral Culture' (Ph.D. Dissertation, National University of Ireland, 2000); '"Whether the White People Like It or Not": Edmund Burke's Speeches on India', *Éire-Ireland: An Interdisciplinary Journal of Irish Studies*, 37, 3–4 (Fall/Winter 2002), pp.187–206; 'The Image of a Relation in Blood: *Párliament na mBan* & Burke's Jacobite Politics', *Eighteenth-Century Ireland: Iris an Dá Chultúr*, 15 (2000), pp.98–119.

3

Speaking from behind the Scenes: Edmund Burke and the Lucasians, 1748–49

HELEN BURKE

> Observe, the Audience is in Pain,
> While *Punch* is hid behind the Scene,
> But when they hear his rusty Voice,
> With what Impatience they rejoice.
>   Swift, 'Mad Mullinex and Timothy' (1728)

In a letter that he wrote to Richard Shackleton on 14 January 1748, William Dennis made the following excited announcement about an upcoming 'war' that he and his two Trinity College friends, Edmund Burke and Beaumont Brenan, were planning to wage on the Theatre Royal and its manager, Thomas Sheridan, in the interest of liberating the stage from 'tyranny' and establishing a more tasteful, and a more Irish, theatre:

> *Arma virumque cano – bella horrida bella.* Nothing else to do, we the tri-umvirate talk of nothing but the subversion of the present theatrical tyran-ny; lend us your pen; you have often drawn it for your own and friends' entertainment; now do it for their assistance and the establishing taste in spite of Sheridan's arrogance or his tasteless adherents. Don't think this gasconade, for we love liberty and consequently hate French customs. No, we tread on firm ground with Irish resolution and perseverance, resolving to pull down Baal from the high places, and that by (what is esteemed uncommon) the force of Irish genius, and establish Irish productions in the place of English trash comedies and French frippery of dances and harlequins, which have been the public entertainments this winter[1]

As he went on to describe this proposed war, Dennis also revealed that it was to be carried on with the covert assistance of 'one Dr. Hiffernan, a poet, philoso-pher and play-wright in this town' and a group of Hiffernan's friends who called themselves 'an association in defence of Irish wit'.[2] And he made it clear that this was to be a guerrilla-style campaign, waged through a variety of liter-ary genres and from a number of different, hidden, locations:

Burke's paper has paved the way; three hundred were sold yesterday. On Monday, Hiffernan in an expostulation from Punch displays Mr. Sheridan in a ridiculous but true light, which will take three papers. Next comes Brennan with a grave inquiry into the behaviour of the manager, which will be backed by Ned [Burke] and I; and thus we will persecute him daily from different printers till the plot is ripe, and we have established liberty on the stage and taste among the people.[3]

In the months that followed, a series of 'papers' that corresponded broadly to this outline rolled off the presses in Dublin, though, for whatever reason, the co-conspirators evidently changed the order of attack. The Burke 'paper' that 'paved the way' in the campaign, the above letter reveals, was *Punch's Petition to Mr. Sh-n, to be admitted into the Theatre Royal*, a piece that Hiffernan had already persuaded the Dublin printer, Joseph Cotter, to publish anonymously,[4] and the allusion to 'yesterday' in the above suggests that this text was published on 13 January 1748. On 28 January, *The Reformer*, a periodical that appears to have been managed primarily by Burke[5] began to circulate, devoting its first three numbers to attacking Sheridan and his supporters in what could be called a tone of 'grave inquiry', and on 18 February, Hiffernan began his offensive in what could be called the more 'ridiculous' tone of his periodical, *The Tickler*. In March and April, Hiffernan also delivered more directly on his promise to expostulate 'from Punch' when he and his group moved their campaign to the boards of the little theatre on Capel Street and began employing the mimic and puppeteer, Samuel Foote, and the Irish 'wit',[6] Laetita Pilkington, to attack the Theatre Royal – an effort that the Burke faction supported by publishing adver-tisements and 'puffs' for Capel Street in *The Reformer*. There was also a dramatic epilogue to this 'war' in May of the following year (1749). At that time, Hiffernan and a company of 'Gentlemen', who advertised themselves as being 'zealous for their Country's Honour',[7] again used the Capel Street stage to attack the Theatre Royal and its supporters, and, in keeping with the previous year's Punch motif, they used a mock-puppet play (*The Election*) to deliver their satire.

This campaign, as I have suggested elsewhere,[8] is important in Irish theatri-cal history because it reveals the highly contested nature of the eighteenth-century Irish stage but, as I will suggest here, it is also worth re-examining for the light it throws on Edmund Burke's early politics and, more specifically, on his relationship with the radical reformer and populist patriot, Charles Lucas. As is well known, Burke's relationship to Lucas during the latter's campaign to win a seat in the Dublin by-election of 1749 has become a touchstone for discussing whether the young Burke was a conservative or a radical in his early days. In 1798, his earliest biographer, Robert Bisset laid the grounds for the former view when he wrote that Burke began his political career in 1749 by publishing essays that mocked Lucas's style and that showed 'the absurdity and danger' of the reformer's 'leveling doctrines'.[9] During the century that followed, most biogra-phers also uncritically accepted this claim.[10] In the early twentieth-century, however, Arthur Warren Samuels argued that there was no supporting documentary evidence for the Bisset position and, citing the young undergraduate's ardent commitment to classical republican ideals, he proposed the alternate view that Burke was the secret author of a number of *pro*-Lucas tracts.[11] Since that time, scholars have been divided on this issue, with each side citing the lack of definitive evidence on the other side as the grounds for continuing the dispute.[12]

The inability to lay this dispute to rest, however, has less to do with a lack of definitive evidence than the modernist tendency to segregate the domain of the aesthetic from the domain of the political, and when these domains are reintegrated – as they always were for Burke[13] – it becomes quite clear that the young undergraduate was in the anti-Lucas camp. This is not to suggest, however, that Burke was 'conservative' in any simple sense. Writing of Burke's later most famous 'conservative' statement – his *Reflections on the Revolution in France* – Conor Cruise O'Brien persuasively argues that the contradictory styles as well as the intense feeling of this piece come from the suppressed Irish Catholic side of Burke. While most of Burke's counter-revolutionary argument is delivered in a rational, enlightenment, Whig style, O'Brien notes, it is shot through with Gothic, pathetic and ironic strains, and these more emotionally charged styles betray a sympathy with the Irish Catholic cause and a hostility to the very Protestant Whig culture into which he [Burke] was apparently assimilated.[14] The variety of styles and the intensity of feeling in this theatrical campaign, I will argue, can be accounted for by similarly suppressed identifications and hostilities. While the 'grave' essays in *The Reformer* enunciate what appears to be an elitist Irish Protestant reform agenda, what we see ventriloquized through the bitter irony of *Punch's Petition* and through Burke's covert, intertextual dialogue with Paul Hiffernan's *Tickler* is a deep resentment at the 'new men' who were governing Ireland and a yearning for the return of a hereditary elite. In the context of eighteenth-century Ireland, such invocations of tradition always carried a revolutionary charge.

LUCASIAN REFORMERS TAKE THE STAGE, 1747–48

To understand why the theatre became the locus for the first articulation of Burke's politically unstable kind of conservatism, however, it also necessary to understand Charles Lucas's engagement with the theatre in the 1747–48 period. Lucas's radical agenda made him, in many ways, the forerunner of Dr Price, the Dissenting preacher whose anti-aristocratic and anti-popery remarks would later elicit the passionate *Reflections*. And this radical agenda, with all its threatening ramifications for Irish gentlemen with Catholic identifications or affiliations, was first enunciated through the theatrical reform movement of 1747–48.

Lucas turned to the theatre for a platform after the failure of his first political reform campaign in the early 1740s. This campaign, which was undertaken when he was a member of the common council of the Dublin Corporation, was aimed at limiting the oligarchic powers of the lord mayor and aldermen and restoring the ancient rights of Dublin 'freemen', but it ended unsuccessfully after a lawsuit in 1744, and Lucas lost his place on the Corporation. The six-week conflict that broke out at Smock Alley in the spring of 1747, after Thomas Sheridan beat a Connaught gentleman named Edmund Kelly for reputedly assaulting one of the female players, then provided the reformer with a perfect opportunity to regain the public spotlight and renew his attack on oligarchic privilege. When a group of Kelly supporters, who styled themselves the 'Gentlemen', interrupted Sheridan's performance at Smock Alley on 9 February 1747 and demanded an apology from the manager – depending on which source you believe, they were offended either because Sheridan had struck a gentleman or because he had said he was as good a gentleman as any of them – Lucas stood up from his place in the pit and staged a mini-drama on democratic theory and practice. He first gave a speech, the gist of which was (as he later reported himself) *'That it was no longer his [Sheridan's] Quarrel, that he was no Aggressor, and that he should not give up the Public Right by making a base submission to Lawless Rage and Tyranny'*,[15] and he then suggested that, like other public disputes, this dispute should be determined 'by the Majority', through a show of hands by audience members.[16] This strategy was also successful in bringing about the defeat of the 'Gentlemen', at least for that night. After the Kelly faction saw that the majority was against them, they left the playhouse, and Lucas emerged as the defender of 'Public Right'.

In the three *Letters* that he wrote under the pseudonym 'A. Freeman, Barber, and Citizen' (the Barber *Letters*) in the weeks following, Lucas also connected this theatrical reform campaign to the historic English mission to 'civilize' Ireland, and he identified gentlemen from both a native Irish and Old English Catholic background as the barbarian enemy. At one point, for instance, he suggested that this theatrical 'Quarrel' was between those 'whose Ancestors came to subdue the Barbarity of the Natives of this Island' and the 'Offspring' of those 'Savages and Tyrants',[17] and, at another point, he suggested that it must be seen in the light of Dublin's historical struggle to defend itself against a *'Force* of rebellious *Irish* Savages, and degenerate *English'*.[18] If, as Lucas himself noted, some Catholics in his own day 'represented him as a CROMWELIAN',[19] and if some historians have subsequently characterized him as a Protestant extremist,[20] it was also because of his willingness to conjure the spectre of the 1641 rebellion and the recent Jacobite rebellion in these *Letters*. Unless his fellow Protestants took immediate action against these theatrical rioters, he warned, this alliance of 'professed *Papists*' and *'mercenary Converts'* would incite 'a *foreign Invasion*, a *western Insurrection*, or an UNIVERSAL MASSACRE'.[21] These Barber *Letters*, however, also articulated Lucas's emergent, proto-Jacobin brand of patriot politics,[22] leading one to suspect that the 'over the top' rhetoric was at least partially an attempt to deflect attention from this other more subversive agenda. Embedded in his apparently loyalist anti-'Gentlemen' reform rhetoric was also a call for Irish Protestant 'citizens' to make common cause with the Irish Catholic peasantry in opposition to what Lucas perceived as the tyranny of all hereditary elites, whether of Irish *or* English extraction. In his self-vindication in the third Barber's *Letter*, for example, Lucas clearly states that his animosity was not directed at the 'Romanists' or at the 'native Irish' in general but rather at a 'set of People, who vainly boast their ancient pedigree from illustrious *Irish,* or imaginary *Spanish* kings; who like their *Ancestors* keep their subjects, or tenants, in the most abject dependence and slavery'.[23] And as he sympathetically described the plight of this Irish peasantry under their Irish overlords – they have nothing, he wrote, but a 'wretched cottage, and coarse Pasturage for a few happier brutes, on whose blood and milk the poor slaves live, as their masters do on theirs' – he implicitly made a connection between their suffering and that of lower-class, urban Protestants who, he wrote, were also treated as '*Slaves* and *Hirelings*' by city gentlemen.[24] Both groups, he tacitly suggested, were having their blood sucked out of them by a parasitic ruling class, and consequently they should unite – under his leadership – to remove this elite from the playhouse and the broader national arena.

In December of 1747, Lucas also went public with these sweeping attacks on elite tyranny in his *Complaints of Dublin*, an address that he delivered before the Earl of Harrington at the King's Bench, in Dublin. And after these 'complaints' were summarily dismissed – the reformer was told in no uncertain terms not to return to court – he went back to using the Theatre Royal as his political staging ground. Sheridan, who owed Lucas for his help during the previous season's disturbance, was also entirely co-operative. During the 1747-48 season, he apparently permitted Lucas to insert his trademark speeches about 'Liberty' and 'the Constitution' into performances of plays,[25] and it appears that he also allowed Lucas to use his theatre to rally supporters and raise funds.[26] As the playhouse was being transformed into a rallying site for the rapidly expanding population of Lucasians, it also became even more of a 'no-go' area for 'Gentlemen' of an old Irish Catholic ilk, as is evident from the pamphlet, *Mr. Nobody's Anti-Ticklerian Address to Mr. Lucas*. This pamphlet, which appeared in the spring of 1748, ironically praised Paul Hiffernan for his 'Spirit in mounting to the upper Regions [the upper gallery]' at a recent performance so that he 'might be exalted above that haughty *Charley* who "perk'd it at the same time in the Boxes" and was saluted with a loud Clap' whenever he appeared. But it also ominously warned Hiffernan to '[be]ware pumping' at the hands of Lucasians.[27]

'PUNCHING' BACK: THE BURKE/HIFFERNAN
COUNTER-REFORMATION OF 1748

This Lucasian ascendancy at the Theatre Royal, then, provided the political context for Burke's *Punch* pamphlet and for the campaign against Sheridan and his 'tasteless adherents' that the Burke platoon, with the covert aid of Paul Hiffernan and his group of 'Irish wit[s]', launched early in 1748. For the

Burke/Hiffernan group, as for the Lucasians, the Irish theatre served as a metaphorical space for the Irish nation and, as is evident from the title of one of their publications – *The Reformer* – they, like the Lucasians, also believed that this nation stood in dire need of reform. But, whereas the Lucasians envisioned this reform movement being led by 'new men' drawn from the ranks of the Protestant urban class and from the descendants of Cromwellian settlers, the Burke/Hiffernan group envisioned it being led by Ireland's hereditary ruling class – by men drawn (as they themselves were) from the ranks of an Old English and Gaelic, 'professed papist' or 'convert', gentry.

The contours of this gentry form of Irish patriotism are also first discernible in Burke and Dennis's first direct engagement in theatrical politics during the 'Gentlemen's Quarrel' of 1747, though ironically the Trinity duo appeared to be on the same side as Lucas and Sheridan in this dispute. Burke had been among the hundred 'Scholars' who had forced a number of the Connaught 'Gentlemen' to kneel and apologize for their behaviour in the College yard on the morning of 13 February 1747,[28] and around the same time, Dennis had written a pamphlet, *Brutus's Letter to the Town*, supporting the manager and condemning his opponents. If we look closely at the two friends' comments on their involvement in this 'Quarrel', however, it becomes clear that their objection to the Kelly faction's behaviour had a different ideological basis from Lucas's. In assuming the persona of Brutus to speak to the 'Town' and in speaking a language of the 'Rights and Liberties' of the 'Individual',[29] Dennis certainly was drawing on the Whig rhetoric that was the mainstay of Lucas's brand of patriotism. But in arguing that Kelly and his supporters had 'acted contrary to all Rules of Modesty and Good-breeding', Dennis also invoked traditional standards of gentry behaviour as the norms by which their behaviour should be measured and condemned, and in faulting this faction for raising a 'Tumult in the City, when we were scarce cool'd, when the apprehension of Civil War was just allay'd',[30] he also hints that his objections were linked to a concern for the well-being of the Catholic population. Two years previously, during the time of the Jacobite invasion, the city had indeed been rocked by fears of a 'Civil War', and Catholic gentlemen had been closely monitored for any sign of 'Tumult'.[31] Burke, who had expressed dismay at that time at the prospect of Jacobite gentlemen being punished for their part in the rebellion,[32] and who was, as we can gather from his later remarks, alarmed by the government's promotion of Protestant zealotry during the '45,[33] may also have been thinking of these recently cooled tensions when he undertook the disciplining of these riotous Connaught gentlemen. In any case, he was careful to emphasize to Shackleton that he and the 'Scholars' only became involved when it became clear that 'no ties of honour or Religion could bind em [the Kelly faction]'[34] – a statement that indicates that his participation in the 'Gentlemen's Quarrel' was, in effect, in *defence* of traditional values and a traditional form of society. 'Ties of honour' and 'Religion', of course, were the mainstays of traditional societies.

This Catholic-inflected traditionalism is even more pronounced in *Punch's*

Petition to Mr. Sh- n, to be admitted into the Theatre Royal, and his anti-Theatre Royal stance in this text suggests that, by the winter of 1747, Burke had come to see the Smock Alley 'reformers' – Sheridan, Lucas and their supporters – as a greater threat to social order and stability than Kelly and his faction. At its most obvious level, *Punch's Petition* is an attack on the 'low' entertainment that prevailed at Smock Alley during the 1747–48 season. The Dublin stage was, in fact, dominated by harlequins and French dancers at this time so that in having a puppet petition to join Sheridan's company – Punch wants to sign up, he says, because his own puppet booth has been driven out of business by the Theatre Royal – Burke is drawing attention to the prevalence of this kind of 'illegitimate' entertainment in the theatre and satirizing the manager for catering to 'low' taste. When these kind of satiric attacks were launched in eighteenth-century England, there was also a conservative class politics behind them. Writers who complained that Punch was invading the theatre, or who critiqued 'lowness' or 'dullness' in drama or poetry, were generally attacking the emerging middle-class who were assuming the political and cultural roles formerly held by the 'wits' or the aristocratic elite.[35]

Discursive forms that were conservative in England, however, as has been often noted, sometimes took on a different, more subversive valence in Ireland because of that country's different politics and history, and this was also the case with this kind of Punch satire. By the time Burke wrote his pamphlet at mid century, there was a tradition among Irish writers of using Punch to ventriloquize Irish Protestant grievances at the mismanagement of Ireland[36] and, as Swift's poem, 'Mad Mullinex and Timothy' (1728), illustrates, such critiques could also encompass Protestant leaders who deliberately stirred up Protestant bigotry and anti-Catholic paranoia for their own political ends. The 'Timothy' alluded to in the title of Swift's poem was the Irish MP Richard Tighe and, throughout the poem, Swift ridicules this statesman for being a Whig fanatic, a man who is obsessed with '*Popish* Craft', with 'the *Pretender*', and 'With Plots; and *Jacobites* and Treason'.[37] He drives this attack home, then, by finally comparing Tighe's behaviour to the antics of Punchinello, a puppet character notorious for stirring up the whole puppet booth with his pranks:

> Thus *Tim*, Philosophers suppose,
> *The World consists of Puppet-shows;*
> Where petulant, conceited Fellows
> Perform the part of *Punchinelloes*;
> So at this Booth, which we call *Dublin*,
> *Tim* thour't the *Punch* to stir up trouble in;
> You Wrigle, Fidge, and make a Rout
> Put all your Brother Puppets out,
> Run on in a perpetual Round,
> To Teize, Perplex, Disturb, Confound.
> Intrude with Monkey grin, and clatter
> To interrupt all serious Matter.[38]

In 1747, however, another rising Irish Whig politician, Charles Lucas, was invoking the Jacobite spectre and stirring up alarm in both Catholics and Protestants at the Theatre Royal, and by having his Punchinello plead to be admitted to this same 'booth' in a pamphlet that resembled a formal political petition (each paragraph begins with 'That…), Burke was drawing attention to this fact, while also suggesting the illegitimacy and danger posed by Lucas's and Sheridan's brand of political and cultural leadership. Dublin readers who were familiar with the Swiftean ironic tradition and who had witnessed Lucas's recent grandstanding at Smock Alley would also have seen the political 'Punch' behind Burke's first pamphlet, even though it seemed to be concerned with purely theatrical affairs.

It is worth noting that, some fourteen years later, when Burke explicitly commented on Lucas's brand of leadership, he also drew on the imagery of 'low' entertainment to express his contempt for this reformer. 'If the latter mountebank should now descend from his stage', Burke wrote of Lucas in a letter to Charles O'Hara in 1761, 'it would be of great service to his character; which, if he returns to the usual unhealthy soundness of his intellects, will infallibly come to be known by the dullness of his admirers; and thus his medical quackery will cover the blunders of his political'.[39] By labelling Lucas a 'mountebank', Burke implied not only that the populist reformer was a medical quack (by this time Lucas had earned a medical degree) but also a political quack, and he implicitly associated his brand of populist patriotism with the 'low' entertainment of the street and the fair. Mountebanks were street entertainers as well as salesmen, and they frequently used harlequins, clowns and other comic acts on their outdoor stages to attract an audience for their fraudulent wares.

If the Punchinello in Burke's first publication points to the ascendancy of such fraudulent leaders on the Irish cultural and political stage, however, this figure also points to the exclusion of the 'ingenious Native' and, as is evident both from this pamphlet's title and from the following passage, this *Petition* was also a hurt plea to include such subjects in the public arena:

> he [Punchinello] trusts as you [Sheridan] value yourself on the Love of your Country, that you will encourage an ingenious Native preferable to a Foreigner, as your Petitioner is descended from the Ancient British Harlequins, who have had Possession of this Stage long before these Italian Performers were heard of, and that it is not his want of Merit, but his being Body and Soul of Irish Manufacture, which makes him neglected, he being able to shew more Feats of Agility, and has besides that advantage over them, that to his admirable Postures he adds his admirable Wit, a Quality they don't even pretend to.

At one level, this can be read as Burke's plea on behalf of his friend, Beaumont Brenan, an 'ingenious Native' who had recently submitted a play to the manager and who was still anxiously waiting to see this play produced (in the 14

January letter cited at the opening of this essay, indeed, Dennis explicitly stated that the friends were alarmed by the thought of *Punch's Petition* going to
press 'for fear it might hurt Brenan if there was any suspicion of Burke being
the author').[40] But as an 'ingenius Native' and 'admirable Wit' who is simultaneously of 'Ancient British' descent and 'of Irish Manufacture', and who is
'neglected' merely because he has this ancestry, the Punchinello in Burke's text
is also suggestive of the more general situation of the Old English and Irish
Catholic gentry in eighteenth-century Ireland; and it is this class's neglect –
their exclusion from the theatrical, cultural and political realm – that is also
indirectly protested here. An Irish Catholic sympathy sounds however obliquely through this ventriloquism act, adding a note of pathos that complicates this
particular Punchinello's 'wit'.

It was possibly because he recognized these 'ingenious Native' strains in
Burke's 'wit', too, that Hiffernan – an Irish Catholic medical doctor who had
received much of his initial education in a clerical college in Montepellier –
persuaded Cotter to publish *Punch's Petition* (Dennis noted in his 17 January
letter that Hiffernan had characterized it as a 'humorous, sharp piece'[41]). And
similarly, it seems likely that it was Burke's early upbringing among the Irish
Catholic community in Cork that led him to admire[42] and support this native
Irish man of letters as he began to direct his satirical volleys at Lucas, Sheridan
and their supporters in the pages of *The Tickler*. If *The Tickler* is discussed at
all today, it is solely in connection with the by-election of 1749, and it is generally asserted that Hiffernan entered on the anti-Lucas, pro-Aldermen side of
this political fray for purely monetary gain.[43] As Dennis's letter reveals, however, *The Tickler* began as part of the Burke/Hiffernan theatrical campaign in
the spring prior to Lucas's election bid, and the repeated allusions to the Barber
Letters in this publication make it clear that Hiffernan's hostility to Lucas had
its source in the latter's anti-'Gentlemen' rhetoric of 1747. Hiffernan indeed
cites 'the elegance and Politeness of the *BARBERS LETTERS*' as his literary
model in the ironic dedication to Charles Lucas in the collected edition of *The
Tickler*, and when he responded to those who were criticizing him for unfairly
satirizing Lucas in the sixth issue of his paper, he also explicitly mentioned
(among other inflammatory actions) the 'incendiary apothecary's indiscrimi-
nate abuse of 'a whole province'.[44] The 'whole province' that Lucas had
'abused', of course, was the native Irish gentry-dominated province of
Connaught.

Much of the satire that Hiffernan directed against Lucas and his theatrical
supporters in *The Tickler* in the spring of 1748 also resonates with the satire that
Gaelic poets directed at the 'new men' that governed Ireland in the wake of the
Cromwellian plantation, and like these other marginalized Irish 'wits',
Hiffernan depicted the new social and political upstarts – in this case, Lucas and
his chief supporters, Sheridan and the newspaper publisher, George Faulkner –
as buffoons, churls and vicious clowns. There are clear continuities between the
Pairlement Chloinne Tomáis (The Parliament of Clan Thomas) satiric genre,[45]

for example, and the 'mock heroic description of a ridiculous *Apotheosis*',[46] that Hiffernan drew in the fifth issue *The Tickler*, a description that imagines Lucas leading a grotesque 'patriot procession' from his house on Ormond Quay to Essex Bridge, and then staging his death – he jumps into the Liffey —in an effort to show his 'citizen' supporters that he is as 'great' a man as their hero, Cromwell.[47] The theatrical imagery and the emblems of violence that pervade this description – Lucas is dressed in wigs and costumes borrowed from the playhouse, and he is supported by Sheridan and a group of players and constables who are armed with 'truncheons' and 'protended staves'[48] – also underscore what Hiffernan takes to be the inauthentic and repressive nature of Lucas's brand of populist leadership, and this imagery became even more pronounced in later issues. In the last *Tickler*, which appeared on 20 October 1749 after Lucas had fled the country, Hiffernan referred to the reformer as a 'bellowing phantom, [a] poor player, that strutted, and fretted his hours in halls, and now is heard no more' and, as Burke would do later, he compared Lucas's political abilities to those of a '*mountebank* who held forth on a '*street-stage*'.[49]

That Burke shared Hiffernan's outlook on this political reformer in 1748 is also apparent from the anti-Lucasian commentary that is woven through the pages of *The Reformer*, a commentary that appears both in the paper's advertisements and in the essays themselves. In the essay section of the first three issues, as the Dennis letter had promised, *The Reformer* took issue with every aspect of Sheridan's playhouse. Ireland had become an 'Empire of *Dulness*', it announced,[50] and the playhouse epitomized this trend with its 'dull' and immoral entertainments, its poor actors and its uncivilized audience. The Hackball advertisement that appeared after the 'grave' essay in the first issue of *The Reformer*, however, suggested that (as with the first Punch pamphlet), there was a political as well as aesthetic dimension to this attack on 'Dulness'. When *The Refomer* announced that a print of Hack-ball, 'the Head of the *Mendicant* Order, and of obstreperous Fame in this City' was being published by subscription, it was clearly being ironical since, in real life, Hack-ball was a street character, one Patrick Carregan, the reputed king of Dublin's beggars.[51] And when it mentioned that the 'great Original' for this print lived at Ormond Quay, it appeared, at first, to identify Sheridan as its satiric target. The manager was living at Ormond Quay at this time and, during the previous year, as we have seen, his 'obstreperous Fame' – his claim to being a 'gentleman' – had set the city in an uproar. But Charles Lucas also lived at Ormond Quay at this time (Sheridan was actually lodging in Lucas' house), and this satire further pointed in his direction when it alluded to a 'Fellow Citizen of *some Eminence* [who had] to pay the entire Expence himself' for a similar print. In 1747, Lucas had commissioned a portrait of himself from the painter William Jones, and this portrait (subsequently made into a print) had also portrayed the reformer as a 'Citizen of *some Eminence*'.[52] Subsequent satires in *The Tickler* also clearly identified Lucas as the object of this Hack-ball satire. In the second issue of *The Tickler*, for example, Hiffernan used an announcement from Hack-ball to satirize Lucas's announcement declaring that he had been authorized to collect trade taxes in Dublin.[53] And Hiffernan drew on the Hack-ball conceit later the same year when he satirized the Lucas print in the frontispiece of his collected edition of *The Tickler*.[54]

If present-day readers have consistently missed this political subtext in *The Reformer* – and thus also the young Burke's hostility to Lucas – it is undoubtedly because they have believed Hiffernan when he stated in the first issue of *The Tickler* that he alone was responsible for this Hackball advertisement,[55] and because they have taken at face value the hostile statements that Burke and Hiffernan directed at one another in their respective papers as part of their strategy to conceal their alliance. This mock-fight began in the first issue of *The Tickler* when this paper accused *The Reformer* of being one of Sheridan's 'noisy clappermen' or supporters.[56] In its fifth issue, then, *The Reformer* piously denied this charge, proclaiming its alarm and dismay that anyone would ever consider it to be a 'Party' paper.[57] Even in the very issue that *The Reformer* asserted its political innocence, however, it also continued a subversive interplay with Hiffernan and his paper. This fifth issue, like six other issues of *The Reformer*, carried an advertisement for subscriptions to Hiffernan's *Reflexions on the Structure and Passions of Man*,[58] and in its essay section, it also painted a portrait of Sheridan partisans that conformed to *The Tickler*'s dark outlook on this group of 'reformers'. This description occurs as the 'Reformer' purports to describe a journey that he undertook through Dublin coffeehouses in an effort to ascertain whether the public shared *The Tickler*'s view that *The Reformer* was a 'Party' paper. In most sites he visited, the 'Reformer' reports, he encountered indifference rather than hostility but the situation took a dramatic change for the worse when he entered the last, most socially-diverse, coffee-house. There he heard a 'clever tall Fellow' publicly praising the manager and denouncing the author of *The Reformer* as a 'Scoundrel,' and when the 'Reformer' himself stepped forward and expressed his belief that such expressions were 'unworthy of a Gentleman', the speaker threatened to hit him with a 'Cudgel'. The 'Reformer' then withdrew and grew 'silent' after hearing from a bystander that 'this angry Person was one of the Manager's Partizans, who had it in his Commission to abuse all who dared dislike his Proceedings'. But the victorious Sheridan supporter went 'boisterously vapouring all over the House' until people from every walk of life in the coffee house (politicians, tradesmen, lawyers, divines, gentlemen, critics, beaux, pedants) were drawn into the controversy, including, as the 'Reformer' notes, 'a little Gentleman, with a black Wig, and of sower Aspect, whom I took to be either a Physician or Apothecary, [who] said it [*The Reformer*] was so malevolent, that the Authors ought to be purg'd for the Spleen'.[59] An 'Apothecary' who demands that his opponents should be 'purg'd', however, is also clearly a figure for Lucas (an apothecary by trade) who had demanded the weeding out of his 'Gentlemen' opponents a year earlier. Like Hiffernan in *The Tickler*, Burke suggests that a universe dominated by this 'sower' 'Apothecary' and by Sheridan's violent partisans is a depraved and dangerous world, one in which true 'Reformers' are threatened and silenced.

In issues four to nine of *The Reformer*, Burke also articulated the gentry alternative to Lucas's populist patriotism and, in so doing, he brings out the Irish Catholic political agenda that was always implicit in Hiffernan's Lucasian satire – an agenda about which this Catholic gentleman (like other contemporary Catholic apologists) could never speak without undermining his loyalist cover.[60] In a recent essay in which he reconsiders the politics and content of Burke's paper, Thomas McLoughlin argues persuasively that *The Reformer* was not just a plea for a better theatre but 'a plea for a humane and Irish-based socio-economic order in which Arts and Sciences have a central position', and he also notes that *The Reformer* sees the involvement of the upper classes as the key to this change.[61] This argument is also borne out by an analysis of the central issues of this paper. The fourth issue of *Reformer*, for example, roundly denounces the 'Nobility and Gentry' for not patronizing Irish 'Manufacture' (either commercial or artistic);[62] the seventh issue of *Reformer* condemns the 'Great' for callously indulging in their 'Pageantry' and 'luxurious lives' while the poor peasants live in unprecedented squalor and poverty;[63] and the ninth issue of *Reformer* paints a picture of a 'Nation sinking into Ruin and Misery, while whose those who are bound to promote its Advantage, by Birth, Gratitude and Interest are spending its Revenues' abroad.[64]

However, in arguing that these kinds of protests take their meaning *exclusively* from an Irish Protestant patriot tradition of dissent – the tradition of protest established by Molyneux, Swift, Berkeley and Madden[65] – McLoughlin overlooks the dialogue between the Reformer and his friend, 'Asper', in the central sixth issue of *The Reformer*, a dialogue which suggests that Burke's critique derives equally from a native Irish gentry source.[66] Details in this exposition leave little doubt that 'Asper' is a pseudonym for Hiffernan,[67] and it is Hiffernan's particular native Irish gentry brand of alienation that is apparent in his gloomy description of the present ruling class. In Asper's critique of a 'Gentry' who have lost the 'Taste of true Glory' and who neglect the 'fine Arts' because they are 'constantly employed in the Study of accumulating Wealth, or idly spending it',[68] for example, it is possible to hear the complaint of the traditional Gaelic writer against the mercenary 'new men' who have displaced the old elite. And in the following passage, which describes the consequences of this neglect, it is possible to catch another glimpse of the upside-down, nightmare world of both *Parliament Clan Thomas* and *The Tickler*: 'Fustian', 'Faction' and the 'leaden-headed Fellows' who approve *Clarissa* in this passage are scarcely disguised references to Sheridan, Lucas and George Faulkner, the triumvirate who ruled over the empire of dullness in *The Tickler*:

> How many good Things have been the Objects of the publick Censure? How many of the vilest have met general Approbation? Else sure *Fustian* playing would never be term'd *Genius, Faction, Spirit*; nor a Set of leaden-headed Fellows, the lowest of Mankind, set up for Men of Taste; nor

Books the vilest in their nature [here he mentioned *Clarissa* and some
other modern Pieces] be accepted and universally read. These things shew
the Flood of Barbarism to be at the highest, and 'tis vain to oppose it.
There is a Fatality in all Things, some Ages shine with the Light of
Science and Virtue, while others are buried in the grossest Darkness.
These mutually and naturally succeed each other as Night does Day; and
when it comes to any Nation's Turn to fall into Ignorance, Experience
shews it can no more be avoided than the Change of the Seasons.[69]

Though the 'Reformer' responds to Asper's tirade with a mild disclaimer – he
counters Asper's 'melancholy Prospect' with remembrances of 'the many
Societies we see formed for the Support of Useful Trades and Charities' – he
nevertheless acknowledges the validity of his friend's vision: 'the more I considered it, the more Reason I had to fear the Truth of my Friend's Assertions'.[70]
And with this acknowledgement, Burke makes it clear that his reformist discourse is a double-voiced one – a critique that draws its force from the dispossessed Irish Catholic, as well as Irish Protestant patriot traditions. Asper's
lament is another 'caoineadh ar chéim sios na nuasal' [lament for the fallen
noblility], and by including this 'caoineadh' in his paper, the 'Reformer' adds
a 'Gothic' undercurrent to his Whiggish patriot discourse.

BEHIND THE SCENES AGAIN? *THE ELECTION*, 1749

As noted above, *The Reformer* also continued to offer support for Hiffernan's
group when this group began to launch their satirical attacks from Capel Street
theatre in March and April,[71] and there are also hints that Burke continued his
relationship with this Capel Street group the following year, as the Dublin by-
election began to be fought out on the Irish stage. After Lucas announced his
candidacy for a vacant parliamentary seat in August 1748, *The Tickler* (which
continued to be published long after *The Reformer* ceased publication) immediately accused Sheridan of making 'interest for his friend *Charley*',[72] a charge
that appears to be accurate in the light of the manager's decision to stage Henry
Brooke's *Jack the Giant Queller* the following March, at the height of the
Dublin by-election campaign. Brooke was Lucas's chief propagandist during
this campaign,[73] and this new ballad opera, which showed a peasant hero leading a popular revolution against the corrupt giants who ruled his native land,
was a scarcely concealed allegory for the Lucasian political mission. Like the
earlier Barber's *Letters*, this Lucasian piece also articulated a daring kind of
populist Irish patriotism that cut across ethnic and religious lines, and the inter-
jection of traditional Irish music – some of it with Jacobite associations –
throughout the piece again suggested that Lucas saw himself as the leader of
both the Catholic and Protestant Irish masses.

  In May, then, Capel Street began staging a 'live' puppet-show play called

The Election[74] that satirized Lucas and his election campaign, and the similarity of tone between this mock-puppet play and the writing that emanated from the paper war of the previous year suggests that the same group of writers and 'Irish wits' were responsible for this anonymous work. Like *The Tickler,* for example, this three-act satire focused chiefly on Lucas, Sheridan and Faulkner, who are here represented by the characters Firebrand, Fustian and Puff; and like both *The Tickler* and *The Reformer*, this play suggested that this triumvirate of dullness were threatening to bring about the 'the utter Dissolution of the Society'[75] with their desire to assume a leadership role in political and cultural affairs. Mimicry and parody are also this play's dominant mode of critique – there are long passages parodying Lucas's campaign speeches, for example[76] – and this too suggests a continuity with the previous year's opposition.

Most intriguingly, however, from the point of view of establishing where Burke was in 1749, there is also a Punchinello in this play, and like the Punchinello that opened the Burke/Hiffernan campaign the previous year, this play's Punch is both a resentful and a plaintive figure whose grievances stem from theatrical as well as broader political injustices. The most immediate referent for this character's bitterness is the 1747 'Gentleman's Quarrel'. We hear during the play, for example, that Fustian has ordered Punch to be locked up because – like Kelly in this dispute – he dared question this player's right to be called a gentleman,[77] and when Punch finally appears on the stage to give the play's epilogue, having, by his own admission, 'broke loose at length' from his captors,[78] his complaints against the town seem to be that of the aggrieved Connaught 'Gentlemen'.

> Can ye bear then, ye Royst'rers of the Town,
> To see your once lov'd Actor hunted down?
> When a vile Player, through his own Default,
> Had half this City's Rage upon him brought;
> Beaus, Belles, and Scholars, did at once unite,
> To this Fellow's fancy'd Merit Right.
> But when true Wit, as just as e'er was stamp'd
> Is by a set of sordid Schemers cramp'd,
> Not one of you will set your Throats a Bawling,
> Or brandish Stick to keep his Cause from falling.
> So well this strange Inconstancy of you,
> Does prove, Alas! This Observation true,
>   'Excess of Merit makes the Brave to fall,
>   'And proves more hurtful than no Parts at all.' [79]

'Beaus, Belles, and Scholars' had also supported a 'vile Player' (Sheridan), during the 1747 dispute and, like Punchinello, Kelly was hunted down, beaten, pumped and finally imprisoned.

But when Punch berates his genteel audience for their inaction as 'True Wit' was 'cramp'ed', and when he alludes to the 'hurtful' 'fall' of 'the Brave', he would also seems to be referring to the more general marginalization and oppression of 'True', that is, native Irish, writers and gentlemen in contemporary Ireland, and in this context, the 'vile player' and 'schemers' also signify Lucas and the 'new men' whose rise on the national stage was predicated on the exclusion of this traditional elite. That Burke felt such a sense of betrayal and 'hurt' at Lucas's political ascendancy is also clear from his later remarks on this topic. Again, in a letter to O'Hara in 1761, he wrote that he was unable to understand 'that spirit which could raise such hackneyed pretences, and such contemptible talents as those of Dr. Lucas to so great a consideration, not only among the mob, but, as I hear on all hands, among very many of rank and figure', and he also added: 'I feel myself hurt at this, and the rather as I shall be obliged from decency and other considerations to hold my tongue.'[80] The Punchinello of *The Election* is another such 'hurt' and 'cramp'd' figure, and the muffled grief and rage that sounds through his speech suggests that the young Burke was once again – either literally or metaphorically – behind the scenes during the anti-Lucas campaign of 1749.

NOTES

1. Dennis to Richard Shackleton, 14 Jan. 1747 (O.S), in James Prior, *The Life of Oliver Goldsmith, M. B., from a variety of original sources* (Philadelphia: E.L. Cary and A. Hart, 1837), p.315.
2. Ibid., pp.316–17.
3. Ibid., pp.317–18.
4. Ibid., p.316.
5. See T.O. McLoughlin, 'Did Burke Write *The Reformer*?' *N&Q*, NS, 39, 4 (Dec. 1992), pp.474–7.
6. For Laetita Pilkington's reputation as a 'Wit', see Arch Elias, 'Male Hormones and Women's Wit: The Sex Appeal of Mary Goddard and Laetita Pilkington', *Swift Studies*, 9 (1994), p.14. Mrs Pilkington wrote satire which her son, Jack, delivered on stage.
7. *The Dublin Courant*, 28 Feb.–4 March 1749.
8. See my *Riotous Performances, The Struggle for Hegemony on the Irish Stage, 1712–1784* (South Bend, Indiana: University of Notre Dame Press, 2003), Chaps 5 and 6.
9. Robert Bisset, *The Life of Edmund Burke* (London: George Cawthorn, 1798), p.19.
10. See James Prior, *Memoir of the Life and Character of the Right Honourable Edmund Burke with Specimens of his Poetry and an estimate of His Genius and Talents Compared with Those of His Contemporaries* (London: Baldwin, Craddock & Joy, 2nd edition, 1826), pp.33–4; Peter Burke, *The Public and Domestic Life of the Right Hon. Edmund Burke* (London : Ingram, Cooke, 1853 – The National Illustrated library, Vol.31), pp.10–11.
11. A.P.I. Samuels, *The Early Life, Correspondence and Writing of the Rt. Hon. Edmund Burke* (Cambridge: Cambridge University Press, 1923), pp.180–202, 389–95.
12. For a summary of this dispute to date, see Sean Murphy, 'Burke and Lucas: An Authorship Problem Re-Examined', *Eighteenth-Century Ireland*, 1 (1986), pp.143–56. Murphy himself argues that Burke was a Lucas supporter.
13. See for example, Tom Furniss, *Edmund Burke's Aesthetic Ideology: Language, Gender and Political Economy in Revolution* (Cambridge: Cambridge University Press, 1993); and Luke Gibbons, *Edmund Burke and Ireland: Aesthetics, Politics, and the Colonial Sublime* (Cambridge: Cambridge University Press, 2003).
14. Conor Cruise O'Brien, 'Introduction', in *Reflections on the Revolution in France* (London: Penguin, 1968), pp.33–49.
15. Charles Lucas [A. Freeman, Barber and Citizen, pseud.], *A Letter to the Free-Citizens of Dublin* (Dublin, 1747), p.7.
16. Benjamin Victor, *The History of the Theatres of London and Dublin* (London, T. Davies, 1761), vol.1, p.114

17. Lucas, *A Letter to the Free-Citizens of Dublin*, p.5.
18. Charles Lucas, *A Second Letter to the Free Citizens of Dublin* (Dublin, 1747), p.8.
19. Charles Lucas, *A Third Letter to the Free Citizens of Dublin* (Dublin, 1747), p.4.
20. See, for example, W.E.H. Lecky, *A History of Ireland in the Eighteenth-Century* (London, 1913 ed.), vol.1, p.461; and R.B. MacDowell, *Irish Public Opinion 1750–1800* (London, 1944), pp.11, 17.
21. Lucas, *A Second Letter to the Free Citizens of Dublin*, p.10.
22. For the proto-Jacobin elements in Lucas's writing, see Sean Murphy, 'Charles Lucas, Catholicism and Nationalism', *Eighteenth-Century Ireland*, 8 (1993), pp.83–102.
23. Lucas, *A Third Letter to the Free Citizens of Dublin*, p.16.
24. Ibid., pp.17, 11.
25. *The Tickler*, 3 (3 March 1748), p.17; *The Election* [Dublin, 1749], pp.35–6. *The Tickler* references throughout this essay refer to *The Tickler* collection (Dublin, 1748).
26. *The Tickler*, 6 (29 April 1748), p.49; Esther Sheldon, *Thomas Sheridan of Smock-Alley* (Princeton: Princeton University Press, 1967), p.329.
27. *Mr. Nobody's Anti-Ticklerian Address to Mr. Lucas* (Dublin, 1748), pp.14, 15.
28. Burke to Richard Shackleton, 21 Feb. 1747, *Correspondence*, vol.i, pp.83, 84.
29. [William Dennis], *Brutus's Letter to the Town* (Dublin, 1747), p.2.
30. Ibid., pp.3, 4.
31. For a discussion of the monitoring of Catholics during the '45, see Burke, *Riotous Performances*, pp.119–26.
32. Burke to Richard Shackleton, 26 April 1745, *Correspondence*, vol.i, p.63.
33. In his *Letter to a Peer* (1782), Burke would later denounce the Chesterfield administration for 'stimulating with provocatives, the wearied and half exhausted bigotry of then parliament of Ireland' during this period, *The Field Day Anthology of Irish Writing*, (Ed. Seamus Deane) [Derry: Field Day Publications, 1991], vol.1, pp.820–1.
34. Burke to Richard Shackleton, 21 Feb. 1747, *Correspondence*, vol.i, p.83.
35. See Robert M. Krapp, 'Class Analysis of a Literary Controversy: Wit and Sense in Seventeenth-century English Literature', *Science and Society*, 10 (1946), pp.80–92; Peter Stallybrass and Allon White, *The Politics and Poetics of Transgression* (Ithaca: Cornell University Press, 1986), p.110.
36. See also *Punch's Petition to the Ladies* (Dublin, 1724).
37. Jonathan Swift, 'Mad Mullinex and Timothy', in Harold Williams (ed.), *The Poems of Jonathan Swift* (Oxford: Clarendon Press, 1937), vol.3, pp.774, 775.
38. Ibid., p.777.
39. Burke to Charles O'Hara, 10 July 1761, R.J.S. Hoffman, *Edmund Burke, New York Agent with his Letters to the New York Assembly and intimate correspondence with Charles O'Hara 1761–1776* (Philadelphia: American Philosophical Society, 1956), pp.278–9.
40. Dennis to Richard Shackleton, 14 Jan. 1747, pp.316–17.
41. Ibid., p.316.
42. The Burke poem, entitled 'To Dr. – H', dated 6–19 Feb. 1748, is almost certainly directed at Hiffernan since it appears to refer to his *Reflections on the Structure and Passions of Man* in its opening stanza:

> Say, H –n, for thou canst truly say,
> To thee is given to know
> The Structure of Man's Passions, & display
> The source from whence they flow.

This poem also lauds its subject for his knowledge of 'Physick', and it suggests that Burke thought of Hiffernan as a great poet: 'The Delian God to thee alone/His Various Excellence have shewn,/For in thy Breast in decent order lie/Physick, Philosophy, & Poetry' (cited in *Writings and Speeches*, vol.i, p.31).
43. See *The European Magazine*, 35 (Feb. 1794), p.110.
44. *The Tickler*, 6 (29 April 1748), p.45.
45. For a discussion of this genre of Gaelic satire, which savagely mocked social upstarts, see Vivian Mercier, *The Irish Comic Tradition* (Oxford: Clarendon Press, 1962), pp.155–71.
46. *The Tickler*, 6 (29 April 1748), p.46.
47. *The Tickler*, 5 (18 March 1748), pp.24–9.
48. Ibid., p.26.
49. *The Tickler*, 35 (20 Oct. 1749).
50. *The Reformer*, 1 (28 Jan. 1748), p.1.
51. See Patrick Fagan, *Dublin's Turbulent Priest: Cornelius Nary 1658–1738* (Dublin: Royal Irish Academy, 1991), p.198.

52. For a reproduction of this print, see Burke, *Riotous Performances*, p.175.
53. *The Tickler*, (26 Feb. 1748), pp.13–14.
54. This frontispiece depicts Lucas being 'tickled' by a grinning, ragged man in what was clearly a satirical rendering of the Jones portrait of the previous year. For a reproduction of this print, see Burke, *Riotous Performances*, p.176.
55. *The Tickler*, 1 (18 Feb. 1748), p.7.
56. Ibid., p.1.
57. *The Reformer*, 5 (25 Feb. 1748), p.1.
58. Ibid., p.4.
59. Ibid., pp.2–3.
60. Charles O'Conor and John Curry, for example, also used loyalist rhetoric to make the case for Catholic emancipation.
61. Thomas McLoughlin, 'The Context of Edmund Burke's *The Reformer*', *Eighteenth-Century Ireland*, 2 (1987), p.43.
62. *The Reformer*, 4 (18 Feb. 1748), pp.1–3.
63. *The Reformer*, 7 (10 March 1748), pp.1–4.
64. *The Reformer*, 9 (24 March 1748), pp.2, 1–3.
65. McLoughlin, 'The Context of Edmund Burke's *The Reformer*', pp.51–5.
66. *The Reformer*, 6 (3 March 1748), p.1.
67. For the identification of 'Asper' as Hiffernan, see also Samuels, *The Early Life, Correspondence and Writing of the Rt. Hon. Edmund Burke*, p.172.
68. *The Reformer*, 6 (3 March 1748), p.1.
69. Ibid., pp.1–2.
70. Ibid., p.2.
71. For an extended discussion of this campaign, and *The Reformer's* support for it, see Burke, *Riotous Performances*, pp.183–95.
72. *The Tickler*, 9 (8 Sept. 1748).
73. See Jacqueline Hill, *From Patriots to Unionists: Dublin Civic Politics and Irish Protestant Patriotism, 1660–1840* (Oxford: Clarendon Press, 1997), pp.106–8.
74. The parts of the puppet characters were performed by 'a Company of Gentlemen' (*The Dublin Courant*, 29 April–2 May 1749; 10–23 May, 1749).
75. *The Election*, p.7.
76. Firebrand's long 'Oration' in the first act, and his written 'Address' in the second act for example, are satires of Lucas's election speeches (*The Election*, pp.17–20, 26–9).
77. Ibid., p.44.
78. Ibid., p.63.
79. Ibid., p.68.
80. Burke to Charles O'Hara, 3 July 1761, in Hoffman, *Edmund Burke, New York Agent*, p.277.

4

Edmund Burke and Trinity College:
Lifetime Ties and Later College Commemoration[1]

L. M. CULLEN

Edmund Burke's name looms large in the history of Trinity College, and when in the nineteenth century, it wished to give its ethos a public face, the college chose Burke and Goldsmith, and not others, to stand at its portals on College Green. Strictly speaking Burke, rather like Lecky, another name in the College's panoply of genius, is a figure external to its ongoing life, inevitably so as he never taught there. His subsequent known visits were very edifyingly mainly to the library and to Thomas Leland, the senior fellow who most frequently assumed what was at this time the somewhat informal annual officership of librarian. Burke's standing of itself, of course, would make him a figure to which the College could safely resort when it felt either vulnerable or simply wanted to vaunt the greatness of its graduates. He would certainly have shown the College to his son in 1786, but that is a guess, not a documented fact of Burke's brief – and last – visit to Ireland, the sole one which was prompted by personal motives alone.[2] Decided at short notice, it was cut short only because the parliamentary session in London resumed earlier than had been expected. In Irish terms Burke was far to the left of centre. His honorary doctorate at the end of 1790 owed more to the goodwill of its turbulent provost John Hely-Hutchinson than to the appeal of Burke's *Reflections on the French Revolution* which was popular with conservatives in both islands, and the carefully-chosen terms of the citation in the College registry are clearly from the pen of the wily Hely-Hutchinson and three decades' knowledge of Burke.[3]

The College, more conservative in the nineteenth century than in the eighteenth, was more comfortable with Burke in the Hist (student debating society or 'club' founded in 1747 by Burke) than in the front square and outside its portals than inside its walls. In 1897 the centenary of his death seems to have gone officially unnoticed. It was the Hist, not the college, which commemorated him, and in December, not in July, the month of his death. The college itself did so only in the Trinity Monday discourse of 1900, and it honoured Grattan in 1901. In the politics of the time the purpose of taking him up publicly was to mitigate or undo its increasingly conservative image, which appeared more and more opposed to all the aspirations of an increasingly nationalist Ireland, a task made the more urgent by the quickened pace of political pressures in favour of a radical university reorganization.

Edmund Burke, like his great friend and admirer, Adam Smith, has suffered the stigma of being paraded as the father of conservatism. Like Smith he is in the good sense of the word subversive, and an unsparing critic of entrenched position and vested interest. The *Reflections on the French Revolution* shocked many of his admirers who saw it as out of character with his thought. Burke's contacts in his post-student days were with figures who were innovative, or at some stage of life, had been so. Three of them stand out. The first was John Monck Mason, a student contemporary of Burke's with whom he renewed acquaintance in the early 1760s when Mason was a member of Parliament. The second was Thomas Leland, elected to fellowship in 1746, in other words during Burke's student days, and who was in the 1760s Burke's closest contact in the College and party to a grand design for the history of Ireland, the purpose of which was political as much as scholarly. The third was Hely-Hutchinson, whom Burke first knew in Hely-Hutchinson's early political career at the outset of the 1760s. In his brief visit in 1786 the provost was one of the first figures that Burke hoped to meet; as it happened, Hely-Hutchinson was out of town, the shortened visit made a meeting impracticable and the regrets remain enshrined in prose expressing real feeling and not just conventional loss.

Burke's youth is usually described as obscure in detail. Yet the fact is that we know much of him as an undergraduate, and of the six who joined him in 1747 in founding the Club, the parent of the future Hist.[4] However, interesting though they are, Burke and his fellow-members stand in total isolation from the student body at large. In a curious way, either the Club provided a training for several students who lacked the charmed backing or social assurance of broad acres, or more probably, as I suspect, the student body itself in its intimate as opposed to rumbustious moments, was chronically cliquish and there were simultaneously several of these societies. The record of this one survives by combination of chance, the genius of its founding figure, and above all Burke's fascination with politics and parliamentary procedure and dedication to writing things down. Sons of landed gentry were absent from this particular little club; we cannot trace at the time his early friendship with Monck Mason, or his acquaintance with Leland, beyond the fleeting observation in 1746 that Leland in the competition for election to fellowship 'answered exceedingly well'. In fact, we know Leland was unanimously elected.

The real contrast is between our often rather full knowledge of Burke up to the end of his undergraduate career, and the sheer scarcity of detail for the years from 1748 to 1759, when Burke's career becomes well-documented once more. *The Reformer*, the journal which he launched in January 1748, suspended publication in April of the same year.[5] However, he expected to resume later in the year, as the last issue announced that 'the thinness of the town for the ensuing summer, obliges us to discontinue this paper until next winter, during which time, subscriptions will be taken by the printer hereof.' Something happened in the interval. As a letter in 1759 refers to eleven years absence from Ballyduff, Co. Cork, the inference is that he left Ireland before late 1748, as if he had remained he would certainly have continued his annual visitations to his mother's home there. It is these years, 1748 to 1759, that are puzzling; most obscure of all are the years from 1748 to 1755.

Journalism and politics, and in Burke's case the two go together, may well have been the attraction. The fact that late 1748, as the Irish parliament met only every second year, would not be a parliamentary season may have been an added incentive to leave. Did he leave in the casual way many other contemporaries did for London, or did he leave for a London which had more politics and more journalism than Dublin? A hint in a letter in 1757 points to contact with Lord Egmont, a peer with north County Cork lands, and Burke was writing pamphlets. Obscurity in these years is a reminder of the sheer difficulty of advancement for someone not conventionally a member of a social and political establishment, who for some reason abandoned the orthodox path of finishing a legal education as a basis for entry to political life. We must remember that times were changing, and that before Burke left, Charles Lucas showed how a career might be based on journalism, a pattern that Wilkes in London later emulated. Forty years previously, Swift in London had hoped to make a career of ecclesiastical advancement through journalism in the Tory cause. Burke in some senses is the lay, and in material terms, more successful, exponent of the same talent and path. His quarrel with his first-known, but almost certainly not his first political employer seems to have revolved in essence around the question of whether Burke's talents would be devoted exclusively to his patron's political interest, or to a concurrent pursuit of his own concerns. He was always to believe in ideas; he read and wrote to a degree which would have been impossible for major party political managers, given the crushing social and business demands on their time; and his advocacy in speeches, letters and writings is attractively but unrealistically the naive one that argument and reason of themselves can change the world. In a peculiar sense, he had, and from a not dissimilar background, some of the make-up of the very revolutionaries whom he later criticized in his *Reflections*.

His success, already anticipated by the well-got social circle in London that he had acquired by the end of the 1750s, is measured in his position of private secretary to a chief secretary in two Irish parliamentary seasons in the early 1760s, and in the influence wielded in this ostensibly obscure role as secretary to the holder of an office which itself was only in the 1760s beginning to become one of serious parliamentary management. If there were limits to how far he could go, his career – and its Irish dimension was simply the accident of Irish office acquired by a capable and rising politician who had retained Burke as a secretary – reflects how patronage was moving beyond the hiring of conventional legal abilities to recruitment of talent with the pen.

If his college career unfolded in a Dublin already enlivened by the early turmoils of Lucas's new journalism, it was just as much or even more influenced by the fact that it coincided with the gestation of Jacobite invasion of Scotland, its course in 1745–46 and its aftermath. At its end in April 1746, the invasion was, in Burke's words, 'the most material, or rather the only news here'. The confident and detached policy of Chesterfield, dispatched in October 1745 to Ireland as a lord lieutenant capable of handling a crisis, was vital to the calm public response. On a report of a rising in Connaught, looking at his watch, his response was that 'it's now 9 o'clock and time for them to rise, so I am inclined to believe your intelligence is true'. The O'Flaherty, geographically the most remote chieftain of Gaelic lineage, from the suspect and lawless far side of the Corrib, was received at the viceregal court as a symbolic gesture of order in the remote west; and Chesterfield observed memorably that Miss Ambrose, a young lady with charming eyes, was the only dangerous papist he knew. However, this Olympian approach, vindicated by the fact that a rising did not occur, did raise the question as to what policy should be, not only for now but also for the future. The fact that for the first time in a crisis (and disregarding the most recent precedent of closure amid tensions in 1744) the chapels had not closed by order, made the question central. There were those who wanted the laws enforced with vigour and those who, like Chesterfield, felt that these laws were already antiquated. In a subtle way, the background issue was the future of the Penal Laws. In April 1746, when the invasion had been thrown back and defeated, Burke wrote that 'tis indeed melancholy to consider the state of those unhappy gentlemen who engag'd in this affair, who have thrown away their lives and fortunes and destroyed their families in what I believe they thought a just cause'. These sentiments were preceded by the words, 'I am sure I share in the general compassion', which hints at the outlook in Dublin and above all in Trinity. By July, now reading in the summer vacation in the Library, he was writing that 'I have read some history. I am endeavouring to get a little into the accounts of this our own poor country'.

The student body in Burke's student days was remarkably varied. If it included two sons of the Maude family, who led the hard-line Tipperary faction that Burke was to battle in 1761–62, it also included two sons of Anthony Malone, the parliament's most brilliant lawyer and the first member to question the purpose of the Acts. Contemporaries also included two men who in their later lives were both magistrates of deepest reactionary hue, the clergyman Robert Owen, one of Wexford's first Orangemen, battered or tortured by the Wexford rebels in 1798, and the layman Ambrose Power, murdered by the Whiteboys in Tipperary in 1776. However, Burke's friends Monck Mason and Leland more accurately anticipated the immediate future. Over the 1750s there followed remarkable undergraduates who in later life were to back changes in Irish society. In the 1760s, themselves, Andrews, the MP/Provost described by a political contemporary as 'an excellent politician never out of his road' and Leland formed part of a circle which also embraced Monck Mason, Sir Lucius O'Brien and Hely-Hutchinson. It was the more effective because it worked with government: its members tinged, not altogether unattractively, with hues of ambition and openness, are a good mirror to the modernity of the age.

Burke's small circle of six fellow students in the Club, which first met on 21 April 1747, were motivated more by the urge to learn to debate than by the external issues themselves. However, the general compassion informed the topics they chose; the Club debated the issue of leniency for the rebels twice in May 1747 and Burke lauded the role of Chesterfield in the following month. Two of the members were to take holy orders, a reminder that clergymen should not be seen, as they have been, simply as a bastion of the establishment. Clergymen – Anglican, Catholic or Presbyterian – were the educated men of the age; married clergymen in their family circle created a milieu with a taste or respect for learning, and it was they and their offspring, female as well as male, rather than the gentry as such who provided the backing for learning. After the 1798 rebellion, it was not simply graduates of the college, but clerical graduates who were the most outspoken supporters of the policy of reconciling rebels by Cornwallis, the Chesterfield of another troubled year in Irish history. They included Bishop Joseph Stoke of Killala, a humane and gifted fellow whose portrait handsomely graces the smoking room adjoining the Common Room; James Gordon, a learned and polished curate in Wexford; and James Little, the gentle and scholarly rector at Lackan, where the French landed in 1798, whose account of the rebellion, taking long to write because his house had been destroyed by the rebels, never got beyond manuscript.

The College's open atmosphere almost certainly is the basis of Burke's abiding belief that political circumstances were ripe for change, and that only a small handful of politicians in political society stood against it.[6] In the 1790s, when the great momentum for change had become politically sensitive in an age of revolution on the two sides of the Atlantic, the college's student body was to be found on the opposing sides in the debate on the great questions of the age, questions which indeed still trouble Irishmen. Students and scholars were identified with the radical public meetings of protest over the recall of the liberal or Whig lord lieutenant Fitzwilliam in 1795, and by 1798 there were four United Irishman societies in the College. The Orange Order was introduced to Dublin by undergraduates. In attributing this at a later date to Armagh undergraduates – who were not numerous – returning to College after the summer vacation, William Blacker was modestly or discretely underplaying his own personal role in the phenomenon. Though Catholics could not attend until 1793 because of an unacceptable oath, the fact is that Catholics were there in some numbers in the 1780s and early 1790s, which suggests that the college under its maverick Provost had with calculation turned a blind eye.

If the College in Burke's student days was opening to the great issues of a new age, he was in the same years observing directly the fury of Munster politicians, to whom he later referred distastefully as 'mongril' landlords amid, as he put it, 'the horrors of a Munster circuit', meaning in effect the initiation by the grand jury of County Cork of legal actions in the assizes in those years of the early and mid-1760s in which a parliamentary season was either about to open or was already in session. Spending his youth in his mother's Nagle family home of Ballyduff in Co. Cork, and visiting it every summer in the vacation from Trinity, he well knew the temper of the county and the lack of the 'general compassion' he found in Trinity. His Nagle relatives were a small circle of propertied Catholic families holding broad acres in the strongly Protestant society of north Cork. Though discriminated against legally, their wealth and social position ensured that they participated fully in the social life of the season, which revolved around the summer assizes. As these coincided with the summer vacation, Burke as a politically awakening youth spent every one of the vacations certainly to 1747 in Cork. In the politically troubled summer of 1745 we find him writing that 'after I arrived the races of Mallow took up three days of my time. After this the assizes of Cork, during which I had scarce a moment's time on my hands'. The following year from Caranatta in Cork we have an attractive little account of 'murdered sleep with dancing these three nights past that I can hardly hold up my head, which you will doubtless say I never did'. By the end of July, he was at Ballyduff, and we can guess that 'my mother's calling me to go away with her' was to yet another event in the social whirl. In 1747, four letters to him in County Cork from a friend went unanswered. We know there were tensions in north Cork, and the fear of papist conspiracy was part of the conversation in Cork somewhat in the way that the rhetoric of sermons in Dublin to commemorate the massacres that followed the outbreak of rebellion in Ulster of 23 October 1641 reached a high pitch in 1745 and 1746. As we know from other evidence, it was the sermons of these years which convinced the fashionable Catholic medical doctor John Curry of the necessity to tell the real truth of 1641 if opinion were to be made ready to accept political change.

Coming back to Ireland as private secretary to the chief secretary William Gerald Hamilton in 1761–62 and 1763–64, Burke was intimately involved in the political issues, which, as they revolved around the Catholic question, foundered on the bedrock of Cork and Tipperary opposition.[7] The two surviving documents in relation to an alleged Catholic conspiracy and the remarkable special commission to Munster in the spring of 1762, whose purpose was to take the administration of justice at the time of the spring assizes out of the hands of the local gentry – Burke's 'mongril' gentry – are not in the State Papers, but in Burke's private papers. He seems to have written the famous four-hour parliamentary speech by Hamilton which was delivered in the spring of 1762, and in 1764 he had prepared a long draft paper on the penal laws which is probably a fuller working out of the ideas in the 1762 speech. Monck Mason, a friend from college days, with Sir Lucius O'Brien, introduced the decisive first mortgage bill. Intended to allow Catholics to lend money on the security of land, had it been passed into law it would have made the repeal of the entire property code inevitable, as creditors all too often become the legal owners of property, and the measure was to be reintroduced in subsequent sessions.

Opposition to change and the continued emphasis by opponents on conspiracy and on the danger of massacre made it necessary to look into the massacres. Burke claimed as early as 1771 that it was he who prevailed on Thomas Leland to write a history of Ireland: 'I really thought our History of Ireland so terribly defective that I did, and with success, urge a very learned and ingenious friend of yours and mine in the University of Dublin to undertake it.' He told his close friend Bishop Markham that the bishop was in error in thinking that Burke's views were simply a repetition of those of his friends:

> They know little or nothing of the Irish history. They have never thought on it at all; I have studied it with more care than is common, and I have spoken to you on the subject, I dare say 20 times ... Indeed *I have* my opinion on that part of history, which I have often delivered to you; to every one I conversed with on the subject, and which I mean still, to deliver whenever the occasion calls for it. Which is 'That the Irish rebellion of 1641 was not only (as our silly things called Historys call it), not utterly *unprovoked* but that no History, that I have ever read furnishes an instance of any that was so *provoked*'. And that 'in almost all parts of it, it has been extremely and most absurdly misrepresented'.[8]

Leland and Burke went over the depositions in person in the College library, and twenty-eight years later Burke was still able to go into detail about the individual documents relating to Armagh events of 1641. He could also recall purchases made of documents of the period from a dealer in old furniture. He may have been the central figure in the purchases because he could repeat the conversation with the old man 'who was very curious and intelligent'. In his almost conspiratorial Irish visit from August to October 1766 (to recruit the remarkable legal team of young men who successfully defended Irish Catholics charged with treason), he gave Leland's college address to his English acquaintances as the means of contacting him. In the following years he continued to meet Leland in London, and he was probably also the person who introduced Leland to Johnson, and gave him Irish manuscripts. Leland (a senior fellow at thirty-nine years of age in 1761) was for Burke, we must remember, a congenial friend.[9] He was, on contemporary evidence, the reputed author of a historical romance published in 1762, and was said 'in agreeableness of familiar letter writing' to have few equals.[10]

Burke's role as prime mover in regard to study of the massacres drew him into study of the wider historiographical issues. These interests, still very much alive in the early 1770s, were to recur in letters to General Vallencey in 1786: he still shared the interest in publishing the 'ancient Irish Historical Monuments', since unless 'something of this is done, criticism can have no secure anchorage'. It was he who introduced Leland to the two most scholarly members of the Catholic committee, Curry and O'Conor. By 1766, Charles O'Conor had dined with Dr Leland and as he told George Faulkner, editor of the *Dublin Journal*,

viewed with pleasure in his dining room as fine a portrait of you as hands

could draw. He is a very learned and what is infinitely better, a very
worthy man ... To unite all parties in these kingdoms in one creed of civil
faith is possible, nay very practicable, and it were to be wished that those
who oppose such an union in civil orthodoxy assigned any one instance
wherein it could be hurtful to Britain or Ireland.

By 1767, O'Conor was using the library and in his visits remarkably had experienced also the civility of the provost. He was in subsequent years entertained
by Leland in his scholarly retreat at Rathmichael where he became prebendary.[11]

In a way of which we are not fully clear, the lord lieutenancy of Townshend
in 1767–72, like that of Halifax in 1761–62 was, among other things, intended to
advance the case of the Catholics. Within days of coming to Ireland in the autumn
of 1767, the rough soldier Townshend had visited the bookshop of the publisher
Faulkner who stood at the centre of Dublin intellectual life; Leland almost immediately entered his retinue as chaplain. Both Burke and O'Conor spoke with
warmth of the lord lieutenant, in his stormy years in Dublin. The liberal wind of
change in the corridors of the draughty Castle was quickly detected by the finely attuned antennae of conservatives. Significantly, too, Burke, with his Geiger
counter for measuring intolerance, sensed from London a gradual hardening of
feeling in conservative circles against Catholics. He was writing in defence of
Catholics again in 1776, and in that year he had briefed Arthur Young who was
embarking on his Irish tour, and whose later book not only paraphrased Burke's
words, but seemed at one point to repeat a remarkable paragraph from *The
Reformer* of 1748.

However, whatever about access to or advance made in the corridors of
power, the direct return on historical study of the massacres was poor. Burke
and the Catholics were disappointed with Leland's history, of which they had
such high hopes, when it appeared in 1773.[12] Burke noted later that the 'the
mode of doing it varied from his first conceptions'. Yet there was also a real
intellectual point in Leland's favour. If some of the old works republished in the
1760s maintained that more Protestants had been massacred in 1641 than actually lived on the island, the view of O'Conor, Curry and Burke was that there
had been no massacre at all, and in the good Irish partisan fashion of seeing one
side, but not both, as capable of mayhem, they devoted much energy to docu-
menting a massacre of Catholics in Islandmagee in Co. Antrim and of seeing it
as the catalysing force of the savagery of the war. O'Conor and Curry, themselves turned into hardened and ungenerous figures by the zealots they
opposed, never forgave Leland. They had quite unscrupulously obtained unau-
thorized access to the proofs of his book at the printers, and when it appeared
they had ready from Leland's own London publisher a condemnation of it.
Leland's scholarly reputation was to suffer even contemporaneously, though to
modern eyes Leland's sin is more that of opting for scholarly than political purpose. In differing from his friends on the evidence for a massacre of Catholics
at Islandmagee in Co. Antrim, the book seemed to them a betrayal: it provided

ammunition for those who saw Catholics as the perpetrators of crime. In controversial terms, which study of history was on both sides, it belied his underlying moderate purpose or could even be used to undermine it, a flaw in Burke view in 1774 due to 'his great distance from affairs, which makes him ignorant of the true situation of men'.[13] Curry also criticized Leland for giving the customary sermon on the anniversary of the rebellion in the parliamentary session of 1771. Yet for a ticklish commemorative occasion for a variegated and volcanic political audience, Leland's sermon was skilfully crafted, and behind the formality of the address, it was a consummate liberal political discourse.[14]

The College was never far from Burke's thoughts. Decades later, he hoped that the manuscripts he had collected had been deposited in the library. He knew all its provosts. As an incoming undergraduate, he met Provost Baldwin: to a young man in 1744, the Provost inevitably appeared an 'old sickly-looking man'. He knew Provost Andrews, a very active MP, who in 1766 mentioned Burke in a letter to Hely-Hutchinson 'in the highest terms'. Burke knew Hely-Hutchinson well from 1761 onwards. In the summer assizes of 1762, Hely-Hutchinson, a barrister as well as MP, went on the Munster summer assizes in the knowledge of the cases pending there and with the approval of Hamilton, Burke and Mason.[15] Andrews and Hely-Hutchinson were both in some way, like Leland and Faulkner, party to the great enterprise in the Catholic cause in which Burke was variously a cog and a prime mover.

In 1774, Burke emerges as a backer of Leland for Provost. The ailing Provost Andrews died at last at Shrewsbury on 12 June. Two days later, Leland wrote to Burke and three other letters followed. He asked Burke to enlist the support of Bishop Markham in England (whose acquaintance Leland had probably made though Burke in London). Burke, describing Leland to Markham as 'my old friend ... a very learned and in all other respects a very well-informed man', saw the approach as ill-considered as Markham had no real political say. The Board's meeting on 23 June was a purely formal one to arrange the funeral, and it could not at that meeting address the question of a successor. It was, however, left no time to consider the matter of a successor, as Hely-Hutchinson was parachuted by the government into the office. Some months later in a sharp observation to Hely-Hutchinson, in saying with candour that 'I had always thought that this office is best suited to a man of the ecclesiastical gown, and a mere academic', Burke was, in effect, making clear that his support had lain with Leland. This view of the office was to be repeated in 1794 at a time when he had no personal loyalty to a candidate for office. The conservative or loyalist Westmorland administration had in mind a political nomination in 1793 and the new London coalition in London in 1794, though intended to be a reforming one for Ireland, was no better because of its dilemma in having two men in England to reward and its desperate need to find a job for the second of them. To Earl Fitzwilliam, Burke's political patron, about to step into the shoes of the outgoing lord lieutenant, he observed, that the post should not be filled 'jobbishly and improperly' as was proposed, by a man who was an outsider both to Ireland and to the

College; and he pointed out that Hely-Hutchinson at least had been a graduate of the College. He added that 'this intrusion of an absolute stranger, by dispensation, can be justified only by some unfitness of the statutable members of the body for that Office'. He was adamant about the standards of the College: 'Fellowships are not obtained by favour in Dublin; nor by a blind and partial election. That place is obtained by a very rigid course of study, under which more than one has died, and after a publick examination of the strictest kind, made in the Theatre, and in the face of a numerous, attentive, and often very critical audience.' He went on to defend the College: 'Dublin never did, at any time, possess so many fellows, not only unexceptionable for morals and learning, but of very high and just reputation for both.' These statements were made more in remembrance of his undergraduate days and the early 1760s, and of poor Leland who had died in 1785, than of the college in the 1790s of which he had no personal knowledge.

Made by a man who from those days wanted change and a place in Ireland for Catholics, they are a reminder that Trinity always remained in his eyes a living and tolerant institution. Almost a century later, the undergraduate careers of both Douglas Hyde and John Millington Synge remind us that, far from being a rigid institution, it exercised a very positive role in the formation of young, critical and innovative minds. Even at the very end of the nineteenth century, there were eddies and currents beyond the circle of those seven deadly sins, the Senior Fellows, and in the twentieth century, the aspirations associated with Edward Gwynn, provost from 1927 to 1937, and the achievements brought to fruition, a generation later, by Provost McConnell and his backers, came from within the College, not from outside. That would indeed have been in Burke's view the college that he knew and respected. His friendships in the College and the liberal views of politicians such as Sexton Pery (a future speaker of the Commons whom he came to know in the early 1760s and an open man on the Catholic question) and Hely-Hutchinson were to be the basis of an abiding belief held by Burke even into the 1790s that advances were held up solely by the vested interest of a handful of politicians.

NOTES

1. This text is based on the Trinity Monday discourse in Trinity College, Dublin, in May 1997, in commemoration of the bicentenary of Burke's death. Footnotes are given sparingly. The main sources are the Burke Correspondence, both the Copeland edition and the Charles William, Earl Fitzwilliam and Sir Richard Bourke *Correspondence* of 1844. They are usefully supplemented by A.P.I. Samuels, *The Early Life, Correspondence and Writings of the Rt. Hon, Edmund Burke* (Cambridge: Cambridge University Press, 1923), and R.J.S. Hoffman, *Edmund Burke, New York Agent, with his letters to the New York Assembly and intimate correspondence with Charles O'Hara* (Philadelphia: American Philosophical Society, 1956).
2. On Burke's little-known visit of 1786 see L.M. Cullen, 'Burke's Irish Views and Writings', in Ian Crowe (ed.), *Edmund Burke: his life and legacy* (Dublin: Four Courts Press, 1997), p.74.
3. Trinity College Dublin, MUN/V/5/5, Board minutes, 11 Dec. 1790, honouring him as 'a powerful advocate of the constitution, as the friend of public order and virtue, and consequently of the hap-

piness of mankind and in testimony of the high respect entertained by the university, which had the honour of his education, for the various endowments of his mind and for his transcendant talent and philantrophy'.

4. For these years, Samuels' *Early Life*, is a very full source.

5. This rare journal is reproduced in Samuels, *Early Life*, pp.297–329.

6. On Burke's proneness to the conspiracy theory of history, see L.M. Cullen, 'Burke, Ireland and Revolution', *Eighteenth-century Life*, 16, n.s.1 (Feb. 1992), pp.22, 36–7.

7. On the Munster background, see Cullen, 'Burke, Ireland and revolution', pp.28–33; L.M. Cullen, 'The Blackwater Catholics and County Cork Society and Politics in the Eighteenth Century', in P. O'Flanagan and C.G. Buttimer, *Cork: History and Society* (Dublin: Geography Publications, 1993b), pp.535–84.

8. *Correspondence*, vol.ii, pp.284–5, post 9 Nov. 1771, There is a redundant 'not' in the third line of the quotation, and the use of inverted commas also suggests that Burke was repeating views he had conveyed to Markham in their conversations.

9. Leland in fact brought back the manuscript to Dublin (two volumes, the Lloyd Mss). They are referred to in the introduction to Thomas Leland, *Sermons on Various Subjects* (Dublin, 1788), vol.1, p.xxvi.

10. The best summary of Leland's career is contained in the introduction to the three volumes of Leland's sermons, published by subscription in 1788.

11. Charles O'Conor's correspondence has a number of references to the College and to the Leland and Burke connections. C.C. and R.E. Ward (eds), *The Letters of Charles O'Conor of Belanagare*, 2 vols (Ann Arbor, 1980).

12. Thomas Leland, *History of Ireland from the Invasion of Henry II* (London, 1773), 3 vols.

13. Leland was well aware of his departing from the views of his friends, stating that the reader 'who may have the curiosity to enquire after those authorities, on which I have stated this transaction differently and with more precision, will find them among the depositions of the county of Antrim, from the middle to the latter end of the volume'. (*History of Ireland*, vol.3, p.129n). Burke's view, if anything, hardened with time, if we are to give weight to what he set out to his son in 1792. *Correspondence between 1844 and 1797* ed. Charles William, Lord Fitzwilliam and Richard Bourke, vol.ii, (London 1844) p.441, quoted in *Correspondence*, vol.vii, p.285 note. The differences between Leland and the Catholic leaders really stemmed from the interpretation of this single episode, central to their arguments not only that Catholics were innocent of massacre, but that there had been at the very outset a massacre of Catholics in Island Magee. In other words massacre had started with the Protestants rather than Catholics. Curry's *Occasional remarks on certain passages in Dr Leland's History of Ireland in a letter to M-F- esq* (London, 1773) is a much less judicious assessment than Leland's. O'Conor and Curry, of course, along with Burke, denied that there had been any massacre of Protestants. Leland noted both that Protestant accounts had exaggerated the massacres by Catholics, and that in regard to the Island Magee killings of Catholics the 'popish writers have represented it with shocking aggravation'.

14. The text of the sermon is reproduced in the published collection of Leland's sermons.

15. Hamilton had noted to Hely-Hutchinson, about to go to Munster for the assizes in July 1762, that 'I am sure you have too much firmness and humanity to let those who are innocent be made a sacrifice to party and to personal resentment'. See Public Record Office of Northern Ireland Report on Donoughmore Mss, p.78 (T, 3459.C/1/40).

5

Burke's Irish Connections in England

ELIZABETH LAMBERT

The ages of five or six to eleven are among the most impressionable in a child's life. During these years he or she acquires a sense of self as an accountable moral agent; in fact, certain religious traditions define the period as 'coming to the age of reason'. It is also the time when the child is very conscious of the concept of justice – or injustice – and becomes aware that inequality is an unhappy fact of life. Edmund Burke developed in this essential way when he lived in the Blackwater country under the care of his Catholic uncle, Patrick Nagle.

Burke was not a robust child, and the periodic flooding of the river Liffey next to their Dublin home made his parents worry for his health. For this reason, they sent him to live with his maternal relatives, the family of Patrick Nagle, in the Blackwater area of County Cork.[1] Certainly in the larger picture of Burke's life, his time with the Nagles is a mere blip on the screen, and, admittedly, the term 'some five years', as reported by Burke's biographers could mean either 'sporadically', or 'continually'. Nevertheless, a closer study of the Blackwater years and of the first decade of Burke's life in England reveal the significance of that period and of Burke's Irish connections in his life and career.

In terms of the kind of man Burke became, two aspects of his life with Patrick Nagle are significant. The first is the fact that the Nagles were Catholic and were living under the strictures of the penal laws against Roman Catholics. Burke had a special love for his Uncle Patrick and voiced the highest praise for him years later when Patrick was dying:

> We shall all lose, I believe, one of the very best men that ever lived; of the clearest integrity, the most genuine principles of religion and virtue, the most cordial Goodnature and benevolence, that I ever knew ... I really think he is the person I should wish myself, or anyone I greatly loved, the most to resemble. This I do not say from the impression of my immediate feeling, but from my best Judgment; having seen him at various times of my Life, from my Infancy to the last years.[2]

Observing Patrick Nagle and listening to the talk of his more rebellious cousins, Burke learned about the coping mechanisms that came with being second-class citizens under threat.[3]

The second aspect of Burke's experience among the Nagles in the Blackwater country is that he developed a love of the land and experienced the challenges and satisfactions of that particular way of life. As a young man newly arrived in England, he wrote to a friend that he wished Providence had blessed him with 'a few paternal acres', and termed agriculture 'my favourite study and my favourite pursuit'.[4] Because of these early experiences among the Nagles, ownership of property and privilege merged in Burke's mind with questions of identity.

The three main branches of the Nagle family were the Nagles of Monanimy, the Nagles of Annakissey, and the Nagles of Clogher. Burke lived with the Nagles of Monanimy in Ballyduff, but the Nagles of Annakissey were only some two or three miles distant, in the village of Ballygriffin. Members of the family also fanned out all over the Blackwater Valley and into the city of Cork. Moreover, there was a significant contingent of them in France. Some had served in the French army, and one Richard Nagle acted as Secretary of State in the court of St Germain-en-Laye. By the eighteenth century there was a strong branch of the Nagle family in Cambraie.

The family was also a mixed lot in terms of wealth. They were not, as Dixon Wector asserts, 'a band of poor relations who often applied for and received help from the statesman in his heyday'.[5] Uncle Patrick seems to have been a fairly prosperous farmer, was educated, and later took an active interest in English politics when Burke sent him London newspapers. In the previous generation David Nagle of the Nagles of Annakissey managed to secure a great deal of land and wealth by circumventing the Penal Laws governing property, thus providing well for his descendents in Ballygriffin. Similarly, Joseph Nagle[6] was a wealthy merchant in the nearby city of Cork. In the eighteenth century Cork was a city of opposites with a thriving, educated merchant population, and a commensurately poor and brawling population whose social problems were exacerbated by the transient seamen going in and out of the port. Paradoxically, the Penal Laws that forbad Irish Catholics to own land did not restrict their commercial ventures. Hence Dutch, Italian, Spanish, French, and Portuguese ships, as well as English, took on provisions in Cork's harbours and provided its Catholic merchants with opportunities for making a significant amount of money. Joseph Nagle was in this class. Success had its price, though, because Cork was one of the areas where the Penal Laws were firmly enforced. According to Nano Nagle, her uncle, Joseph was 'the most disliked by the Protestants of any Catholic in the kingdom',[7] and his house had been searched more than once on one pretext or another.

This Nano Nagle became a shadowy but, at the same time, substantial entity in the lists of those Nagles who touched Burke's life. She and her sister Anne had been sent to a Benedictine convent school in France for further education.

After schooling the two women remained there, living among the many Irish ex-patriots in Paris, and returned to Ireland only upon their father's death in 1746. Since that branch of the Nagle family lived only two miles away from Patrick Nagle's home, we can presume that the women's decision to stay in France, and the make-up of the Irish community in Paris, was a topic of conversation in the family and that young Burke was aware of the implications as to why his cousins were there and why they chose to remain.

In 1750 Burke left Ireland to study for the bar at Middle Temple in London. The following six or so years have been styled as 'the missing years' in Burke's biography for there are only some thirteen letters from this period and a few other writings. What we do know is that during these years Burke formed life-long attachments, the most important of which was Jane Nugent, his future wife. We also know a significant number of Burke's fellow students at Middle Temple were Irish.

According to the Register of Admissions to Middle Temple, in 1750 when Burke was admitted there were nineteen Irish and three Americans among the group of forty-seven. In the following year fifteen were admitted, six of whom were Irish, one Scot and one American. Several of the Irish had been fellow students at Trinity. The Americans came from Virginia, Maryland, Pennsylvania and South Carolina. Among them was William Franklin, the illegitimate son of Benjamin Franklin. Conversations with his fellow students from the colonies probably piqued Burke's interest in going to America because he mentions it several times in his correspondence of 1757. And he continued to pursue the idea that a career in writing was compatible with a law career. In her biography of Wolfe Tone, Marianne Elliott notes that 'the Middle Temple was known more for its resident writers, of whom Cowper, Goldsmith, Sheridan and Fielding were the most notable, than its great legal minds'.[8] That atmosphere would have done nothing to quiet the 'fatal itch' that made him scribble.

Outside of Middle Temple itself there was a strong network of Irish in the London of the 1750s, and we know that Burke's father, Richard, had business connections there. From the beginning Burke was a beneficiary of this Irish network. The sureties to Edmund's bond at Middle Temple were John Burke of Serjeants Inn, Fleet Street, and Thomas Kelly of Middle Temple. John Burke and Edmund's father, Richard Burke, may have had business dealings. Through John Burke and Kelly, Burke met Joseph Hickey, another barrister, and when he became ill within months of his arrival in England, Hickey put him in touch with his good friend and noted Irish physician Dr Christopher Nugent.

Nugent was a Catholic physician and Governor of the Bath General Hospital. Contemporary accounts accord him full laurels for his medical expertise and tranquil, pragmatic personality. Sir John Hawkins, not one to be easily pleased, describes Nugent as 'a physician of the Romish communion and into practice with persons of that persuasion. He was an ingenious, sensible, and learned man, of easy conversation, and elegant manners. Johnson had a high opinion of him and always spoke of him in terms of great respect.'[9] Indeed,

Samuel Johnson loved Nugent and enjoyed his easy and learned conversation as one of the first members of the Literary Club.

In 1752, two years after he began study at Middle Temple, Burke wrote an epistle to Dr Nugent in which he celebrated Nugent's character as well as his medical skill. The speaker asserts Nugent both 'restored his life and taught him how to live'. In the closing lines of the poem the speaker expresses a need for the Doctor's friendship, 'and Hers no less'. The 'her' is described a few lines later as one 'in whom just Heav'n has joined, / The weakest body, with the firmest mind' and is saluted as 'Our fair and Absent friend'. Nugent's daughter, Jane Mary is the woman so celebrated.[10] Burke seems to have fallen in love instantaneously and completely. Although he and Jane were not married for another five years, in 1757, there is never mention of another woman in his life.

Given the fact that Christopher Nugent was a known Catholic, it has also been presumed that his daughter Jane was also a practicing Catholic. Thus biographers have unhesitatingly asserted that Burke's wife was a Catholic. Little attention has been paid to the implications of such a situation or known evidence to the contrary. According to Penal Law on the books at the time, if a Protestant married a Catholic he could not become a barrister or solicitor, much less a Member of Parliament. Furthermore, when the Duke of Newcastle told Lord Rockingham that his new secretary, Edmund Burke, was a papist, Burke immediately went to Rockingham and offered to resign rather than put him in an awkward situation. Acknowledging that 'several of his connections were Roman Catholics', he 'disclaimed that persuasion for himself and *all the members of his family, save his mother and sister*' (emphasis mine). One could charge that Burke's excluding his wife from the list of Catholic connections was a case of saving his own neck or, in this case, his job. That charge falls away in light of the following.

According to genealogist Basil O'Connell's research, Dr Nugent, a Catholic, had married a Presbyterian, Jane Leake of Holycross, in 'a run-away match' because of their different religions. According to custom at the time, in mixed marriages daughters were raised in the mother's faith and sons in the father's. Hence Jane Nugent would have been raised in her mother's Presbyterian faith. Sir James Prior, one of the earliest and the most reliable of Burke's biographers, states that at the time of the marriage, Jane's mother 'stipulated for the free enjoyment of her own religion [and] for the privilege of educating her daughters in the same tenants'.[11] We do not know when Jane's mother died, but when Burke met her she was the only woman in the family. As such, and as a loving daughter, Jane could quite possibly have been attending Mass with her father. Nevertheless, as Burke's wife, solid evidence establishes her as a practicing Anglican.

Religion aside, Jane was the presiding woman in the house when Dr Nugent was practicing medicine in Bath in the 1740s and 1750s. Given her father's profession and his practice of treating patients in his home, she more than likely had to deal with domestic arrangements, financial matters, changing schedules, delayed meals, and people in and out of the house at all hours. Furthermore, Dr Nugent had achieved a reputation as an eminent physician and author of a recognized treatise on hydrophobia; hence she became accustomed to distinguished visitors and their interesting conversations. According to a character Burke wrote of her, Jane entered into these discussions, 'informing them to whom she listened for Information'.[12] And the wonderful sense of humour that emerges so frequently in her correspondence had to charm the young Burke.

Jane needed and used every one of these skills as Burke's wife when, in later years, she docketed correspondence, entertained visitors of all sorts, and handled domestic arrangements for their house in London as well as for the Beaconsfield estate. She also took on the role of spokesperson in correspondence with Lord Rockingham and Bristol constituents when Burke was on the road or pressed with other business and handled the always-precarious finances of the family, leaving Burke's mind, as he said in his will, 'free to prosecute my publick Duty, or my Studies, or to indulge in my relaxations or to cultivate my friends'.[13]

Jane's voice in her largely unpublished correspondence is firm, competent, knowledgeable, warm, and demonstrates a marvellous sense of humour. Most of all, she was a loving wife to Burke and excellent mother to their surviving child, Richard.[14] These impressions are validated by those who came into contact with her, such as a Bristol constituent who reported, 'Mrs. Burke is very pleasing and extremely affable, and is sensible ... The time before dinner was employed in conversation in which Mrs. Burke took part'.[15]

Another account, albeit a decidedly slanted one, is given by Hester Thrale whose visit to Burke coincided with the General Election of 1774 when Burke left his guests to attend to public matters and returned in a few hours 'much flustered with liquor', as were her husband and several others. Mrs. Thrale sniped at Jane Burke's not leaving the room immediately after dinner as a more proper hostess would have done; the general shoddy state of housekeeping – 'their Black a moor carries Tea about with a cut finger wrapt in Rags'; noted that 'Mrs. Burke drinks as well as her husband' and finished her account with a shot at the Irishness of it all: '[they are] always like Foreigners somehow: dirty and dressey, with their Clothes hanging as if on a Peg'.[16] While the tenor of Mrs. Thrale's account reverberates with class prejudice, it does support other evidence that Jane and Edmund Burke shared a compatibility not typical of many eighteenth-century marriages.

One other all-important connection from Burke's early days in London was William Burke, son of John Burke who was one of the sureties to Edmund's bond at Middle Temple. William Burke, or Will as he is often called, quickly became Burke's constant companion and was called 'kinsman' by him although their exact relationship is not clear. Initially Will was a constant presence in Burke's life as his fellow student at Middle Temple and then as a companion in their common search for political position. He also seems to have been an originator of get-rich schemes and was politically and financially ambitious for them both. Because of this close association early on in Burke's career, the tendency has been to think of William Burke as a life-long house guest, sharing Burke's living arrangements. In reality, William was in India for eleven years and spent only a brief period with the Burkes upon his return. In important ways, Edmund and Will were opposites. Will was volatile, prejudicial and disingenuous. To a certain extent Burke shared the volatility and certainly was prejudiced in favour of those he loved and respected. However, falseness or self-centred calculation was not part of his character. To be fair, one must also note that Will was a supportive and faithful friend to Burke in ways that appear absolutely contrary to his negative qualities. Will's beneficent attributes were not generally known, however, and the public often linked Edmund with him as a companion of the roistering speculator Lauchlin Macleane.

Of Scots and Welsh heritage, Lauchlin Macleane was born in County Antrim in Ireland sometime between May 1728 and May 1729 (the records were destroyed in the Irish Troubles of 1922). By the 1760s, he had been a classics scholar, general medical practitioner, regimental surgeon, army contractor, customs officer, land speculator and stock market gambler on the grand scale. He had also lived in North America and in the West Indies. Although he was known to be corrupt and utterly ruthless, he had a personal charm that drew others of like interests to him. Will Burke and Edmund's younger brother Richard were so drawn and, as we know, lost their financial shirts in the India Stock crash of June 1769 when they over-invested with Macleane's encouragement. According to James Macleane, Lauchlin's biographer, Edmund's association with the man was peripheral, perhaps as much from personal choice as from life's circumstances because he characterizes Burke as one who, 'In an age of roistering, unprincipled rakes, he stood out as a model of marital fidelity, clean living and moral integrity'.[17]

That may have been, but some of his contemporaries tarred Burke with the same 'Irish Adventurers' brush as they did brother Richard and kinsman William. The slur comes from an account that Laetia Hawkins wrote about her father, Sir John Hawkins, Samuel Johnson's biographer. She said that Hawkins called them 'Desperate venturers':

> 'The Burkes' as the men of that family were called ... were, as my father termed them, 'Irish Adventurers', and came into this country with no good auguries, nor any very decided principles of action. They had to talk their way in the world that was to furnish their means of living.[18]

Included in this slur was Dick Burke, Edmund's younger bother. Scholars designate him as 'Richard Burke Sr' to distinguish him from Burke's son, Richard Burke Jr. Dick Burke had settled in England in the 1750s. In 1763 he was appointed Collector of Customs in Grenada and in 1770 bought a tract of land on St Vincent. Because the climate was bad for his health and his finances unstable, he was discharged as Collector for Grenada and returned to England.

He was admitted to Lincoln's Inn on 12 November 1771 and in 1777 was called to the Bar. Through the years he was a part of Edmund's professional and social life even while pursuing a political career of his own. When he died in 1794, Richard was Recorder for Bristol. That was his professional life. In private he was a gambler and a self-confessed procrastinator but a man possessed of a lively wit and affectionate heart. The critical public only saw the fist half of that equation: the younger brother who depended upon his talented older brother for a career and a livelihood. Hence, as Burke moved more and more into public view, his Irish connections became part of his persona. And friends and enemies alike viewed them as a detriment.

Gilbert Elliot's description of the 'train' that followed Burke evokes a mental image that is at once humorous and telling in terms of Burke's characteristic loyalty to those he loved. Elliot's description features Burke's son Richard, 'who is quite *nauseated* by all mankind', brother Richard, 'oppressive with animal spirits and brogue', cousin Will Burke, 'a fresh charge on any prospects of power Burke may ever have', and, concludes the list with a description of Mary French, Burke's niece, as 'the most perfect she Paddy' ever caught.[19] Frances Burney has filled in the picture of Burke's niece when she described meeting her at Mrs Crew's:

> When we left the Dining Parlour to the Gentlemen, Miss French seized my Arm, without the smallest previous speech, & with a prodigious Irish brogue, said 'Miss Burney, I am so glad you can't think to have this favourable opportunity of making an intimacy with you! I have longed to know you ever since I became rational!'[20]

(One cannot help but wonder if Burney was indulging her flair for comedy in the last statement.) She concludes the account with the acknowledgement that Miss French was 'a handsome Girl & seems very good humoured' and expresses the hope that the 'soft-mannered & well bred & quiet Mrs. Burke will soon subdue this exuberance of forwardness and loquacity'. The only one in Burke's family who escapes Elliot's pen is Jane Burke, and the reason is apparent in Burney's description of the 'soft-manner and well bred' Mrs Burke – the same qualities Hawkins, Johnson's biographer, approved of in her father, Dr Nugent.

It was not enough that Burke's name was associated with some of the infamous Irish in London, but in 1770 the activities of his Nagle relatives in Ireland seeped into and affected his life in England. As William Gerard Hamilton's secretary, Burke had been in Ireland during the winters of 1761 and 1764 and had begun the *Tract on the Popery Laws* published, as we know, posthumously. Then in February 1765 he had quarrelled bitterly with Hamilton and resigned his pension. Within four months he was employed as secretary to the Marquis of Rockingham, and, as noted above, that position was in jeopardy when the Duke of Newcastle charged Burke with being a papist. While Burke immediately countered the charge, he knew that his Irish background and

Catholic connections in Ireland were being investigated. In the 1760s the activities of several of his Nagle relatives could not bear scrutiny.

Nano Nagle, in defiance of the Penal Code, had secretly established schools in the poorest sections of Cork and was trying to form a congregation of religious sisters to secure her work. James Nagle was under investigation in the Father Nicholas Sheehy treason case when Sheehy was hanged, drawn and quartered on charges of inciting to riot and rebellion. Garrett Nagle was arrested on suspicion of aiding and assisting the White Boys – the agrarian group formed to protest large-scale enclosure of common lands and whose activities had become more threatening than tearing down pasture fences. Another Garrett – Garrett Atty Nagle – had abducted a protestant heiress and was in danger of being hanged. Evidence in Burke's papers and correspondence attest to his disgust with the Sheehy case, considering the trial as a travesty of justice and the execution as barbaric. There is also a letter in Burke's papers from one James Buxton, executed as a conspirator with Sheehy, asserting that he could have been pardoned if he had given evidence against James Nagle.

Genealogist Basil O'Connell writes of that phase in the Nagle family and states, 'in desperation and fear of persecution, the Nagle family had some organized plan to protect themselves'.[21] The plan was simple enough: in 1765 four Nagles conformed to the Established Church; among those conforming were James and Garrett. In the meantime, Patrick Nagle had appealed to Burke for help in Garrett Atty Nagle's case – the abduction of the heiress. Writing to his uncle, Burke assured him that 'there is no one Step on earth in my power that I would not gladly take to give ease [to your mind]', but acknowledged that any efforts he would take would, in Garrett's case, come to naught because at this time his own intentions were just as suspect as those of his Irish connections.[22]

In that letter to Patrick Nagle Burke spoke of 'industrious endeavours, which malice and envy, (very unprovoked indeed) have [been] used to ruin me'. Given the following sequence of events, one cannot dismiss Burke's complaint as neurotic. In the summer of 1766 he had been in Ireland with his wife, son and brother and had attended a three-day family gathering at which Nano Nagle – the illegal schoolmistress and founder of a religious order – had been present. The following October he complained about those whose 'purpose was, since they were not able to find wherewithal to except to my Character for the series of years since I appeared in England, to pursue me into the Closest recess of my Life, and to hunt even to my Cradle in hope of finding some blot against me'.[23] While one may charge Burke with indulging in hyperbole – 'even to my Cradle' – evidence suggests that there was a certain legitimacy to his claim.

For one thing, the charge that Rockingham had hired a papist seems to imply that Burke had been a Catholic from birth. Furthermore, in Ireland, his childhood friend Richard Shackleton had been asked by interested parties to write a biographical account of Burke that would include details about his 'family Connections, religion and General Character'. One can surmise that those anonymous individuals were in the pay of those determined to discredit Burke

A reading of Shackleton's sketch discovers that the subject of religion frames the account, beginning with the third sentence where Burke's mother is identified as being from 'a popish family' and concluding with an extended defence of Burke's Protestantism. It was exactly the sort of thing that Burke had feared and, in fact, predicted four years earlier when he heard that Shackleton had been approached for information. He had told him that, if religion were a leading part in the account, the topic would cause suspicion since the subject was 'not in the general thoughts of men of publick business'. He attributed the inquiry to the 'malice of my Enemies' and not to a casual desire for information about a public man. The fact that the popish connection had been used to discredit him with Rockingham lends credence to Burke's contention that his enemies were hunting for evidence 'even to his cradle' to use against him. It may have been that during his visit to Cork in the spring of 1766, his Nagle relations had spoken of such inquiries. Expediency might dictate that at this juncture Burke quietly separate himself from the Nagles and/or make himself less conspicuous as an Irishman. That was not in his make-up. Joseph Farington records in his diary the observation that 'Burke has associated in a domestic way very much with Irish people and has a strong prejudice in their favour'.[24] The Nagles were among the most significant of these domestic associations.

Various members of the family became part of the household in the course of their travels. The most prominent of them was Captain Edmund Nagle of the Royal Navy who stayed with the Burkes when not on duty. But it is his cousin, Edward Nagle, son of his cousin Walter Nagle and Burke's junior by some thirty years, to whom posterity owes an accurate account of Burke's last year and final hours as he took on the duties of amanuensis and functioned as companion and keeper of the gate.

Edward Nagle is first mentioned in a 1779 letter in which Burke tells a relative that he was unable to provide for him and his brother James, who were at that time students at the Catholic school in Staffordshire. In spite of Burke's professed inability to do something for the boy, when Nagle next appears in Burke's correspondence he is a clerk in William Windham's office.[25] Then in November 1796, nine months before his death, Burke told correspondents that he was using 'the hand of my friend and kinsman, Nagle' because he was too weak to sit at his desk. To others he spoke of Nagle as a 'confidential friend' as well as relative.

In his capacity as Burke's amanuensis, Nagle recorded Burke's last thoughts on the Pitt administration, France and Ireland in letters to Lord Fitzwilliam, William Windham and French Laurence. He was also Burke's hand in letters to friends and was a witness to his will. During June and July 1797 Nagle wrote, sometimes several times a day, to Burke's intimates in London keeping them apprised of Burke's deteriorating physical condition. Hence if anyone was privy to Burke's final state of mind on matters political, personal and spiritual, Edward Nagle was. For this reason, Nagle's unpublished correspondence at the time of Burke's death serves as a corrective to the several rumours then circulating about Burke's state of mind and religious preference at the time of his death.

One of these instances is the account that Burke, in a final and complete state of hallucination, asked to be buried where an invading French army could not find his grave and desecrate the body. That he made such a request is true, but what is not as well known is that it was made when Burke was in a temporary feverish state and that those around him were horrified by such a request. We have Nagle's account of the incident in a series of unpublished letters between John Alexander Woodford, who was at Beaconsfield with Nagle, and William Windham in London. Woodford reported that Nagle told Burke that 'he should not consider this as his last Directions unless he again repeated them tomorrow, nor does he mean to say anything of them if Mr. Burke's death should happen without anything further being said by him on the subject'.[26]

It is also Edward Nagle's correspondence with Windham that puts to death the rumour that Burke died a Roman Catholic because of a death bed conversion, attended by the Rev. Thomas Hussey. Sometime during the day of 8 July 1797 Nagle wrote to William Windham in London describing Burke's steadily deteriorating condition and then asked Windham to tell Rev. Hussey the state of things at Beaconsfield,

> but beg him on no account to come here. If anything should happen it would go into the world that Mr. B had a P___t with him at his last moments, and you know such ever were his intentions. But I'll leave you to manage this and doubt not but you will feel with me the necessity of Dr. Hussey's keeping away.[27]

Burke died within a few hours of Nagle's writing to Windham, thus it is clear that the Rev. Hussey had not attended Burke in his last illness and, in fact, those around Burke were determined to keep him away. It is also worth noting that Nagle was a Catholic but determined to follow and to respect Burke's wishes. Fittingly, this Nagle was at Burke's bedside when he died early in the morning of 9 July 1797, and was, with Jane's brother Jack Nugent, a chief mourner in the funeral procession.

Another Irish domestic link that provided assistance during the last years of Burke's life was the Hickey family. As noted above, Burke met Joseph Hickey soon after he arrived in England to study at Middle Temple. Hickey had three children: William and the twin girls, Ann and Sarah. William was in India when Will Burke was there and his memoirs from that period are valuable for Hickey's view of events during the Hastings period.[28] The twins, Ann and Sarah lived much at Beaconsfield from the late 1780s, and Ann frequently acted as Burke's secretary. The few pieces of her surviving correspondence show her to be lively as well as intelligent. The two women lived with Jane Burke for several years after Burke died and took a house in Beaconsfield to be near her in her last years. William Hickey joined them there, and his memoirs give a touching picture of the elderly Jane Burke, lame from arthritis, but frequently visited by old friends and younger protégés of her husband.

All of these Irish associations do much to elucidate Burke's character. Like many of his fellow countrymen, Edmund Burke arrived in England wearing his Irish nationality as an unambiguous form of identity. Unlike many of them, he did not play down his Irishness by taking elocution lessons to get rid of his brogue or strive to keep his relatives in a 'decent obscurity', as a contemporary recommended. One could argue that it would have been fruitless to do so. His enemies were significant in terms of numbers and had no intention of discounting his Irishness – the golden coin for their satire. That may be, but why, in Burke's case was his nationality such an issue when, in others of his countrymen, it was not even a subject for comment? Edmond Malone, the Shakespeare scholar, slipped easily in the stream of England's intellectual milieu, and contemporaries seem to have ignored completely the fact that he was Irish.

One obvious answer is that Burke never seemed to leave individuals unaffected: usually he was either hated or loved. While his friend Samuel Johnson was magnanimous in his estimation of the way Burke impressed people, saying that he was 'great by nature', others were not as generous. In correspondence with Warren Hastings, Paul Benfield ranted against the 'damned Paddy', and wished for ways to 'shut his mouth'. In the 10 March 1786 issue of the *Morning Herald* Burke was called a 'brazen itinerant Hibernian', and from 1770 he was a ripe subject for caricaturists who exploited his nationality, his supposed Roman Catholicism, and his perceived political inconsistency.

But his supporters were also many and influential. Party leaders such as Lord Rockingham, the Duke of Portland, and later, Lord Fitzwilliam admired Burke's character as well as his intellectual talents. And contemporaries such as George Canning attest to the strong, personal following he had among younger members of the House of Commons as well as individuals from all ranks and elements of society. Gilbert Elliot, in a letter to his wife, marvels at Burke's success in spite of significant limitations: '[Burke is] a sort of *power* in the state ... [and in] Europe even though totally without any of those means or the smallest share in them, which give or maintain power in other men'.[29] Elliot was speaking fact: Burke did not come from a family who had power and influence to do something to help his political career. Moreover, his Irishness exacerbated the situation.

What was there about Burke that drew so many to him? Certainly there are many viable responses to this question and many permutations to each answer. However, among these many, Burke's clear sense of self figures significantly. James Boswell caught a manifestation of Burke's unflinching sense of self when he recorded a conversation at the 8 April 1788 meeting of Johnson's Literary Club. According to Boswell's journal, there was an extended discussion of the various dynamics operating in Parliament: the effects of a good speech on most of the members, the part interest had to play in a member's decisions, and the willingness of members to be open to opposing arguments. Burke participated in the general discussion and at one point made an interesting departure in terms of himself: 'I believe in any body of men in England, I should have been in the Minority; I have always been in the Minority'.[30] Clearly the context was political, but the expression – 'in any body of men in England' – lends itself to a wider interpretation.

This is not to say that he thought of himself as belonging to an intellectual or socially inferior class. He never gave that impression, and while on occasion he did rant about the perverse behaviour of the Irish, for example, citing the senseless malice of the Sheehy case, he never sought to divest himself of the plain ways that garnered the criticism of those such as Mrs Thrale. Furthermore, he did nothing to discourage or to explain away such perceptions. In fact, he had a policy of never defending himself or his actions. When Boswell once urged him to do so, Burke refused and elucidated:

> My character must stand on its own Base, or it cannot stand at all. Apologies, defences, and minute discussions cannot serve it ... one of the most known and most successful ways of circulating slander is by stating charges, and anticipating defences, where nothing can come to proof, where there is no judge, and where every man credits and carries away what he pleases, and according to the measure of his Malice.[31]

For an individual to sustain this sort of indifference to the ways of public opinion requires courage and a significant amount of self-control. But this stance also bespeaks a certain peace with self and a proper pride in the acknowledgement of one's real talents. Furthermore, these are character traits that generate the kind of devotion in others that Canning describes: 'he had among all his great qualities that for which the world did not give him sufficient credit, of creating in those about him very strong attachments, as well as unbounded admiration'.[32] Undoubtedly, Burke's power and influence with those in high places was an attraction to many who may have otherwise cheerfully ignored him. Nevertheless, his dedication to an ideal, his unambiguous responses to the ideas and the characters of others, as well as his passionate love and loyalty of family members and intimate friends, kept those attached to him who either shared the same traits and ideals or who welcomed honest disagreement. There is no denying that these characteristics were natural to Burke's personality and to his particular emotional constitution. But they are also reminiscent of the people among whom he spent some five impressionable years of his childhood. Thus there is a certain validity to speak in terms of cause and effect when describing Burke's mature character as owing much to his years in the Blackwater Valley of County Cork.

68   EDMUND BURKE'S IRISH IDENTITIES

NOTES

1. Genealogists have been unable to trace Burke's family on his father's side, and it appears as though there was no interaction between Burke and his paternal relatives.
2. *Correspondence*, vol.i, p.346.
3. Revisionist historians argue that the Penal Laws were erratically enforced. Nevertheless, the fact that they were on the books and could be used constituted a threat to Irish Catholics. It was a fear that, in many cases, was justified.
4. *Correspondence*, vol.i, p.152.
5. Dixon Wector, *Edmund Burke and His Kinsmen: A Study of the Statesman's Financial Integrity and Private Relationships* (Boulder: University of Colorado Press, University of Colorado Studies, ser. B, 1939), p.5.
6. T.J. Walsh, *Nano Nagle and the Presentation Sisters* (Kildare Ireland: Presentation Generalate, 1980), p.25 n.2.
7. Ibid., p.45 and n.2.
8. Marianne Elliott, *Wolf Tone: Prophet of Irish Independence* (New Haven: Yale University Press, 1989), pp.46–7.
9. Sir John Hawkins, *The Life of Samuel Johnson, LL. D* (London, 1787), p.179.
10. For a detailed description of Jane Nugent Burke's life and character see Elizabeth Lambert, *Edmund Burke of Beaconsfield* (Newark: University of Delaware Press, 2003).
11. James Prior, *Life of the Right Honourable Edmund Burke*, 5th edition (London, 1872), p.49.
12. Edmund Burke, *A Notebook of Edmund Burke*, ed. H.V.F. Somerset (Cambridge: Cambridge University Press, 1957), pp.53–7.
13. *Correspondence*, vol.ix, pp.375–6.
14. A second son, Christopher, named for Jane's father, was born on 14 December 1758 but died in infancy.
15. Hugh Owen, *Two Centuries of Ceramic Art in Bristol* (London, 1925), pp.217–18.
16. Hester Lynch Piozzi, *Thraliana: The Diary of Mrs. Hester Lynch Thrale (Later Mrs. Piozzi) 1776–1809* ed. Katharine C. Balderston, 2nd edn, 2 vols (Oxford: Oxford University Press, 1951), vol.I, p.475.
17. James Maclean, *Reward Is Secondary: The Life of a Political Adventurer and an Inquiry into the Mystery of 'Junius'* (London: Hodder and Stoughton, 1963), p.137.
18. Thomas Copeland, *Our Eminent Friend Edmund Burke* (New Haven: Yale University Press, 1949), p.46.
19. The Countess of Minto, *Life and Letters of Sir Gilbert Elliot*, 3 vols (London, 1874), vol.2, p.136.
20. Frances Burney, *The Journals and Letters of Fanny Burney* (Madame D/Arblay) ed. Joyce Hemlow *et al.* 12 vols (Oxford: Clarendon Press, 1972–84), vol.1, pp.199–200.
21. O'Connell also points out the relationship of the Nagle crises to that of Burke's career.
21. O'Connell also points out the relationship of the Nagle crises to that of Burke's career.
22. *Correspondence*, vol.i, p.216.
23. *Correspondence*, vol. I, p.273.
23. *Correspondence*, vol. I, p.273.
24. Joseph Farington, *Faringtos Diary* ed. James Greig, 8 vols (London, 1922–28), vol.I, p.103.
25. William Windham (1750–1810) protégé of Burke. Later (1806) appointed Secretary for War.
26. BL. ADD. MS. 37, folios 195, 197, 199, 201 and 203.
27. Edward Nagle to William Windham, 8 July 1797. With permission of the Sheffield Archives, Sheffield, England and the Director of Libraries and Information Services.
27. Edward Nagle to William Windham, 8 July 1797. With permission of the Sheffield Archives, Sheffield, England and the Director of Libraries and Information Services.
28. Peter Quennell, *The Prodigal Rake: Memoirs of William Hickey* (New York: Dutton, 1962).
29. The Countess of Minto, *Life and Letters of Sir Gilbert Elliot*, vol.2, p.136.
30. James Boswell, *Life of Johnson*, edited by George Birkbeck Hill, revised by L.F. Powell, 4 vols. (Oxford: Oxford University Press, 1934–64), vol.III, p.235.
31. *Correspondence*, vol.v, p.258.
32. Quoted in Lord Malmesbury, *Diaries and Correspondence of Lord Malmesbury* (London, 1844), vol.3, p.398.

6

The 'genuine voice of its records and monuments'?: Edmund Burke's 'interior history of Ireland'

SEÁN PATRICK DONLAN

In 1792, Edmund Burke noted that over the previous century 'as the English in Ireland began to be domiciliated, they began also to think they had a country'.[1] Such 'settler patriotism' had, in fact, developed centuries before with the 'Old English', the descendants of the Anglo-Normans who would remain largely Catholic after the Reformation. The process repeated itself with later 'New English' and Scottish arrivals, especially seventeenth-century Protestant settlers and soldiers rewarded with Irish plantations. In the eighteenth century, this patriotism intersected with a number of other strands of political discourse, often simply dialects of wider British and European usages.[2] At its core was the belief in an inherent superiority, both religious and political, over Catholics as well as a concern for Protestant security. In England, 'ancient constitutionalism' effectively involved projecting into the past the perceived virtues of contemporary legal and political structures. In Ireland, Protestant patriots joined this to the Old English constitutional tradition, to conquer theory, classical republicanism and, ever so gradually, natural rights. Each of these rhetorics were complicated by seventeenth-century land settlements and the confessional divide they had cemented. Each provided a vocabulary in which the legitimacy of existing Irish institutions could be critiqued or defended. Each of these languages were also intimately connected with Irish historiographical debates.[3]

In the early and unpublished, but much circulated, *Tracts on the Popery Laws* (c.1759–65?), Burke expressed his lifelong resentment of:

> those miserable performances which go about under the names of Histories of Ireland ... [which] would persuade us, contrary to the known order of Nature, that indulgence and moderation in Governors is the natural incitement in subjects to rebel. But there is an interior history of Ireland, the genuine voice of its records and monuments .... For they even now show to those who have been at the pains to examine them, and they may show one day to all the world, that these rebellions were not produced by toleration,

but by persecution – that they arose not from just and mild government, but from unparalleled oppression.[4]

Burke spent considerable energy ensuring that such a history was told.[5] His views on the course of Irish history may be partially reconstructed from his scattered, but extensive, comments on the subject and his relationships with Irish antiquarians and historians. This 'interior' history was neither especially novel nor always accurate. But concepts critical to Burke scholarship – the relationship between laws and manners, the obligations of conquest and colonialism, the ancient constitutions of Britain and Ireland, property and prescription – may take on added significance in light of his Irish experiences and his views on its past. In addition, if Burke should not be read exclusively through this (or any other) lens, contextualizing him in this way may also assist in understanding the complex varieties of Irish and British identities in the eighteenth century.

A VANITY COMMON TO ALL NATIONS

There is little that is not speculative, and speculated on, concerning the events of Burke's early life. After spending a decade engaged in legal study and writing in England, he briefly returned to Dublin in the early 1760s to work as private secretary to William Gerald Hamilton (1729–96), then Irish Chief Secretary. While there, Burke befriended many in Irish politics as well as a number of antiquarians and historians.[6] Among the latter, the most important were Charles O'Conor of Belanagare (Cathal Ó Conchobhair, 1709/10–91) and Dr John Curry (c.1702–80). O'Conor descended from Roderick or Rory O'Connor (Ruaidhrí Ó Conchobhair), the last nominal high king of Ireland defeated in the Anglo-Norman conquest of the twelfth century. He also suffered personally the effects of the penal or 'Popery' laws, restricting in various ways the religious practice, education and property ownership of Catholics and dissenters. If O'Conor exemplified the remnants of an aristocratic, agrarian Gaelic Ireland, Curry was more representative of the urban Catholic middle class at mid-century, successful despite the penal statutes. The two were friends and founding members of the Irish Catholic Association (later the 'Catholic Committee'), whose attempts to secure change of the penal laws Burke supported and assisted.[7]

In addition to political pamphlets, both O'Conor and Curry wrote revisionist histories of Ireland that were no less important to the 'Catholic question'.[8] O'Conor especially was at the centre of Irish historiography for much of the century. In his *Dissertations on the Antient History of Ireland: wherein an account is given of the origine, government, letters, sciences, religion, manners and customs, of the antient inhabitants* (1753, second edition 1766), he maintained, with the Irish bardic historiographical tradition, an early Spanish or 'Milesian' settlement of Ireland. More importantly, he defended the existence of an early Irish civilization at a time of British barbarism. This was subsequently undermined by the assaults of the Scandinavian ancestors of the Anglo-Normans. O'Conor argued that with the invasions of Norsemen and Normans, it was only native manners – their social mores, practices and institutions – that kept the nation from savagery.

But if O'Conor defended the civility of the Irish past, he saw its improvement and its future as inextricably linked to Britain. A Hanoverian loyalist, his writing employed contemporary commonwealth and republican language. In the *Dissertations*, he whiggishly projected English models of government, complete with 'glorious revolutions' and 'patriot kings', into the Irish past. This created a native Irish constitution still more ancient, and no less problematic, than that of England. O'Conor also sought to assuage Protestant fears. In both his historical and polemical writings, he projected a Gallican outlook that distinguished Irish from Roman Catholicism, spiritual from temporal spheres. He also made less explicitly Catholic use of bardic sources. On the other hand, he noted that the constitutional history of Ireland drawn on by New English patriots was a largely Old English achievement. O'Conor pointed out, too, the irony of critiquing Ireland's traditional Brehon laws for inhibiting economic progress when the penal laws did so by design, thus placing many Irish (once more) outside of the equal protection of English law.

O'Conor also encouraged Dr Francis Stoughton Sullivan (1719–66), Trinity's first professor of feudal and common law, to begin a translation of the *Annála Ríoghachta Éireann* (*The Annals of the Kingdom of Ireland* or *The Annals of the Four Masters*), the most extensive digest of ancient Irish scholarship, into Latin.[9] Though Burke was probably following O'Conor's lead, the historian repeatedly credited him with suggesting literal translations of ancient Irish materials to insure their preservation.[10] Burke and O'Conor corresponded and 'Mr Burke of Wendover' paid a visit to O'Conor when he returned to Ireland in 1766.[11] The second, considerably expanded, edition of the *Dissertations* (1766) noted Burke's encouragement and was sent to him in England. O'Conor would subsequently edit a posthumous edition of Curry's *An Historical and Critical Review of the Civil Wars in Ireland* (1786), citing Burke's *Letter to a Peer of Ireland* ('Letter to Lord Kenmare', 21 February 1782) in the introduction.

Although arguably more polite, historical disputes in eighteenth-century Britain were no less polemical than those of Ireland. Burke's historical 'sense' is frequently acknowledged, indeed exaggerated, while his historical writings are often overlooked. In 1758, he began editing (1758–64?) the *Annual Register,* to which he contributed detailed 'historical' accounts of current events, not least of the 'Seven Years War' (1756–63).[12] His most important historical works, the incomplete and unpublished '*Essay Towards an Abridgement of the English History*' (1757–62?) and a brief fragment on English law (c.1757), were written in the period between the two editions of O'Conor's *Dissertations*. In both works, Burke was critical of the belief in English insularity and exceptionalism. As befitted the author of *A Vindication of Natural Society, or, a view of the mis-*

eries and evils arising to mankind from every species of artificial society, in a letter to Lord ****, by a late noble writer (1757), Burke saw the liberty of the ancient Britons as lawlessness closer to that of the Amerindians than to modern Europe.

The public myth of the English 'ancient constitution' had reached maturity in the constitutional crises of the seventeenth century, but was no less popular in the eighteenth. At its core was the belief in the continuity, often quite substantial, of English law with the ancient past. This included a balanced constitution of king, lords and commons, the 'Gothic' legacy of the free Germanic tribes, including the Saxons. In numerous, ingenious ways, apologists denied that the Franco-Normans effected any essential discontinuity. They did this partly to deny that laws could be altered by royal fiat, validating both Norman alterations and monarchical privileges. The more 'philosophical' approach of Burke's writings problematized the belief in perennial principles and immemorial institutions linking the British present with the English past.[13] He even acknowledged the civilizing effect of the Norman conquest on the 'rude and barbarous' Saxons through the resulting 'communication' with the continent.[14] Here as elsewhere, however, Burke avoided the more narrowly legalistic casuistry of his contemporaries, both English and Irish. Ending his abridged history with the Magna Carta, this historical view of the English government was very different from the more vulgar Whiggery of other contemporary British histories. As would become clear as a Rockingham Whig, Burke saw the essential constitutional moment in the settlement of the 'Glorious revolution'. This did not deny the development of the laws, adjusted to circumstance over time, but neither was it dependent on continuity with the Saxon past. His focus was on modern, not ancient, liberties.

The complexity and convolution of thought in English ancient constitutionalism was paralleled in Irish debates, many of which were simply variations on the theme. Perhaps due to the unreliability of the bardic histories and numerous gaps in the historical record, Burke was also more cautious in his claims about Irish history than was O'Conor. Burke's section on Ireland in his English history suggests that he did not always agree with the Irish historian.[15] Appropriately perhaps given his views on prescription, Burke seems ultimately little concerned about the ancient past or origins of either island. The Irish, he wrote, 'lay claim to a very extravagant antiquity, through a vanity common to all nations. The accounts, which are given by their ancient chronicles, of their first settlements are generally tales confuted by their own absurdity.'[16] While he accepted a Milesian settlement, he notes that 'In cases of this sort rational conjectures are more to be relied on than improbable relations. It is most probable that Ireland was first peopled from Britain. The coasts of these countries are in some places in sight of each other. The language, the manners, and religion of the most ancient inhabitants of both are nearly the same.'[17] In relation to England, Burke suggested that Ireland's ports were 'better known than those of Britain in the time of the Romans', though he does not imply that this was very meaningful.[18]

Unlike Catholic writers who saw the Milesians as a superior civilization,

Burke minimized distinctions between them and earlier settlers in Ireland. 'The Milesian colony,' he wrote, 'whenever it arrived in Ireland, could have made no great change in the manners or language, as the ancient Spaniards were a branch of the Celtae, as well as the old inhabitants of Ireland'.[19] He noted, too, that the Irish 'were much more addicted to pasturage than agriculture, not more from the quality of the soil, than from a remnant of the Scythian manners'.[20] While Celts and Scythians were often conflated in eighteenth-century writings, the Scythians were typically associated with barbarism. In addition, the Irish language, with which it is reasonable to suggest he had some familiarity, was 'not different from that of all other nations, as Temple and Rapin, from ignorance of it, have asserted'.[21] This may reflect his awareness of the Welsh antiquarian Dr Edward Lhwyd (1660–1709) who showed that the Irish language was related to those of Europe.[22] It also, however, places Burke somewhat closer to those Irish Protestant writers (especially in the 1780s) who emphasized the importance of ancient British settlements in Ireland. But whereas for some commentators this emphasized the barbarity of Irish manners, for Burke, it seems more likely that it pointed to the irrelevance of such origins.

In his historical writings, Burke was more convinced than were many of his British and continental contemporaries – Montesquieu, Voltaire, Hume and Gibbon – of the gradual, cumulative and rational nature of European progress.[23] There was also little anti-clericalism in Burke's *Abridgement*. Indeed, he emphasized the role, both pious and political, of the institutional church and even the papacy in European progress. The 'first openings of *civility*', he wrote, 'have been every where made by religion'.[24] He believed this to be true even in pre-Christian times, and goes to surprising lengths to commend the Druids.[25] The positive image of a corporate Druidic priesthood Burke presents is in many ways the reverse of that offered earlier in the century by countryman John Toland (probably born Seán Ó Tuathhalláin, 1670–1722), in his *Specimen of the Critical History of the Celtic Religion* (published posthumously in 1726). It was also less ambiguous than O'Conor's treatment in the *Dissertations*.[26] In relation to Ireland, however, Burke said little about the pre-Christian era. While'[t]he Druid discipline anciently flourished in that island; in the fourth century it fell down before the teaching of St Patrick; then the Christian Religion was embraced and cultivated, with an uncommon zeal'.[27]

THIS NOBLE ISLAND

Whatever level of pagan civility this may suggest, Burke clearly saw Christianity in Ireland to have been of great importance. Without claiming that the Irish saved civilization, he believed that 'the contemplative life' of Irish Christianity 'and the situation of Ireland, removed from the horrour of those devastations, which shook the rest of Europe, made it a refuge for learning, almost extinguished every where else'.[28] Irish decline was not simply the result of internal institutional 'corruption':

> Science flourished in Ireland during the seventh and eighth centuries. The
> same cause, which destroyed it in other countries, also destroyed it there.
> The Danes, then Pagans, made themselves masters of the island, after a
> long and wasteful war, in which they destroyed the sciences along with
> the monasteries, in which they were cultivated.

The defeat of the Norsemen did not end this Irish dark age:

> By as destructive a war they were at length expelled; but neither their
> ancient science nor repose returned to the Irish; who falling into domes-
> tic distractions as soon as they were freed from their foreign enemies,
> sunk quickly into a state of ignorance, poverty and barbarism; which must
> have been great, since it exceeded that of the rest of Europe. The disor-
> ders in the church were equal to those in the civil economy, and furnished
> a plausible pretext for giving Henry a commission to conquer the king-
> dom, in order to reform it.[29]

If against many (though by no means all) eighteenth-century Protestant commentators, Burke suggested an early, civilized Christianity, he acknowledged
more explicitly than his Catholic colleagues the 'disorders' of the Irish church
and 'civil economy', even if this had an external source.[30]

As in Britain and much of Europe, settlement, invasion and conquest were
constant motifs in eighteenth-century Irish thought.[31] Burke's *Abridgement*, too,
is divided into three sections neatly enveloping the conquests of Britain by the
Romans, the Anglo-Saxons and the Normans. While his discussion of Ireland
is brief, it is difficult not to see parallels with English history.[32] He notes, in fact,
that the conquest of England stood 'as a single event in history, unless, perhaps,
we may compare it with the reduction of Ireland some time after by Henry the
Second'.[33] The many myths associated with the Norman conquest of England
corresponded with those of Irish Protestant circles. As many in Ireland were
descendants of these Old English, this was even more complicated than in
England. Dominating Irish debate throughout the eighteenth century was the
argument that no legally meaningful conquest of Ireland had occurred. Ireland
was a kingdom, at least constitutionally, and not a colony.

The most popular origin myth of Irish Protestant patriotism was exemplified
by William Molyneux (1656–98). His *Case of Ireland's being bound by Acts of
Parliament in England stated* (1698) mixed historical/legal precedent and, in
language pregnant with future meaning, the natural rights language of his friend
John Locke. In this account, Ireland had voluntarily acquiesced to, or compacted with, the Anglo-Normans. Alternatively, Molyneux suggested that the native
Irish (or at least their aristocracy, the political 'nation') were almost wholly
replaced by settler stock. In either event, they retained, under a composite
monarchy, the same rights as other kingdoms. Ireland's not so ancient Anglo-

constitution was comprised of its own Magna Carta, common law, and 'gothic' parliament. In this regnal patriotism, as suspect as the English thought it drew upon, Ireland was entitled to legislate for itself. Molyneux was not the first of the New English to appropriate the constitutional history of Old English parliamentarians.[34] The largely New English parliament of 1692 had similarly adopted the rhetoric of its Jacobite predecessor. The fact that British monarchs never gave any political support to such ideas did nothing to curb the enthusiasm of Protestant patriots.[35] Nor did its failure to account for, among other things, the constitutional moment of 1688, in which the London parliament installed William and Mary as joint monarchs for both islands.

Burke argued, in line with contemporary Catholic historians, that an English conquest – the first, it appears, of several – had occurred in the twelfth century.[36] The invasion of Ireland came about from the same type of native 'faction and discontent' that had brought about first Saxon and later Norman influence in England.[37] As he relates it, Henry II (1133–89) had long had designs on Ireland. After the brutal murder of Thomas Becket by the King's allies, the English King hoped to recover the good graces of the pope by seizing Ireland (1169–1172) ostensibly to reform the Irish church and collect Peterspence.[38] Indeed, many earlier English commentators had seen Irish Catholicism as little more than a thin veil over native paganism and barbarism. Burke's analysis was more pointedly political. Henry 'well knew, from the internal weakness and advantageous situation of this noble island, the easiness and importance of such a conquest'.[39]

Dermot McMurrough (Diarmuid Mac Muireadhaigh), king of Leinster, involved in one of many domestic disputes with 'Roderic, King of Connaught, and Monarch of Ireland', requested Henry's assistance.[40] A force led by 'Richard, Earl of Striaul, commonly known by the name of Strongbow' landed in Ireland. With Henry's sanction and McMurrough's support:

> With an incredible rapidity of success they reduced Waterford, Dublin, Limerick, the only considerable cities in Ireland. By the novelty of their arms they had obtained some striking advantages in their first engagements; and by these advantages they attained a superiority of opinion over the Irish, which every success encreased. Before the effect of this first impression had time to wear off, Henry, having settled his affairs abroad, entered the harbour of Cork with a fleet of four hundred sail, at once to secure the conquest, and the allegiance of the conquerors. The fame of so great a force arriving under a prince, dreaded by all Europe, very soon disposed all the petty princes, with their King Roderic, to submit and do homage to Henry.[41]

Indeed,

> The bishops and the body of clergy greatly contributed to this submission, from respect to the Pope, and the horrour of their late defeats, which they began to regard as judgments.[42]

He added, however, that Irish resistance continued for more than four centuries. The effective conquest was presumably made with the defeat of Hugh O'Neill in the Nine Years War (1594–1603), though Burke may have meant Cromwell or even William of Orange.

Papal involvement in the original Anglo-Norman invasion of Ireland, by granting England authority through the Bull *Laudabiliter* (1155) created problems for eighteenth-century Catholics and Protestants alike. Following the work of James Ussher (1581–1656), Protestant archbishop of Armagh, many in the established church presented an image of an enlightened, pre-Norman and non-Roman Christianity. Yet again, this paralleled earlier English arguments. The post-reformation Irish church could thus be seen as a restoration of an historic Celtic institution. Burke appears to have agreed with Ussher.

> The most able antiquaries are of opinion, and Archbishop Usher, whom I reckon amongst the first of them, has I think shewn, that a Religion not very remote from the present Protestant persuasion, was that of the Irish, before the Union of that Kingdom to the Crown of England. If this is not directly the fact, this at least seems probable, that Papal authority was much lower in Ireland than in other Countries. This was made under the authority of an arbitrary grant of Pope Adrian, in order that the Church of Ireland should be reduced to the same servitude with those that were nearer to his See.[43]

Dr Ferdinando Warner (1703–68) an English Protestant ecclesiastical historian who had worked with O'Conor on a history of Ireland, and may have met Burke briefly in the early 1760s, argued along similar lines.[44] This represented another example of the Irish Protestant nation's selective adoption of elements from English, Old English and native traditions.

With the exception of the expatriate Jacobite Abbé James MacGeoghegan (1702–63), Catholic historians typically thought it better to avoid these issues.[45] Burke was among the few Irish writers to point out that Adrian IV (Nicholas Breakspear), the pope who had given Henry authority, was himself English. It was not unusual 'that an ambitious Monarch should make use of any pretence in his way to so considerable an object'.[46] This had been true, too, of the Franco-Norman invasion of England. But, in Ireland,

> What is extraordinary is, that for a long time, even quite down to the Reformation, and in their most solemn acts, the Kings of England founded their title wholly on this grant ... [I]n the submission of the Irish Chiefs to Richard IId mentioned by Sir John Davis, [the Irish bound] themselves ... to the Kings of England ... supposing the Pope as the superior power.[47]

The very Roman Catholicism of Ireland was, Burke seems to have believed, the result of two events: first, the invasion of the 'Old English', more Roman Catholic than the native Irish Catholics themselves and second, the forceful (post-Reformation) imposition of Protestantism on both Old English and Gaelic alike.

TWO ADVERSE NATIONS

Central to the bardic tradition was the apocryphal *Lebor Gabála Érenn* (the *Book of the taking of Ireland* or *The Book of Invasions*), chronicling the arrival of various peoples to Ireland. Employing numerous Gaelic scribes, Francis Stoughton Sullivan had begun a critical translation of the work, incomplete at his early death in 1766. A mytho- or pseudo-history of the invasion and settlement of the Milesians (c.1000 BC) – via Egypt, Scythia, the Caspian, the Maeiotic marshes, and Spain – it was compiled in the same century as the Anglo-Norman conquest. English or British commentary on Ireland for this period was extensive and hostile. The historian-ecclesiastic Giraldus Cambrensis (Gerald de Barri/Barry or Gerald of Wales, c.1146–1223) visited Ireland first in 1183 and then in 1185, accompanying Prince John. His writings, especially the *Expugnato Hibernica* (c.1180s), portrayed the barbarity of the comparatively non-urbanized, decentralized Irish as justification of the conquest. This hostility and the fabulous nature of his descriptions of the island in the *Topographia Hibernica* (1186) did not prevent the works from becoming canonical visions of the 'wild' or 'meere Irish'.

Elizabethan writers such as Edmund Spenser (c.1552–99) and William Camden (1551–1623) continued this criticism in a somewhat more humanistic, if no less hostile, vein. Spenser, best known as the author of the *Faerie Queen* (1590–96), had served as an administrator in Ireland and seems to have been related to Burke through his mother's family.[48] In his *View of the Present State of Ireland* (1598), he recommended military terror against, and famine of, the native Irish. Camden's incorporation of Giraldus' works in his *Britannia* (1602), coinciding with the defeat and subsequent submission of Hugh O'Neill (1550?–1616), the Earl of Tyrone, in the Nine Years War (1594–1603), re-ignited controversy over the 'barbarism' of the native Irish. The war marked the last major resistance of Gaelic Ireland to English rule. Coupled with the 'flight of the earls' (1607) and the unsuccessful revolt of Sir Cahir O'Doherty (1608), this Tudor conquest made manageable an extensive programme of plantation and colonization. This was especially true in Ulster, the most stubbornly Gaelic of Ireland's four provinces. With the elimination of a Scottish threat by the accession of James I (VIth of Scotland) to the English crown, England gained effective political control in Ireland it had not previously enjoyed or at least long maintained. It also permitted, and was secured by, subsequent legal changes that saw the virtual elimination of native Brehon laws throughout Ireland in favour of the application of English common law.

Especially important to eighteenth-century interpretations of the Irish past
was Sir John Davies's (1567–1624?) *A discovery of the true causes why Ireland
was never entirely subdued [and] brought under obedience of the crown of
England until the beginning of his Majesty's happy reign* (1612).[49] With numerous English critics, the Welshman argued that Irish law and manners – especially 'tanistry' and 'gavelkind' – prevented social and economic progress. In
the *Discovery*, he celebrates Ireland's 'final' conquest. It confirms and probably embellishes his role, as Attorney-General of Ireland, in the judicial 'conquest' of the Brehon laws. They illustrate, too, the complicated relationship
between positive law, the commands of the common law, and custom. Within
the English legal tradition, Davies' *La primer discours des cases et matters in
ley* (1615) is frequently cited for the proposition that the common law was
'nothing else but the *Common Custome* of the Realm'.[50] But this was still too
clearly untrue in the Irish kingdom. Among jurists, it was a legal humanist
commonplace, long before Montesquieu's *L'esprit des loix* (1748), that laws
were and ought to be matched to the history and manners of a people. Davies,
and even Spenser, said as much. In practice, however, they sought to fit the Irish
to English laws and manners.[51] The process was, in fact, very similar to that
which had occurred in Wales in the previous century.

Davies' critique was neither racial nor confessional. It was aimed at Irish
manners rather than Irishmen. While he was sharply critical of the process of
Gaelicisation, or 'degeneration', of the manners of the Old English in Ireland,
the *Discovery* could be, and was often, read as a plea for the 'rule of law' in
Ireland. This was invariably, however, the rule of English law. Even Burke
would use Davies in this way. His 'Speech on conciliation with America (22
March 1775)', an attempt to get the British administration to alter its American
policy, was among his most positive portrayal of British-Irish history. He said:

> This benefit of English laws and liberties, I confess, was not at first
> extended to *all* Ireland. Mark the consequence. English authority and
> English liberties had exactly the same boundaries. Your standard could
> never be advanced an inch before your privileges. Sir John Davis [sic]
> shews beyond a doubt, that the refusal of a general communication of
> these rights, was the true cause why Ireland was five hundred years in
> subduing; and after the vain projects of a Military Government, attempt-
> ed in the reign of Queen Elizabeth, it was soon discovered, that nothing
> could make the country English, in civility and allegiance, but your laws
> and your forms of legislature. It was not English arms, but the English
> constitution, that conquered Ireland.[52]

In a much cited, arguably rhetorical, passage, Davies praised the lawfulness of
the Irish. His critique explained Irish barbarism institutionally, as the weakness
of English government due to the extensive local powers given to the lords of
the Irish palantines, coupled with the failure to incorporate the native Irish into

the protection of its law. The work remained an important source for Irish debates in the eighteenth century, quoted selectively by Protestants and Catholics alike.

But Davies' gloss ought not obscure the deep hostility he felt towards Irish culture. Neither should Burke's parliamentary rhetoric, which contradicts many of his other comments on the conquest(s) of Ireland. In his *Letter to Sir Hercules Langrishe* (1792), published in support of limited Catholic enfranchisement in the aftermath of the revolution in France, Burke underscored his belief in the long-standing hostilities between natives and newcomers. Speaking of the Glorious Revolution, he wrote:

> For a much longer time than that which had sufficed to blend the Romans with the nation [the Gauls] to which of all others they were the most adverse, the Protestants settled in Ireland considered themselves in no other light than that of a sort of colonial garrison, to keep the natives in subjection to the other state of Great Britain. The whole spirit of the revolution in Ireland, was that of not the mildest conqueror. In truth, the spirit of these proceedings did not commence at that aera, nor was religion of any kind their primary object. What was done, was not in the spirit of two religious factions; but between two adverse nations.[53]

He continued by mentioning the 'Statutes of Kilkenny' (1367). These had outlawed the adoption of Irish manners by English settlers and forbid their social intercourse with the Gaelic Irish. While these may have been primarily aimed at limiting the Gaelicisation of the Old English, Burke argued that they showed

> that the spirit of the popery laws, and some of their actual provisions, as applied between Englishry and Irishry, had existed in that harassed country before the words Protestant and Papist were heard of in the world. If we read Baron Finglas, Spenser, and Sir John Davis, we cannot miss the true genius and policy of the English government there before the revolution, as well as during the whole reign of Queen Elizabeth. Sir John Davis boasts of the benefits received by the natives, by extending to them the English law, and turning the kingdom into shireground. But the appearance of things alone was changed. The original scheme was never deviated from for a single hour.[54]

If this suggests a questionable uniformity of policy across centuries, Burke's comments are important. The great defender of the modernity of Europe's *ancien régime,* and indeed of British imperialism, portrayed Ireland, if only rhetorically, in quasi-colonial terms.[55]

But Burke was not uncritical of Irish custom and had little sentimentalism for a romantic Celtic past. As noted, the Brehon laws remained at the centre of eighteenth-century debates on ancient Irish civility. Burke regretted that evidence of the laws was destroyed or was not better documented, as 'there is no doubt but many things of great value towards determining many questions relative to the laws, antiquities and manners of this and other countries had been preserved'.[56] This is not to say, however, that he was sympathetic to them. Burke was critical of both 'tanistry' and 'gavelkind'. Tanistry, the traditional, elective system of kingship whereby an heir-apparent was elected by the tribe to succeed, was, Burke wrote, 'attended with very great and pernicious inconveniences', and the 'Monarch of all Ireland, [was] raised to that power by election, or more properly speaking, by violence'.[57] Though a universal – or at least European – element in systems of property and successions, it was among numerous outdated Irish customs retained long after analogous manners were given up on the continent.

Burke, in fact, made use of a similar analysis to critique both Whig and Tory accounts of English constitutional history.[58] 'Gavelkind', a legal term borrowed for the Irish context from an analogous practice in Kent, was more strictly related to real and personal property than to governance. It involved paritable inheritance, the equal division of property between all male children. Gavelkind stood in sharp contrast with English primogeniture and appeared to undermine both financial and governmental economies of scale. If Burke said little about the practice in his *Abridgement*, he criticized it shortly afterwards in its new guise in the penal statutes. In general, he might have found little fault in O'Conor's argument that earlier Irish manners could be appropriate for the times. But he noted that many Irish customs were 'much in the strain of Eastern policy' and when 'these and many other of the Irish institutions ... came to degenerate, [they were] well calculated to prevent all improvement, and to perpetuate corruption, by infusing an invincible tenaciousness of ancient customs'.[59]

Burke understood the real limitations of the British constitution, both ancient and modern, in Ireland as well as in America and India. Throughout his work, he noted the negative effects and positive obligations of conquest and colonialism on the 'metropolitan' and settled country alike.[60] Borrowing heavily from traditional civic critiques, his Irish and Indian criticism focused extensively on the character of empire and the dangers of financial and constitutional 'corruption' brought home to London. But he was not anti-imperial or anti-colonial. In fact, as is clear from his English history, conquest and colonialism could even spur progress through 'communication' with other nations.[61] Ideally, as in England and other parts of Europe, it would also absorb the best of its composite parts to form one people. 'Time has, by degrees, in all other place and periods', he wrote in the 1790s, 'blended and coalited the conquered with the conquerors'.[62] Ireland's unique religious complexity made a reassessment of the confessional state necessary, but this merely suggested the importance of the integration of Irish Catholics into the British *ancien régime*. The Irish nations were to be treated fairly, but Ireland was and ought to remain a subordinate kingdom.

OLD VIOLENCE

The events of seventeenth-century Ireland gave arguments defending social privileges on the basis of origin myths of ancestry and military superiority, largely abandoned in European historiography, continuing force. Ireland's long seventeenth century began with the Nine Years War and the plantations that followed. The remaining years of the century saw the Eleven Years War (October 1641–April 1652, including the rebellion of 1641 and Cromwell's campaigns), Restoration and the Irish Act of Settlement (1662), the Williamite wars, and the enactment of the Irish penal statutes. Catholic writers of the century, often clerical émigrés on the continent, sought to defend Irish traditions against the New English (*Nua Ghail*). Indeed, the Old English (the *Fionn-Ghall* or 'fair-foreigners'), often Gaelicised over the centuries, were increasingly absorbed into a wider identity with the native Irish (*Gaeil*). This new collective, confessional identity as fellow Catholics and Irishmen (*Éireannaigh* or the Latin *hibernos*) – loyal to the English crown – set them in opposition to the more recently arrived New English and Scottish. Interestingly, much of the criticism of Spenser and Davies had also been directed towards the 'English-Irish', both old and new. As throughout Europe, these identities were very fluid, complex creations of political, religious and socio-economic factors.

With its numerous plantations and confiscations, seventeenth century Ireland experienced a fresh wave of British, overwhelmingly Protestant, colonization. In response, Old English writers, most notably Geoffrey Keating (Séathrún Céitinn, c.1580–c.1644) and John Lynch (c1599–c.1673) sought to integrate the earlier Anglo-Normans into the historical settlements of ancient Ireland (as in the *Lebor Gabála Érenn*). In line with contemporary European humanism and histories, Keating's *Foras feasa ar Éirinn* (*Compendium of Wisdom about Ireland* or *A basis of Knowledge about Ireland* [c.1633–36]) combined legendary and mythical materials to tell the story of Ireland from creation to the arrival of the Anglo-Normans. Widely available in manuscript, his style and thought were both very influential. He preserved much of the early, often credulous tradition, but critiqued the caricatures of Giraldus, Spenser, et cetera.[63] Lynch, Catholic archdeacon of Tuam, translated Keating into Latin (1660) and wrote his own *Cambrensis Eversus; or, refutation of the authority of Giraldus Cambrensis on the history of Ireland* (1662) against Giraldus and later Elizabethan historians of Ireland. Neither writer was uncritical of native Irish customs such as tanistry and gavelkind.

Like the *Annála Ríoghachta Éireann* of the same period, and many subsequent Irish histories, seventeenth-century accounts reflected contentious contemporary events. Many of the constitutional opinions adopted by later Protestant patriots originated in the Old English arguments in mid-century. Both before and during the ill-fated Confederation of Kilkenny (1642), these combined loyalty to the crown and a defence of limited parliamentary autonomy.[64] While there remained tensions, both Keating and Lynch sought in their works to integrate the Old English culturally and politically with the native community. Keating accepted a *translatio imperii* through Rome and the concomitant claim to sovereignty in Ireland, though this was not based on the need for reform of the Irish church. A century before Burke's *Tracts*, Lynch based his claim on prescription.[65] Property claims, even those originating in crime, were sanctioned by time and long possession. There was, as a result, little separating the claims of the Old English from newer arrivals, including Cromwellians, 'but time'. Burke would, of course, made a similar defence of property, including the Cromwellian and Williamite settlements. When Captain Thomas Mercer, an Ulster Protestant Whig, challenged his opposition to the confiscations of Catholic properties in revolutionary France, Burke responded:

> But these are donations made in 'ages of ignorance and superstition'. Be it so. It proves that these donations were made long ago; and this is *prescription* ... It is possible that many estates about you were originally obtained by arms ... a thing almost as bad as superstition, and not much short of ignorance; but it is *old violence*; and that which might be wrong in the beginning, is consecrated by time, and becomes lawful. This may be superstition in me, and ignorance; but I had rather remain in ignorance and superstition than be enlightened and purified out of the first principles of law and natural justice.[66]

Deeply critical of the seventeenth-century confiscations in Ireland, Burke argued, on the basis of prescription, against radical changes in property ownership. He did so even when he believed them to have originated in 'old violence'.

Many disputes about the Irish past involved not English, but Scottish writers.[67] While the Irish and Scottish had once embraced a pan-Gaelic identity, this altered significantly with their different historical experiences, not least the Reformation. Among other issues exacerbated by this division, antiquarians and historians debated the priority of settlements between Ireland and Scotland and vied for the legacy of a learned Christian past, the intellectual tradition of ancient 'Scotia'. As James VI of Scotland and a fellow Milesian, James I could be integrated genealogically into an ancient Irish royal dynasty settled (in the sixth century) in the Scottish colony and preceding an English kingdom. This made the seventeenth-century accommodation with the English crown easier for many Irish. This was true, too, of Roderic O'Flaherty's (Ruaudhrí Ó Flaithbheartaigh, 1629–1718) *Ogygia sen rerum Hibernicarum Chronologia Land* (completed c.1655, published 1685), dedicated to the future James II. Encouraged by Lynch and assisted in publication by Molyneux, O'Flaherty combined a wide array of primary sources, while linking Irish and European affairs. The work was also written in Latin to ensure a wider continental audience and his reputation was such that Lhywd later visited him (c.1700).

O'Flaherty underscored, too, the significance of the Tudor conquest.[68] A century later, O'Conor issued O'Flaherty's *The Ogygia Vindicated, against objections of Sir George Mackenzie* (1775), restating the Irish account of this colonization of Scotland.

Burke's activities intersected with contemporary variants of these Irish-Scottish disagreements. Shortly before he entered Parliament, the poems of James Macpherson (1736–86), presented as the work of a third-century poet, Ossian, re-ignited these debates. While the primitivism of the works fit the universal stages of progress from rudeness to refinement suggested by Scottish historians and philosophers, they contradicted the, largely Irish Catholic, defence of civility before English conquest and commerce. For these historians, a civilized antiquity and Celtic Christianity could suggest the possibility of reconciliation between a more Gallican Catholicism and the established church. Irish decline, and a stronger Roman Catholicism, had been imposed from without.[69] On the other hand, Irish Protestant historians of the 1780s would consciously align themselves with the theory of stadial progress, relegating native traditions to savagery. It was Irish progress, and often its Protestantism, that were imports. Burke's response to MacPherson was complex. He was impressed by Ossian and may have first believed the works to be genuine. Under the criticism of friends – Dr Johnson, O'Conor and the Rev Dr Thomas Leland (1722–85) – it became increasingly clear that the poetry was at least partially fabricated.[70]

Burke was also personally and philosophically close to many Scottish thinkers. Indeed, his sense of history is broadly similar to Scottish 'philosophical' and 'conjectural' histories. He was far more sceptical, however, than were his Scottish associates – David Hume, Adam Smith, William Robertson and John Millar – about discrete stages of progress and their prioritization of commerce over manners. In his defence of modern civil – or *civilized* – society, manners were more important than either laws or commerce. Burke consequently remained more supportive of the *ancien régime*, of aristocracy and landed property, paternalism and primogeniture. In Scotland, Burke's fellow *hiberni* Francis Hutcheson (1694–1746), coming from moral philosophy, had earlier challenged the rationalism and egoism of 'modern' natural lawyers. Trained in the law, Burke consistently leavened the 'vulgar' legalisms of contemporary political and moral theory with a variety of other public languages (humanist, polite, et cetera). For both men, this may have an Irish source. Manners necessarily achieve polemical precedence over laws and even commerce when there appeared, as in their own country, law corrupted by faction and commerce constrained by monopoly.

OPPRESSION AND INSOLENCE

Among the leading thinkers and artists of Britain the young Burke befriended by the late 1750s was David Hume (1711–76). Burke's well-known coolness towards the Scottish philosopher-historian may owe less to philosophical or theological differences than to Hume's views on Irish history. Burke shared his scepticism towards England's 'ancient constitution'. He may even have seen Hume's *History* as undermining party-political histories and taking to task both contractualism and the vulgar Whig apologetics of the ancient constitution. In Hume, Burke seemed to see the 'strange chaos of liberty and tyranny, anarchy and order, [from which] the constitution, we are now blessed with, has at length arisen'.[71] With Hume and Robertson, Burke ignored the origin and descent debates between Scottish and Irish historians. But the Irishman saw Hume uncritically repeating the more offensive, prejudicial and inaccurate portrayals of Ireland. In his *History of England* (1754–62), relying heavily on Elizabethan writers and especially Davies, Hume applauded the Anglo-Norman or British 'civilization' of the native Irish.

Especially in his depiction of the Irish rebellion of 1641, Hume was anything but sceptical, credulously exaggerating the Protestant dead from several thousand to several *hundred* thousand. This was many more than lived in Ireland at the time. Shortly after their first meeting, Burke and Hume quarrelled about the rebellion. Burke, an early biographer wrote, 'considered himself, though no Catholic, as referred to on the subject'.[72] Following the effective eclipse of Gaelic Ireland, continuing confiscation and British settlement, the events of the 1640s engulfed both islands in the 'Wars of the three kingdoms'. The wars, rooted in combined confessional and constitutional divisions, brought the extraordinary violence – and many of the soldiery – of the continental Thirty Years Wars (1618–48) to Britain and Ireland. Burke later wrote of the period, the same era Davies had earlier celebrated, that:

> Unheard of confiscations were made in the northern parts, upon grounds of plots and conspiracies, never proved upon their supposed authors. The war of chicane succeeded to a war of arms and of hostile statutes; and a regular series of operations were carried on … in the ordinary courts of justice, and by special commissions and inquisitions; first, under pretence of tenures, and then of title in the crown, for the purpose of the total extirpation of the interest of the natives in their own soil – until this species of subtle ravage, being carried to the last excess of oppression and insolence under [Thomas Wentworth, lord deputy of Ireland and later] Lord Strafford, kindled at length the flames of that rebellion which broke out in 1641.[73]

With O'Conor, Curry and the Scottish writer-historian Tobias Smollett, Burke attempted to persuade Hume to reconsider his account of the English settlements in Ireland.[74] Hume made only minor adjustments in future editions and even these were subsequently muted.

Burke granted Ireland's native and Catholic cultures a status generally denied them by British and Irish Protestant historians. Portrayed as beginning with a series of unprovoked Catholic atrocities, the defeat of Irish insurgents after 1641 acquired providential significance for Protestants. It set the tone for alarm and triumphalism well into the eighteenth century. In this, Sir John Temple's (1600–77) *Irish rebellion* was especially important.[75] Like historians and critics both before (Finglas and Davies) and after him, the New English Temple held high legal office in Ireland, as Master of the Rolls. Compared to the critiques of Spenser and Davies suggesting at least the possibility of the assimilation of the Irish to English manners, Temple portrayed Irish Catholics as irredeemable. He did not seek their integration, but their repression. His book is a colourful parade of priest-led atrocities committed by Catholic men, women and children against innocent Protestants. The work, with those of Edmund Borlase (c.1620–82) and Edward Hyde (1609–74), Earl of Clarendon remained very popular. These were frequently reprinted into the nineteenth century, particularly in periods of anxiety over Protestant security.[76] Works of this sort further sharpened confessional identities in both Britain and Ireland. Burke believed these histories, including Hume's, were inaccurate, the work of factional loyalties, and dehumanizing in their portrayals of the Catholic Irish.

The Catholic perspective on these events, argued most forcefully in the writings of Dr John Curry, was no less partisan. Curry, a descendant of the dispossed Jacobite Ó Corras of Co. Cavan, was a Dublin physician. While Curry reconciled himself with the Hanoverian regime, there remained in his writings a shrillness and sectarian bias absent in O'Conor's works. In his *Brief account from the authentic Protestant writers of the causes, motives, and mischiefs, of the Irish rebellion ...1641* (1747), written in the persona of a moderate Protestant, Curry attempted to re-evaluate the events of 1641.[77] Curry did not deny Catholic brutalities, but argued that they followed similar Protestant atrocities. In this way, he sought to contextualize Catholic actions, suggesting that Protestants, especially Ulster Presbyterians, had been no less brutal. In the 1750s, he became engaged in a public debate with the Protestant historian Walter Harris (1686–1761). As writer and editor-adaptor (1739–45) of the works of Sir James Ware (1594–1666), Harris had adopted a more charitable view of Gaelic sources and early Irish history, permitting Protestants to claim it – as they would increasingly do – as their own. He had also complained of the partisan nature of Irish histories. But Harris responded to Curry's portrayal of 1641 with a vigorous attack, revealing Curry's Catholicism. Like his Protestant opponents who had no access to original Gaelic materials, Curry was unable to review primary sources kept at Trinity College. Unlike O'Conor, he did not avail of Thomas Leland's offer to visit its library.

Burke, who may have known Harris in the 1740s, sided intellectually with Curry, at least in relation to the 1640s.[78] He appears, too, to have arranged to have Curry's *Historical Memoirs* reviewed by Smollett in the English *Critical Review* (1761). In preparing its republication in 1764, Curry also deferred to Burke, offering him the opportunity of 'altering, expunging, or inserting' his notes on the sequence of events in 1641.[79] Burke's opinion is clear. He insisted to William

Markham, later archbishop of York, that he had 'studied [Irish history] with more care than is common'.[80] He wrote "'That the Irish rebellion of 1641 was not only (as our silly things called Historys call it), not utterly *unprovoked* but … no History, that I have ever read furnishes an Instance of any that was so *provoked*." And that "in almost all parts of it, it has been extremely and most absurdly misrepresented".'[81] Burke appears to be one of the few Protestants to question the popular account of these events, though even he did not do so publicly. In his interior history, Burke's focus was not on ancient Ireland, but the period after the Anglo-Norman invasion and, even more importantly, the events of the seventeenth century.[82]

In the 1760–70s, along with O'Conor, Burke strongly encouraged Dr Thomas Leland to write an impartial history of Ireland.[83] Leland was a friend and Burke was probably responsible for the *Annual Register*'s reviews of his early works.[84] While Burke had briefly discussed ancient Ireland in his abridged English history, he advised Leland to focus on the period after the Anglo-Norman invasion of Ireland. He also made available several valuable manuscripts, then in the hands of Sir John Sebright (1725–94), friend and member of Parliament for Bath. Originally from Lhwyd's collection these included numerous early Brehon law tracts.[85] The same texts later provided the foundation for Trinity's Gaelic collection (1786). In 1771, Leland had preached a sermon celebrating the victory of Protestant forces in 1641. These annual, commemorationist histories typically emphasized the barbarity and treason of Irish Catholics and the continuing necessity of the penal laws. While Leland suggested that Catholic actions were the result of Protestant sins, a significant shift in rhetoric, he nevertheless maintained that Catholic superstition was the central cause. Following O'Conor's earlier critiques of James Macpherson, Leland criticized the Scot in his anonymous *An Examination of the Argument Contained in a late Introduction to the History of the Ancient Irish and Scots* (1772). He attacked Macpherson's failure to substantiate his claims for Ossian by producing the originals, a charge others later levelled against O'Conor. Leland defended the use of bardic histories in Irish historiography by noting that classical Greek and Roman writers were generally accepted as authoritative. Different standards, he stressed, were being applied to the Irish annals and historians. When completed, however, Leland's *History of Ireland from the Time of Henry II with a Preliminary Discourse on the antient state of that kingdom* (1773) was less impartial than equivocal.

Leland was, as Burke appears to have been, largely indifferent to claims of a pagan high culture. Nevertheless, citing O'Conor, Leland supported the idea of a learned, early, though not overtly Roman, Christianity. He explained the barbarism of Irish manners, borrowing heavily from the canonical analysis of Davies, by the weakness of English government following the Anglo-Norman conquest, coupled with a failure to incorporate the native Irish into English law. But Leland described the 1641 rebellion in terms only slightly milder than had Hume. As in his sermon of the same period, he laid the ultimate responsibility for the rebellion on Catholic superstition. He acknowledged subsequent massacres of Catholics and criticized English policy, but wrote that '[a]n enthusiastic hatred of the Irish was the natural and necessary consequence' of their actions.[86]

With O'Conor, Curry and other associates, Burke, explicitly thanked in Leland's work, was deeply disappointed.[87] When his son Richard (1758–94) returned to Ireland in the 1790s to act as agent for the Catholic Committee, Burke told him:

> Let an honest and sure hand copy for you the whole of the affadavits (so far as they relate to Armagh) contain in the rascally collection in the College relative to the pretended Massacre in 1641 particularly an account of the correspondence with Owen O'Neil then in Flanders, which is in a longish piece. The affidavits relative to the besieging and the taking the Church of Armagh from Saturday October the 23d (as I think) to the Tuesday following; I am sure wicked as they are, and mostly hearsay, they refute fully the false stories produced on their Credit by Temple. Leland went over them with me…; We agreed about them; but when he began to write History, he thought only of himself and the bookseller – for his History, was written at my earnest desire – but the mode of doing it varied from his first conceptions.[88]

Leland's work may even have influenced Hume to return to a harsher view of 1641 in the final edition of his English history (published posthumously 1778).

NATIONAL HATRED AND SCORN

The second half of the seventeenth century was no less contentious than the first. Whereas before the Eleven Years War, Catholics had still owned a majority of the 'real property' or land of Ireland, by the beginning of the eighteenth century they held less than a fifth. While there were past and contemporary European parallels, this was more akin to the Franco-Norman conquest of England than the Anglo-Norman or Tudor conquests of Ireland. By Burke's time, as a result of the penal laws, Catholics held less still. This was of particular significance to him, though on quite conventional European lines. Property, especially landed and agricultural property, was considered by many of the period to be valuable for its role in governance (rather than as any type of neo-Lockean right). Considerations of social utility – though *not* utilitarianism – and the public good were at its core. The offices and duties of property ownership were no simple *noblesse oblige* or the so-called 'imperfect' obligations of moral and jurisprudential thought. Landed property provided a security from influence and corruption. They were also the attempt, with a long pedigree in political thought, to join private interest and public duty. An aristocracy seeking fame and honour, rather than wealth, was an interested ward of political and public virtue. While its divisions were largely along confessional lines, this was little different in Ireland. The commercial humanism Burke exemplified sought to balance the stability and corporate experience of a hereditary aristocracy with the energy and talent of a 'natural' aristocracy of merit, of men like Burke.

This was not without its complications, particularly in eighteenth-century Ireland.[89] With many other Catholic Irish, Burke's maternal relations, the Nagles, had lost much of their land in the seventeenth century. Criticizing the Irish Protestant ascendancy in the 1790s, he wrote that

> They revive the bitter memory of every dissention which has torn to pieces their miserable Country for ages … They would not wantonly call on those phantoms, to tell by what English Acts of Parliament, forced upon two reluctant Kings, the lands of their Country were put up to a mean and scandalous auction in every goldsmith's shop in London, or chopped to pieces, and cut into rations, to pay the mercenary soldiery of a Regicide Usurper. They would not be so fond of titles under Cromwell, who if he avenged an Irish rebellion against the sovereign authority of the Parliament of England, had himself rebelled against the very Parliament whose sovereignty he asserted, as much as the Irish Nation, which he was sent to subdue and confiscate, could rebel against that Parliament, or could rebel against the king, against whom both he and the Parliament which he served and which he betrayed, had both of them rebelled.[90]

The 1640s had confirmed the shift from ethnic to confessional identities. Along with the deaths of a fifth or more of the Irish population from war and famine, the aftermath of the Cromwellian conquest brought a revolutionary shift in property ownership. While some was returned following the Restoration, the Irish Act of Settlement (1662) largely reinforced the new order. Ironically, this rewarded the parliamentarians and Cromwellian republicans who had opposed the Crown, rather than Catholic loyalists. These events may have influenced Burke's thoughts on confiscations in his own day. He was clearly sympathetic to those who lost their property and place in Ireland. But precisely because he understood the repercussions of such acts, he was reluctant to encourage another cycle of confiscation and chaos. 'I shall never praise', he wrote his son, 'confiscation or counter-confiscations as long as I live'.[91]

Burke always saw the 'Glorious revolution', rather than any Saxon golden age, as the critical watershed in British constitutional history. But, in Ireland, the events of 1689–91 had a very different significance. Williamite victory over the Jacobites further secured Protestant control of Irish property and politics. Burke wrote that he did not think that the deprivation of some millions of people of all the rights of citizens, and all interest in the Constitution, in and to which they were born, was a thing comfortable to the declared principles of the Revolution ... In England it was the struggle of the great body of the people for the establishment of their liberties, against the efforts of a very small faction, who would have oppressed them. In Ireland it was the establishment of the power of the smaller number, at the expense of the civil liberties and properties of the far greater part, and at the expense of the political liberties of the whole. It was, to say the truth, not a revolution, but a conquest, which is not to say a great deal in its favour. To insist on every thing done in Ireland at the Revolution, would be to insist on the severe and jealous policy of a conqueror, in the crude settlement of his new acquisition, as a permanent rule for its future government. This, no power, in no country that ever I heard of, has done or professed to do – except in Ireland; where it is done, and possibly by some people will be professed.[92]

Another letter of the 1790s noted that,

The Irish again rebelled against the English Parliament in 1688; and the English Parliament again put up to sale the greatest part of their estates ... If the principle of the English and Scottish resistance at the Revolution, is to be justified (as I sure it is) the submission of Ireland must be somewhat extenuated. For if the Irish resisted King William, they resisted him on the very same principle that the English and Scotch resisted King James.[93]

The guarantees of the 'Treaty of Limerick' (1691), which had ostensively secured Jacobite property, pardoned treason and prohibited lawsuits, were largely ignored by Irish Protestants. For Burke, this was a further disregard of the 'civil liberties and properties' of the Catholic majority.[94] And if a standing army of thousands, supported by Irish taxation, was obnoxious to much Irish (and British) thought, many Irish Protestants accommodated themselves in exchange for the security and financial benefits it entailed.

For Burke, the medieval invasions of England had brought attendant benefits in joining it to Europe. The advantages of the Cromwellian and Williamite re-conquests were perhaps less clear to many in Ireland.[95] By 'the issue of' 1641, Burke wrote,

by the turn by which the Earl of Clarendon gave to things at the restoration, and by the total reduction of the kingdom of Ireland in 1691; the ruin of the native Irish, and in a great measure too, of the first races of the English, was completely accomplished. The new English interest was settled with as solid a solidity as any thing in human affairs can look for. All the penal laws of that unparalleled code of oppression, which were made after the last event, were manifestly the effects of national hatred and scorn towards a conquered people; whom the victors delighted to trample upon, and were not at all afraid to provoke.[96]

All of these events preceded the penal laws (themselves modelled on English laws). For all the rhetoric, often exaggerated, of the *Tracts*, Burke understood that the penal statutes were not the cause of Irish Protestant hegemony, but its security. Never published, several versions of the work circulated in the following decades among members of English and Irish administrations.[97] Many of these statutes passed effectively into desuetude, but, as O'Conor knew firsthand, they were never entirely a dead letter.[98]

While Burke brought to his analysis in the *Tracts* considerable intellectual, legal and rhetorical abilities, his arguments closely reflected those of the Catholic Committee. With them, he paid particular attention to the fragmentation and insecurity of Catholic property-holding and sought to show how the laws undermined the economic interests of Ireland generally.[99] The penal laws were a 'departure from the Spirit of the common Law' and 'entirely change the course of *Descent* by the common Law. They abrogate the right of *primogeniture*; and … substitute a new Species of Statute Gavelkind'.[100] The laws played on family division by encouraging, though less successfully than was perhaps intended, additional conversions and confiscations. The expectation was, Burke argued, that 'the Landed property of Roman Catholicks should be wholly dissipated'.[101] It is at least ironic that a form of gavelling, earlier criticized as undermining native improvement, should become the means of promoting or maintaining the decline in Catholic property-holding. It was, Burke wrote, 'as if the Law had said in express terms, "Thou shall not improve"'.[102] He also knew that the penal laws left surprisingly little restriction on trade, a point that had not gone unnoticed or uncriticized by Protestants. As would be clear in the *Reflections on the Revolution in France and on the proceedings in certain societies in London relative to that event* (1790), such a 'monied' interest, Catholic or otherwise, was not an unalloyed good.

In the context of eighteenth-century British politics, the Whig Burke was neither a radical nor a reactionary, but a reformer. Indeed, while such labels are anachronistic, on many issues – economic reform, religious tolerance, slavery, and criminal law – it was not Burke, but his constituents, who were 'conservative'. But many of his earliest comments on the meliorist reform with which he is associated came in discussing the necessity of change in the *Tracts*.[103] More specifically, his remarks on Irish Catholicism anticipate later comments on 'prescriptive' religion. Religion, perhaps like manners more generally, 'is not believed because the Laws have established it; but it is established because the leading part of the community have previously believed it to be true'.[104] Catholicism was 'the old Religion of the Country, and the once Established Religion of the State'.[105] Criticized in early centuries for their failure to adhere rigidly to Roman Catholicism, Irish Catholics now suffered for their faithfulness to Rome.[106]

In the *Tracts*, Burke appealed to reason, natural law and history. But the perversion of the legal and social orders by the penal statutes was no small concern. When he later wrote Curry refusing £300 from the Catholic Committee for his assistance, Burke claimed that his 'uniform principle' was 'an utter abhorrence of all kinds of public injustice and oppression, the worst species of which are those which being converted into maxims of state, and blending themselves with law and jurisprudence corrupt the very fountains of all equity, and subvert all the purposes of Government'.[107] In the 1790s, Burke would insist on the creation of a Catholic landed class and what Richard called a 'communication of constitutional privileges'.[108] For Burke, the seventeenth century began with the elimination of the Brehon tradition, arguably to improve the mores and material goods of the native Irish (and 'degenerated' Old English) through equal treatment under law. It ended with the legislative attempt, admittedly piecemeal, confused and often ineffective, at eroding or containing Irish Catholicism and commerce.

REJECTED ALLEGIANCE

If built on quasi-colonial foundations, Ireland in Burke's day as closely resembled other European social structures. Both the Protestant and Catholic 'nations' remained aristocratic, though this was complicated by the confiscations of the seventeenth century. The possibility of subaltern grievances checked by the social and political institutions of Protestant Ireland cannot be dismissed. Publicly, however, the Catholic majority acted throughout most of the eighteenth century to effect reform within the existing political order, rather than through violence. Indeed, as with much of Europe, patterns of deference and paternalism were common and there is little to indicate significant resistance to existing authority until the 'revolution in France'.[109] Jacobite loyalties, to an alternative British monarch, had a limited political impact within Ireland. Unlike Scotland, Ireland played no significant part in the rising of 1745. It was arguably to endure less explicit brutality as well, experiencing nothing like the Spenserian levels of repression exacted in the 'pacification' of the highlanders. Particularly with the Seven Years War (1756–63) against Catholic France, Irish Catholics became increasingly vocal in their protestations of loyalty to the British state. This was accelerated by papal decisions to omit mention of James II in briefs for appointment to Irish sees and refuse recognition of Charles Edward as king of Great Britain and Ireland on the death of James III in 1766. Burke did not deny the reality of Irish poverty and suffering.[110] He was, however, generally dismissive of the threat of the Stuarts and there is scant evidence of Jacobitism, latent or active, in his thought.

In fact, writing after the French revolution, Burke saw the source of Irish Jacobinism in '[p]enury and irritation, … scorned loyalty, and rejected Allegiance'.[111] Whether his analysis of the Irish situation was accurate or not, the emphasis was consistently on Catholic loyalty and unnecessary Protestant alarm. It was Irish Protestants who were quick to interpret domestic disturbances as political and sectarian in nature or, at least, to exploit that interpretation. This was particularly true in the 'Whiteboy' disturbances – those involved wore white shirts over their clothing – in rural Munster of the 1760s.[112] These quickly became charged by the Dublin government with sectarian overtones. Burke, then in the country as personal secretary to Hamilton, appears to have privately undertaken the defence of Catholics. While he spent considerable energy in the effort, he could not prevent fresh confiscations and conversions, or the 'judicial murder' of Fr Nicholas Sheehy (1728–66). To Charles O'Hara (1705–76), friend and member of the Irish House of Commons, Burke expressed considerable anger over these 'fictitious terrors of state'.[113] The disturbances were followed by the republication of the most bitter and biased Protestant histories, including Hume's account of 1641. While in Dublin, Burke visited its libraries and booksellers for additional historical materials and subsequently began an account of the events. He later discontinued the work, perhaps because Curry had taken up a similar project.[114] While the repression of the Whiteboys appears exceptional, Burke seems to have been deeply affected, continuing to refer to the events of the 1760s for the next three decades.[115]

Given such experiences, it is not surprising that Burke – along with many Irish Catholics – may have seen London, rather than Dublin, as the best site for effecting reform on both islands. Having completed his English history only up to the period of the Magna Carta, Burke had already disturbed numerous popular legal and political myths, both English and Irish. If he considered writing an Irish history in the years before entering Parliament, he would have seen similar obstacles.[116] After entering Parliament, he maintained extensive connections to Ireland and remained an authority on its history in the eyes of his contemporaries. While the demands of parliamentary business and the necessity of political compromise ensured that O'Conor and Curry were not always pleased with him, Burke remained in correspondence with his Irish allies. This included Irish Protestant politicians, though Burke never expressed sympathy with patriot histories and often strongly disapproved of their constitutional aims.[117] He was much more concerned with the political influence of the overwhelmingly Protestant 'Volunteers', a militia raised 'without commission of the crown' in the 1770–80s, than he had been with the Whiteboys.[118]

Burke corresponded, too, with the Irish antiquarian and physician Sylvester O'Halloran (1728–1807).[119] In hopes perhaps of a civil pension, O'Halloran provided genealogical information on the Burkes of Limerick. He sent Burke 'a large silver ring & a seal Antique' from County Tipperary and an 'old fresco from an ancient Irish abbey'.[120] O'Conor also appears to have introduced Burke to Thomas O'Gorman (1732–1809), doctor, antiquary, genealogist for European expatriates, honorary member of the Royal Irish Academy and 'Chevalier' of France.[121] Burke continued to collect numerous 'monuments' of the Irish past throughout his lifetime. In 1790, as an exception to a general bar to honorary membership, he was made a member of the Royal Irish Academy (founded in 1785).

As late as the 1780s, Burke was dragged into Irish historiographical debates.[122] In their argument for an early, civilized Ireland, O'Conor and O'Halloran were joined by the eccentric Englishman Charles Vallancey (1725?–1812). Vallancey arrived in Ireland as an army officer and was unsympathetic to the cause of Catholic reform. But he had become an important stimulus to the study of Irish history and the collection of ancient texts and artefacts. On the basis of specious linguistic analysis linking Irish with Punic (Cathaginian), he argued that the distant ancestors of ancient Irish civilization were the Phoenicians.[123] Linked to wider European debates about language and 'culture', these theories and much of the bardic tradition came under renewed criticism from a new generation of Irish Protestant historians in the 1780s. These were not unconnected to contemporary debates. Most notable was the Rev. Dr Edward Ledwich (1738–1823), vicar of Aghaboe (Co. Westmeath). Against Vallancey, he suggested a 'Northern' or 'Scandian' system in which Ireland was originally populated by Scandinavian barbarians. As a corollary to this, civilization in Ireland came with the arrival of the Anglo-Normans. Not above fabricating his own evidence, he also represented a conservative backlash in the wake of the constitutional changes of the 1780s.[124] Ledwich 'gothicised' the Irish past, attempting to show that the Brehon laws were Germanic in character and origin. Less clearly, Burke had made a similar claim two decades before in the *Abridgement*.[125] Indeed, with William Beauford and the Rev. Drs Thomas Campbell (1733-95) and Daniel Beaufort, Burke may have combined both Milesian and Northern, if not necessarily Cathaginian, theories.[126]

Vallancey corresponded with Burke as early as 1783. Crediting the 'judicious antiquary' O'Conor, Burke reaffirmed the importance of

> literal translations into Latin or English, by which they might become proper subjects of criticism; and, by comparison with each other, as well as by the examination of the interior relations of each piece within itself, they might serve to shew how much ought to be retained, and how much rejected. They might also serve to contrast or confirm the histories, which affect to be extracted from them, such as O'Flaherty's and Keating's ... Until something of this kind is done, that ancient period of Irish history, which precedes official records, cannot be said to stand upon any proper authority.[127]

Vallancey later sent Burke a copy of his *Vindication of the history of ancient Ireland; wherein is shewn, I, The Descent of its old Inhabitants from the Paeno-Scythians of the East, II, The early Skill of the Paeno-Scythians, etc., III, Several Accounts of the Ancient Irish Bards* (1786).[128] Burke responded with a kind, but cautious letter, reaffirming the importance of translations.[129] O'Conor, to whom Vallancey proudly showed Burke's letter, noted that it was '[l]ike

every other intellectual performance of that great man (for he is great) ... highly judicious'.[130] Perhaps because Burke and O'Conor were so judicious,
Vallancey was oblivious to their doubts.

    Another churchman, Thomas Campbell was incumbent in Clogher, Co.
Tyrone and a friend of Dr Johnson and of Thomas Percy (1729–1811) Bishop
of Dromore (Co. Down). Campbell's *A Philosophical Survey of the South of
Ireland* (1777), owned by Burke, was written in the guise of an Englishman and
perceived as 'liberal'. By the 1780s, however, Campbell had begun another
work critical of Vallancey and O'Conor. While it is unclear what Burke knew
of these events, Campbell visited him in England in 1787. The two discussed
Campbell's plan for an Irish history. As he had with Leland, Burke advised him
to begin with the Anglo-Norman invasion. He lent both encouragement and
papers – initially compiled by George Carew (1555–1629), the first Earl of
Totnes – relating to the events leading up the Irish Rebellion. Ignoring this
advice and siding with Ledwich, Campbell entered the debates on Irish origins,
publicly attacking Vallancey and O'Conor. Vallancey subsequently printed
Burke's letter as evidence of his support. But Campbell interpreted the letter
differently, perhaps more accurately. He gathered the materials of the dispute,
including the letter, and published them in his *Strictures on the Ecclesiastical
and Literary History of Ireland* (1789). He dedicated the book to Burke implying, as had Vallancey, his agreement. Burke was, it appears, disgusted.[131] In an
'Agenda' for Richard Burke in Ireland, the first item the senior Burke noted
was to 'get the Books out of Dr Campbells hands. Let him not triffle with you.
I have trifled in giving them to him!'[132]

                    LET TIME DRAW HIS OBLIVIOUS VEIL

In sketching Burke's 'interior history', we must be wary either of making too
much of limited evidence or of taking his account as accurate and objective. He
appears to have been largely uninterested in, or critical of, the origin narratives
of either Britain or Ireland. There is little to indicate, for example, that he felt
the defence of ancient Irish civility important. Against at least some Catholics,
he believed the early Irish church to have been largely independent from Rome.
But if Burke's scepticism about Ireland's historiography is genuine, he never
adopted other historical views associated with Irish Protestantism. He argued
that Ireland had been conquered, although he often used legal language in a
rhetorical sense, and seems to have maintained a generally 'Catholic' – perhaps
even 'Old English' – interpretation of the events of the seventeenth century. His
hostility here and elsewhere was directed less to England than to the more
recently settled 'English in Ireland'.[133]

    A century before, the Protestant-dominated Irish parliament of 1692 had
refused to burn records of the so-called 'Patriot parliament' of 1689, composed

of Old English Jacobites. These New English sought to ensure that Catholic barbarity would not be forgotten. At the end of the eighteenth-century, Irish Protestants still insisted on the relevance of history to Irish affairs. Burke denied that Catholics were themselves obsessed with history and wrote to Richard:

> one would think they [the Irish Protestant Ascendancy] would wish to let Time draw his oblivious veil over the unpleasant modes by which lordships and demesnes have been acquired in their, and almost in all other countries upon earth. It might be imagined, that, when the sufferer (if a sufferer exists) had forgot the wrong, they would be pleased to forget it too; that they would permit the sacred name of possession to stand in the place of the melancholy and unpleasant title of grantees of confiscation.

But almost immediately he added,

> History records many things which ought to make us hate evil actions; but neither history nor morals, nor policy, can teach us to punish innocent men on that account. What lesson does the iniquity of prevalent factions read to us? It ought to lesson us into an abhorrence of the abuse of our own power in our own day; when we hate its excesses so much in other persons and in other times. To that school true Statesmen out to be satisfied to leave mankind. They ought not call from the dead all the discussions and litigations which formerly inflamed the furious factions which had torn their Country to pieces; they ought not to rake into the hideous and abominable things which were done in the turbulent fury of an injured, robbed, and persecuted people, and which were afterwards cruelly revenged in the execution, and as outrageously and shamefully exaggerated in the representation, in order, an hundred and fifty years after, to find some colour for justifying them in the eternal proscription and civil excommunication of a whole people.[134]

Burke found it no easier than did other Irish Protestants or Catholics to forget, to draw the veil over, the Irish past.

NOTES

An earlier version of this article was delivered at a *Burke Society of America/Newington-Cropsey Foundation* conference (Washington, DC: 21–22 Nov. 2003). My thanks to Michael Brown, Michael Griffin, Padraig Lenihan, Fred Lock, Caoilfhionn Ní Bheacháin and Clare O'Halloran for their comments on subsequent drafts.

1. *Writings and speeches,* vol.ix, pp.616.
2. J. Leerssen, *Mere Irish and Fíor-Ghael: Studies in the Idea of Irish Nationality, its Development and Literary Expression Prior to the Nineteenth Century* (Cork: Cork University Press, 1996, 2nd edn), esp. pp.294–383. See also S.J. Connolly (ed.), *Political Ideas in Eighteenth-century Ireland* (Dublin: Four Courts, 2000) and S. Small, *Political Thought in Ireland 1776–1798: Republicanism, Patriotism, and Radicalism* (Oxford: Clarendon Press, 2002).

3. See C. O'Halloran, *Golden Ages and Barbarous Nations: Antiquarian Debate and Cultural Politics in Ireland, c.1750–1800* (Cork: Cork University Press, 2004). See also C. Kidd, *British Identities before Nationalism: Ethnicity and Nationhood in the Atlantic World, 1600–1800* (Cambridge: Cambridge University Press, 1999), esp. Chap. 7.
4. *Writings and speeches*, vol.ix, pp.478–9.
5. See the numerous Irish titles listed in S. Deane (ed.), *Sale Catalogues of Libraries of Eminent Persons: Volume 8 – Politicians* (London, 1973) and the 'Catalogue of the Library of the late Right Hon. Edmund Burke' in Oxford's Bodleian Library (Ms. Eng. Misc. d. 722).
6. N. Lebow, 'British Historian and Irish History', *Éire-Ireland*, 8 (1973) pp.3–38, esp. 27–9.
7. Curry to Burke (6 Aug. 1779) in the Burke Papers of the Wentworth Woodhouse Muniments (hereinafter 'WWM Bk P') at the Sheffield Archives, 1/1189.
8. C.D.A. Leighton, *Catholicism in a Protestant Kingdom: A Study of the ancien régime* (New York: St Martin's Press, 1994), chaps 5–6; T. Bartlett, *The Fall and Rise of the Irish Nation: The Catholic Question 1690–1830* (London: Gill and Macmillan, 1992), esp. Chaps 4–5.
9. Burke may have known Sullivan. 'You will be sorry', Thomas Leland wrote Burke, 'to hear that our poor friend Sullivan has been laid on his Back some Months by a dreadful paralytic stroke'. Leland to Burke (9 Jan. 1766) in WWM Bk P 1/77.
10. See C.C. Ward and R.E. Ward (eds), *The Letters of Charles O'Connor of Belanagare* (Ann Arbor: University Microfilms International, for Irish American Cultural Institute, 1980), letters 377, 379, 389, 392 and 428. There are numerous other references to Burke. This is abridged as R.E. Ward, J.F. Wrynn and C.C. Ward (eds), *The Letters of Charles O'Conor of Belanagare: A Catholic Voice in Eighteenth-century Ireland* (Washington: Catholic University of America, 1988).
11. Ward and Ward, *The Letters of Charles O'Connor of Belanagare* (1980) and Ward et al., *The Letters of Charles O'Connor of Belanagare* (1988), letter 152.
12. Here, as elsewhere, Oliver Goldsmith borrowed liberally. R.W. Seitz, 'Goldsmith and the Annual Register', *Modern Philology*, 31 (1933–34), pp.183–94.
13. Cf. T.O. McLoughlin, 'Edmund Burke's *Abridgement of English history*', *Eighteenth-Century Ireland/Iris an dá chultúr*, 5 (1990), p.57.
14. *Writings and speeches*, vol.i, pp.430, 399. Probably a classical commonplace, 'rude and barbarous' was a centuries-old trope in British writing about the Irish.
15. 'Ireland, before the English conquest, though never governed by a despotic power, had no Parliament.' *Writings and speeches*, vol.iii, p.139.
16. Ibid., vol.i, p.509.
17. Ibid., vol.i, p.510.
18. Ibid., vol.i, p.509. He wrote that Ireland was 'less praised for corn than pasturage, in which the soil is more rich and luxuriant. Whilst it possesses these internal means of wealth, it opens on all sides a great number of ports, spacious and secure, and by the advantageous situation inviting to universal commerce. But on these ports, better known than those of Britain in the time of the Romans, at this time [that is, that of the Anglo-Norman conquest] there were few towns, scarce any fortifications, and no trade that deserves to be mentioned.' Ibid.
19. Ibid., vol.i, p.510.
20. Ibid., vol.i, p.512.
21. Ibid., vol.i, p.510. Without confirming any facility with Irish, numerous texts in Burke's library catalogues suggest an interest in the language.
22. Burke owned Llwyd's *Archaeologia Britannica, an Account of the Languages, Histories, and Customs of the original Inhabitants of Great Britain* (1707). It included Irish language materials.
23. The young Burke had criticized Voltaire, not as a radical *philosophe*, but a poor historian. He was critical of Voltaire's pretensions to knowledge of the past and the suggestion 'that none but well peopled and civilized Nations make conquests on each other'. Edmund Burke and William Burke, *A Note-book of Edmund Burke: poems, characters, essays and other sketches in the hands of Edmund and William Burke now printed for the first time in their entirety*, H.V.F. Somerset (ed.) (Cambridge: Cambridge University Press, 1957), p.119. Instead, he wrote, the 'very contrary of which is rather true'. Ibid. For Voltaire's relationship to Ireland and his negative views of the Irish, see G. Gargett's contributions to G. Gargett and G. Sheridan (eds), *Ireland and the French Revolution, 1700–1800* (Basingstoke: MacMillan, 1999).
24. *Writings and speeches*, vol.i, p.349 (italics added).
25. On the Druids, see gen. *Writings and speeches*, vol.i, pp.349–59, 392. Burke praises, too, early Christians who built on pagan foundations, for displaying a 'perfect understanding of human nature'. Ibid., vol..i, p.395.
26. Burke owned Toland's *Life of Milton* and '*Harrington's Works*, with his Life by Toland'.
27. *Writings and speeches*, vol.i, p.510.

28. Ibid., vol.i, pp.511, 511.
29. Ibid.
30. See D. Ó Corráin, *Ireland before the Normans* (Dublín: Gill and Macmillan Ltd, 1972).
31. For the experiences of Ireland, as well as Scotland and Wales, see R.R. Davies, *Domination and Conquest: The Experience of Ireland, Scotland and Wales 1100–1300* (Cambridge: Cambridge University Press, 1990).
32. See gen. ibid., vol.i, pp.508–14.
33. Ibid., vol.i, p.427.
34. See Richard Burke's comments in 'On the state of Ireland' in *Correspondence of the Right Honourable Edmund Burke* (London: Francis & John Rivington, 1844), vol.iv, pp.78–9.
35. Burke's claim to have 'endeavour[ed] to get a little into the accounts of this our poor country' at Trinity may have echoed, perhaps ironically, Molyneux. Letter to Richard Shackleton (12 July 1747) in *Correspondence*, vol.i, p.68. Cf. Molyneux's 'my own Poor Country' in J.G. Simms (ed.), *Colonial Nationalism, 1698–1776: The Case of Ireland Stated by William Molyneux* (Dublin: Cultural Relations Committee of Ireland, 1977 [1698]), p.24. Again, this phrase may be a classical commonplace.
36. Cf. 'On the right of settlements or conquered countries to be bound by the laws of the metropolitan or dominant country' in WWM Bk P 27/46 (citing Sir John Davies).
37. *Writings and speeches*, vol.i, p.511. '[E]ach clan forming within itself a separate government'. Ibid.
38. On Beckett, see Ibid., vol.i, pp.500, 503–7.
39. Ibid., vol.i, p.509. Cf. William Burke's 'Notes on Ireland' in WWM Bk P 40 (distinguishing, as had Molyneux, 'compact' from 'conquest').
40. *Writings and speeches*, vol.i, p.512.
41. Ibid., vol.i, p.513.
42. Ibid.
43. Ibid., vol.ix, p.469. Burke owned Ussher's *Britannicarum ecclesiarum antiqutates* (*A discourse of the religion anciently professed by the Irish and the British*, 1639) as well as Louis Augustin Alemand's *Historia monastique d'Ireland* (Paris, 1690).
44. The first volume of Warner's Irish history received a generally favourable review in the *Annual Register*. Burke believed that Warner, who accepted the notion of a civilized pre-Christian Ireland, taught 'us (for the mutual advantage of both countries) to lay aside prejudices against, and jealousies of Ireland and gives us the following fine lesson in politics, that fair and equal dealing to all the parts of an empire, is the true interest of the whole'. *Annual Register* (1763), p.258 (second pagination). The second volume, *The History of the Rebellion and Civil-war in Ireland* (1767) seems to have followed party lines, especially in relation to the rebellion of 1641. Burke also quoted Warner in his discussion of 'Fingal' in *Annual Register* (1761), pp.276, 277.
45. O'Conor and Curry corresponded with MacGeoghegan, and Burke owned his *Histoire de l'Irlande, ancienne et moderne, tire des monuments les plus authentiques* 3 vols, (Paris, 1758–63). See V. Geoghegan's comments on Burke and MacGeoghegan in 'A Jacobite History: The Abbé MacGeoghegan's *History of Ireland*', *Eighteenth Century Ireland/Iris an dá chultúr*, 6 (1991), p.49.
46. *Writings and speeches*, vol.ix, p.469.
47. Ibid., vol.ix, pp.469–70.
48. Perhaps because of its harsh prescriptions, the *View* remained unpublished in Spenser's lifetime. It did, however, circulate in manuscript. Burke and his contemporaries would have been familiar with the edited (and muted) version published in Sir James Ware (ed.), *Ancient Irish Histories* (1633), the unabridged text not being in print until the nineteenth century. 'Spencer' and 'Upton's Spencer's *Faerie Queen*' are included in the Bodelian catalogue.
49. Burke owned the 1789 edition of William Camden's *Britannia, sine Florentissimorum Regnorum Angliae, Scotiae, Hiberniae, et Insularum Adjacentium ex intima antiquitate Chorographica Descriptio* (1586), edited by Richard Gough.
50. 'Preface' to the anonymous translation, *A Report of Cases and Matters in Law* (Dublin, 1762), p.3.
51. Cf. Burke's letter to R. Burke (*post* 19 Feb. 1792) in *Writings and speeches*, vol.ix, p.650.
52. Ibid., vol.iii, p.140.
53. Ibid., vol.ix, p.615.
54. Ibid., vol.ix, pp.615–16. Finglas (1480?–1540) was baron of the Irish Exchequer and chief justice. Finglas'*Breviat of the getting of Ireland and of the decaie of the same*, written in the sixteenth century, was published in the first volume of Walter Harris (ed.), *Hibernica: or, some antient pieces relating to Ireland, never hitherto made publick* (1747). The second volume (1749) at least was owned by Burke. A third volume was prepared in 1752, but remained unpublished at Harris' death.
55. On the Irish *ancien régime* debate, see Connolly, *Religion, Law and Power: The Making of Protestant Ireland* (Oxford: Clarendon Press, 1992); Connolly, 'Eighteenth-century Ireland: Colony

or *ancien regime?*', in D.G. Boyce and A. O'Day (eds), *The Making of Modern Irish History: Revisionism and the Revisionist Controversy* (London: Routledge, 1996), pp.15–33; Leighton, *Catholicism in a Protestant Kingdom*; J. Hill, *Dublin Civic Politics and Irish Protestant Patriotism, 1660–1840* (Oxford: Clarendon Press, 1997). On Irish revisionism generally, the best introduction remains C. Brady (ed.), *Interpreting Irish History: The Debate on Historical Revisionism 1938–1994* (Dublin, 1994). See also Boyce and O'Day (eds), T*he Making of Modern Irish History*.

56. *Writings and speeches*, vol.i, p.433. See Burke's letter to Charles Vallancey (29 Nov. 1786) in *Correspondence*, vol.v, p.292.

57. *Writings and speeches*, vol.i, p.511. '[I]t was obviously an affair of difficulty to determine who should be called the worthiest of the blood; and a door being always left open for ambition, this order introduced a greater mischief than it was intended to remedy.' Ibid.

58. Ibid., vol.i, pp.325 and 433.

59. Ibid., vol.i, p.512.

601.In this respect, his participation with William Burke on *The Account of the European Settlements in America* (published anonymously, 1757) deserves greater, more careful attention. As the Irishman's role is still unclear, note O'Conor's letter to Charles Ryan (*post* 8 Oct. 1777), instructing him to 'read Mr. Burke's book'. Ward and Ward, *The Letters of Charles O'Connor of Belanagare* (1980) and Ward *et al*, *The Letters of Charles O'Connor of Belanagare* (1988), letter 295.

61. See *Writings and speeches*, vol.v, p.402.

62. 'Letter to Sir Hercules Langrishe' (1792) in Ibid., vol.ix, p.614. 'This is contradicted, more or less, by the history of every country in Europe, without exception. They have almost every one of them been conquered; in every one of the conquerors appropriated to themselves the lands, and the civil and military administration; and yet, when this was done, the natives, by degrees, have been raised from slavery to freedom, from freedom to property, and from property to privilege, not only without the invasion of the usurped possessions, or the subversion of established authority, but with all those advantages which make Europe what it is. Ireland is in the same circumstances.' Richard Burke, 'On the state of Ireland', in *Correspondence of the Right Honourable Edmund Burke*, vol.iv, p.94.

63. Burke refers knowingly and critically to both Keating and Roderic O'Flaherty in a letter to Charles Vallancey (15 Aug. 1783) in *Correspondence*, vol.v, pp.109–10. Keating's work was translated into English almost immediately by Michael Kearney (c.1589–?) and later, poorly, by Dermot O'Connor (Diarmaid Ó Conchubhair, ?c.1729–33).

64. The second volume of Harris' *Hibernica* contained the important seventeenth-century tract, 'A declaration how, and by what means, the laws and statutes of England, from time to time, came to be in force in Ireland'.

65. B. Cunningham, 'Representations of King, Parliament and the Irish People in Geoffrey Keating's *Foras Fease an Éirinn* and John Lynch's *Cambrensis Eversus* (1662)' in Ohlmeyer, *Political Thought in Seventeenth-century Ireland*, esp. p.145.

66. *Correspondence*, vol.vi, p.95. See his discussion of the Ascendancy and 'the solid rock of prescription; the soundest, the most general, and the most recognized title between man and man that is known in municipal or in publick jurisprudence', in *Writings and speeches*, vol.ix, pp.657–8.

678.On the different historiographical responses, see O'Halloran, *Golden Ages and Barbarous Nations*, esp.pp.28–40, 97–124, and Kidd, 'Gaelic Antiquity and National Identity in Enlightenment Ireland and Scotland', *English Historical Review*, 90 (1994), pp.1197, 1198.

68. Burke owned O'Flaherty's *Ogygia sen rerum Hibernicarum Chronologia Land* (1685).

69. See the comparison between Scottish and Irish ancient constitutionalism in Kidd, *Subverting Scotland's Past: Scottish Whig Historians and the Creation of an Anglo-British Identity, 1689–c.1830* (Cambridge: Cambridge University Press, 1993), pp.123–8.

70. See Burke's letter to Thomas Percy (24 March 1772) in F.P. Lock, 'Unpublished Burke Letters (II), 1765–97', *English Historical Review*, (1999) pp.636–57, 639–40.

71. *Annual Register* (1761), p.301 (second pagination).

72. Bisset, *Life of Edmund Burke* (London, 1800, 2nd edn), vol.ii, pp.425–6. Indeed, Hume may have aimed a later passage on the rebellion at Burke. 'There are indeed three events in our history', he wrote, 'which may be regarded as touchstones of partymen. An English Whig, who asserts the reality of the popish plot, an Irish Catholic, who denies the massacre in 1641, and a Scotch Jacobite, who maintains the innocence of queen Mary, must be considered as men beyond the reach of argument or reason, and must be left to their prejudices.' *The History of England, from the invasion of Julius Caesar to The Revolutions of 1688* (Indianapolis: Liberty Press, 1778 edn [1762]), vol.iv, p.395.

73. *Writings and speeches*, vol.ix, pp.615–16.

74. D. Berman, 'David Hume on the 1641 Rebellion in Ireland', *Studies*, 65 (1976), pp.101–12.

75. The Bodelian catalogue lists Temple's *Irish Rebellion* and 'Temple's works, 2 vols'.
76. Burke owned both 'Borlace's Irish rebellion' – possibly *TheRreduction of Ireland to the Crown of England* (1675, an abridged chronological history), but more likely *A History of the execrable Irish Rebellion trac'd from many preceding acts to the grand eruption ... 1641, and thence to the Act of Settlement 1662* (1680, incorporating Clarendon's unpublished work) – and, at least, Clarendon's posthumous *History of the Rebellion and Civil Wars in England* (1702–1704). He also owned '*Remarks on Clarendon*'.
77. Burke owned '*Memoirs of the Irish Rebellion*' (probably Curry's *Historical Memoirs of the Irish Rebellion in the Year 1641, in a letter to Walter Harris, Esq.* [1758]), *An Historical and Critical Review of the Civil Wars in Ireland from the Reign of Queen Elizabeth to the Settlement under King William* (1775), and the posthumous revision by O'Conor of 1786.
78. M. Fuchs suggests that Burke may have known Harris and Thomas Wright (1711–86), English author of *Louthiana, or an Introduction to the Antiquities of Ireland* (1748). M. Fuchs, *Edmund Burke, Ireland, and the Fashioning of Self* (Oxford: Voltaire Foundation, 1996), p.215. Harris had, with Dublin's Physico-Historical Society, advertised the publication of James Simon's *An essay on towards an historical account of Irish coins, and the currency of foreign monies in Ireland. With an appendix, containing the several statutes, proclamations, and patent relating to the said monies* in Burke's *Reformer* (1748). Simon's book is included in the Bodelian catalogue.
79. Curry to Burke in WWM Bk P 1/32 (15 Dec. 1764) and 1/37 (24 Feb. 1765). While Burke is credited by Curry for showing him how to use Temple's account in their favour, it is unclear whether Burke followed up with any suggestions for the revision.
80. To Dr William Markham (*post* 9 Nov. 1771) in *Correspondence*, vol.ii, p.285. The inverted commas are in the original.
81. Ibid., vol.ii, p.285. For a brief look at the period after the rebellion, see T.C. Barnard, *The Kingdom of Ireland, 1641–1760* (Basingstoke: Palgrave Macmillan, 2004).
82. The Burke archives contain numerous materials relative to the 1640s. See Weston's description in 'Edmund Burke's Irish History: A Hypothesis', *Publications of the Modern Language Association of America*, 77 (1962), p.401 n.40 (citing 'Fitzwilliam MSS., Bk. 27d'). Among other works already listed, Burke owned *Life and Letters of Ulrick [de Burgh], Marquis of Clanrickard, ... lord lieutenant of Ireland and commander-in-chief of King Charles during the rebellion* (1757).
83. Burke owned Leland's *History of Ireland, Demosthenes's Orations* (1771), and *Life of Phillip of Macedon*, 2 vols (1775). On Burke's encouragement, see Leland's letters in WWM Bk P 1/297 (22 March 1770) and 1/301 (19 May 1770).
84. W.D. Love, 'Charles O'Conor of Belanagare and Thomas Leland's "philosophical" history of Ireland', *Irish Historical Studies*, 13 (1962), pp.1–25.
85. See W.D. Love, 'Edmund Burke, Charles Vallancey and the Sebright Manuscripts', *Hermathena*, 95 (1961), pp.21–35.
86. Thomas Leland, *The History of Ireland from the Invasion of Henry II with a Preliminary Discourse on the antient state of that kingdom*, 3 vols (1773), vol.iii, p.128.
87. This makes it unlikely Burke wrote the review in *Annual Register* (1773), p.253 (second pagination).
88. To R. Burke (20 March 1792) in *Correspondence*, vol.ii, p.104.
89. Burke questioned whether the Irish Ascendancy were 'not *alone* sufficiently the people to form a democracy; and ... *too numerous* to answer the ends and purposes of *an aristocracy*'. *Writings and speeches*, vol.ix, p.601.
90. Ibid., vol.ix, pp.654–5. Note that Burke also owned Thomas Harris' *Life of Cromwell*.
91. *Writings and speeches*, vol.ix, p.657.
92. Ibid., vol.ix, p.614.
93. To R. Burke (*post* 19 Feb. 1792) in ibid., vol.ix, p.656.
94. On the 'Articles' or 'Treaty of Limerick', see ibid., vol.ix, pp.471–5.
95. For a reflection on the impact of the Williamite conquest on Irish historiography, see Hill, 'Politics and the Writing of History: The Impact of the 1690s and 1790s on Irish Historiography', in D.G. Boyce, R. Eccleshall and V. Geoghegan, *Political Discourse in Seventeenth- and Eighteenth-century Ireland* (London: Palgrave MacMillan, 2001), pp.222–39. Note that the Jacobite Hugh Reily's (1630?–95) *Ireland's Case Briefly Stated*, written in the 1690s and later known as *The Impartial History of Ireland*, was later published in Dublin with Burke's 'Speech to the Electors of Bristol' (1780).
96. *Writings and speeches*, vol.ix, pp.615–16.
97. The *Tracts* are included in Ibid., vol.ix, pp.434–82. See also WWM Bk P 27/205, listing the penal laws in outline and quoting Blackstone.
98. Curry to Burke (7 June 1778) in WWM Bk P 1/1062.

99. *Writings and speeches*, vol.i, pp.481–2. See the curious 'Hints on circulation' contrasting, without reference to religion, the aggregation of wealth in the gentry from 1685–1762 and concluding that '[t]he gentry and commonality had in 1685 pretty near an equal division of the wealth of the kingdom, now the proportion is changed as 10 to 3'. F(M) xxiv.24 of the Fitzwilliam (Milton) Burke Collection at the Northampton Record Office. Note that Burke owned the New English economist Sir William Petty's *'Tracts relating chiefly to Ireland*, Dublin 1769'.

100. *Writings and speeches*, vol.ix., pp.437, 436 (to 'proceed, ad infinitum').

101. Ibid., vol.ix, p.437.

102. Ibid., vol.ix, p.477. O'Conor made explicit the unfavourable contrast between Hume's 'declamation against the Tanistry Laws ... [and] the Popery Laws since King William's demise'. Ward and Ward, *The Letters of Charles O'Connor of Belanagare* (1980) and Ward et al., *The Letters of Charles O'Connor of Belanagare* (1988), letter 107.

103. 'Laws, like houses, lean on one another', 'Veneration of antiquity is congenial to the human mind', et cetera. *Writings and speeches*, vol.ix, pp.453, 467.

104. Ibid., vol.ix, p.466.

105. Ibid., vol.ix, p.465.

106. Ibid., vol.ix, p.468. 'No country, I believe, since the world began', he wrote 'suffered so much on account of Religion; or has been so variously harassed both for Popery and for Protestantism'. Ibid., vol.ix, p.471.

107. To Curry (14 Aug. 1779) in *Correspondence*, vol.iv, p.118.

108. 'On the state of Ireland', in *Correspondence of the Right Honourable Edmund Burke*, vol.iv, p.9. See gen. ibid., pp.93–7.

109. For the 'moral economy' in the Irish context, see Bartlett, 'An End to Moral Economy: The Irish Militia Disturbances of 1793', in C.H.E. Philpin (ed.), *Nationalism and Popular Protest in Ireland* (Cambridge: Cambridge University Press, 1987), pp.191–218; and E. Magennis, 'In Search of the "moral economy": Food Scarcity in 1756–57 and the Crowd', in P. Jupp and Magennis (eds), *Crowds in Ireland, c. 1720–1920* (London: Macmillan Press Ltd, 2000), pp.190–1.

110. Cf. Burke's early comments in the seventh issue of *The Reformer* in *Writings and speeches*, pp.96–101 with WWM Bk P 8/173 and the 'State of Ireland in the 1770s' at WWM Bk P 8/192–3 (note that Burke did not visit in the 1770s).

111. To the Rev. Thomas Hussey (*post* 9 Dec. 1796) in *Correspondence*, vol.ix, p.162.

112. J.S. Donnelly, 'The Whiteboy Movement 1761–5', *Irish Historical Studies*, 21 (1978), pp.20–59; J.S. Donnelly, 'Irish Agrarian Rebellions: The Whiteboys of 1769–76', *Proceedings of the Royal Irish Academy*, 83 (1983), pp.293–332;

113. To O'Hara (12 June 1766) in *Correspondence*, vol.i, p.256. See also *Writings and speeches*, vol.ix, p.602 and O'Conor to Burke (25 April 1765) in Ward and Ward, *The Letters of Charles O'Connor of Belanagare* (1980), letter 145. Cf. R. Burke, *Correspondence of the Right Honourable Edmund Burke*, vol.iv, p.74.

114. See 'A candid enquiry into the causes and motives of the late riots in the province of Munster, together with a brief narrative of the proceedings against the rioters, anno 1766' in WWM Bk P 8/1. It is also included in the *Correspondence of the Right Honourable Edmund Burke*, vol.i, pp.41–5. The Burke archives contain numerous materials relative to the period. See also R. Burke, 'On the State of Ireland', in ibid., vol.iv, pp.74–6.

115. See D. Dickson, 'Jacobitism in Eighteenth-century Ireland: A Munster Perspective', *Éire-Ireland*, 39 (2004), pp.38–99, especially his comments on Burke on pp.98–9.

116. See Weston, 'Edmund Burke's Irish History: A Hypothesis', esp. p.397.

117. Cf. the analysis of anti-patriot writing in S.J. Connolly, 'Precedent and Principle: The Patriots and their Critics', in Connolly, *Political Ideas in Eighteenth-century Ireland*.

118. To Thomas Burgh (1 Jan. 1780) in *Writings and speeches*, vol.ix, p.558. See gen. P.D.H. Smith, 'The Volunteers and Parliament, 1779–84', in Bartlett and D.W. Hayton (eds), *Penal Era and Golden Age: Essays in Irish History, 1690–1800* (Belfast: Ulster Historical Foundation, 1979), pp.113–36.

119. Burke owned 'O'Halloran's *History of Ireland* (1772)', presumably *An introduction to the study of the history and antiquities of Ireland: in which the assertions of Mr Hume and other writers are occasionally considered* (1772). O'Halloran also wrote *Ierne defended* (1774), against Leland, and *A general history of Ireland, from the earliest accounts of to the close of the twelfth century* (1775).

120. J.B. Lyons, 'The Letters of Sylvester O'Halloran (second part)', *North Munster Antiquarian Journal*, 9 (1962–63), p.41.

121. See WWM Bk P 1/43 and 1/1669–1.

122. This is discussed at length in W.D. Love, 'Edmund Burke and an Irish Historiographical

Controversy', *History and Theory*, 2 (1962–3), pp.180–98.

123. For an atypically generous perspective on Vallancey, see J. Lennon, 'Antiquarianism and Abduction: Charles Vallancey as Harbinger of Indo-European Linguisitics', *The European Legacy*, 10 (2005), pp.5–20.

124. Cf. N. Vance, 'Volunteer Thought: William Crawford of Strabane', in Boyce, Eccleshall, and Geoghegan, *Political Discourse in Seventeenth- and Eighteenth-century Ireland*, pp.257–69.

125. Tanistry, he wrote, 'prevailed in Ireland, where the Northern customs were retained some hundreds of years after the rest of Europe had in a great measure receded from them. It continued in force there, until the beginning of the last century.' *Writings and speeches*, vol.i, p.433.

126. Burke owned Beaufort's *Memoir of a Map of Ireland, illustrating the topography of that kingdom* (1792). The book marked out the locations of the Protestant churches of Ireland and included a commentary incorporating the Milesian and Gothic views. Burke's copy contained notes in his hand.

127. To Vallancey (15 Aug. 1783) in *Correspondence*, vol.v, pp.109–10. 'As told of Ireland – the beginning of its antient history, for which we are obliged to Keating, must be given up.' Letter to Vallancey (29 Nov. 1786) in ibid., vol.v, p.292 (on Keating).

128. Vallancey's *Vindication* was volume 14 of his *Collectanea de Rebus Hibernicus* series. Volumes are included in the library catalogues.

129. To Vallancey (29 Nov. 1786) in *Correspondence*, vol.v, pp.290–3.

130. To Joseph C. Walker (18 or 19 Dec. 1786), in Ward and Ward, *The Letters of Charles O'Connor of Belanagare* (1980), letter 427.

131. Vallancey wrote asking Burke to explain his earlier correspondence, but his precise answer is unknown. Vallancey's citation, in volume five of the *Collectanea*, of Burke's regret 'that heats are kindled among wise and learned men, upon subjects, which, in themselves, seem the least of all others of a nature to rouze the passions' was hardly proof of support. Burke to Vallancey (*post* 8 Oct. 1789) in *Correspondence*, vol.vi, p.29. It is also clear that Burke knew better.

132. To R. Burke (20 Mar 1792) in *Ibid.*, ii.104. Burke owned Campbell's *Philosophical Survey of the South of Ireland, in a series of letters to John Watkinson, MD* (1777) and *Strictures on the ecclesiastical and literary history of Ireland* (1789)). Burke also owned the 1789 edition of Camden's *Britannia* to which Campbell contributed.

133. This summary is based, in part, on that of Hill, 'Popery and Protestantism, Civil and Religious Liberty: The Disputed Lessons of Irish History 1690–1812', *Past & Present*, 118 (1988), pp.96–129.

134. To R. Burke (*post* 19 Feb. 1792) in *Writings and speeches*, vol.ix, pp.653 and 655–6. The 'miserable Natives of Ireland, who ninety-nine in a hundred are tormented with quite other cares, and are bowed down to labour for the bread of the hour, are not, as gentlemen pretend, plodding with antiquaries for titles of centuries ago to the estates of the great Lords and 'Squires, for whom they labour'. Ibid., vol.ix, p.657. See gen. ibid., vol.ix, pp.654–8.

7

Burke and the Irish Constitution

EAMON O'FLAHERTY

Burke's constitutional thought has always attracted attention. It is fair to say that his enormous output and influence in the refashioning of British politics and political theory in the later eighteenth century has bequeathed a contested legacy. Although it is possibly true of Burke that no man was ever more like himself, it is also true that Burke was a pragmatist in politics as well as an ideologue. Many commentators have been impressed by the apparent consistency of Burke's vision of politics and the constitution. It is one of the obvious dangers of intellectual biography that the biographer is almost obliged to dwell on the integrity of the subject. Thus from his early substantial work in aesthetic philosophy in the 1750s, to his final outpourings against Revolutionary France and the Irish governing system in the 1790s, Burke's thought has often been enclosed in an architecture which relates each part of his work to the whole. Burke's own sensitivity to any charge of expediency or inconsistency contributes not a little to this impression. On many occasions throughout his political career Burke was forced to defend himself against such charges. He was especially obliged to do so as a new man, one virtually without any natural connections in British society, forced to balance party commitment and connections with an ideal of independence and personal honour.

Burke's personal and public position interacted in an important way in his involvement with Irish politics. A primary area of development of Burke's constitutional ideas centred on his concern with the interdependence of justice and sovereignty in the relations between England and the subordinate parts of the British Empire. From the 1760s Burke was concerned at defining the constitutional relationships against a background of his direct political involvement. The parallels between the assertion of constitutional rights by the American colonists and the development of Patriot politics in Ireland were recognized by most opposition politicians in Ireland at the time. Burke even briefly hoped that Ireland might act as a mediator in the Imperial quarrel, although the subsequent behaviour of the Irish opposition and the North ministries in England showed this to have little basis in reality. Burke had relatively little sympathy with the Irish opposition and his distance from Ireland was more than just a product of physical absence. In part Burke's divergence from Irish party politics and ideology reflected the priority of other concerns most of the time, but an essential element in understanding Burke's attitudes was his radical difference of perspective on Irish affairs from his Irish contemporaries, which was at once rooted in his knowledge of the country and its history formed in the 1760s, and in his concern with the place of Ireland in the Imperial system. Burke's attitudes to Irish politics and the Anglo-Irish governing system were complex and subject to considerable modification throughout his career. Certain key themes dominated Burke's views on Ireland from the beginning of his political career in the early 1760s. The Whiteboy disturbances in Munster in the 1760s and the early stages of the Roman Catholic campaign against the Penal Laws provoked Burke's first writings on Irish affairs. Burke spent two lengthy periods in Ireland as private secretary to William Gerard Hamilton between 1761 and 1764, but after his breach with Hamilton in 1765 and the beginning of Burke's connection with Rockingham, Burke spent very little time in Ireland. His direct involvement in Irish politics diminished, although he continued to maintain an extensive circle of Irish correspondents and, probably in 1767, wrote an account of the Whiteboy disturbances in Munster.[1]

Burke's first major work on Ireland, The Tracts Relating to Popery Laws of 1765, was also his first major work of political and constitutional thought, offering a powerful criticism of the Penal Laws against Roman Catholics in Ireland. The Tracts, which were published posthumously, offered a variety of arguments to prove the injustice and impolicy of the system whereby the Catholics were subjected to severe civil and religious disabilities in order to ensure the security of the Protestant government of the kingdom. Having described in detail the extent of the system, Burke proceeded to indict the system as a violation of the fundamental principles of natural justice. The code was unlike any other system of religious persecution operating in Europe in that its effective object was the majority of the population: 'it is well worthy of a serious and dispassionate examination, whether such a system, respecting such an object, be in reality agreeable to any sound principles of legislation, or any authorized definition of law'.[2] Burke's argument about the imperfections of the code is that they are, by their bizarre perfection, subversive of the utilitarian object on which all law and justice are originally based – the welfare of the community.

> The true weakness and opprobrium of our best general Constitutions is, that they cannot provide beneficially for every particular case, and thus fill, adequately to their intentions, the circle of universal justice. But where the principle is faulty, the erroneous part of the law is the beneficial.[3]

Thus a law against the majority of the people invalidates the purpose of law itself and becomes a national calamity, violating the principles of equity and utility, 'where the greatest and most ordinary benefits of society are conferred as privileges, and not enjoyed on the footing of common rights'.[4]

Contrasting Ireland, supposedly governed by the rule of law, with Louis XIV's

France leads Burke to a passionate statement of the fundamental importance of religious conviction and association in human society and the irrationality of such an extensive system of persecution. 'A Constitution against the interest of the many, is rather of the nature of a grievance than a Law.'[5] Burke's emphasis on utility and equity and the need for laws to be interpreted on the basis of their congruence with elementary principles of justice was thus rather similar to the more radical Physiocrat position enunciated by Dupont de Nemours in 1767:

> It is clear that any judge who took it upon himself to inflict penalties on his fellows by virtue of obviously unjust laws would be guilty of fault. Judges, therefore, should measure the ordinances of positive law against the laws of essential justice which govern the rights and duties of all men ... before taking it upon themselves to give judgement according to those ordinances.[6]

In addition to the primary argument just outlined, Burke also provided a detailed critique of the Popery Laws in the Tracts, which focussed on the economic consequences of the legislation affecting property rights and on the historical evolution of the Penal Laws from the period of the Williamite war. Burke's argument in the first case was pragmatic rather than constitutional. The Popery Laws were condemned as impolitic because of their damaging effects on the spirit of industry and improvement essential to national prosperity. Damage to public prosperity consequent on the laws against property was also damaging to the interest of Great Britain, which 'whilst they subsist, can never draw from that country all the advantages, to which the bounty of Nature has entitled it'.[7] In addition to this pragmatic argument based on a view of Irish economic problems, Burke also examined the historic basis of the Penal Laws in contested views of recent Irish history and the Glorious Revolution. Even if the Penal Laws were not contrary to natural law, they could be shown, 'on another and almost as strong a principle [to be] unjust, as being contrary to positive compact and the publick faith most solemnly plighted'. Burke's arguments here turned on the specific charge that the Popery Laws were a violation of undertakings given to the Catholics by King William in the Treaty of Limerick in 1691. The Treaty of Limerick was, according to Burke, binding on the king and his successors with or without the sanction of parliament. When, in the reign of Queen Anne, the government permitted acts of parliament to be passed which violated the Treaty, it was all the more guilty because it possessed a power under the Irish constitution of preventing such legislation from passing through parliament. Here Burke was referring to the procedures under Poynings' Law, originally enacted in 1494, whereby the crown exercised ultimate control over the passage of legislation through the Irish parliament.

Burke thus indicted the parliament for violating the solemn and binding undertaking made by the king, and indicted the administration and indirectly the king and his successors, for permitting such a breach of faith despite the constitutional safeguards contained in Poynings' Law.

To say nothing further of the ministry, who in this instance most shame-fully betrayed the faith of Government, may it not be a matter of some degree of doubt, whether the Parliament, who do not claim a right of dissolving the force of moral obligation, did not make themselves a party in this breach of contract, by presenting a Bill to the Crown in direct violation of those articles so solemnly and so recently executed, which, by the Constitution, they had full authority to execute.[8]

In accepting Poynings' Law as a central element of the Irish constitution, Burke was at variance with a long tradition in eighteenth-century Irish political and constitutional thought which resented the idea that Ireland was a subordinate or dependent kingdom, and which was to play a considerable role in the formation of the ideology of the Patriot opposition in the 1760s and 1770s. The Tracts thus elaborated two of the key themes in Burke's attitude to the Irish constitutional debate of the 1760s and 1770s – a view of the constitutional dependence of Ireland which was congruent with Burke's evolving views of the eighteenth-century British Empire which was in many key respects at variance with Irish Patriot ideas, and a tendency to regard the treatment of the Catholic majority as a major flaw in Irish politics. This combination of a metropolitan, imperial perspective and a concern for Catholic rights rooted in his own personal experience and family connections placed Burke at an increasing remove from the Patriot ideology which was to dominate the political debate in Ireland in the 1770s and 1780s.

Burke's attitude to the Irish constitutional crisis of the 1770s and 1780s has remained somewhat obscure, despite the amount of attention paid to his attitude to Ireland. It has been assumed by some authors that Burke, as a patriot and an Irishman, was broadly in favour of the patriot movement for legislative independence that dominated Irish politics and Anglo-Irish relations between 1776 and 1789.[9] More recently, historians have stressed the ambiguity of Burke's relationship with the Irish confessional state, and the degree to which key themes in Burke's thought can be traced to formative Irish experiences and influences.[10] Analysing Burke's position on the constitutional question in this period is complicated by the fact that he devoted less time to Irish affairs, with the single exception of the Catholic question, in this period than at any other stage in his career. Burke's party commitments in England influenced his position on several key issues in Anglo-Irish politics in this period, often leading Burke to oppose measures that were supported by the Irish patriot opposition. In such circumstances Burke's position was sometimes determined by political expediency. Burke gave out a number of apparently contradictory signals on Irish constitutional affairs throughout his career. At a key point in the constitutional crisis of the early 1780s, Burke seems to have been left in the dark about government policy, which made his immediate comments on the concessions of 1782 rather guarded and cryptic. Burke's party commitments in Britain, and the prospect of Anglo-Irish political alliances in the early 1780s, further complicated matters and limited Burke's freedom of action. Not until the early 1790s did Burke attempt to play a leading role in Irish affairs, by which stage his view of the situation was coloured by his crusade against the French Revolution.

Shortly after he entered parliament in December 1765 Burke successfully opposed an attempt to extend restrictions on Irish woollen exports and unsuccessfully supported efforts to remove restrictions on the sugar and soap trade.[11] In the 1767–68 session of parliament Burke spoke against the government's scheme to augment the Irish army establishment, the original source of the conflict between Viscount Townshend and the Irish undertakers. In his speech to parliament in November 1767, Burke used the occasion to refute the suggestion that the army augmentation would benefit the Irish gentry 'because the country was in a great degree R. Catholic, and therefore a rotten part of the British dominions'. Burke used this opportunity to voice his indignation at the injustice of the official reaction to the Whiteboy disturbances and to point the finger at the real problems of Ireland:

> As to the rottenness of the country; if it was rotten, I attributed it to the ill policy of government towards the body of the subjects there. That it would well become them, to look into the state of that kingdom; especially on account of a late black and detestable proceeding there.[12]

Burke's ambivalence towards the conventions of Irish Protestant politics was apparent in his highly individual stance on the augmentation scheme. In his speech of February 1768 against the army augmentation scheme, Burke's objections were very different from those of the Irish opposition, stressing the 'danger and impropriety' of leaving an arrangement so essential to the security of the Empire as the army augmentation under the control of the Irish parliament.[13]

But Burke's ideas on Ireland in this period continued to be overshadowed by his indignation at the execution on dubious evidence of Fr Nicholas Sheehy and four others accused of Whiteboy activity in March 1766, the 'black and detestable proceeding' that he referred to in his speech of November 1767. The previous year, writing to his main Irish confidant Charles O'Hara, Burke was dismissive of Irish constitutional reform bills emanating from the Patriot opposition, but he was clearly distancing himself from Ireland as a result of the conduct of the Sheehy trial:

> You think well of Ireland, but I think rightly of it … I am told that those miserable wretches whom they had hanged died with one voice declaring their innocence: but truly for my own part, I want no man dying, or risen from the dead, to tell me that lies are lies, and nonsense is nonsense. I wish your absurdity was less mischievous and less bloody.[14]

In this context Burke's opposition to the Octennial Act, limiting the duration of the Irish parliament, gives a significant insight into his attitude to Irish constitutional reform. Remarking that the concession was an act of madness by the British government 'equalled only by the Phrensy of your country which desired it', Burke went so far as to argue that the act constituted 'a virtual repeal of the most essential parts of Poynings' Law'.[15] In his reaction to the augmentation measure and the Octennial Act, Burke echoed the twin concerns of the Tract on the Popery Laws – a critique of the Irish governing system which stressed the importance of the imperial connection, given constitutional permanence in Poynings' Law.

Yet in his belief in the subordination of the Irish parliament, Burke also believed that there was an appropriate division of functions between the British and Irish legislatures. In a speech on Irish banking in the House of Commons in December 1770, Burke argued that such a complex subject as the Irish banking system ought properly to be considered solely by the Irish parliament: 'it is an affair too much of the interior polity and oeconomy of that country, it is not proper for the Parliament here'.[16] There are clear echoes here of the position adopted by Burke in his draft speech of 1766 on the government of the American colonies, where he drew a distinction between the 'speculative idea of a right deduced from the unlimited nature of the supreme legislative authority' and the 'practical, executive exertion of this right' which may be 'impracticable, may be inequitable and may be contrary to the genius and spirit even of the constitution which gives this right'.[17]

Burke's attitudes to Poynings' Law can also be viewed against the background of considerable constitutional debate within the Irish parliament in the preceding fifteen years. The discussion of Poynings' Law also involved the court and country contests of mid-eighteenth century Irish parliamentary politics. In 1757 Edmund Sexton Pery, one of Burke's closest Irish correspondents in the 1770s and 1780s, introduced a bill in the Irish House of Commons attempting to limit the powers of the Irish Privy Council under Poynings' Law. This effort, which was easily defeated by the administration,[18] was based on an interpretation of the law that sought to expand the power of parliament against that of the executive. Pery's initiative was itself part of the political aftermath of the showdown between the Irish parliament and the administration on the right to initiate legislation in the Money Bill disputes of 1751–56. In a sympathetic account of Pery's initiative, the lawyer and future politician John Monck Mason, who was an old friend of Burke's, gave an essentially historical interpretation of the system, arguing that its original purpose had been to preserve the rights of parliament and the crown against encroachment by English governors. Mason echoed the denial made by Pery and his supporters that the system gave the Irish Privy Council the right to suppress or alter heads of bills originating in the Irish parliament before transmitting them to England for consideration by the Privy Council there.[19] In 1770, in the wake of another bruising contest between the parliament and the executive arising from the army augmentation proposals of Viscount Townshend and resulting in the proroguing of parliament, Robert French of Monivea, who had supported Pery's motion in 1757,[20] argued that

> instead of abridging the constitutional rights of the people, [Poynings'
> Laws] strengthened, confirmed and considerably enlarged them ... they
> were intended to connect this kingdom for ever to the crown of Great
> Britain, so as to promote the mutual welfare and to strengthen the securi-
> ty of both kingdoms ... if ever there was a wise political compact between
> the crown and the people, this was one.[21]

Burke's idea of the relationship between the subordinate and imperial jurisdiction was developed at length in his opposition to the Irish Absentee Tax
proposed, as a popular measure, by the Irish administration in 1773. Burke's
opposition to the tax was no doubt influenced by the fact that his patron
Rockingham was a substantial Irish landowner and was one of five peers who
wrote a letter to Lord North opposing the proposed bill. Yet Burke's constitutional arguments against the Absentee Tax, in a letter written in October 1773,
are consistent with his arguments about imperial unity developed in an
American context in the previous decade. While dwelling at length on the
practical and political consequences of dismantling the unity of the Empire by
penalising those who chose to reside in England (a principle that could just as
easily be applied in reverse), Burke's primary argument was based on his idea
of the balance of constitutional relationships. In order that 'the several bodies
which make up this complicated mass are to be preserved as one Empire, an
authority sufficient to preserve that unity ... must reside somewhere: that somewhere can only be in England'.[22] Burke acknowledged the existence of real Irish
grievances in the Anglo-Irish relationship, implicitly pointing to the commercial regulations governing Ireland which, as 'restrictive regulations' were 'great
oppressions, as well as great absurdities', but suggesting that Ireland, as the
weaker kingdom, should beware of dismantling imperial structures based on
common justice in pursuit of the redress of other grievances. 'Justice is the
shield of the weak; and when they choose to lay this down, and fight naked in
the contest of mere power, the event will be what must be expected from such
imprudence.'[23] Significantly, in the light of his earlier invocations of Poynings'
Law, Burke saw the Absentee Tax as the result of a 'municipal Legislature
considering itself as an unconnected body'.[24]

Burke's increasing preoccupation with the American crisis pushed Irish
affairs into the background during the 1770s, but the similarities between the
position of the American colonies and Ireland were made explicit by Burke in
his Speech on Conciliation with America of March 1775, where he offered a
rather idealized image of Ireland's harmonious place in the imperial system to
effect a contrast with the government's policy towards the American colonies.
Ireland was portrayed as the fortunate recipient of every benefit of the Anglish
constitution:

> almost every successive improvement in constitutional liberty, as fast as
> it was made here, was transmitted thither ... It was not English arms, but

the English constitution, that conquered Ireland. From that time, Ireland has ever had a general parliament, as she had before a partial parliament ... This has made Ireland the great and flourishing kingdom that it is; and from a disgrace and burthen intolerable to this nation, has rendered her a principal part of our strength and ornament.[25]

The effusiveness of Burke's picture of the Irish constitution in 1775 stands in marked contrast to the tenor of his earlier and later writings.[26]

Later the same year Burke made the extraordinary suggestion that the Irish parliament could act as a mediator in the quarrel between Britain and America by addressing the king in favour of conciliation and voting to withhold grants of money for troops employed outside Ireland.[27] Burke's image of an Irish constitution in which 'every thing was sweetly and harmoniously disposed through both islands for the conservation of English dominion and the communication of English liberties'[28] may even have reflected a genuine optimism about Ireland, rather than simply a rhetorical contrast. Burke was aware of the initiatives for a partial repeal of the Penal Laws in Ireland from the mid 1770s. In the summer of 1778 he devoted enormous efforts to ensuring the smooth passage of Luke Gardiner's Catholic Relief Act of 1778 through the British privy council. The Relief Act of 1778 removed the main restrictions on Catholic ownership of property, and Burke had high hopes, which were widely shared in Ireland, that further reform of the system was not far off. Writing to Pery in August 1778 after the bill had passed its final stages in the Irish House of Commons, Burke took a similarly optimistic tone – although one that differed in detail from the image of the Irish constitution presented in the Conciliation speech of 1775. The removal of the first of the Penal Laws was for Burke the beginning of a process of political transformation in Ireland: 'You are now beginning to have a Country; and I trust you will complete the design. You have laid the firm honest homely rustick of Property; and the rest of the building will rise in due harmony and proportion.'[29] A combination of factors vitiated Burke's optimism of the later 1770s and revealed Burke's profound misgivings about the Patriot movement for constitutional reform and the prospects for further Catholic relief.

Burke's response to the constitutional crisis in Anglo-Irish relations between 1778 and 1783 revealed both the extent of his ambiguous attitude to the Irish reformers and the distance imposed by his own position in British politics. As the substance of the debate moved from commercial concessions in the late 1770s to constitutional concessions, including an attack on Poynings' Law in the early 1780s, to radical proposals for parliamentary reform after 1782, Burke's misgivings became more apparent. As we have already seen, Burke had drawn attention to the fact that restrictive regulations imposed on a subordinate kingdom could indeed be oppressive, but neither prudence nor justice suggested that these oppressions warranted a repudiation of the subordination of Ireland within the Empire. Burke's support for generous commercial concessions to Ireland involved him in considerable political risk. His active support for a substantial concession to Irish opinion by removing restrictions on Irish trade brought him into conflict with his own supporters in Bristol, and ultimately cost him his seat there.

In April and May 1778 Burke defended his policy in Two Letters on the Trade of Ireland addressed to the Bristol merchants. Burke justified his support of the concessions on Irish trade in terms of moderation, prudence and equity. The prudential element in Burke's argument for concession to Ireland on trade was one that was echoed later in Burke's career by his arguments in favour of the conciliation of the Irish Catholics in the aftermath of the French Revolution. In the crisis of the empire caused by the failure to conciliate America, Burke argued that the prudent course was 'to give all possible vigour and soundness to those parts of it which are still content to be governed by our councils'. Given that 'communities must be held together by an evident and solid interest', Burke concluded that a timely concession freely given would avert the impression that might be given 'that Great Britain can in no instance whatsoever be brought to a sense of rational and equitable policy but by coercion and force of arms!'[30]

In evoking the threat of armed force in 1778, Burke was referring obliquely to the rise of the Volunteers in Ireland. When in 1779 the extra-parliamentary pressure represented by the volunteering movement grew much stronger, partly in response to the failure of the British parliament to satisfy Irish political demands, Burke and Rockingham found themselves at cross purposes. In May 1779 Rockingham drafted a motion in favour of concession to Irish demands which alarmed Burke in that it seemed 'highly indiscreet and dangerous' to suggest that the government ought to enlarge the concessions to Ireland in order to appease the Irish demands for reform: 'in Gods Name where is the Necessity that Parliament should lose all appearance of Grace and dignity in the manner of making its concessions?'[31]

In the event North's government ultimately capitulated to sustained pressure both from within the Irish parliament and from outside. In November Burke and the Rockingham Whigs were kept guessing about the government's policy on Irish trade. Speaking in parliament on 6 December in the wake of the Irish parliament's demonstration of defiance and support for the armed societies, Burke struck a gloomy note, painting a picture of supreme constitutional irresponsibility by the ministry and demonstrated his lack of sympathy with the Volunteers: 'it was a principle ascertained by the constitution ... that let men be armed by the state or by themselves, they cannot act or assemble but under a commission of His Majesty'. Burke associated himself with the Irish Lord Chancellor's refusal to vote for the Irish resolution thanking the Volunteers and protested that he would never support any concessions to Ireland that were contrary to the interests of Britain.[32]

The Rockingham Whigs were taken by surprise when North produced radical new proposals for concessions in December. Uncertain how to respond, Burke, Fox and Rockingham largely kept silent in the ensuing debate and this resulted in considerable opprobrium directed at Burke in Ireland. In a lengthy defence of his conduct in the form of a letter to Thomas Burgh, which was published in 1780, Burke was injured and indignant at the criticisms of his behaviour made in Ireland, but despite his eagerness to demonstrate the consistency of his conduct, Burke effectively repeated his criticism of the unconstitutionality of the Volunteers. Burke was scathing about 'those, who ... have improved the critical moment of their fortune, and have debated with authority ... at the head of forty thousand men'.[33] It is highly probable that Burke saw in Ireland's 'new military force' a revival of the spirit of intolerance and persecution which he had condemned in Ireland during the 1760s, and which formed one aspect of his indictment of the Popery Laws.

It is hard to know just how well informed Burke was about the nature of political volunteering in Ireland in 1779, although he may have been aware of the largely Protestant nature of the volunteer corps. However he clearly saw the concessions of 1779 as a capitulation to armed force which might ultimately be as destructive to Irish interests as to the unity of the Empire. In defending his silence to Burgh – as he later had to defend his support for concessions in the Guild Hall speech at Bristol delivered in September 1780 – Burke also indicated that the surrender of British authority to the threat of force was an important factor in his embarrassed silence. Frightened into concession, the British parliament 'made an universal surrender of all that had been thought the peculiar, reserved, uncommunicable rights of England'.[34] In April the Irish constitutional offensive continued with Grattan's motion declaring the sole legislative competence of the Irish parliament and Barry Yelverton's motion for the partial repeal of Poynings' Law.

Burke's experience of the first phase of the Irish constitutional crisis had exposed him to criticism from several sources. Politically, he and the opposition had been outmanoeuvred by North on the concessions to Ireland, and his position in Bristol suffered irreparable damage, resulting in the loss of his seat. Burke's optimism on the progress of Catholic relief also suffered a setback during the course of 1780, when he had been caught up in the Gordon riots in London in June. The effect of this on Burke is apparent in his defence of his political principles in the Bristol Guildhall speech of September 1780, two thirds of which he devoted to a lengthy justification of his support for the English Catholic Relief Act of 1778. In reflecting on the consequences of the Irish Relief Act, Burke emphasized the unifying effects of toleration in an implicit contrast to the disruptive effects of the Protestant Association and the turmoil of the American crisis. The Irish Relief Act,

> this first faint sketch of toleration ... completed in a most wonderful manner the re-union to the state of all the Catholicks of that country. It made us what we ought always to have been, one family, one body, one heart and soul, against the family-combination, and all other combinations of our enemies.[35]

Burke was also disappointed with the second instalment of Catholic relief legislation passed by the Irish parliament and expounded his criticisms in February 1782 in a letter to Lord Kenmare which was later published. Although the 1782 Relief Act granted further concessions to Catholics, Burke's reaction was negative and critical by comparison with the optimism of his 1778 letter to Pery about the new country. The letter to Kenmare also illuminates the evolution of Burke's attitude towards Irish politics in the aftermath of 1780. At a critical juncture in the evolution of the Anglo-Irish constitutional crisis Burke claimed that his contacts with Irish politicians had ceased and, as far as the Catholic question was concerned 'I know as little of the intentions of the British government, as I know of the temper of the Irish parliament.'[36] Burke argued that the limited concession of the right to religious worship in the 1782 act was vitiated by the exclusion of any relaxation of civil disabilities. By continuing to exclude Catholics from civil functions the bill was 'a renewd act of universal, unmitigated, indispensible, exceptionless disqualification ... It puts a new bolt on Civil Rights; and rivetts it I am afraid to the old one in such a manner that neither, I fear, will be easily loosend.'[37] In the event, Burke's suspicions about the 1782 Relief Act proved justified. The relief measures of 1778 and 1782 had done nothing to end the exclusion of Roman Catholics from the state, and the subsequent history of Irish political attitudes to Catholic relief confirmed Burke's impression that the 1782 act actually double-bolted the door against any inclusion in the commonwealth. This also provides an illuminating context for Burke's distance from the Irish constitutional crisis of 1782.

When Rockingham became prime minister in 1782 they were immediately faced with a renewal of the pressure for further concessions from the Irish opposition. Henry Grattan's speech in the Irish House of Commons in February 1782 attacked the 'tyrranical and unconstitutional assumptions' of the British parliament and reiterated his claim that Ireland was a free people with a distinct kingdom linked to Britain only through the imperial crown.[38] The drastic implications of such rhetoric for Burke's views on the place of Ireland in the Empire are clear, but by this stage Burke's involvement with the formulation of Irish policy was at a low ebb. Grattan's renewed offensive recognized the impending collapse of North's ministry. The new ministry, in which Burke was paymaster general but not a member of the cabinet, was immediately faced with a motion for the repeal of the Declaratory Act at Westminster on 8 April and a unanimous resolution to the same effect by both Irish Houses of parliament. In the parliamentary debate on the Irish crisis, urging time for deliberation: 'The motion before the House went, in some measure, to tear asunder the connection between England and Ireland; and yet the House was to be hurried into a decision in a moment upon a question of such magnitude.'[39] Both in the debate and in a letter to John Hely-Hutchinson written shortly afterwards, Burke also proposed that the repeal of the Declaratory Act would not resolve the issue of the constitutional conflict and that some clear and solid settlement of the differences between the two countries was required.[40]

Burke's involvement, so far as can be judged from the surviving evidence, was peripheral at this critical juncture, but his statement on the need for a more lasting settlement of the Anglo-Irish relationship was quite close to the proposals of Fox, who was far more closely involved in framing the government's response to the crisis:

> My opinion is clear for giving them all that they ask, but for giving it to them so as to secure us from further demands, and at the same time to have some clear understanding with respect to what we are to expect from Ireland, in return for the protection and assistance which she receives ... If they mean really well to their country, they must wish some final adjustment which may preclude further disputes.[41]

Burke spoke in favour of Fox's motion for the repeal of the Declaratory Act on 17 May, but much of his reported speech was concerned with justifying his own position in the vicissitudes of recent years. Yet Burke's distance from the measures adopted by the ministry was eloquently expressed in a letter to the Duke of Portland, the Irish lord lieutenant, in which he stated that as far as Irish affairs were concerned he was 'more completely uninformed about everything that is going on, than I thought it was possible for one that lived in London to be'. Burke also claimed that he had not been aware of the cabinet's intentions until a meeting at Fox's house on the night before the motion of 17 May.[42]

Burke's rather lukewarm and detached attitude to the Grattanite revolution of 1782 was modified in the aftermath of the concessions of that year. But despite his belief in the necessity of some permanent settlement to avert the dangers to the Anglo-Irish connection, Burke expediently supported the opposition to Pitt's proposal for an economic settlement between the two kingdoms embodied in the commercial propositions of 1785. After 1790 Burke's interest in Ireland was rekindled by the emergence of the Catholic question in Irish politics. In the intervening period Burke had been increasingly preoccupied with his campaign to expose the corruption of the East India Company, a cause which dominated his career from 1783 to 1790. Burke's attack on the position of the Company, first enunciated in 1783, argued forcefully for the pre-eminence of justice and the chartered rights guaranteed by the constitution over the specific Charter of the Company.

In terms redolent of the assertion of the priority of the public welfare over systems of law which were inimical to the public good in the Tracts on the Popery Laws, Burke condemned the theory that an attack on the company's charter was a violation of right:

> The rights of men, that is to say, the natural rights of mankind, are indeed sacred things ... If these natural rights are further affirmed and declared by express covenants, if they are clearly defined and secured against chicane, against power, and authority by written instruments and positive engagements ... they partake not only of the sanctity of the object so secured, but of that solemn public faith itself, which secures an object of

such importance. Indeed this formal recognition by the sovereign power of an original right in the subject can never be subverted, but by rooting up the radical principles of government, and even of society itself.

The charters in question are the fundamental charters of the constitution, such as the Magna Carta, which Burke argues are 'very fitly called the *chartered rights of men*'.[43] Five years later, in his opening speeches on the impeachment of Warren Hastings before the House of Lords, Burke made his famous assault on 'geographical morality' – the contention that different standards of justice apply in India, despite the fact that Hastings went there as a British governor and not 'as a subdahar, as a bashaw of three tails'. Once again Burke exhibits a prior standard of justice inherent in the constitution over-riding specific systems, which tend to deprive the subject of the fundamental benefits of constitutional government.

Burke's return to Irish affairs in the 1790s was motivated by a concern that the iniquities of the Irish governing system, which he had hoped to see reformed in the 1770s, were in danger of exposing Ireland to the contagion of French revolutionary ideas. Burke retained close contacts with the leaders of the movement for the relaxation of the Penal Laws in Ireland and was instrumental in having his son Richard appointed agent of the Catholic Committee in 1791. In ways reminiscent of his attitude to prudent concessions on Irish trade in 1778, Burke believed that a timely grant of political rights to Catholics might cement their loyalty to the state and prevent an alliance of disaffected Catholics and republican radicals. Burke's attitude to Catholic rights went much farther, however, and produced his most sustained body of analysis of the Irish governing system in the context of a discussion of the constitution. Burke's Letter to Sir Hercules Langrishe was published early in 1792 as the Catholic campaign for political rights was beginning to encounter serious opposition among Irish politicians. The Letter was ostensibly a reply to a liberal Protestant who had misgivings about the wisdom of granting concessions and the potential danger to the security of the Irish governing system. Burke argued that the British and Irish constitutions were not oligarchical, given the existence of a popular element, but that the exclusion of any substantial body of people – much less the majority of the population – would create a multitude who were excluded 'not from the state but from the British constitution'.[44]

In a review of Irish history since the twelfth century Burke argued that the fundamental principles of English government in Ireland had been adapted to conditions prevailing there at various times. In an inversion of the arguments used by the promoters of the idea of Protestant Ascendancy to justify the exclusion of the Catholics from the constitution, Burke argued in favour of the constitutional changes of 1782 as representing a gradual 'domiciliation' of the English interest in Ireland. 'The true revolution to you, that which most intrinsically and substantially resembled the English revolution of 1688, was the Irish revolution of 1782.'[45] Having conceded property to the Catholics in 1778–82,

Burke argues that prudence and justice dictate that they be admitted to the franchise.

> Then, since our oldest fundamental laws follow, or rather couple, freehold with franchise; since no principle of the Revolution shakes these liberties ... since the principles of the Revolution coincide with the declarations of the Great Charter ... since the King's coronation oath does not stand in his way to the performance of his duty to all his subjects ... since no nation in the world has ever been known to exclude so great a body of men (not born slaves) from the civil state, and all the benefits of its constitution; the whole question comes before Parliament as a matter for its prudence.[46]

Burke's rehabilitation of the Revolution of 1782 may be seen as an attempt to couch his criticism of the denial of constitutional benefits to the majority of the population in a language acceptable to a rational if misguided adherent to a sectarian constitution. Yet the fundamental argument about the prudence and justice of an inclusive system reveals Burke's sense that the universally-applicable principles of the British constitution over-ride the sectional interests evident in the contested history of Ireland. The exclusion of a majority from the benefits of the constitution is a contradiction in terms, analogous to the charge of geographical morality with which Burke indicts the conduct of Hastings and the East India Company.

The tone of Burke's Letter addressed to Langrishe was in marked contrast to that which he adopted in an unpublished and unfinished letter to his son Richard, written a month later. The contrast between the conciliatory stance adopted by Burke in the former and the indignation of the latter conceal a common basis of argument about the relationship between justice and the constitution. The principal difference lay in Burke's castigation of the theory and practice of Protestant Ascendancy in the letter to Richard Burke. As before, Burke dwells with some feeling on the turbulence of Irish history and the sufferings of the native inhabitants, including 'those confiscations, with the memory of which the gentlemen who triumph in the acts of 1782 are so delighted'.[47] But even here Burke also writes as an Anglican and a defender of the transcendent virtues of the British constitution, which he saw as a universal benefit in his idea of empire. The psychic mystery of Burke's deep sympathy for the victims of oppression and injustice, probably dating from his earliest affective ties in Ireland, thus merge with the orator and statesman proud of his place at the centre of the Empire.

> Is it because I love the Church, and the King, and the privileges of Parliament, that I am to be ready for any violence, or any injustice, or any absurdity in the means of supporting any of these powers, or all of them together? Instead of prating about Protestant ascendancies, Protestant Parliaments ought, in my opinion, to think at last of becoming Patriot Parliaments.[48]

NOTES

1. L.M. Cullen, 'Burke, Ireland and Revolution', *Eighteenth Century Life*, 16 (1992), p.40.
2. 'Tracts Relating to Popery Laws', *Writings and speeches*, vol.ix, p.453.
3. Ibid., p.454.
4. Ibid., p.459.
5. Ibid., p.462.
6. Pierre Samuel Dupont de Nemours, *De l'origine et progres d'une science nouvelle* (1767), in Mario Einaudi, *The Physiocratic Doctrine of Judicial Control* (Cambridge, 1938), pp.44–5.
7. 'Tracts Relating to Popery Laws', *Writings and speeches*, vol.ix, p.456.
8. Ibid., p.473.
9. William O'Brien, *Edmund Burke as an Irishman* (Dublin, 1924); T.H.D. Mahoney, *Edmund Burke and Ireland* (Harvard, 1960).
10. Conor Cruise O'Brien, *The Great Melody; A Thematic Biography and Comment Anthology of Edmund Burke* (London: Sinclair-Stevenson, 1992); Michael Fuchs, *Edmund Burke, Ireland and the Fashioning of Self* (Oxford: Voltaire Foundation, 1996); Luke Gibbons, *Edmund Burke and Ireland; Aesthetics, Politics and the Colonial Sublime* (Cambridge: Cambridge University Press, 2003)
11. Burke to Charles O'Hara, 24 May 1766, *Correspondence*, vol.i, pp.254–5; F.P. Lock, *Edmund Burke: Volume I, 1730–1784* (Oxford: Clarendon Press, 1998), p.225.
12. Burke to O'Hara, 27 Nov. 1767, ibid., vol.I, p.337; L.M. Cullen, 'Burke's Irish Views and Writings', in Ian Crowe (ed.), *Edmund Burke, his Life and Legacy* (Dublin: Four Courts Press, 1997), pp.69–70.
13. Burke to O'Hara, 20 Feb. 1768, *Correspondence*, vol.i, p.343.
14. Burke to O'Hara, 24 May 1766, ibid., p.256
15. Ibid., p.343.
16. Speech on Irish Banking, 17 Dec. 1770, *Writings and Speeches*, vol.ix, p.486.
17. *Works*, vol.ii, p.47; see also Richard Bourke, 'Liberty, Authority and Trust in Burke's Idea of Empire', *Journal of the History of Ideas*, 61 (2000), pp.453–71.
18. *History of the Irish Parliament*, 1692–1800, vol.iv, p.56.
19. John Monck Mason, *Remarks upon Poyning's Law and the manner of passing bills in the parliament of Ireland* (Dublin, 1758), pp.6–10, 31–4.
20. Ibid., p.32.
21. Robert French, *The Constitution of Ireland and Poynings Law explained* (Dublin, 1770), pp.3–4.
22. Letter to Sir Charles Bingham, 30 Oct. 1773, *Writings and speeches*, vol.ix, p.488.
23. Ibid., p.494.
24. Ibid., p.491.
25. Speech on conciliation with America, *Writings and speeches*, vol.iii, p.140.
26. See O'Brien, *The Great Melody*, p.190.
27. Burke to the Duke of Richmond, Aug. 1774, *Correspondence*, vol.iii, pp.217–20.
28. Speech on conciliation with America, *Writings and speeches*, vol.iii, p.158.
29. Burke to E.S, Pery, 12 Aug. 1778, *Correspondence*, vol.iv, p.15.
30. Letter to Samuel Span, *Writings and speeches*, vol.ix, pp.508–9.
31. Burke to Rockingham, 9 May 1779, *Correspondence*, vol.iv, pp.70–1.
32. *Writings and speeches*, vol.ix, pp.540–2.
33. Ibid., p.548.
34. Speech at Bristol Previous to the Election, 1780, *Writings and speeches*, vol.iii, p.631.
35. Ibid., p.401.
36. Burke to Kenmare, 21 Feb. 1782, *Writings and speeches*, vol.ix, p.566.
37. Ibid., pp.567, 579.
38. *Parliamentary Register*, vol.i, pp.266–9.
39. *Writings and speeches*, vol.ix, p.581.
40. Burke to Hely-Hutchinson, *post* 9 April 1782, *Correspondence*, vol.iv, p.440.
41. Fox to Richard Fitzpatrick, 28 April 1782 in John Derry, *Charles James Fox* (New York, 1972), p.140.
42. Burke to Portland, 25 May 1782, *Correspondence*, vol.iv, pp.454–5.
43. Speech on Fox's East India Bill, 1783, *Writings and speeches*, vol.v, p.384.
44. *Writings and Speeches*, vol.ix, p.600.
45. Ibid., p.617.
46. Ibid., p.628.
47. Letter to Richard Burke, *Writings and speeches*, vol.ix, p.656.
48. Ibid., p.650.

8

Burke, Goldsmith and the Irish Absentees

MCHAEL J. GRIFFIN

> Here lies our good Edmund, whose genius was such,
> We scarcely can praise it, or blame it too much;
> Who, born for the Universe, narrow'd his mind,
> And to party gave up, what was meant for mankind.
> Oliver Goldsmith, *Retaliation* (1774)

A few months before his death, Oliver Goldsmith read parts of *Retaliation* to Hugh Boyd, requesting his opinion. Boyd told him that he thought its sections relating to the Burkes – Edmund, Richard and William – were too severe, and that their publication 'would not only put an end to the friendship which subsisted between them and Goldsmith, but likewise disturb the harmony which prevailed in the Club'.[1] Goldsmith accepted Boyd's suggested emendations, and the lines that appeared were not as damaging as those deleted. On hearing of Goldsmith's death on 4 April 1774, Edmund Burke is reported to have burst into tears; still, it seems, friendly enough with Goldsmith, Burke did not take too churlishly the former's cruel line, which decried Burke's narrowing his mind so that he could give up to the Rockingham party 'what was meant for mankind'.[2] Goldsmith, more than many, might have known; their acquaintance and developing friendship between the 1740s and the 1770s spanned that 'narrowing'.

That Goldsmith and Burke were good friends in London is well known. They were both of Johnson's circle. Less studied are their shared origins at Trinity College, Dublin. It has been presumed that this mutual background was not known to them in advance of their displacement to the London scene.[3] Burke entered Trinity College in April of 1744; Goldsmith, in June of the following year. No correspondence between the two from those days is known to exist – very little of Goldsmith's correspondence exists in any case; nor can we be sure how well they knew each other in Dublin. However, Goldsmith's reputation as an entrepreneurial balladeer, rioter and host would probably have been known throughout the college. Their backgrounds were similar: they were both Anglicans with inflections of familial Catholicism. Their statues stand together on the green of Trinity College Dublin as testaments to a presumed equivalence in Anglo-Irishness, but in the case of both men there are traces of the Gaelic and Jacobite rural milieu of their childhoods. Burke is 'a product of his Gaelic Jacobite upbringing and his Patriotic Irish education' at Trinity.[4] And Goldsmith is closer to this world than is commonly appreciated. His family's Protestantism was a century old; theirs was an Anglicanism not separate from the Gaelic, Jacobite culture which surrounded them in the Irish midlands.[5] The greatest influence in Goldsmith's early life was his uncle Thomas Contarine, a friend of the historian of Gaelic Ireland Charles O'Conor,[6] at whose house it is thought that a very young Goldsmith met Carolan, the blind harpist and subject of one of his later journalistic essays.

Given the general acceptance of his status as a great Anglo-Irish author in Yeats' Protestant pantheon, and the politically obscuring plagiarism of much of his prose, such aspects of his cultural background are routinely ignored. Graham Gargett argues that Goldsmith's reproduction of Voltaire's Humean anti-Irish sentiment in his *History of England* 'indicates that any nationalist, Catholic, genes in his character were singularly inactive'.[7] Samuel Johnson's view, however, is more to the point. Thinking him an excellent compiler, he found the idea of Goldsmith doing original research faintly comical. In 1778, he remarked that Goldsmith was 'at no pains to fill his mind with knowledge. He transplanted it from one place to another; and it did not settle in his mind; so he could not tell what was in his own books.'[8] That Goldsmith took anti-Irish sentiments from Voltaire does not necessarily tell us anything at all about his political outlook or his views on Ireland. He also thieved liberally from David Hume. Though he found Hume's thought generally repulsive, he was happy to take what he needed from him in his professional writing. Burke was at greater liberty to research a challenge to anti-Irish historiography than Goldsmith; as an historian, the latter was nothing if not hackish.

The Traveller (1764) and *The Deserted Village* (1770), rather than the great, unoriginal mash of his histories, are the keys to Goldsmith's politics. Both poems lament destruction of a pastoral order brought about by luxury and spurious notions of 'liberty'; and both describe mass emigration to the New World as inevitable consequences. 'Biographically', writes Roger Lonsdale, 'his two major poems, both written with painstaking care and with no immediate financial motive, almost certainly represent what he himself considered the only true manifestations of his literary integrity and talent'.[9] Both poems have as their first person an exile; both lament the decay of organic social modes and their destruction by commercial notions of 'liberty'. Both, in effect, are emotionally Jacobite poems; and both are of a piece with the political philosophy of Burke's *Reformer*.

These parallels help to explain the longer context (the immediate occasion is well known)[10] of Goldsmith's markedly barbed swipe at Burke in *Retaliation*. The mild invective recalls a very recent difference of opinion. A year before *Retaliation* was composed, Goldsmith had almost imperceptibly engaged himself on a campaign for the taxation of Irish absentees. Burke had, in the 1740s, lambasted the negligence and luxuriance of the Irish absentees, but had decisively sided with Rockingham's landed interest when a tax on their Irish earnings was mooted in 1773. It is the long divergence in their approaches to this topic over the decades that best explains Goldsmith's cutting comment in *Retaliation*.

To clarify this divergence of opinion, it is best to divide the relationship of Burke and Goldsmith to Ireland into two sections, corresponding to two decades: the 1740s and the 1770s. It is suggested that the political protest of *The Deserted Village* (1770) is a product, not just of the poet's experiences in the Irish midlands, but also of the intellectual culture of Dublin in the 1740s. Those two aspects interacted with the Dublin publication in 1740 of Laurence Whyte's poetry, which described widespread denudation and emigration caused by absentee-ism and rack-renting. Goldsmith was also influenced by the political content of Burke's *Reformer* (1748). Not only did Goldsmith read *The Reformer*; I suggest that, in all probability, he contributed his first published poem, anonymously, to the *Reformer*'s fourth number.

In 1729, the Irish Patriot Thomas Prior excoriated the wanton luxury of Irish absentee landlords, by claiming that they:

add Insult to ill Usage; *they* reproach us with our Poverty, at the same Time, that *they* take away our Money; and can tell us, we have no Diversion or Entertainments in *Ireland* for them, when they themselves disable us from having better, by withdrawing from us.

   But 'tis to be hoped, that our Legislature will take Care, that these Gentlemen, who spend their Fortunes abroad, and are thereby the greatest, and almost only Cause of its Poverty and Distress, shall not be the only Persons favoured, and exempted from paying the Taxes thereof.[11]

Prior's writing may have influenced Jonathan Swift's complaint – composed in the early 1730s, first published in 1762 – regarding 'the Folly, the Vanity, and Ingratitude of those vast Numbers, who think themselves too good to live in the Country which gave them Birth, and still gives them Bread; and rather chuse to pass their Days, and consume their Wealth, and draw out the very Vitals of their Mother Kingdom, among those who heartily despise them'.[12] The culture of disdain for the absentees was broad, intense in Dublin's patriotic circles, and diffused throughout the countryside. Laurence Whyte's poems, published in 1740, were circulating in Dublin as Goldsmith and Burke were studying in Trinity College. In the preface to 'The Parting Cup, or, The Humours of *Deoch an Doruis*', Whyte sketches the culture of hospitality among the native gentry in Goldsmith's native Westmeath, before critically narrating the decline of that hospitality from 1688 to 1740, and including a severe admonition to those landlords who spend their money abroad, thus impoverishing the country that sustains their luxurious lifestyles.

Canto 4 of the poem is a sustained critique of the destruction wrought by the

Absentees. Extracting excessive rents from a tenantry to which they show no filial affection or duty, the men of wealth and pride allow the dereliction of rural Ireland. The processes described presage *The Deserted Village*:

> Depopulating ev'ry *Village*,
> Where we had *Husbandry* and *Tillage*,
> Fat *Bacon*, *Poultry*, and good *Bread*,
> By which the *Poor* were daily fed.
> The *Landlords* then at ev'ry *Gale*,
> Besides their *Rent*, got *Nappy Ale*,
> A hearty welcome and good *Chear*,
> With *Rent* well paid them twice a Year.
> But now the Case is quite revers'd,
> The *Tenants* ev'ry day distress'd,
> Instead of living well and thriving,
> There's nothing now, but *leading, driving,* –
> The *Lands* are all *monopoliz'd*,
> The *Tenants* racked and sacrific'd,
> Whole *Colonies* to shun the Fate,
> Of being oppress'd at such a Rate
> By *Tyrants* who still raise their Rent,
> Sail'd to the *Western Continent*,
> Rather than live at home like slaves,
> They trust themselves to Wind and Waves

The rack-renting landlords are 'too well bred to live at home',[13] Whyte writes ironically; preferring what Goldsmith might call 'the long pomp'[14] of London and Paris masquerades, they are financed in their extravagance by Irish rents:

> These *Absentees* we here describe,
> Are mostly of our Ir___sh Tribe,
> Who live in *Luxury* and *Pleasure*,
> And throw away their *Time* and *Treasure*,
> Cause *Poverty* and Devastation,
> And sink the *Credit* of the *Nation*,
> A *Nation* sunk for Want of *Trade*,
> A Foot-stool to her *Neighbours* made;
> And yet our *Gentry* all run wild,
> And never can be reconcil'd,
> To live at home upon their Rent,
> With any Pleasure or Content.[15]

Goldsmith drew poetical and political inspiration from the milieu and the substance of Whyte's poem;[16] the Dublin reading public would be well used to complaints such as those emanating from the Thomas Prior's Dublin Society regarding the negligence of a luxurious and feckless gentry.

It was in the 1740s, these Trinity years, that Burke's views on the land, the Irish peasantry, and the gentry would have been most accordant with those of Whyte, and by extension, Goldsmith. In the evenings following their discussions of Trinity student disturbances in Dublin (of which Goldsmith was a known leader, almost certainly known to Burke),[17] Burke introduced to his club a bill 'to tax the absentees ten per cent of their estates', claiming such a tax to be 'the only means of preserving some part of the little money in the kingdom, which, appropriated to the Dublin Society, might prove a great advantage to it'.[18] Thematically continuous with this resolution was the fourth number of the *Reformer*, in which Burke differentiates between party and public-spiritedness, a distinction which provides a basis for his critique of absentee-ism:

> We are very easy about those who for this Reason brand us with the name of *Party*, and equally despise the Appelation, and those who give it, unless they mean, that by their dulness they have made all Persons of Taste a Party against them, and then we glory in the Title. But 'twas no Hatred to particular Persons, but a love of the *Publick* that gave life to this Design; and we would endeavour, as much as in us lies, to infuse the same Spirit into our Readers.
>
> Hospitality and *Public-Spirit* have the same Source, namely, the Love of Mankind; yet 'tis no less certain than surprizing, that we who are remarkable for the former, discover very little of the latter, tho' it seems more strongly enforced by Nature, yet thro' an odd Perverseness, all People are welcome to our Favour, but those whom Nature and their own merits make worthy of it; while several of the Nobility and Gentry, in whose Power alone it is to prevent this Evil, are not only passive, but assistants to it, as if conscious of the Poverty and Infamy their Behaviour raises to their Country, they fly it and bestow their Riches, where, as they are less wanted, the People are less thankful for them.

The love of mankind, then, is perverted through the wilful irresponsibility of the nobility. The general tenor of the *Reformer* is one of patriotism, inflected with a critical pastoralism. Appropriate to this inflection, a poem 'On the Several Conditions of Life' appears at the end of *Reformer* No.4, and is included by Burke for being 'moral and ingenious':

> With even hand has all disposing Fate,
> Pleasure and Pain annex'd to every State:
> Kings who Dominion with their Maker share,
> Tho' free to govern, live the Slaves of Fear;
> While Peasants whom no regal Cares invade
> Find their Contempt with Safety well repaid;

Content when lodg'd within the poor man's Breast,
Equals his worst of Fortunes with the best;
While the rich Wretch whose Wishes nought confines
In Midst of Plenty as in Want repines.

To heal his Wounds the Soldier gets a Name,
And dies in battle but to live in Fame;
The Hopes of Heaven cheers the suff'ring Saint,
While keen Remorse the Sinner's Pleasures taint;
The Bard whose Labours are with Genius crown'd,
Oft sees his Worth in Seas of Envy drown'd,
Saint-like he voluntary Want must chuse,
Not reap, till dead, the Profits of his Muse.[19]

A.P.I. Samuels has asked whether this was Goldsmith's poem.[20] Goldsmith is reputed to have made some of his way in Trinity by selling poems, though such sales are now impossible to trace. Nonetheless, the poem is quite probably by Goldsmith. Quite apart from the promising stylistic similarities – uncluttered heroic couplets, dialectically weighted[21] – to both of Goldsmith's major poems, the philosophy of the poem is straightforwardly Goldsmithian.

The Deserted Village replays one image in particular, in which a returned soldier weeps 'o'er his wounds and tales of sorrow' in a scene of pastoral generosity and safety. The image of the reward as 'crowning' is also one which figures in ideal scenes of calm retirement in the later poem. The vision is one of patriarchal monarchy, of a protective Kingly prerogative, which leaves the peasant to the felicitous safety of innocent ignorance. Goldsmith's late Jacobitism manifests itself generally in a type of Tory Monarchism, one which, in *The Traveller*, curses that hour, 'when first ambition struck at regal power'.[22] Disgusted by the Whig oligarchy and the way of the world since '88, Goldsmith painted a pastoral order wherein everyone had their load to bear; wherein, more importantly, everyone knew which load was *theirs*. The duty of the powerful to the poor is essential to this pastoral vision. For Goldsmith, it is normative; in Ireland it was not, in the 1740s, a reality. That 'On the Several Conditions of Life' should appear in a particularly sharp number of the *Reformer* (No.4), wherein the Absentees are vilified, gives the poem a critical edge that, intrinsically, it lacks.

The Traveller internationalizes the thesis of 'On the Several Conditions of Life' to demonstrate that what holds within countries also holds comparatively. For every benefit of power, there is responsibility. For every simple pleasure of rustic working life, there is limitation. This idea of 'content'[23] runs throughout the poetry, linked in critical antagonism to the concept of luxury. Luxury, in turn, is a euphemism for the decline of patriarchal monarchy and the dialectical probabilities of exploitation and insubordination. Burke's idea of real national wealth is precisely Goldsmith's; Goldsmith's, at this point, precisely Burke's:

> The Riches of a Nation are not to be estimated by the splendid Appearance or luxurious Lives of its Gentry; it is the uniform Plenty diffused through a People, of which the meanest as well as the greatest partake, that makes them happy, and the Nation powerful.[24]

According to these principles, the *Reformer* No.7 of 10 March 1748 again linked poverty and destitution in Ireland to the luxury of the nobility and the gentry. Echoing Swift's *Short View of the State of Ireland* (1727), Burke observes that wealth has not diffused as it should through the Irish population, and claims that few countries in Europe can equal the poverty of the Irish peasantry, a poverty all the more scandalous when thrown into sharp relief by the excesses of the rich. Irresponsible wealth, as Goldsmith would put it later, is 'but a name'/ That leaves our useful products still the same'. The men of 'wealth and pride'[25] indulge a luxury which destroys the poor. More particularly, the villain is the rich man who displaces the rural poor with his expansive landscape garden; but the depiction of such social irresponsibility is inspired equally by the Absentee who, in luxurious oblivion, drives his tenants to emigration.

If the pastoralism of 'On the Several Conditions of Life' acquires political momentum in the context of the organ in which it was published, so does the pastoralism of *The Deserted Village* develop a critical edge in relation to the processes of denudation it describes. For many Irish observers – from W.B. Yeats to Seamus Deane – it is the soft pastoralism of *The Deserted Village*, and not its political argument, which defines and delimits the poet's stance. Referring to *The Deserted Village*, Deane insists that Goldsmith's Ireland is not

> the Ireland of the penal Laws and of occasional famines, agrarian disturbances and judicial murders. It is an idyll, comparable to his view of Irish society of which *The Deserted Village* is the appealing remnant ... Blandness is converted to sweetness and the nostalgia is believed to refer to an actual society, English or Irish, that had been degraded by the onset of the new world of the agricultural and industrial revolutions. Goldsmith was anxious to support the idea that the form of liberty gained in England in 1688 was a commodity that had been exported to Ireland.[26]

The Deserted Village, however, is not a real idyll. The poem's Irish context is that of the 1740s, the last decade that Goldsmith spent in his native country, a decade characterized by famine. The landowners in Ireland are luxuriously, blissfully unaware of the 'imploring famine' of 1740–41, the 'wretched matron, forced, in age, for bread,/ To strip the brook with mantling cresses spread'.[27] Goldsmith's vision is of a country ruined by the waste of the peasantry's potential, the population distraught, hungry and driven to emigration by a general neglect. Ireland, in the years before Goldsmith began his studies at Trinity, was oftner visited with famine, than any other country under heaven, and every famine attended as a natural and necessary consequence, with a pestilence that sweeps away its inhabitants in prodigious numbers, who also croud out to *America*, and elsewhere, so fast, that it is in danger of being unpeopled in a little time; that as to it's wealth, it is one of the poorest countries in the world.[28]

Goldsmith left Ireland in 1752, never to return. He fancies strange revolutions at home; but such disturbances are, he reckons to himself, figments of distanced imagination. For English critics in 1770, *The Deserted Village* has little to do with contemporary reality. One reviewer congratulated its 'most beautiful structure, though we think it is built upon a very sandy foundation; or rather, it is a rainbow castle in the air, raised and adorned solely by the strength of the author's imagination; for we cannot believe, that this country is depopulating, or that commerce is destructive of the real strength and greatness of a nation'.[29] In his substantial account of the circumstances of the poem's creation, however, William Cooke recalls Goldsmith's remark two days into the poem's composition: 'Some of my friends', he told Cooke, 'differ with me on this plan, and think the depopulation of villages does not exist – but I am myself satisfied of the fact. I remember it in my own country, and have seen it in this.'[30]

The reality of the poem is that of the Ireland which effectively produced both Burke and Goldsmith intellectually: an Ireland of poverty, famine and absenteeism. And whereas both men would have agreed on the need for a tax on absenteeism in the 1740s, Goldsmith knew that by 1773 Burke had given up on that belief due to party affiliation. Goldsmith's poetry echoes John Brown's disdain for party, corruption and luxury.[31] Burke affects to dispense with such outmoded Toryism in his *Thoughts on the Present Discontents* (1770), which famously makes the case for party government.

In 1773, the Irish House of Commons, following on a proposal from the patriot Colonel John Blaquiere (1732–1812), proposed a tax of two shillings on every pound on net rents earned by Irish estates owned by landlords who did not reside in Ireland for six months of every year. It was quietly agreed at a poorly-attended cabinet meeting that, should the Irish send over such a proposal, the North Ministry would urge the King to authorize the tax. The prominent landholders to be affected would include the Marquis of Rockingham, whose townhouse in Grosvenor Square quickly became the centre of opposition to the measure. Since 1765, Burke had been private secretary to Rockingham. In the opposition to the absentee tax, Burke was the primary agitator, accumulating petitions and assisting in the drafting of letters representative of the absentees' interests.

There are two interpretations of Burke's mature opposition to the absentee tax. One version might simply place his opposition in the context of party affiliation and self-interest. The other version sees this episode in the context of Burke's adhesion to a general imperial principle. Regarding the first version, it bears reminding that Burke was himself an absentee at this stage, though on a very small scale. He inherited his brother Garrett's estate in Clogher, in Cork, in 1765, the same year as he allied with the Rockingham Whigs. By the time of the 1773 proposal, Rockingham's estates in Ireland yielded £14,000 pounds a year; Burke's, the comparatively negligible sum of £500. 'It may therefore look', writes Conor Cruise O'Brien, 'as though their opposition was dictated by material interests'.[32] For O'Brien's Burke, however, it was the principle of the thing, a principle of stability through union. Burke's guiding principle, with Ireland and America, was to minimize exploitation in the context of the imperial connection.

For Burke, unease in the American colonies loomed large, and it was crucial that the centre held. 'The position which he took on this Irish business', writes Mahoney, 'was in perfect consonance with that which he had been holding in reference to America'.[33] Only England could exercise power in ways that would keep the empire unified. If any other parliament took it upon itself to authorize and collect taxes for its own administration, the empire itself would gradually fracture. Secondly, such a tax would discourage intra-imperial mobility, with the result that marriages, and bonds of affection and inheritance would be lost: those factors that for Burke were the stuff of strong international relations. Burke wrote to Rockingham on 29 September that it would be ridiculous 'to understand it as any thing else than a measure of administration, notwithstanding their pretended wishes of a more agreeable mode of Supply'. This letter is perhaps his most substantial missive on this issue. Burke derides the plan as 'preposterous', and possibly resulting in the 'derangement of the whole contexture of this Empire considerd [sic] as a well orderd [sic], connected, and proportiond [sic] body'. People would, he speculated, be seduced by the 'superficial appearance of Equity in this Tax, which cannot fail to captivate almost all those who are not led by some immediate Interest to an attentive examination of its intrinsick merits': the absentees themselves. A tax on absenteeism acknowledged that Ireland and England were separate political and administrative entities. Absentee landlords would, according to Burke, be driven back to Ireland and would therefore not be in a position to represent the interests of Ireland to parliament in England. If this tax were allowed, it would mean that Ireland would be setting a legislative precedent for the empire as a whole. Such imperatives were deemed by Burke to properly reside in England itself; citizens of the empire should be able to reside wherever they wished, in any of His Majesty's dominions. Burke's arguments are by turns alarmist and affective, and in both senses just woolly enough to warrant suspicion. On 30 October 1773 Burke wrote to Sir Charles Bingham in Dublin:

> One of the most odious parts of the proposed absentee tax is its tendency to separate friends, and to make as ugly breaches in private society as it must make in the unity of the great political body ... We shall be barbarized on both sides of the water if we do not see one another now and

then. *We* shall sink into surly, brutish Johns, and *you* will degenerate into wild Irish. It is impossible that we should be wiser, or the more agreeable; certainly we shall not love one another the better for this forced separation, which our ministers, who have already done so much for the dissolution of every other sort of good connexion, are now meditating for the further improvement of this too well-united empire. Their next step will be to encourage all the colonies, about thirty separate governments, to keep their people from all intercourse with each other and with the mother country. A gentleman of New York, or Barbadoes, will be as much gazed at as a strange animal from Nova Zembla or Otaheite; and those rogues the travellers will tell us what stories they please about poor old Ireland.

A tax as proposed is 'a virtual declaration that England is a foreign country'. 'Is there a shadow of reason', Burke demanded, 'that because a Lord Rockingham, a Duke of Devonshire, a Sir George Saville [sic], possess property in Ireland, which has descended to them without any act of theirs, they should abandon their duty in parliament, and spend their winters in Dublin?'[34] The question was more rhetorical than it should have been. Absentees would not necessarily have to return to Dublin. They would just have to pay tax on their lands' earnings in Ireland.

George Savile himself acknowledged as much. Though invoked by Burke in his letter to Bingham, Savile agreed with neither Burke nor Rockingham on the issue. An owner of property in Fermanagh and Tyrone, he refused to sign up with the opponents of the tax because he doubted that the measure was a bad one for Ireland, though it certainly was for England and for the absentees. On 5 November 1773, he explained himself to Rockingham:

We are two nations, not one. In money matters absolutely, in some matters hostile, for we have a separate purse. If *you* was to be taxed in Northamptonshire for not living there, it would be absurd; but if Northamptonshire had a separate purse, and all her landlords went and enriched neighbour counties, I don't know exactly how far I should think I might go if I were a Northamptonshire man.

If, in considering the two nations as hostile, I am right in excusing *them*, the same argument condemns the approbation of it here; for if it be good for Ireland, as having a separate interest, to make her landlords reside, or to impoverish them who do not, it is for every reason just as bad for England, and England has the power.

The argument deduced from the right of residing where one will, *within the dominions*, is, I likewise think, carried full as far as it will bear. I am a prisoner, it is true, if I am forbid by the state to use my right of travelling about, but a tax upon wheels is not an infringement upon liberty. I know I am a little sophistical in stating it thus, and I mean to be as much beyond the truth as one may, as that argument of the *impeachment of liberty* is the other. The truth may be between them, but, doubtless, if a State finds that, by a number of its subjects enjoying their property in one particular way they become less useful to their country, a tax may surely be laid to *compensate* to the public the *difference*; and whether the pernicious luxury be in wearing *foreign ruffles* or breathing *foreign* air, I may be taxed in the consumption of it ... This is what I have to argue, speaking as a *resident* Irishman. Ireland *contra* Great Britain is the idea the plan continually suggests to me, and, this hostility once established, I am bound to confess that England might double tax all persons who, having English estates, live in Ireland. When America begins to entice our rich, as it does now our people, we shall have this last proposition more fairly before us.[35]

The case of Ireland, then was the case of the American colonies, and potentially of the empire as a whole. Savile was, according to MARIUS, a correspondent in the *Public Advertiser*, a man of 'strict Principles', whose honesty in this matter was to be compared positively with the private interest of Rockingham, and by implication, Burke. Rockingham had a cheek 'to interest the Public in his Private Affairs'.[36] PHILO-MARIUS augmented the argument two days later:

We know, Sir, that Ireland has been principally ruined by the Management of the Retainers of the English Proprietors of vast Tracts of Land in that Country. The unfortunate People, by having the whole Fruits of their Industry carried out of the Country by the avaritious Exactions of men, who farm whole Estates from such as the Marquis, are first reduced to Beggary and Distress, and then are obliged to trust themselves to the Ocean to seek in a foreign Country that Relief which their own had denied. Hence proceed those emigrations that have deprived Ireland of a third Part of her Inhabitants; and hence those extensive Deserts which cover the best Parts of that unfortunate Kingdom.

When the Proprietor resides upon his Estates he barters back his rents for the Industry of his Tenants; but when the whole is carried to another Country, the Heart for want of the Return of the Blood, loses its Pulse, and the Body Politic languishes, and at last expires.[37]

In a similar vein, William Petty, Earl of Shelburne (1737–1805), though an Irish absentee himself, was in favour of the tax, having been convinced by Chatham of its merit on two points: the tax meant that absentees would be forced to make a contribution to the country from which they derived so much of their wealth; and, secondly, colonial parliaments should decide their own taxation.

Shelburne and Savile, then, both absentees, stood aloof from the Rockingham campaign against the tax – Savile for reasons of principle; Shelburne, in Burke's view, out of a spurious populism. On first being asked to sign the anti-tax petition, Shelburne wrote to Chatham on 17 October 1773: 'I naturally distrust my own judgment, where I am so deeply interested; and at any rate, I should be sorry to pay a greater regard to myself than becomes a liberal man, or may be likely to meet the public; who are not too apt to extend their feelings, even in cases of oppression, where the case does not exactly apply to the whole, or a majority of the whole'. Rockingham had called to Shelburne, and he to Rockingham twice to discuss the issue, but Shelburne stuck to his abstention: to Chatham Shelburne declared his principle that he did 'not conceive that Ireland or America can ever gain by the interposition of parliament' in Westminster:

> The Ministers, I understand, are come round to join with the most violent in condemning the policy, and I suppose will not be less ready to join them in upholding Poyning's Act, and all the old doctrine of the dependence of Ireland upon England, in all cases whatsoever. I shall therefore be very anxious to know how far the reservation I have stated meets your Lordship's idea, as I expect whatever debate occurs will turn upon that, or some other distinction which may be offered in favour of the supreme authority of the mother-country.[38]

Shelburne's views of the tax were oppositional, but only coyly so; his own estates in Ireland were worth £18,000. Horace Walpole documented Shelburne's duplicity in the absentees affair. In reality opposed to the tax, like Rockingham, for reasons of personal finance, he claimed to have been convinced of its merits by Chatham, who argued that the Irish parliament had not exceeded its remit, and that the solicited interference of the British parliament would be unjust, unconstitutional and injurious to Anglo-Irish relations. Shelburne played the role of double agent. Even though he acceded to, and campaigned for, Chatham's interpretation of the tax issue, he also quietly sought to encourage Burke to write against the tax to save the absentees, including himself, money.[39] He was, in short, two-faced on the issue.

Against Rockingham, he enlisted the services of Goldsmith, who was more determinedly in favour of the tax, as evidenced by a letter from Joseph Hickey to Rockingham. Hickey, Burke's Irish attorney, was active in circulating Absentee lists and corresponding lists of those who might politically be influenced by them. He was one of Burke's closest associates at Grosvenor Square. He wrote to Rockingham on 7 November:

> I have very strong reason to believe, tho' no certain Authority, That Lord Shelburne has employed Dr Goldsmith to write in favor of it. The Dr is become a great advocate for it and has even condescended to consult *me*, as to my thoughts.[40]

Naive in his support for Shelburne, and just as naive in asking Hickey for his thoughts, Goldsmith's enthusiasm for the tax would have irked Burke, as much as Burke's opposition to the tax would have baffled Goldsmith. That Burke had changed his mind is the subject of some nationalist critique, according to which Burke's stance exemplifies his commitment to empire: 'In playing the part he did in this instance', writes Mahoney, 'Burke was clearly placing himself in opposition to the sentiment prevalent among the majority of his former countrymen'.[41] It transpired, however, that many of the tenants had clauses written into their leases which made them liable for any additional taxes. The extra cost would, in today's parlance, be 'passed on' to the tenant. Principle aside, it seems that a tax which should have been generally popular, as Mahoney too readily implies it was, disappeared without any great noise. The absentee tax was defeated, after a muddled debate, in the Committee of Ways and Means of the Irish House of Commons on 25 November 1773. That it died quietly does not necessarily negate its desirability; it was, however, doomed by the iniquitous legal and political situation into which it would have been produced. 'Laws grind the poor', as Goldsmith wrote, 'and rich men rule the law'.[42]

For Burke, the situation had changed in the period between 1748 and 1773. His patriotic disdain for the absentees had been superseded by the compromises of working for them, and his views on their taxation were supplemented by a fraught imperial conviction. Burke was a consistent and conscientious critic of imperial abuse, if not always of the imperial principle. It was this principle that was exercised so severely by the taxation issue. Goldsmith's major poems were consistently anti-imperial; both were ideologically closer to the Burke of the *Reformer* than the Rockingham Burke. The last decade which they both spent in Ireland provide the most clarifying backdrop, not just to *The Deserted Village*, but to that longer process whereby Burke had given up to party certain convictions based on 'love of mankind'.

NOTES

1.   Laurence Dundas Campbell, 'The Life of Hugh Boyd', *The Miscellaneous Works of Hugh Boyd, the Author of the Letters of Junius. With an Account of his Life and Writings* (London, 1800), vol.1, p.188. 'Goldsmith may have made some remarks in private about the financial opportunism of the Burkes.' Dixon Wecter, 'Goldsmith and the Burkes', *Times Literary Supplement*, (12 Feb. 1938), p.108.
2.   Roger Lonsdale (ed.), 'Retaliation', *The Poems of Thomas Gray, William Collins, and Oliver Goldsmith* (London: Longman and New York: Norton, 1969, 1972), p.749.
3.   See Donald Cross Bryant, *Edmund Burke and His Literary Friends* (St Louis, 1939), pp.83–98; though Thomas Copeland writes of their relationship being 'revived' in London in 1757, implying that they were friends at Trinity. 'Introduction', *Correspondence*, vol.i, p.xviii.
4.   Katherine O'Donnell, 'The Image of a Relationship in Blood: Parliament na mBan and Burke's Jacobite Politics', *Eighteenth-Century Ireland: Iris an Dá Chultúr*, 15 (2000), p.100. Burke's ironic style is, for Conor Cruise O'Brien, symptomatic of a 'friction between outer Whig and inner "Jacobite"'. Conor Cruise O'Brien, 'Introduction', *Reflections on the Revolution in France* (Harmondsworth: Penguin, 1969), p.43.
5.   In his 1856 biography Thomas Babington Macaulay contends that Goldsmith
     never showed the least sign of that contemptuous antipathy with which, in his days, the ruling minority in Ireland too generally regarded the subject majority. So far indeed was he from sharing in the opinions and feelings of the caste to which he belonged, that he conceived an aversion

to the Glorious and Immortal Memory, and, even when George the Third was on the throne, maintained that nothing but the restoration of the banished dynasty could save the country.

'Life of Goldsmith' (1856), in Walter Scott, Thomas Babington Macaulay and William Makepeace Thackeray, *Essays on Goldsmith*, ed. G.E. Hadow and C.B. Wheeler (Oxford: The Clarendon Press, 1918), pp.20, 21. On Goldsmith's complicated ancestry, see W.J. McCormack, 'Goldsmith, Biography and the Phenomenology of Anglo-Irish Literature', in Andrew Swarbrick (ed.), *The Art of Oliver Goldsmith* (London: Vision Press; Totowa, New Jersey: Barnes and Noble, 1984), pp.168–94; Patrick Murray, 'The Riddle of Goldsmith's Ancestry', *Studies*, 63 (1974), pp.177–90; and Michael Griffin, 'Delicate Allegories, Deceitful Mazes: Goldsmith's Landscapes', *Eighteenth-Century Ireland: Iris an dá Chultúr*, 16 (2001), pp.104–17.

6.   But insulted nature resumes her own rights and Mr. OConor was too well acquainted with some of the Protestant nobility of this kingdom not to foresee that they would do signal services as soon as an opportunity presented itself for the exertion of their bright talents, manly patriotism and Christian benevolence; happening one day to dine with Mr. Contarine, 'Mr OConor', said the Parson, 'I am glad to see that you like my beef – I hope it is <u>orthodox</u>', 'Sir', said the other 'every thing that is Irish is orthodox' – The reply was so unstudied and so much to the good Parson's taste that filling out a bumper, well then said he OConor here is 'Everything that is Irish is orthodox,, The two gentlemen then unbosomed themselves, the Magic influence of good cheer brightened up new horizons for futurity, fancy revelled in new combinations, the <u>Saturnian</u> reign with all its golden harvest and innocent pleasures was anticipated, the hearts of the two neighbours were expanded by a consciousness that tho' they differed in Religious opinions they differed not thro' worldly but thro' honest motives, and this rendered their convivial happiness more exquisite, it was a feast with fellowship that gave free course to the genial current of the soul.

In manuscript material relating to 'Memoirs of the Life and Writings of the late Ch Oconor of Belanagare Esqr. M.R.I.A., to which is prefixed a short Historical Account of the Family of O'Conor From the Invasion of Henry 2. Compiled Principally from Notes and Extracts taken by Himself From Ancient Writers on Irish History And other Sources hitherto unexplored or not generally known', in the Gilbert Collection MS 203, Dublin City Library, Pearse St, pp.163–4.

7.   Graham Gargett, 'Plagiarism, Translation and the Problem of Identity: Oliver Goldsmith and Voltaire', *Eighteenth-Century Ireland: Iris an dá Chultúr*, 16 (2001), p.95.

8.   Quoted in James Boswell, *Life of Johnson*, ed. G. B. Hill, 6 vols (Oxford: Oxford University Press, 1791, 1934), vol.3, p.253. See also Michael Griffin, 'Oliver Goldsmith and Francois-Ignace Espiard de la Borde: An Instance of Plagiarism', *The Review of English Studies*, new series 50 (1999), pp.59–63.

9.   Roger Lonsdale, '"A Garden, and a Grave": The Poetry of Oliver Goldsmith', in Louis L. Martz and Aubrey Williams (eds), *The Author in his Work: Essays on a Problem in Criticism* (New Haven and London: Yale University Press, 1978), p.9.

10. Unfinished by the time of Goldsmith's death on 4 April 1774, *Retaliation* was begun in January of that year, instigated by epigrammatic sparring with the actor David Garrick at St James's Coffee House. See Roger Lonsdale's headnote, *The Poems of Thomas Gray, William Collins, and Oliver Goldsmith*, pp.741–5n.

11. *A List of the Absentees of Ireland, and the Yearly Value of their Estates and Incomes Spent Abroad. With Observations on the Present Trade and Condition of that Kingdom*, 2nd edn (Dublin, 1729), p.33. The List is 'one of the most important pamphlets of the period. To write and publish it was a courageous step, for it pilloried his own class and many of his intimate friends.' Desmond Clarke, *Thomas Prior, 1681–1751: Founder of the Royal Dublin Society* (Dublin: Royal Dublin Society, 1951), p.16.

12. 'Sermon: Causes of the Wretched Condition of Ireland' (1762), *Swift's Irish Pamphlets: An Introductory Selection*, edited by Joseph McMinn (Savage, Maryland: Barnes and Noble Books, 1991), p.154.

13. Laurence Whyte, 'The Parting Cup, or, The Humours of *Deoch an Doruis*, alias *Theodorus*, alias Doctor *Dorus*, an old *Irish* Gentleman famous (about 30 Years ago) for his great Hospitality, but more particularly in *Christmas* Time', *Poems on Various Subjects* (Dublin, 1740), pp.92, 95.

14. Lonsdale, *The Poems of Thomas Gray, William Collins, and Oliver Goldsmith*, p.687.

15. Whyte, 'The Parting Cup', pp.97–8.

16. James Prior, *Life of Oliver Goldsmith, M.B.*, 2 vols (London: John Murray, 1837), vol.1, pp.39–43.

17. On 21 May 1747, following the arrest, for debt, of one of their number, rioting Trinity students made their way to the Black Dog (Newgate) prison, where shots were fired by the constabulary, killing two non-students who had involved themselves. The college authorities publicly admonished

Goldsmith for his leading part in the riot. On 29 May, the students' club, of which Burke was president, affected stern disapproval of student participation in city rioting. Riots surrounding the Sheridan and Kelly factions after the so-called 'Gentlemen's Quarrel' of January 1747 were symptomatic of conflicts between the establishment and Jacobitism. On the Black Dog Riots, see Arthur P.I. Samuels, *The Early Life, Correspondence and Writings of the Rt. Hon. Edmund Burke* (Cambridge: Cambridge University Press, 1923), pp.142–5. Burke's *Philosophical Enquiry into the Origin of our Ideas of the Sublime and the Beautiful* (1757) features a celebrated passage describing the manner in which communal identity is produced amidst the racket of the crowd: 'The shouting of multitudes has a similar effect; and by the sole strength of the sound, so amazes and confounds the imagination, that in this staggering, and hurry of the mind, the best established tempers can scarcely forbear being bor[n]e down, and joining in the common cry, and common resolution of the croud'. J.T. Boulton is of the opinion that this passage refers to the Black Dog Riots. *A Philosophical Inquiry into the Origin of our Ideas of the Sublime and the Beautiful*, in *Writings and speeches*, pp.250–1n.

18. Declan Budd and Ross Hinds, *The Hist and Edmund Burke's Club: An Anthology of the College Historical Society, the Student Debating Society of Trinity College Dublin, from its Origins in Edmund Burke's Club 1747–1997* (Dublin: The Lilliput Press, 1997), p.165.

19. Edmund Burke, *The Reformer* No.3, *Writings and speeches*, vol.i, pp.84, 87.

20. 'Can it be by Goldsmith? When in Trinity he made a little money by occasionally resorting to ballad writing, and found a market for his productions. He may have responded to the invitation of the *Reformer*. There seems to be notes in the poem which are heard in the *Traveller* and *Deserted Village*, and the dedication of the *Traveller* to his brother Henry shows that "the several conditions of life" were with him a considered theme'. Samuels, *The Early Life, Correspondence and Writings of the Rt. Hon. Edmund Burke*, p.170.

21. Describing Goldsmith's 'Johnsonian balance of achievement and limitation', John G. Hayman proposes that in *The Traveller* 'the couplet form provides a neat unit for Goldsmith's theory of balance'. John G. Hayman, 'Notions of National Characters in the Eighteenth Century', *Huntington Library Quarterly*, 35 (1971), pp.11, 12.

22. Lonsdale, *The Poems of Thomas Gray, William Collins, and Oliver Goldsmith*, pp.656, 683, 654.

23. It may also have a tradition in Westmeath; in Laurence Whyte's poem, the absentees refuse to live at home 'with any pleasure or content'; similarly Samuel Whyte's later 'Impromptu, written on the back of a trencher in the cottage at the crooked Wood, County Westmeath, August, 1773': 'Let wealth regale itself on costly plate,/ cares will intrude and happiness prevent;/ but peasants, who off humble trenchers eat,/ with rosy health enjoy supreme content.' Patrick Fagan (ed.), *A Georgian Celebration; Irish Poets of the Eighteenth Century* (Dublin: Branar, 1989), p.145.

24. *The Reformer*, No.7, p.96.

25. Lonsdale, *The Poems of Thomas Gray, William Collins, and Oliver Goldsmith*, p.688.

26. Seamus Deane, 'Oliver Goldsmith: Miscellaneous Writing, 1759–1774', in Seamus Deane (ed.), *The Field Day Anthology of Irish Writing*, 3 vols (Derry: Field Day Publications, 1991), vol.1, p.660.

27. Evidence of recourse 'to collecting the classic foods of famine', which David Dickson lists as 'docks, cresses, nettles, seaweed, and the blood drawn from live cattle'. David Dickson, 'The Other Great Irish Famine', in Cathal Póirtéir (ed.), *The Great Irish Famine* (Cork and Dublin: Mercier Press, 1995), pp.54–5. See also Michael Drake, 'The Irish Demographic Crisis of 1740–41', in T.W. Moody (ed.), *Historical Studies VI* (London: Routledge & Kegan Paul, 1968), pp.101–24.

28. Philip Skelton, *The Necessity of Tillage and Granaries. In a Letter to a Member of Parliament Living in the County of ——* (Dublin, 1741), p.59.

29. *The Town and Country Magazine; or, Universal Repository of Knowledge, Instruction, and Entertainment*, 2 (1770), p.168. Similar sentiments are expressed in *The Critical Review*, 29 (1770), pp.435–52.

30. William Cooke, 'Table Talk; or, Characters, Anecdotes, etc. of Illustrious British Characters, during the last Fifty Years: Dr. Goldsmith', *European Magazine*, 24 (1793), pp.171–2.

31. See *Estimate of the Manners and Principles of the Times* (London, 1757–58); *Thoughts on Civil liberty. On Licentiousness, and Faction* (London, 1765).

32. Conor Cruise O'Brien, *Edmund Burke*, abridged by Jim McCue (London: Vintage, 1997a, 2002), p.27.

33. T.H.D. Mahoney, *Edmund Burke and Ireland* (Cambridge, MA: Harvard University Press; London: Oxford University Press, 1960), p.58.

34. *Correspondence*, vol.ii, pp.465–6, 468, 474, 476, 477–8.

35. Cited in George Thomas, Earl of Albemarle, *Memoirs of the Marquis of Rockingham and his Contemporaries. With Original Letters and Documents Now First Published*, 2 vols (London: Richard Bentley, 1852), vol.2, pp.232–3.

36. *Public Advertiser*, No.12058 (Monday 13 Dec. 1773).
37. *Public Advertiser*, No.12060 (Wednesday 15 Dec. 1773).
38. Cited in Lord Edmond Fitzmaurice, *Life of William, Earl of Shelburne, afterwards First Marquess of Lansdowne. With Extracts from his Papers and Correspondence*, 3 vols (London: Macmillan and Co., 1875), vol.2, pp.280, 283, 283–4.
39. Horace Walpole, *Journal of the Reign of King George the Third, from the Year 1771 to 1783*, edited with notes, by Dr Doran, 2 vols (London: Richard Bentley, 1859), vol.1, pp.265–6. Walpole claims that he was told of this request by the Duke of Richmond.
40. Wentworth Woodhouse Muniments – Rockingham Papers 3/27. Goldsmith came to know Shelburne through Lauchlan Macleane, a mutual friend of Burke and Goldsmith at Trinity, who became Shelburne's secretary. See Prior, *Life of Oliver Goldsmith*, vol.1, pp.149–52.
41. Thomas H.D. Mahoney, *Edmund Burke and Ireland*, p.51. See also Mahoney, 'Mr Burke's Imperial Mentality and the Proposed Irish Absentee Tax of 1773', *Canadian Historical Review*, 37 (1956), pp.158–66. Burke 'never willingly conceded colonial independence. To that extent, his opposition to the absentee tax can be seen as an example of his concern for the imperial system.'
42. *The Traveller*, in Lonsdale, *The Poems of Thomas Gray, William Collins, and Oliver Goldsmith*, p.653.

9

Edmund Burke's Anglo-Irish Double Vision in *Thoughts on the Cause of the Present Discontents*

NATHAN WALLACE

INTRODUCTION: BURKE'S TERRITORIES

This essay traces the dynamic relationship between Edmund Burke's English and Irish identities through his first great political pamphlet, the *Thoughts on the Cause of the Present Discontents* (1770). Although Burkeans have located motives behind his mature political causes in his earliest Irish experiences, the *Thoughts* has not yet been examined through the frame of Irish Studies.[1] It is my aim in making this connection to open up a way for us to re-think Burke's national and political identities in terms of assimilation to the British imperial system. This should illuminate both the nature of his identities and the contexts from and into which they developed. The core argument here is that the two most famous features of the *Thoughts* – the Double Cabinet conspiracy narrative and the defence of Party politics – operate on public and private levels. On the public level the pamphlet operates as a Rockingham Whig Party Manifesto, and on the private level it operates as a justification of, and guide to, what I call Burke's own assimilation, as an Irish new man, to the English imperial system.

The current resurgence of Irish Studies has brought with it a renewal of critical interest in the Irish Burke, and he has even taken a central place in the theoretical re-formulation of the field.[2] These developments have in turn led to some territorial conversations about Burke's nationality. As has been the case with other Irish writers (from Swift to Wilde to Beckett), the critical habit of regarding Burke as a canonical figure in English Literature sometimes engenders resistance to the suggestion that an understanding of his Irish background might lead to a profound engagement with his thinking or his art. Burke's importance to the history of English Conservatism has obscured the significance of his Irishness for generations of interpreters, and Burke himself commented very little on his background, most likely because it involved familial connections to the Catholic world of Irish Jacobitism.[3] In a 1997 article J.C.D. Clark criticizes Conor Cruise O'Brien's 1968 argument that Burke's rhetorical persona is fired by a peculiarly Hibernian friction between the 'outer Whig' and the 'inner Jacobite'.[4] Clark counters this by insisting that Burke was a 'latitudinarian Whig' rather than a 'slumbering Jacobite'.[5] Clark's resistance to O'Brien's 'inner Jacobite' entails the maintenance of an Anglo-centric reading, as can be seen in his call for historians to '[rescue] Burke from his posthumous conscription into an Irish Catholic cause'.[6] Clark's Burke cannot have Jacobite sentiment or sympathy because an identification with Whiggery is supposed to exclude other possible sympathies, but if we consider that Burke's Whiggery begins in Ireland, the story of his national and political sympathies correspondingly demands greater nuance.

Recent approaches to the interpretation of Jacobite sympathy in Augustan England are a good guide to reconsidering Burke's national identity, because they recognize political sentiment as fluid and they disassociate it from more concrete identifications or political commitments. Toni Bowers, for instance, argues that 'Toryism and Jacobitism tend now to be seen as shifting, relational functions rather than fixed identities'.[7] Burke's Englishness and Irishness should also be thought of as 'relational functions'. Howard Erskine-Hill speaks directly to this essay's concerns when he writes that an emotional Jacobite 'double vision' arises in response to the subject's 'twofold situation', between 'communities of allegiance'.[8] As with Bowers's 'relational functions', Erskine-Hill's 'twofold situation' is a useful term for describing Burke's Anglo-Irish political identity, goals and surroundings. Burke attempts to synchronize his duties by transforming both of his communities. First, Catholic Ireland must accept the Glorious Revolution, but this can only be meaningful if England can learn to practice conciliatory imperial government. When Burke sees this latter transformation fail, as he does in the late 1760s, he becomes distressed on behalf of both countries.

Recovering Burke's Irishness does not mean denying the Englishness he so frequently claimed for himself. This self-identification is crucial to understanding Burke's political identity, and it is therefore no less crucial that we understand the dynamics of this gesture. By identifying his Englishness as an adoption, Burke signals the doubleness of his identity. His trajectory from an Irish context to an adoptive English one is problematic, and it contributes to the double vision with which Burke sees and represents Englishness itself. An Irish Studies approach to Burke ought to enrich our understanding of Burke's Englishness as well; I suggest that his Whiggery, the touchstone of his national identification, is a career-spanning practice of cultural and political border-crossing between his native Irishness and his adoptive Englishness. Although Burke often employed the first person plural 'we English' in his writings and speeches, as Katherine O'Donnell reminds us he pronounced it with an Irish accent.[9] The multifariousness of his political persona was therefore immediately obvious to his contemporaries in ways that have been lost to us. Recovering some of these complexities can expand the range of texts we may associate with Burke's Irishness, so that it may now include his thinking on the English constitution and party politics.

TAKING THE DISCONTENTS PERSONALLY

Burke's English political identity has a significant Irish dimension, but before interpreting this dimension it is necessary to describe the English context into which he insinuated himself.[10] Starting from his employment with the Marquess of Rockingham 1765, Burke was a member of the Opposition for most of his political career. By the late 1760s, therefore, he saw himself as defending the Whig Constitution against the Court Party's renovated programme of Tory absolutism. While Burke was eager to claim common cause with popular outrage over the Court's disqualification of the radical John Wilkes in the Middlesex election, the Rockinghamites were more interested in the issue of the King's prerogative in appointing a Cabinet. George III guarded the right to appoint the Ministry according to his own wishes rather than to those of Parliament. The Rockinghamites, for their part, insisted on the right to form a Cabinet from their own Party (once they made their way into office again), so that they would not lose solidarity or authority while forming a government.[11] They accused the Court of maintaining a 'Double Cabinet' system to undermine both the authority of legitimate government, and the effectiveness of Parliamentary opposition. In the *Thoughts* Burke used the Double Cabinet to justify the failure of the short-lived Rockingham Administration (1765–66), and explain the necessity of an Opposition Party for the survival of constitutional government in England.

It might be objected that reading the *Thoughts* for an interior narrative is inappropriate because the pamphlet had an immediate function as a Rockingham party manifesto. F.P. Lock, for instance, calls it 'a persuasive "speech act" ... shaped to fit its moment' rather than 'a philosophical treatise or a personal testament'.[12] Burke's correspondence shows the unusual degree of time he took, not only in drafting the work, but also in testing his fellow opposition members' responses before publishing it. On reading a draft of it, Rockingham wrote to Burke that the pamphlet 'would take universally, and tend to form and unite a party upon real and well founded principles – which would in the end prevail and re'establish order and Government in this country'.[13] Burke took care not to jeopardize the Rockingham coalition, and an idiosyncratic narrative on his part could have been capable of doing just that.

Even his expressions of angst over the tract's political effectiveness, however, show that the *Thoughts* have a personal significance. He voices fears that his own ideas could alienate rather than persuade his audience from the Opposition's cause. 'I am very far from confident', he wrote to Rockingham, 'that the doctrines avowed in this piece (though as clear to me as first principles) will be considered as well founded; or that they will be popular'.[14] Burke fears that his own viewpoint on the present discontents, 'as clear to me as first principles', will compromise the Opposition rather than strengthen it, despite the fact that he is drafting this viewpoint as a representative party document. Burke also voices his anxiety about the Double Cabinet theory in the *Thoughts* itself. This appears first in his opening, where he notes the 'degree of delicacy' necessary 'to examine into the cause of public disorders' because '[if] a man ... should be obliged to blame the favourites of the people, he will be considered as the tool of power; if he censures those in power, he will be looked on as an instrument of faction'.[15] Not only does he begin by declaring the difficulty of his own critical position – that he could all too easily alienate his audiences – but he also reiterates this critical trepidation even after having denounced the Double Cabinet. 'Whether all this be a vision of a distracted brain', he writes, 'or the invention of a malicious heart, or a real Faction in the country, must be judged by the appearances which things have worn for eight years past'.[16] This call for readers to test this narrative against their own lights is not merely a rhetorical gesture to accommodate sceptics within the Opposition; it also registers a friction between individual and party narratives.

Another reason to doubt that the *Thoughts* contains an interior narrative might be that the Double Cabinet conspiracy theory was not his own invention, any more than he was the first to call the King's Friends 'Janissaries'. These considerations do not, however, preclude the possibility that these elements of the pamphlet resonate with Burke's double identification and assimilation to Englishness. In fact, the *Thoughts* is where Burke articulates an Irish narrative of assimilation through an Opposition Whig vocabulary. Here we can see Burke employing the 'vision' of his own 'distracted brain' – distracted by the process of assimilation to the English imperial system – to dramatize a Rockingham account of the real reasons for England's present discontents. Ironically, the Whig narrative also turns out to have been a 'vision' in the sense that historians have concluded the Double Cabinet theory was unfounded, if politically useful.[17] If the Double Cabinet gives the Opposition Whigs a role to play in the narrative of English liberty, it also gives Burke a role to play in that narrative of Englishness. This also allows Burke to describe English liberty as a reality despite his perception of the nation's present discontents. The Double Cabinet, in short, accounts for the gap separating Burke's ideal and actual English political landscapes. Burke sees England double because he has Irish reasons to idealize the Whig Constitution, and his attempt to reconcile the two Englands lends the pamphlet its rhetorical immediacy.

DOUBLE CABINET AND DOUBLE VISION

The inner narrative of the *Thoughts* tells of his assimilation as an Irishman to the English imperial system, and his hopes of correcting Irish misgovernment through a Whig programme. In addition to consulting with his fellow English Opposition members, Burke also corresponded with fellow Irishmen Charles O'Hara, Dr Thomas Leland and Richard Shackleton about the production and reception of the pamphlet. When Leland wrote a letter criticizing Burke's style due to 'the very extensive communication of the work', Burke responded with an annotation: the *Thoughts* were 'every word bad & good his own'.[18] Burke may not have used ghost writers in the *Thoughts*, but his writing was haunted by Irish history. A shade of this unspoken Irish interior narrative may be detected in O'Hara's suggestion, referring to the tract's popularity, '[f]ew understand it, but 'tis the fashion to like it'.[19] The Irish stakes of the struggle over defining the roles of Crown and Parliament certainly would not have been clear to all of Burke's audiences, but for his purposes they did not have to be.

For Burke Irish government, like that in every part of the empire, depended upon the maintenance of Whig constitutional liberty in England. Five years after publishing the *Thoughts*, Burke described England's constitutional conquest of Ireland as a model that should be followed in America. 'It was not English arms', he writes,

> but the English constitution, that conquered Ireland ... You changed the people; you altered the religion ... but you never altered their constitution; the principle of which was respected by usurpation; restored with the restoration of the Monarchy, and established, I trust for ever, by the glorious Revolution. This has made Ireland the great and flourishing kingdom that it is; and, from a disgrace and burthen intolerable to this nation, has rendered her a principal part of our strength and ornament. This country cannot be said to have ever formally taxed her.[20]

Without going into the ways in which this account is either historically misleading or inconsistent with Burke's other writings on Irish misgovernment under the Protestant Ascendancy, it is worth pointing out that Burke incorporates Ireland as a positive example into a Whig narrative of conciliatory imperial expansionism. Similarly, writing to Thomas Burgh on 1 January 1780, Burke intertwines the narratives of English and Irish constitutional liberty in a way that is both monitory and optimistic. 'If liberty cannot maintain its ground in this kingdom [England]', he writes, 'I am sure that it cannot have any long continuance in yours [Ireland]' because as soon as England loses 'interest in its own' liberty, it will 'look upon yours with the eyes of envy and disgust'.[21] He warns that English constitutional crisis entails a crisis of Irish government, although we know from various other writings that he does not rate the condition of Irish constitutional government as being this healthy.

In the *Thoughts* Burke identifies the Double Cabinet as the hidden cause for the constitutional crisis by which he can account for the difference between the England of his Whig ideal and the England of his disappointing experience. Burke often represents England as having two characters, and this double vision of England derives from his vacillations between pride and disappointment in his adopted country. He has two opposing accounts, for instance, of how he was received in England. He once described England as an adoptive mother, 'generous enough to receive a man into her bosom', but elsewhere he would also bitterly recall being 'obliged to show my passport' there.[22] Burke also saw

England doubly because his political allegiances and affections were split between England and Ireland. As he put it in a 1785 speech, he spent much of his political life trying 'to reconcile, if possible, the two duties' he owed his native and adopted countries, 'should they unfortunately point different ways'.[23] Burke was of two minds, moreover, about how well England was able to govern Ireland. While in 1785 he referred to England as Ireland's 'guardian angel', in 1780 he wrote that he had been horribly disappointed in his hopes of reconciling his two countries through participation in the English system.[24] 'When I came into this parliament', he wrote, 'obscure and a stranger as I was, I considered myself as raised to the highest dignity to which a creature of our species could aspire … [F]irst and uppermost in my thoughts, was the hope (without injury to this country) to be … useful to [Ireland]; which … I thought ill and impolitically governed'.[25] He quickly realized, however, that 'all my power of obliging either my country or individuals was gone', and so 'all the luster of my imaginary rank was tarnished, and I felt degraded even by my elevation'.[26] There is no conclusive resolution to Burke's career-long, dialectical assessment of English national character.

In his *Letter to a Noble Lord*, Burke restates his complicated mission as an Irishman coming to England. 'My endeavour', he writes, 'was to obtain liberty for [Ireland] the municipal country in which I was born, and for all descriptions and denominations in it', and he equates this with the goal 'to support with unrelaxing vigilance every right, every privilege, every franchise, in this my adopted, my dearer and more comprehensive country [England]'.[27] Here Burke's late correlation of English and Irish liberties is consistent with earlier examples. It is also significant here that Burke calls his England 'dearer and more comprehensive' than his 'municipal' Ireland. It means more than that he preferred living in England to living in Ireland. By linking dearness and comprehensiveness, Burke highlights the connection between the affections and imperial authority. Burke wants to say he is 'comprehensively' English, but he is also saying that England as an empire is comprehending more and more nations, whose liberties can only be protected by England's being 'dear'. The more comprehensive the empire, the 'dearer' Burke wants it to appear to the colonial subject. He therefore identifies the task of 'preserv[ing]… rights in this chief seat of empire' with that of preserving those 'in every nation … under the protection, of the British Crown'.[28] Burke's England is Janus-faced, first because it must preserve domestic and imperial liberties, and second because he was never sure that he had successfully preserved the English Constitution well enough that a moral political life might be enjoyed in the colonies. Another way of putting this is that Burke never completed the process of cultural and political assimilation by which he sought to discover England worthy of the political affections he projected onto it. Because England so often failed to govern the colonies morally, Burke could only adopt Englishness provisionally, and he signalled this provisionality through his attachment to the Whig Opposition. For the Rockingham Whigs the English Constitution was an endangered good, and this absent Constitution became for Burke an alternate version of Englishness that he could idealize and associate with his duty to Ireland. The *Thoughts* is Burke's first great statement of oppositionality within the English political landscape, thus marking his hopes of realizing a kinder, gentler English imperium.

The *Thoughts* diagnoses England's present discontents in terms of doubleness, a doubleness manifesting on the one hand as a form of Cabinet government, and on the other as a pair of opposed possibilities between a Whig Constitution and a tyrannical one. In short, a corrupting faction has placed the Constitution in crisis. As in Cicero's Catiline Orations, the Burkean rhetoric of Constitutional crisis employs a medical conceit. In the *Thoughts*, therefore, England's constitution hovers between life and death. Burke attributes the nation's 'political distemper' a 'sinister piety' against parties spread by the King's Friends who thrive parasitically on the nation's 'intestine disturbances'.[29] The body politic is corrupted by an unconstitutional faction, and is nearing its 'crisis', where a decision will have to be made between the Rockingham Whigs and the Court Party. 'If other ideas should prevail', he concludes, 'things must remain in their present confusion; until they are hurried into all the rage of civil violence; or until they sink into the dead repose of despotism'.[30] The trope of doubling between clearly opposed alternatives – life and death, freedom and despotism, virtue and criminality, competence and confusion – is no less characteristic of Burke's language in the *Thoughts* than it is of his many other writings on England's Empire and Constitution.

CEART AND THE CONSTITUTION

In order to describe Burke's full disappointment in English political conditions, it is also necessary to consider what expectations he brought with him from Ireland. As indicated earlier, the spectre haunting Irish Studies analyses of Burke is Jacobitism, and in this section I will describe Burke's expectations in terms of a revenant Jacobitism – which is not to say that he was a Jacobite. In his major study of Irish Jacobitism, Éamonn Ó Ciardha situates Burke as one of the major 'Irish political leaders, [who] generally disavowed Jacobitism … [mocking] the continuing Protestant preoccupation with … the Stuart Pretender, the pope and the king of France, who had all been cut down to size (as he believed) in the course of the eighteenth century'.[31] O'Brien describes Burke's maternal relations, the Nagles as 'Catholic Whigs', who sought a 'rehabilitation of the Catholic Irish within a revised "Revolution settlement"'.[32] Burke, who never considered the Stuart cause a realistic one, saw it as an obstacle to any relaxation of the Penal Code. The Protestant Ascendancy continually punished the Catholic majority for imagined Jacobite treasons, and these punishments in turn alienated the majority from English rule. The imperial conundrum of the Glorious Revolution, for Burke, was that Britain achieved a constitutional monarchy while Ireland was saddled with a tyrannical minority rule. He sought to solve this problem by encouraging the actual extension of English constitutional liberty to Ireland. Taking these disclaimers into account, Irish Jacobitism is still critically useful for the analysis of the Burkean imagination if we define it in less rigid terms than those of supporting the House of Stuart.

Burke disavowed Jacobitism but he was also sympathetic to Ireland's Catholic 'Underground Gentry', in Kevin Whelan's phrase, who were dispossessed by a tyrannical Protestant Ascendancy. In eighteenth-century Ireland Jacobite sentiments often mourned the condition of a displaced Irish nobility more than that of a displaced English monarch. As a member of an ex-Jacobite family of Catholic Whigs, Burke felt that Jacobite virtue of loyalty was itself noble, and should be transferred to the Whig Constitution. In the *Thoughts* Burke declares that at the outset of George III's reign, 'even the zealots of hereditary right' were ready 'to justify a transfer of their attachments, without a change in their principles'.[33] This disavows Jacobitism but also associates Jacobite 'principle' with the ennobling quality of attachment, not far removed from the Whig principle of 'connexion'. A double inheritance from the Nagles couples Burke's Jacobite structures of feeling with a Whiggish strategy for Irish Catholic relief. This combination of sympathies and strategies contributes to Burke's double vision of Englishness, where an Irish sense of attachment informs his engagement with English Constitutional theory.

Seamus Deane notes a paradox that Burke's 'Jacobite strain' should '[coexist] with an unstinted, perhaps extravagant, admiration for the British constitution as established in 1688'; I would argue that the extravagance of Burke's Whiggery derives from that of the Jacobitism it displaces.[34] One way of elaborating on this dynamic will be to invoke O'Donnell's argument about the role of *Ceart*, an important Irish Jacobite concept, in the earliest stages of Burke's education. She suggests that Burke may have encountered the discourse of *Ceart* at the Nagle hedge school, reading *Párliament na mBan*, a Jacobite pedagogical work by Fr Domhnall Ó Colmáin.[35] O'Donnell identifies *Ceart* as 'the Irish expression of "the Spirit of the Laws"', quoting again how in Ó Colmáin's words 'it "keeps people together and binds them peaceably in communion and love with one another"'.[36] The virtue of *Ceart*'s binding power in this passage recalls Burke's praise for 'connexion' in the *Thoughts*. Throughout his political career, Burke was always trying to correct the English lack of conciliatory art. One cognate of *Ceart*, the verb *ceartaigh*, means 'to correct', 'to rectify', 'to amend', as even 'to explain'.[37] What we see in the *Thoughts*, and in Burke's commitment to oppositional politics, is an impulse to correct the errors that mar English (and by extension Irish) politics. The extravagance of Burke's attachment to the English Constitution (his instrument of correction) therefore seems very likely to be informed by *Ceart* as a structure of feeling inherited from a disavowed Irish Jacobite tradition.

If Burke's English Whiggery is oppositional, then we should regard his Irish

Whiggery as corrective. Burke projected his hopes for a corrected Irish political settlement onto the Whig Constitution, and this transfer forms the basis of
his career-long attempt to reconcile English and Irish interests. It also set up the
abiding problem of his life as an adopted Englishman, because it meant that he
could not be at peace as an adoptive Englishman until imperial England lived
up to an unreachable moral standard. Irish Jacobite discourse may not have
been as escapist as many historians have concluded, but the rhetoric of *Ceart*
kingship did tend to idealize the absent Stuart in a way that was hard to test
against experience. Now the English Constitution would have to deliver the
kind of profound rightness in the world that Irish Jacobite ideology once attributed to the Stuarts. When Burke entered English politics, however, he could no
longer so easily declare the Whig Constitution an absent good. If there were any
hope of its being extended to Ireland, the *Ceart* Constitution would have to be
a present reality at the very least in England. Naturally, he did not recognize this
ideal in the English political landscape of the 1760s and so his trust in the reality of an 'absent good' itself came to a crisis. He found a way to maintain his
extravagant regard for the Whig constitution, however, by placing himself in
the political Opposition. This allowed him to declare that the true Whig
Constitution was an absent or endangered good for the English as well as for
the Irish. The Whig oppositional stance, like the Jacobite oppositional stance,
could only explain the vicissitudes of the status quo by distinguishing it from
an idealized *status quo ante*. Instead of holding out for a true King, therefore,
Burke holds out for a true constitution and this ultimately enlivens the
Rockingham Whigs' own phantasmal narrative of persecution – with the ancestral conviction Burke inherited from the Irish (post-) Jacobite hinterland of his
youth.

CONCILIATION AND THE CICERONIAN PERSONA

This section locates a Ciceronian discourse of conciliation in Burke's defence
of the Rockingham Party, and relates this discourse on one hand to Burke's
thinking as an Irishman, and on the other hand to his self-fashioning as a *novus
homo* or 'new man' in the British imperial system. Burke's source for the
language of conciliation is Cicero, but the impetus to theorize a solution to
political woes originates in the colonial Irish landscape of his youth. As seen in
the previous section, notions of connectedness from the Irish aristocratic literary tradition may also be resonating in the background of Burke's Whig vision,
and if so they would also be reinforcing his language of conciliatory government. This Ciceronian vocabulary both authorized and camouflaged Burke's
Irish voice in the British political context. The Ciceronian persona likewise
allowed Burke to speak as a voice of conscience on behalf of the English
Constitution, because Cicero had done the same in his Verrine Orations, in his
defence of the Republic against the Catiline Conspiracy, and in his Phillipics

against Marcus Antonius. While we tend to look at Burke's use of Cicero as a sign of his confident Whig identity, it is worth remembering that his first recorded reference to Cicero is one that expresses uncertainty. 'I know what is good like the Athenians', he tells Richard Shackleton, 'but Dont practice like the Lacædemonians. What would not I give to have my Spirits a little more settled?'[38] It is significant that this early reference would reflect the themes of indecision and competing identities, and that it occurs in a letter where Burke also argues against religious sectarianism.

Burke's Ciceronian persona was something that he boasted of himself, and it was also something that was frequently used against him. For instance, even though Burke self-consciously modelled his unsuccessful Impeachment of Warren Hastings on Cicero's successful prosecution of Verres, the political theatrics of the Trial were heavily satirized.[39] Burke was subject to insult as a Ciceronian new man, as much as he was subject to praise for it. When he purchased Beaconsfield, Edmund and his 'cousin' Will Burke were derided as '*new Men* who have just acquired (God knows how) a small property in the Country', and Burke was called by one Parliamentarian, 'a White Boy, a native of a Bog in Ireland ... The Cicero of the insular Boetia' who, despite his 'Eloquence ... has not the Worth of a Six-pence of property'.[40] Because the Ciceronian parallel was so apt, Burke was capable of giving far more memorably than he got. In 1770, not far from the time that the *Thoughts* were published, Burke claimed the title of new man during a Parliamentary debate. He was responding to a member's insinuation that he was a closeted Jesuit. William Burke reports the speech:

> As to the St Omer's or St Germain's it matters little ... [Edmund] He took himself the appellation of a *Novus Homo*. He knew the envy attending that Character. *Novorum Hominum Inudustram odisti*; but as he knew the envy, he knew the duty of the Novus homo. He then, valuing himself only on his Industry, not his Abilities, shewed he had performed that Duty in endeavouring to know the Commerce, the finances, and constitution of his country ... He expatiated upon the Impropriety and danger of discouraging new Men. This rising merit stamp'd with Virtue would indeed seek to rise, but under the wings of establish'd Greatness, and if their Industry and their Virtue was greater than &c. &c. &c. they must be equal, nay the superior to the lazy something that came by inheritance ... All wise governments have encouraged rising merit, as useful and necessary; we know not in what mountain of Scotland, what bog of Ireland, or what wild in America that Genius may be now rising who shall save this country.[41]

Burke's masterful appropriation of the 'new man' status has a pervasive subtext of an Irishman's attempt to civilize the Empire. First, he shows his solidarity with new men from Scotland and America, at the same time that he parallels English political wisdom with that of Rome. Secondly, he counters the slur on his Irish connections to Catholicism and Jacobitism as red herrings, drawing attention instead to the unseemly resentments attendant upon unwise imperial policy. The imperial valence of this is reinforced by the fact that the Ciceronian quotation '*Novorum...*' comes from one of the Verrine Orations; Cicero is telling the corrupt imperial governor, 'You hate the industry of self made men'.[42]

Cicero was also a compelling model for Burke to inhabit because Cicero also had two countries – one being the colonizer and the other being the colonized. Just as Burke balanced his loyalties between his adopted England and his native Ireland, Cicero balanced his connections between his adopted Rome and his native town of Arpinum.[43] This aspect of Cicero's biography must have also been of interest to Burke as a self-consciously Ciceronian new man with two countries of his own. Also, as a classical figure Cicero occupied a non-sectarian ground adaptable to every facet of complex political personality.[44] Most importantly, however, Burke found in Cicero a model through which a new man might not only rise in the world, but also become a voice of conscience for an Empire. Burke uses Cicero as a philosophical starting point for his criticism of the Penal Code in *Tracts on the Popery* (1765).[45] Using this persona to reconcile his two countries would be a kind of service by which Burke might reconcile his own conscience as he assimilates to the imperial system. Through his vocabulary of conciliation, Burke performs the Ciceronian role of political and rhetorical philosopher, persuading the imperial centre to use persuasion on its imperial periphery. The most celebrated example of this is his *Speech on Conciliation with America*, in which he proposes 'to reconcile' the colonies with 'the mother country', according to a system which is 'far from a scheme of ruling by discord'.[46] The politics of affection and reconciliation are the key to Cicero's theory of government in *De Officiis*, when he writes that 'fear is but a poor safeguard of lasting power; while affection ... may be trusted to keep it safe for ever.'[47]

When Burke extols conciliatory government in the *Thoughts*, he is following Cicero's complex usage of the verb *concilio* and its cognates as they appear mainly in *De Oratore*, *De Amicitia*, and *De Officiis*. The principle of conciliation is essentially rhetorical, and this is unsurprising, considering the fact that Burke and Cicero are both orators before they are political philosophers. Rhetoric, the 'soulbending sovereign of all things,' depends upon a three operations: '*aut docendo aut conciliando aut permovendo*.'[48] E.W. Sutton renders this series as 'instruction or persuasion or appeal to the emotions,' but *conciliando* more specifically entails getting the audience to identify with the speaker (or the advocates' client).[49] Burke describes the sort of man who has the talent for conciliation: 'a man [who] has shewn by the general tenor of his actions, that the affection, the good opinion, the confidence, of his fellow citizens have been among the principal objects of his life.'[50] The art of conciliation is therefore linked to political virtue.

Burke follows Cicero in arguing that the good governor must to conciliate the governed and this could only happen when the conciliator learned the character of the audience. In *De Oratore* Cicero teaches that conciliation requires a thorough knowledge of the audience's character, which only comes after careful examination.[51] This is why for Burke it is necessary that the good governor have a keen interest in the character of the governed and also why descriptions of America and India are so important in Burke's writings on colonial government in those places.[52] 'The temper of the people amongst whom he presides', Burke writes in the *Thoughts*, 'ought to be the first study of a Statesman'.[53] This principle of study is also crucial to Burke in his station as a new man, as he also makes clear in the *Thoughts*: 'Nations are governed by the same methods, and on the same principles, by which an individual without authority is often able to govern those who are his equals or his superiors; by a knowledge of their temper, and by a judicious management of it.'[54] This 'individual without authority' is Burke himself. As a new man, Burke is speaking to equals and superiors in the British political system. He cannot persuade them on the power of any authority of rank, and so he must study their temper and try to win them over to his side.

Ciceronian conciliation also connects Burke's political and metaphysical thinking. The art of conciliatory government parallels the natural conciliations occurring in a series of concentric circles starting with the family and stretching out to circles of friends, political parties, the nation state, and on to the human race. In *De Haruspicum Responsis*, Cicero describes the sacred continuum between familial and political existence as the work of nature's conciliation: 'Our parents, the immortal gods, our fatherland, – to all these nature binds us (*natura conciliat*) at the hour of our birth.'[55] 'The first bond of union', he writes in *De Officiis*, 'is that between husband and wife; the next, that between parents and children; then we find one home, with everything in common. And this is the foundation of civil government (*principium urbis*), the nursery, as it were, of the state (*quasi seminarium rei publicae*).'[56] It is in the spirit of Cicero that Burke writes in the *Reflections*: 'To be attached to the subdivision, to love the little platoon we belong to in society, is the first principle (the germ as it were) of public affections. It is the first link in the series by which we proceed towards a love to our country and to mankind.'[57] Burke's 'germ as it were' echoes Cicero's '*quasi seminarium*' above. Elsewhere in the *Reflections*, Burke quotes Cicero's use of the term 'concilia', used in the announcement that 'nothing of all that is done on earth is more pleasing to ... God ... than the assemblies and gatherings of men ... which are called States'.[58] The State was pleasing to the Gods because it was a *concilium*, the production of a *conciliatio* achieved by Nature connecting humanity to the divine.

In the *Thoughts* Burke defends the Rockingham Whigs in the terms of Ciceronian friendship, drawing on Cicero's argument in *De Amicitia* that friendship is created by virtuous conciliation: '[V]irtue both creates (*conciliat*) the bond of friendship and preserves it'.[59] The virtue of friendship is related to the virtue of the political subject and thus to the virtue of the state, through the mediating structure of political parties. In Cicero good men are attracted to one another in friendship and political parties because virtue is attracted to its own kind. 'Good men', he writes, 'love and join to themselves other good men in a union which is almost that of a relationship and nature'.[60] Such friendships in virtue are marked by 'the most complete agreement (*consensio*) in policy, in pursuits, and in opinions'.[61] Burke echoes the necessity for such consensus within a Party and describes the Ciceronian *consensio* as a Whig virtue. Consensus is the principle of 'connexion' both at Rome and among 'the best patriots in the greatest commonwealths'.[62] '*Idem sentire de re publica*', he writes, invoking an expression from *De Amicitia*, 'was with them a principal ground of friendship and attachment; nor do I know any other capable of forming firmer, dearer, more pleasing, more honourable, and more virtuous habitudes'.[63]

Friendship is necessary to the formation and maintenance of party and government alike because the centripetal forces of leadership and cooperation operate by way of conciliation. 'I set it down as the peculiar function of virtue', Cicero writes, 'to win the hearts of men (*conciliare animos hominum*) and to attach them to one's own service'.[64] In the *Thoughts* Burke also stresses the importance of 'connexion' to the history of English constitutional liberty. He idealizes the 'great connexion of Whigs in the reign of Q Anne', who were in power during 'one of the most fortunate periods of our history'.[65] These Whigs, according to Burke, lived up the Ciceronian ideal because they 'believed that no men could act with effect ... who were not bound together by common opinions, common affections, and common interests'.[66] As inheritors of the old Whig spirit, the Rockingham Opposition Party is inspired by the same principles and the same virtuous feelings that inspired Cicero's patriotic companions during the last days of the Roman Republic. Burke raises the stakes of his argument through historical analogy as well as through reference to classical political theory and therefore claims that the life of his Party is coterminous with that of the English Constitution itself.

This party of conciliation can only be aristocratic, like the Rockingham Opposition, because for Burke hierarchy itself is conciliatory; it starkly contrasts with the alienating procedures of despotic government Burke so poetically details throughout the *Thoughts*. In later writings the conciliatory features of social hierarchy would be contrasted with the distracting effects of Jacobinism, but the next section will show how in the *Thoughts* a party of conciliation, hospitable to the new man, contends with the King's Friends who will only welcome the Janissary.

NEW MAN AMONG THE JANISSARIES

In the *Thoughts*, Burke's double vision of English national character manifests as the critical difference between conciliatory and alienating political practice. This perceived dual personality, split between constitutional virtue and corruption, is also reflected in the pamphlet through two competing figures of imperial assimilation. We usually think of the competing parties in the *Thoughts* as being the King's Men and the Rockingham Whigs, but we can also contrast Burke himself, as a certain kind of political newcomer, with the King's Men who are newcomers of a different sort. That is, we might read Burke's picture of England's constitutional crisis as one in which the political nation must decide on how it wishes to assimilate newcomers. It can either encourage independence and the arts of conciliation by cultivating the Ciceronian *novus homo* such as Burke himself, or it can encourage servility, arrogance and general alienation by introducing a new class of parliamentary Janissaries. The two types cannot coexist in the same political system without one replacing the other, any more than the State can operate effectively under a Double Cabinet. Each type is clearly aligned with a possible constitutional destiny – liberty or tyranny – and Burke locates himself in the narrative of constitutional crisis by identifying himself as one rather than the other.

By 1770, 'Janissary' was already a familiar term of abuse in the Rockingham Whig vocabulary, and in the *Thoughts* Burke uses it in the received way. This epithet could be applied to the political newcomers among the King's Men, those who were elevated to high positions by an overly independent King's obvious need for a plurality of allies. To equate the King's Men with Janissaries was also to equate the English system with an oriental despotism, which Montesquieu had described in *The Spirit of the Laws*. Janissaries – that is, those Ottoman soldiers who acted as the Sultan's personal guard – were literally slaves to the Sultan, and had no political or family connections to anyone but to him.[67] The Rockingham party prided themselves on their independence, and so railed against their opponents' lack of it. The Court Party's 'Janissary' ethos threatened the nobility's independence from the King, and therefore threatened the necessary system of balance within the constitution itself. The presence of Janissaries degraded Parliament's independent spirit, and Burke's complaints about them echo Montesquieu's account of despotic government.[68]

The language of oriental despotism allows Burke to avoid attacking the King directly, while still identifying his growing power as a danger to the constitution. By referring to the Court Party as Janissaries, Burke is associating George III with the Grand Turk – and thus identifying him with absolutism and arbitrary kingship. In the seventeenth and eighteenth centuries, the Janissaries undertook many successful palace coups, and so Montesquieu refers to 'intrigue in those seraglios of the East ... where an old prince who becomes more imbecile every day is the first prisoner of the palace'.[69] By way of this analogy with a debilitated Sultan, therefore, Burke can claim to be defending the King as well as the Constitution from the Court Party. Burke charges that the King is 'a prisoner in his closet', and that he has in no way 'profited by that faction which presumptuously choose to call themselves *his friends*'.[70] According to the laws of conciliation Burke draws from Cicero, the King's Friends are not really friends, and the Court Party are not really a party; the bonds of genuine friendship (political or otherwise) can only arise from the mutual attractions of virtue.

The Janissary trope clashes with the new man trope through Burke's discourse of conciliation. In contrast to the virtuous *novus homo* who supports the hierarchy, the Janissary degrades the social order through alienation. The King's Friends, emboldened by royal support, were allowed to humiliate their social superiors in the Opposition. Therefore '[point] of honour and precedence were no more to be regarded in Parliamentary decorum, than in a Turkish army'.[71] Again to contrast with the new man, the Court Party promotes 'men of no sort of consideration or credit in the country' to the Administration, while conspicuously overlooking 'men of talents to conciliate the people'.[72] The King's Friends enact a kind of perversion of conciliation, because their 'reconciliations' are entirely selfish. 'Like Janissaries', Burke writes, the King's Men 'derive a kind of freedom from the very condition of their servitude', and thereby 'reconcile ... independence, and ... gross lucre'.[73] Instead of cultivating persuasion to conciliate the governed, they reconcile such inappropriate things as 'independence' and 'lucre' in such a way that 'independence' itself is evacuated of positive value. When the system does promote a conciliatory party, as during the first Rockingham Administration, it strips the ministers of their connexions, so that 'nothing can be done by common counsel in this nation'.[74] No new connexions are able to replace the ruined ones, and the nation is left with a disconnected and ineffective ministry. By getting rid of the nation's natural leadership, the Court Party systematically destroys the tools with which Parliament might effectively balance the power of the Crown.

The Janissary/new man conflict reflects Burke's complicated position in the British political system. As an Irishman and the son of a convert, Burke could relate to others who had been forced to break (or at least to hide) their ancestral connexions in order to become successful in the imperial system under which they lived. In contrast to the Ciceronian new man, the Janissary (in Turkish *Yeniçeri*) means 'new troop'. The difference between man and troop is essential here. Instead of embracing enslavement to this new system in order to become powerful, and instead of being a kind of soldier for an absolute ruler, Burke prides himself on his independence and right to resist the Crown. Burke prizes the English or British constitution for allowing him to take part in the political system as a new man with connexions, rather than as a new soldier without connexions. If the British tended to arrive in Ireland as Janissaries, Burke wanted to be the Irishman who appeared in England as a new man, capable of becoming the voice of political conscience in his new *patria*. The Janissary symbolized the kind of new man that he did not want to be called himself. The Janissary is not simply the image of the political neophyte that the Rockinghams most despised – it was also an image of the immigrant from the colonial periphery who assimilates to the imperial metropole. Burke was not ashamed of having made this move, but he did not want to be thought of as having done so with as little virtue or integrity as the Janissaries had.

If Burke was not simply voicing the indignation of his employer when he called the King's Friends to task for their insolence or their disregard for the principles of conciliatory government, neither was he simply thinking of himself as a certain kind of new Englishman in contrast to another kind. He was also drawing on an Irish aristocratic tradition of excoriating the political newcomer. Kevin Whelan argues that Ireland's 'Underground Gentry', such as the Nagles, 'were obsessed, almost to the point of neurosis, with ancestry, family background and the Cromwellian rupture', and that they powerfully disdained 'the *arriviste* Cromwellian landlords – a gentry by conquest not by blood'.[75] The dispossessed aristocrat, replaced by opportunistic newcomers, provided a 'context – the displaced Irish elite nexus of patron, poet and priest', in which 'Irish Jacobitism flourished'.[76] Burke's familiarity with this 'context', this 'elite nexus', (and probably also the poetry), is a clear influence on his attitude towards an independent aristocracy and their blow-in opponents among the Court Party. For this dispossessed Irish gentry, British liberty was an oriental despotism. The Rockingham Whigs resented the imposing arrogance of the Court's political neophytes, but Burke brought his own Irish ancestral rage to the job when he wrote the *Thoughts*.

CONCLUSION: COLONIAL SYMMETRIES

In the *Thoughts* Burke associates the Court Party's corrupting political Creed with the Manichaeism that attends colonial misgovernment. Early on he attacks the Court's rationalization 'we have a very good Ministry, but that we are a very bad people'.[77] The King's Friends are merely invoking the evil of the governed in order to rule out any obligation on their part to make concessions. This line of reasoning, then as now, is particularly insulting to the poorly governed. It is 'no small aggravation of the public misfortune', Burke writes, that the defenders of the misgovernment consider the situation 'to be without remedy'.[78] This echoes Burke's frustration at the Protestant Ascendancy's insistence on aggressive responses to the phantasmal threat of Jacobitism. Burke sees that the argument is calculated to further alienate the governed and further justify tyrannical policy. 'We seem', Burke writes sarcastically, 'to be driven to absolute despair; for we have no other materials to work upon, but those out of which God has been pleased to form the inhabitants of this island'.[79] He could just as easily have been writing about Ireland, and it is surely a subtext. Crucial to the policy of sowing despair is a steady regimen of punishment. 'I hear it indeed sometimes asserted', Burke continues acidly, 'that a steady perseverance in the present measures, and a rigorous punishment of those who oppose them, will in the course of time infallibly put an end to these disorders'.[80] Again the Irish Burke was already familiar with this authoritarian pessimism. As in his Irish writings, Burke here suggests that the blame should not go to the governors or to the governed, but rather to the conspiratorial middlemen who foment misunderstandings in order to arrogate power in the ensuing confusion. Just as the Protestant Ascendancy is responsible for alienating Catholic Ireland from the Whig Constitution, so is the Court Party responsible for alienating the people from King and Constitution.

In the absence of an effective Opposition to facilitate government by conciliation, Burke's England is a colonized country; he refers to 'this garrison of *King's men*, which is stationed, as in a citadel, to controul and enslave it'.[81] This is where Burke's England looks most like his Ireland. In his 1792 *Letter to Sir Hercules Langrishe*, he would write that the Ascendancy 'considered themselves in no other light than that of a colonial garrison, to keep the natives in subjection to the other state of Great Britain'.[82] Although he could never say this in reference to Ireland, in the *Thoughts* Burke writes that the garrison in England must 'be leveled with the ground'.[83] Here Burke acknowledges that his party mirrors the King's Men in at least one unflattering way: the Rockingham Whigs are also a garrison. 'I admit', writes Burke, 'that people frequently acquire in such confederacies a narrow, bigoted, and proscriptive spirit ... [however, i]f a fortress is seated in an unwholesome air, an officer of the garrison is obliged to be attentive to his health, but he must not desert his station'.[84] Burke's attempt to reconcile his Irish and English duties by way of the Rockingham Whig project does not result in unmixed sense of *Ceart*. He admits that he must hold his nose from the 'unwholesome air' that comes from adopting some of his new English connexions, and indeed that he must become a kind of military occupier himself.

Burke's denunciation of the Double Cabinet is so powerful because it comes from an attempt to reconcile his distracted political personae and to correct his double vision of England. As a defender of the Whig constitution Burke denounces the absolutism of the Double Cabinet, but drawing on resentments from his unspoken Irish Jacobite hinterland, Burke denounces the King's Friends as a swarm of Janissaries, new men gone wrong, and agents of imperial immorality. The *Thoughts* can accommodate so many Irish subtexts ultimately, however, because the Double Cabinet theory was the Rockingham Whigs' narrative of defeat. It operates both as a call to political arms and also as a visionary lament. In each of these capacities it offered much-needed coherence to a group of gentry who regarded themselves as politically dispossessed. Burke was famously predisposed to identify with any group that could be characterized in this way, and while the marginalization of the Opposition Whigs was wholly different from that of Ireland's Catholic underground gentry, he did find a way of applying his Nagle sympathies to his new leader. In making the Rockingham complaint his own, Burke overstates the case so magnificently that at times the King's Men seem to be colonizing England. On the other hand, Burke's engagement with this narrative leads him to adopt the language of imperialism along with that of constitutionalism. This marks a limitation in Burke's critique of empire, but it is a starting place for revising the displaced Irish dimension to Burkean Englishness.

NOTES

I wish to thank Chris Vanden Bossche, Seamus Deane, Luke Gibbons, Sara Crosby, Katherine O'Donnell and Seán Patrick Donlan for their responses to this essay at various stages.

 1. For some of the most recent literary critical and theoretical analyses, see S. Deane, *Strange Country* (Oxford: Clarendon Press, 1997), T. Eagleton, *Heathcliff and the Great Hunger* (New York: Verso, 1995), L. Gibbons, *Edmund Burke and Ireland* (Cambridge: Cambridge University Press, 2003), and W.J. McCormack, *From Burke to Beckett: Ascendancy, Tradition and Betrayal in Literary History* (Cork: Cork University Press, 1994), C.C. O'Brien, *The Great Melody* (Chicago: University of Chicago Press, 1992), and K. O'Donnell, *Edmund Burke's Irish Accent* (forthcoming). For a political scientist's approach to Burke as liberal theorist of imperialism, which also warns against a critical over-emphasis on the Irish background, see U. Mehta, *Liberalism and Empire: A Study in Nineteenth Century Political Thought* (Chicago: University of Chicago Press, 1999), specifically p.165.
 2. Deane, *Strange Country*, identifies the *Reflections* as 'a foundational text' in the 'plot' of Ireland's 'national literature' (p.1). Gibbons, *Edmund Burke and Ireland*, takes Burke's work on the sublime as the start of a project for envisioning an alternative Irish Enlightenment. McCormack, *From Burke to Beckett*, takes Burke as a starting point for theorizing a Protestant Ascendancy literary history, while Eagleton, *Heathcliff and the Great Hunger*, explores Burke as a theorist of hegemony to be worked out in an Irish colonial context. One indicator of how these critical interventions have influenced our view of the Irish canon can be seen in S. Regan, *Irish Writing: An Anthology of Irish Literature in English 1789–1939* (Oxford: Oxford University Press, 2004). A contrary indicator might also be seen in P. Muldoon, *To Ireland, I* (New York: Oxford University Press, 2000).
 3. O'Brien, *The Great Melody*, p.27: 'the socio-religious border-zone in which he was brought up, was of a kind about which he felt it safest to be silent'. Because the evidence is suggestive but not conclusive, scholarship on the Irish Burke is split over the question of whether Burke's father Richard was a Catholic who conformed to the Church of Ireland out of political expediency, and whether he was the same Richard Burke who gave legal counsel to James Cotter, a Jacobite who was judicially murdered in 1720. For analyses of Burke exploring what it might mean if these suggestions about Richard Burke are true, see O'Brien, *The Great Melody*; O'Donnell, *Edmund Burke's Irish Accent*; and Gibbons, *Edmund Burke and Ireland*.
 4. O'Brien, 'Introduction', to Edmund Burke, *Reflections on the Revolution in France* (New York: Penguin, 1968). O'Brien observes that Burke's 'furious irony' derives from '[f]riction between outer Whig and inner "Jacobite"', – and that it reflects the double vision of Burke's 'Irish predicament, with its striking contrasts between pretences and realities' (p.44). O'Brien also holds that Burke's 'middle ground', where he 'harmonizes' these two impulses, allows him to achieve the tone which is best suited to addressing 'the landed proprietors of England' (p.46) – precisely the audience Burke also has in mind in the *Thoughts*.
 5. J.C.D. Clark, 'Religious Affiliation and Dynastic Allegiance in Eighteenth-Century England: Edmund Burke, Thomas Paine and Samuel Johnson', *ELH*, 64, 4 (1997), pp.1029–67, pp.1039–40.
 6. See Clark, 'Religious Affiliation', p.1035.
 7. T. Bowers, 'Jacobite Difference and the Poetry of Jane Barker', *ELH*, 64, 4 (1997), pp.857–69, p.857.
 8. H. Erskine-Hill, 'Twofold Vision in Eighteenth-Century Writing', *ELH*, 64, 4 (1997), pp.903–24, pp.909–10.
 9. Also on the cultural politics of this accent see Deane, *Strange Country*, pp.63–5.
10. On Burke's rhetoric and theory of Party in the *Thoughts*, and his relationship to the Rockingham Whigs, see J. Brewer, 'Party and the Double Cabinet: Two Facets of Burke's Thoughts', *Historical Journal*, 14 (1971), pp.479–501, and 'Rockingham, Burke and Whig Political Argument', *Historical Journal*, 18 (1975), pp.188–201; D. Bryant, 'Burke's Present Discontents: The Rhetorical Genesis of a Party Testament', *Quarterly Journal of Speech*, 42 (1956), pp.115–26; J. Fitzgerald, 'The Logical Style of Burke's *Thoughts on the Present Discontents*', *Burke Newsletter*, 7 (1965), pp.465–78; F.P. Lock, '"The Organ of a Discontented Faction": Burke's *Thoughts on the Cause of the Present Discontents*', in G. Schochet, P. Tatspaugh and C. (eds), *Empire and Revolutions* (Washington, DC: Folger Shakespeare Library, 1993), pp.121–39; F. O'Gorman, 'Party and Burke: The Rockingham Whigs', *Government and Opposition*, 3 (1969), pp.92–110; C. Reid, *Edmund Burke and the Practice of Political Writing* (Dublin: Gill and Macmillan, 1985); C. Robbins, 'Burke's Rationale of Cabinet Government', *Burke Newsletter*, 7 (1965), pp.457–65; and R. Willis, 'Some Further Reflections on Burke's Discontents', *Studies in Burke and His Time*, 11 (1970),

pp.1417–27.
11. The King won the political struggle over who might choose the Cabinet in 1770, and he would do so again in 1784, when he dismissed the highly popular Charles James Fox. See P. Thomas, *George III: King and Politicians 1760–1770* (Manchester: Manchester University Press, 2002); and J. Cannon *The Fox-North Coalition: Crisis of the Constitution, 1782–84* (Cambridge: Cambridge University Press, 1969).
12. Lock, 'The Organ of a Discontented Faction', p.122.
13. Letter from Rockingham (15 Oct. 1769), *Correspondence*, vol.ii, p.92.
14. Letter to Rockingham (*post* 6 Nov. 1769), *Correspondence*, vol.ii, p.109.
15. Burke, *Thoughts on the Cause of the Present Discontents*, in Harris (ed.) *Pre-Revolutionary Writings* (Cambridge: Cambridge University Press, 1993), p.116.
16. Ibid., p.141.
17. To see how unusual this was not, see G. Wood, 'Conspiracy and the Paranoid Style: Causality and Deceit in the Eighteenth Century', *The William and Mary Quarterly*, 39, 3 (1982), pp.401–41.
18. See Burke's annotations to Letter from Dr Leland to Burke (11 June 1770, Sheffield MSS, Burke 1–160). Quoted in Brewer, 'Party and the Double Cabinet', p.484.
19. Letter from O'Hara to Burke (10 May 1770 Sheffield MSS, Burke 1–156a). Quoted in Brewer, 'Party and the Double Cabinet', p.495.
20. Burke, *Speech on Conciliation with America* in Harris (ed.) *Pre-Revolutionary Writings*, p.242.
21. *Writings and speeches*, vol.ix, p.547.
22. Ibid., p.590 'generous...'; p.163 'obliged...'.
23. Ibid., p.590.
24. Ibid., p.591.
25. Ibid., p.561.
26. Ibid., pp.561–2.
27. Ibid., p.167.
28. Ibid.
29. Burke, *Thoughts*, p.149: 'political distemper'; p.153: 'sinister ... disturbances'.
30. Ibid., p.192.
31. É. Ó Ciardha, *Ireland and the Jacobite Cause, 1685–1766: A Fatal Attachment* (Dublin: Four Courts Press, 2002), p.368.
32. O'Brien, *The Great Melody*, p.23.
33. Burke, *Thoughts*, p.127.
34. Deane, 'Introduction' to 'Edmund Burke (1729–97)', in S. Deane (ed.) *The Field Day Anthology of Irish Writing* (Derry: Field Day Publications, 1991), vol.1, p.808: 'It may be that his defence of the old monarchical system in Europe was the last brilliant flare of the Irish Jacobite dream of a restored monarchy, in which catholic Ireland would play its full part and regain its lost privileges. Yet this Jacobite strain in Burke coexists with an unstinted, perhaps extravagant, admiration for the British constitution as established in 1688.'
35. O'Donnell, 'The Image of a Relationship in Blood: *Párliament na mBan* and Burke's Jacobite Politics', *Eighteenth Century Ireland/ Iris an da Chultur*, 15 (2000), pp.98–119, p.112: 'Whether or not the young Burke studied Ó Colmáin's *Párliament*, the fact remains that its discussion of political concepts central to Jacobite thinking are markedly similar to his depiction of key facets of the British constitution.' If Burke did know the text, however, its resonance would have been terrific in Burke's imagination given the fact that it was written for, and dedicated to, the young James Cotter (see Note 3 for debate on Cotter).
36. O'Donnell, 'The Image of a Relationship in Blood', p.113. For more on *Ceart* and Ó Colmáin, see B. Ó Buachalla, 'The Making of a Cork Jacobite', in P. O'Flanagan and C. Buttimer (eds), *Cork History & Society: Interdisciplinary Essays on the History of an Irish County* (Dublin: Geography Publications), pp.469–97. For a historical linguistic analysis of *Ceart* and related terms or concepts, see P. McQuillan, *Native and Natural: Aspects of 'Right' and 'Freedom' in Irish* (Notre Dame: University of Notre Dame Press).
37. N. Ó Dónaill, *Foclóir Gaeilge-Béarla* (Baile Átha Cliath: Mount Salus Press, 1977).
38. Letter to Richard Shackleton (15 Nov. 1744), *Correspondence*, vol.i, p.32. The reference is to *De Senectute*, and he is writing from Trinity College Dublin.
39. N. Robinson, *Edmund Burke: A Life in Caricature* (New Haven: Yale University Press, 1996) pp.83, 93. For more on Burke's use of Cicero in the Impeachment, see H.V. Canter, 'The Impeachments of Verres and Hastings: Cicero and Burke', *Classical Journal*, 9 (1914), pp.199–211; G. Carnall, 'Burke as Modern Cicero', in G. Carnall and C. Nicholson (eds), *The Impeachment of Warren Hastings* (Edinburgh: Edinburgh University Press, 1989), pp.76–90; and E. Samet, 'A Prosecutor and a Gentleman: Edmund Burke's Idiom of Impeachment', *ELH*, 68, 2 (2001), pp.397–418.

40. Quoted in F.P. Lock, *Edmund Burke: Volume I, 1730–1784* (Oxford: Clarendon Press, 1998), p.272.
41. Letter from William Burke to William Dennis (3–6 April 1770, reporting debate in Parliament, 2 April 1770), *Correspondence*, vol.ii, pp.128–9.
42. The editors make this identification; the passage is *In Verrem*, III, 4, 7.See Letter from William Burke to William Dennis (3–6 April 1770, reporting debate in Parliament, 2 April 1770), *Correspondence*, vol.ii, p.128.
43. Arpinum was conquered by Rome in the fourth century BC and was still being assimilated into the empire during Cicero's lifetime. The Romans kept it for more than a century as a *civitas sine suffragio*, and a century before Cicero's birth they granted it citizenship and made it a *praefectura*. Rome made Arpinum a *municipium* when Cicero was a boy.
44. M. Fuchs, *Edmund Burke, Ireland, and the Fashioning of Self* (Oxford: Voltaire Foundation, 1996), p.293. Fuchs argues that by using Cicero Burke tries, however unsuccessfully, to 'win the unreserved approbation of the Catholics', who consider the Penal Laws unjust because they disenfranchise the island's majority, and also 'win that of the Protestants', who will recognize in Cicero's contractual language 'an argument which had been part and parcel of their [Whig] mental equipment since the events of 1688–1689'.
45. *Writings and speeches*, vol.ix, p.456. Burke argues that the Penal Laws go against Cicero's criteria of 'utility and equity' as the 'only two … foundations of Law'.
46. Burke, *Speech on Conciliation*, p.210.
47. Cicero, *On Duties*. Trans. W. Miller. (Cambridge: Harvard University Press, 1913),p.191.
48. Cicero, *De Oratore Books I, II* Trans. E. W. Sutton. (Cambridge: Harvard University Press, 1942), p.333'soulbending…'; p.434 'aut…'
49. Cicero, *De Oratore*, p.435. Cicero elaborates on this meaning with '*ante quam de re diceremus, initio conciliandos eorum esse animos, qui audirent*,' (98), which Sutton translates: 'before speaking on the issue, we must first secure the goodwill of the audience' (99).
50. Burke, *Thoughts*, p.146.
51. Cicero *De Oratore*, pp.330–1.'In order to explore the feelings of the tribunal' he writes, 'I engage wholeheartedly in a consideration so careful, that I scent out with all possible keenness their thoughts, judgments, anticipations and wishes, and the direction in which they seem most likely to be led away most easily by eloquence.'
52. Burke, *Speech on Conciliation*, p.212. Burke argues for government according to the character of the governed rather than according to abstract principle.'[W]e must govern America, according to that [American] nature, and to those [American] circumstances; and not according to our own imaginations; not according to abstract ideas of right.' His descriptions of America, like those of India, are over-determined. For a post-colonial critique of Burke's descriptions of India, see Sara Suleri, *The Rhetoric of English India* (Chicago: University of Chicago Press, 1992).
53. Burke, *Thoughts*, p.117. Harris's editorial note identifies Burke's 'temper of the people' as a translation of Tacitus' Annales Book 4 chapter 33: 'it is necessary to know the nature of the crowd, and by what means they are to be controlled'.
54. Burke, *Thoughts*, p.117.
55. Cicero, *De Haruspicum Responsis* in *Pro Archia Poeta, Post Reditum in Senatu, Post Reditum Ad Quirites, De Domo Sua, De Haruspicum Responsis, Pro Plancio*, translated by N. Watts (Cambridge: Harvard University Press, 1923), p.393.
56. Cicero, *On Duties*, p.57.
57. Burke, *Reflections on the Revolution in France: A Critical Edition*, edited by J.C.D. Clark (Stanford: Stanford University Press, 2001), p.202.
58. Burke, *Reflections*, p.262. Burke is quoting from the *Dream of Scipio*.For the passage and its translation by Keyes, see Cicero, *De Re Publica, De Legibus*, translated by C. Keyes (Cambridge: Harvard University Press, 1928), pp.264–5.Keyes renders *concilia*, cognate with conciliare, as 'assemblies'. The state itself, as well as all the assemblies which build up to the state, are functions of natural conciliation.
59. Cicero, *De Amicitia*, in *De Senectute, De Amicitia, De Divinatione*, translated by W. Falconer (Cambridge: Harvard University Press, 1923), pp.206–7.
60. Ibid., p.161.
61. Ibid., p.125.
62. Burke, *Thoughts*, p.185.
63. Burke, *Thoughts*, p.185.'*Idem sentire de re publica*' references (rather than quotes) an expression uttered in the negative by Laelius in *De Amicitia*. See Cicero, *De Amicitia*, pp.144–5. Falconer translates the expression: 'entertain the same political views'. It could also be rendered as 'think the same way about the constitution'.
64. Cicero, *On Duties*, p.185.

65. Burke, *Thoughts*, p.186.
66. Ibid., pp.186–7.
67. From the fourteenth century Janissaries had been recruited by way of a child-tithe on Christians in the Balkans and Anatolia, but by the early eighteenth century this tithe was no longer in practice, and the marriage restrictions were also relaxed.
68. Burke, *Thoughts*, p.125: 'It is the nature of despotism to abhor power held by any means but its own momentary pleasure; and to annihilate all intermediate situations between boundless strength on its own part, and total debility on the part of the people.'
69. Montesquieu,. *The Spirit of the Laws*, edited by A. Cohler, B. Miller and H. Stone (Cambridge: Cambridge University Press, 1989), p.63.For more on Europe's double image of the Grand Turk as being at once all-powerful in public but compromised in private by the intrigues of the Seraglio and the Janissary Guard, see A. Grosrichard, *The Sultan's Court: European Fantasies of the East*, translated by Liz Heron (New York: Verso, 1998).
70. Burke, *Thoughts*, p.154 'a prisoner...'; p.158 'profited...'.
71. Ibid., p.126.
72. Ibid.
73. Ibid., p.141.
74. Ibid., p.151.
75. K. Whelan, *The Tree of Liberty: Radicalism, Catholicism and the Construction of Irish Identity 1760–1830* (Notre Dame: University of Notre Dame Press, 1996), p.10.
76. Ibid., p.11.
77. Burke, *Thoughts*, p.119.
78. Ibid.
79. Ibid., pp.119–20.
80. Ibid., p.120.
81. Ibid., p.183.
82. *Writings and Speeches*, vol.ix, p.615.
83. Burke, *Thoughts*, p.183.
84. Ibid., p.185.

10

Burke, Ireland and India:
Reason, Rhetoric and Empire

F.P. LOCK

Burke prided himself on his consistency. Since he habitually spoke of himself with (to modern ears) gratingly excessive modesty, this claim needs to be taken seriously. Yet there is perhaps no quality which critics, from Thomas Paine to the present day, have been readier to deny him. Thomas Moore gave the charge memorable expression in his *Memoirs of Sheridan*:

> His mind indeed, lies parted asunder in his works, like some vast continent severed by a convulsion of nature, – each portion peopled by its own giant race of opinions, differing altogether in features and language, and committed in eternal hostility with each other.

Moore sweetened this criticism by likening Burke's 'versatility' to Shakespeare's, achieving 'such a versatility of application' that no statesman could be at a loss to find 'some golden sentence from Burke, either to strengthen his position by reasoning or illustrate and adorn it by fancy'.[1] The earliest critics of Burke's consistency posited a contradiction between his earlier writings and speeches, which championed 'Whig' or libertarian ideals, and the 'Tory' opinions of the *Reflections on the Revolution in France* (1790) and its successors. Most recently, the theory has been reformulated in psychological terms. Isaac Kramnick was the first to identify a Burke divided against himself, the giant races of opinions fighting an internal psychomachia.[2] Kramnick's aim was to rescue Burke from the then conventional 'conservative' interpreters of his thought, and to redeem him as an unconscious subversive. Without necessarily accepting Kramnick's Freudian and Marxist paradigms, several later critics have developed his notion that emotional, suppressed, perhaps even unconscious undercurrents may better represent the 'true' Burke than the surface, 'official' meaning of his writings and speeches. The most comprehensive psychological reading of Burke in this vein is Conor Cruise O'Brien's.[3] O'Brien attributes Burke's concern for India to feelings of guilt at having been complicit with the oppression of Ireland by the Protestant minority.[4] Most recently, Luke Gibbons has likewise sought to identify Burke with the oppressed Catholic majority in Ireland and, by extension, with the oppressed peoples of India.[5] These interpretations make Burke much more strongly 'Irish' (in a certain sense), and much more stridently anti-imperialist and anti-colonialist than he appears in previous readings. Given the proliferation of post-colonial cultural studies, the emergence of a post-colonial Burke was to be expected. Indeed, this is so much a Burke for our time, that (to borrow a phrase from an earlier book of O'Brien's) a 'suspecting glance' is needed.[6]

Broader questions than Burke's treatment of Ireland and India are also at stake. In reading and interpreting Burke, how much weight should we give to what may be regarded as no more than the surface meaning of his statements, and how much to inferences, implications and extensions that may be deduced from what he actually says? O'Brien often argues from silences and inferences, and admits that his account of Burke's motivation is 'hardly susceptible of proof'.[7] Gibbons, even more disarmingly, admits that he is reading Burke 'against the grain', travelling the 'unapproved roads' of Burke's mind.[8] Both approaches, different as they are in many respects (where O'Brien is more speculative, Gibbons is more textual), delve so deep as to obscure some of the most prominent contours of the Burkean mindscape. This essay is intended as a corrective reminder of some of those contours. Without denying Burke's sympathy for the oppressed, whether in Ireland or in India, it aims to reinstate the primacy of the rational, public, official Burke. It argues that his attitudes and actions were primarily determined and driven by rational conviction; that the powerfully emotive force of his rhetoric should be understood as a conscious rhetorical strategy, not as expressive of emotional identification or submerged loyalties; and that, while critical of the practice of empire, he accepted empire as part of a providential order that, upon the whole, operated for the benefit and improvement of mankind.

Two important preliminary considerations are the question of Burke's Irishness and his personality. Several recent studies have stressed his strong links to the indigenous culture, rather than to the Anglo-Irish establishment. In particular, much has been made of the period he may have spent with his maternal relatives, the Nagles, in the Blackwater country.[9] Certainly, the Nagles were important to Burke. He never repudiated that side of his inheritance, and he remained eager to help the Nagles in need. Yet how deeply the Nagle background affected him remains open to question. Hard information about those early years is scanty, most of what we possess deriving from what James Prior was told by anonymous informants in the 1820s. Burke is said to have spent about five years (1735–40, when he was aged from five to ten) with the Nagles at Castletownroche, near Cork, and to have attended a village school there.[10] O'Brien regards Burke's attendance at what he interprets as a 'hedge' school as a formative cultural influence.[11] Perhaps so, but the inference, indeed the existence of the school, is highly speculative. The two educational institutions Burke is known to have attended were both firmly Protestant: Ballitore, established by an English Quaker; and Trinity College, Dublin, a bastion of the establishment. Some of his later letters express an affectionate nostalgia for the Blackwater and the Nagles.[12] Yet Burke left Ireland at the age of 20, to make only four return visits, two of a few months, two of a few weeks. As early as practicable, he escaped from an Irishness with which he could not fully identify, and determined to make a career in England. As soon as he had the remotest prospect of affording it, he bought a country estate to reinvent himself as an English country gentleman. Describing this rather grandiose self-gentrification to his friend Richard Shackleton, he called it an attempt to 'cast a little root'.[13] Although he never in fact achieved complete acceptance or integration into English society, remaining something of an Irish outsider, he thereafter identified his primary loyalty as to England.[14] While he retained his sympathies for the Irish, and especially for the Catholics, and frequently promoted their cause at some cost to his own self-interest, he came to see Ireland from an English point of view. He was certainly no Irish nationalist in the modern sense. Unequivocally and consistently, he argued that, in 'the nature of things' (one of his favourite arguments), Ireland could not be substantially independent. The facts of geography made Ireland more dependent on Britain than were the American colonies. Speaking of America, Burke often uses language suggestive of the empire as an association of nearly co-ordinate bodies, over which the imperial centre exercised only a general superintendence. Speaking of Ireland, his language emphasizes its subordination.[15]

Assessments of Burke's personality are inevitably subjective. But there is ample evidence that his elective affinities were aristocratic and patrician. He viewed society not as an aggregate of isolated individuals, but as a network of overlapping kinship and patronage relationships. These relationships, and the institutions that mediated between the individual and society, gave meaning and purpose to the individual's endeavours.[16] Burke himself was soon multiply connected, to patrons above and clients below. The familiar parallel with Cicero extends beyond their rhetoric. Like Cicero, he was self-conscious about being a 'new man'; he accepted the system as he found it; and (most relevant here) he accepted the obligation to help clients. Even before he bought his estate, he began a career as a patron by financing the Irish painter James Barry's extended period of study in Italy.[17] Such philanthropic enterprises (which he could ill afford) characterized him throughout his life. They testify to his sense of the obligations imposed by his position as a highly privileged member of society. Burke's larger-scale efforts on behalf of oppressed peoples, whether in Ireland or India, were rational undertakings in this spirit, based on the careful accumulation of evidence and arguments. That is why he took so long to abandon his earlier stance in defence of the East India Company. Burke was a man of generous sympathies, unusually capable of feeling for the oppression and injustice from which others, even far away others, suffered. But his efforts on their behalf were determined by his reason and his sense of moral responsibility, not by his feelings.[18] For all his rhetoric of deference and self-abnegation, Burke was extraordinarily self-certain and self-righteous. He viewed the world from a point of view of assured superiority. For example, he often contrasted the feelings of the majority (which were likely to be right) with their inability to reason on them. Reasoning was the preserve of the few.[19] His sympathy for, and efforts on behalf of, the disadvantaged and the downtrodden, whether individuals or peoples, derived from powerful feelings, from pity, anger and indignation, but also from a reasoned sense of his public and private duties. Dissenting from the common view expressed by Pufendorf, Burke argued that, though the time and choice was a matter for individual discretion, 'charity' was an absolute, not an 'imperfect' obligation.[20]

Burke felt passionately and deeply. In an age that valued gentlemanly reserve, he was often regarded as extravagantly emotional, too given to overt displays of feeling, and was even suspected of madness. He was often prejudiced, and could be obtuse and oblivious to the feelings of others. Yet if his style was often highly charged with emotion, his feelings did not determine either his attitudes or his ideas. Thomas Babington Macaulay, with his usual fondness for an aphoristic antithesis, claimed that Burke 'generally chose his side like a fanatic, and defended it like a philosopher'.[21] The reverse is rather true. Burke was not, as Macaulay supposed, captured by an India of his imagination. He was convinced of the case against Hastings, and against the misgovernment by the East India Company, by a mass of documentary evidence. Only after he had taken his side, and begun his crusade, did Burke come to behave like a fanatic, increasingly unable to accept that there could be another stance to the case. Since so much has recently been made of Burke's emotional loyalties, the rational basis of his convictions is worth stressing. His world view was theological, but his was a reasoned theology. In the 1790s, his hostility to Jacobinism (which he equated with atheism) was partly based on his conviction that, without a belief in God, there could be no sanction for the moral law. God, Burke believed, had created the moral order to which mankind must conform.[22] This morality was the same everywhere. Burke repudiated the idea that there could be a 'Geographical morality' in which an act might be wrong in Europe but right in India. Political principles were likewise everywhere the same, though they were embodied in different social structures. Moral feelings were generally right, and reliable, and gave universal access to intuitive truths. But because people differ more in their capacity for reasoning than in their ability to feel, societies need to be guided by statesmen who can apply prudence and principles to the problems of politics. The many can feel an evil or a grievance or an oppression, but only the few can reason about how best to remove or to alleviate it.[23] Burke's was a politics of reason, but not *a priori* reasoning. His reason took account of differences of circumstances, history and culture. Post-colonial critics have rightly stressed Burke's sensitivity to cultural differences, and he has been called 'the most multicultural European of his era'.[24] If this is true, Burke's cross-cultural sympathies did not prevent his also holding to certain universal values. When these came into conflict with local customs, they were accorded precedence. In the Bengal Judicature Bill that he drafted in 1781, for example, a measure that is generally respectful of Indian practices and susceptibilities, he prohibited the standard Islamic punishment of mutilation.[25]

Indeed, much of his case against Hastings was based on the assumption of a universal moral law. One of his fundamental criticisms of the theorists of the French Revolution was that they applied supposedly 'universal' ideas with no regard to circumstances. His own attempts to reconcile local custom with universal law illustrates what has been called his 'principled pragmatism'.[26]

Burke was also a profoundly religious man, for whom religion was a choice of reason as well as a matter of faith. His religion offered a coherent and cogent account of the world and of man's place in it. Religion taught him to accept inequalities and apparent inequities and anomalies as part of the divine plan, as revealed in history; and particularly to respect prescription and property, the foundations of social stability. Religion also taught him that men have duties, to which they ought to subordinate their wills. Burke's religion was thus anti-individualistic, and disposed him to be more sympathetic to Roman Catholicism and Hinduism than were most of his Protestant contemporaries. Besides being the faiths of majorities, Roman Catholicism and Hinduism shared another element that made them highly congenial to Burke's habits of mind. Both are highly social and hierarchical in nature, and both (unlike the kinds of Protestantism that Burke most disliked) are strongly anti-individualistic.[27] This is not to imply that Burke respected religion only, or mainly, for its social utility.[28] Yet he greatly valued the social function of religion, and thought that governments ought to be concerned to protect and promote it.[29]

Burke's predilection for Roman Catholicism has been the more extensively canvassed. In his own time, he was often accused of being a crypto-Catholic, and many later writers have detected leanings towards Catholicism.[30] Yet there is no necessary connection between thinking well of a religion and accepting its claims to be true. Burke thought highly of Hinduism, yet was never suspected of being a closet Hindu. Catholicism and Hinduism were religions of the many. Burke was convinced that the many needed a religion, and in particular that they needed one to which their loyalty was instinctive rather than reasoned. They therefore needed the religion in which they had been educated. For most people, the loss of faith in their first religion was likely to mean the end of religious faith altogether. In Ireland, there was no longer any question of the mass conversion of Catholics to Protestantism. Their faith was threatened by Jacobinism, which would lead to atheism.[31] Burke's sympathy for the Catholic majority was sharpened by his intense and active dislike of many aspects of Irish Protestantism, which in 1792 he denounced as 'nothing more or better than the name of a persecuting faction, with a relation of some sort of theological hostility to others, but without any sort of ascertained tenets of its own'.[32] Burke was especially hostile to the notion of a 'Protestant Ascendancy', which he perceived as a mere excuse for domination and oppression.[33]

For Burke, there was no conflict between reason and religion, because reason, properly employed, supported religion, and religion, properly understood, was reasonable. The 'reason' he detested was the abstract, metaphysical reasoning of the geometricians of the French Revolution. Burke's own reasoning, like all reasoning, was grounded on certain truths that he regarded as self-evident or axiomatic. But the way he developed those first principles was logical. Admittedly, Burke's use of logical argument is less remarkable than his rhetoric. As a reasoner, some of his contemporaries were his equals or his superiors. As a rhetorician, he is the only writer in English who can be compared to the great classical exemplars, Demosthenes and Cicero. This has naturally meant that his rhetoric has received most attention. Further, since his use of the emotional and ethical appeals is more memorable than his use of the rational appeal, emotional and psychological interpretations of Burke can seem plausible. From his writings and speeches, passages of highly charged emotions are readily selected, and they can give a misleading impression of the general tenor of his argument. This is especially true of the often-hyperbolic rhetoric of his speeches at the trial of Hastings. The role of logic, and of supporting evidence, in Burke's rhetoric therefore needs emphasis. A quality on which Burke valued himself more often even than for his consistency was his industrious gathering of information.[34] His passion for information is evident at every stage of his career, and on every subject with which he became concerned.[35] On India, above all, the volume of information that he collected, read and absorbed is remarkable, as the briefest survey of his Select Committee reports, or of the evidence adduced at the trial of Warren Hastings, will suffice to demonstrate. When he published his *Speech on the Nabob of Arcot's Debts* (1785), he added documentary appendices that are as long as the speech itself.[36] These sources are for the most part quite unsensational. Yet they form the bedrock on which Burke constructed his interpretations and arguments. Equally, the canard that Burke was ill informed about the French Revolution has now been rendered untenable.[37]

Even on the subject of Ireland, which Burke knew at first hand, he was at pains to be fully and minutely informed. When he decided to write against the Penal Laws, for example, he eschewed the easy method of general denunciation for a minute dissection of their details, which is all the more telling for its factual density.[38] Everyone knew that the Catholics were much the largest religious denomination in Ireland, though no exact figures were available. Burke supported a project for an 'exact enumeration', praising it as 'a Work of the greatest Use to every Statesman and every man who chooses to perfect himself in the knowledge of public Œconomy', and proposing that it record occupation as well as religion. Burke's motives were mixed. He wanted hard figures to reinforce his claims on behalf of the Catholic majority, to be sure. But his suggestion that the census be extended to include economic information testifies to a more disinterested belief in the political and social value of information.[39]

For all his appetite for information, as a public man Burke was a rhetorician rather than a researcher. His political writings and speeches are all intended to persuade rather than to inform. They exemplify Aristotle's definition of the art of rhetoric as 'a capacity to see, in each case, what are the available means of persuasion'.[40] His arguments and evidence represent not necessarily what Burke himself thought most persuasive, but what he believed would most powerfully affect his audience. No feature of his speeches has provided more persuasive evidence for his supposed anti-imperialism than his use of atrocity stories. Uday Singh Mehta observes that there is 'scarcely a page' in Burke's voluminous writings and speeches on India that is not suffused with 'a simple but piercing concern with brutality, exploitation, the humiliation of women, the avarice of the company and its parliamentary patrons, the corresponding effect of destitution and the arbitrary use of unjust power'.[41] Luke Gibbons draws attention to some of the more sensational stories of torture used by Burke on the fourth day of his opening speech.[42] Mehta concluded that, although Burke 'did not oppose the empire in the sense of calling for its immediate dismantling', the 'tenor of his thought' presents a 'significant challenge' to imperialism.[43] While 'scarcely a page' is an exaggeration, Burke was undoubtedly fond of employing sensational material. Yet however his vivid descriptions of the mistreatment of Indians may now be read, or were understood by some auditors at the time, Burke himself seems not to have meant them as indictments of colonialism, but rather as acts of guilty individuals. Gibbons links the Hastings atrocities with a seemingly parallel passage in Burke's speech on 6 February 1778, condemning the use of Indian allies.[44] In the American speech, Burke did intend the incident to be generalized: he was arguing against the war as a whole, not complaining of an isolated incident. Employing barbarous allies in some sense typified the criminality and misdirection of the war. The Indian atrocities are described at greater length, and with greater vividness of detail (*enargia* is the rhetorical term). Certainly, they were meant to arouse pity for the victims, and to provoke outrage against the perpetrators. To the extent that they embody the general charge in an almost palpable particularity, they operate in a similar way. But a crucial difference is that Burke's aim was to convict Hastings of avoidable crimes, rejecting his 'reason of state' argument that the end justified the means. If colonial rule were not possible without the use of violence and the exercise of arbitrary power, Burke's moral indictment would be fatally weakened. He therefore demonizes Hastings, as he did later the Jacobins, for having made a 'fond election of evil'. In his *Speech on Fox's India Bill* (1 December 1783), Burke offered a 'Magna Charta' for India, evidently confident that, in the right hands, an empire could be ruled morally and benevolently, with due regard to the rights and interests of its inhabitants.[45]

Burke's repeated use of material of this kind suggests that, apart from its powerful rhetorical value, he responded to it with a horrified fascination. Yet this fascination has no necessary link to colonialism. His earliest use of such a story is the passage in the *Account of the European Settlements in America* (1757) describing the tortures inflicted by (North American) Indians on their captives, a passage practically transcribed from Lafitau.[46] Deeply affected by such stories himself, Burke was confident that they would likewise impress his auditors. But he also wanted to convince them, not that colonialism inevitably entails oppression (the likely conclusion of a modern reader), but that where Hastings had failed, others might succeed.

Burke's rhetoric of excess thus serves to strengthen and reinforce his reasoned arguments. In particular, his frequent use of *enargia* and hyperbole is a self-conscious rhetorical strategy, designed to achieve two important effects: to give particularity, a 'local habitation and a name', to crimes that were committed far away and to people otherwise unknown to his audience; and to emphasize the enormity of the crimes, which no language can adequately express. To identify a rhetorical strategy is not to imply that Burke was insincere, or his emotions factitious. As Horace had recognized, 'si vis me flere, dolendum est/primum ipse tibi'. Undoubtedly, Burke believed in the truth of his atrocity stories, and felt strongly about the injustice they represented. The danger is that, if these passages are taken together, out of their contexts, they make Burke appear more virulently and vehemently ant-imperialist than a careful reading of the speeches as a whole suggests.[47] Burke's rhetoric of atrocity served a purpose: to capture the minds and feelings of his auditors. It must not be ignored or minimized, but neither should it be allowed to usurp the weight of the whole argument.

The framework for understanding Burke's view of conquest, empire and colonization is his providential view of history. Providence, 'which strongly appears to have intended the continual intermixture of mankind', implanted in the human mind various means of effecting this purpose. Burke's examples are 'a sort of migratory instinct', 'the spirit of conquest', avarice, curiosity and pilgrimage.[48] In this list, 'the spirit of conquest' appears as a 'natural' human trait, not necessarily in itself either good or evil. Burke does not imply that any particular empire, in itself, enjoyed providential approval. Evil empires, like bad kings, could equally serve the ends of Providence. But conquest often worked to spread civilization, and Burke was not reluctant to praise 'good' conquests, conquerors and empires.[49] The British Empire was certainly in that category. Indeed, the value he placed on the Empire is abundantly attested by the efforts he expended to preserve it. In the context of the 1770s, Burke's consistent opposition to the policy of coercion meant that he was regarded as pro-American. He is sometimes said to have welcomed, or approved, or 'recognized without regret' the inevitability of American independence.[50] This was by no means the case. The Declaration of Independence made him 'sick at heart', and as late as 1778 he hoped against hope that it could be rescinded, and that the colonies would return to the British fold.[51] Since he was prepared to offer the Americans almost every concession in an effort to avert independence, he clearly valued even a nominal imperial relationship. With regard to Ireland, Burke likewise advocated trade concessions, but disapproved of the granting of legislative independence in 1782.[52] In relation to India, despite regarding 'our Indian government' as 'in its best state a grievance', and its actual practice as having been destructive both to India itself and to Britain, Burke never seriously contemplated withdrawal. 'But there we are', he declared, 'there we are placed by the Sovereign Disposer: and we must do the best we can in our situation. The situation of man is the preceptor of his duty.'[53] This recurrent concern for the preservation of the Empire hardly suggests that Burke suffered 'anxieties' about its morality.[54] Empire imposed moral obligation, and the 'anxiety' Burke felt about it concerned its failure to fulfil the moral obligation of its providential mission. But despite a miserable record of misrule and abuse, in Ireland of longstanding, in America and India of more recent date, Burke refused to despair of the institution itself. In the face of overwhelming evidence to the contrary, he believed in the possibility of its redemption. This belief in the beneficence of empire is consistent with the generally hierarchical and communitarian nature of his thought. Countries, like individuals, exist not in a vacuum, nor in a Hobbesian struggle of all against all, but as members of an informal international association. In the 1790s, Burke frequently invoked this idea to justify interference in the internal affairs of France. Drawing an analogy from the 'law of civil vicinity' (which justified an invasion of another's property to prevent damage to one's own), Burke applied the principle to what he called 'the grand vicinage of Europe', 'the great Commonwealth of Christendom', and 'the community of Europe'.[55] Holding a weak theory of national sovereignty enabled Burke to contemplate empire and colonization as natural, and possibly benign, historical events.

Burke has been called an 'enlightened imperialist'.[56] Empire was justified and validated by being exercised responsibly and, in the last resort, as part of the providential plan. He conceived the British Empire as a hierarchy in which power resided at the top, with the British Parliament at the imperial centre in London, and was mediated through local institutions, the nature of which would vary with local circumstances. Imperial rule did not require the explicit approval, or indeed participation, of those who were governed, though such participation might be appropriate (as he thought it was in America and in Ireland). In India, however, representative institutions made no part of the 'ancient constitution', and Burke never advocated their introduction.[57] While he believed that imperial power, like all political power, was a trust, to be exercised for the benefit of those ruled, the common exercise of government did not require popular approval. Prescription was a sufficient foundation.[58] (Burke did not deny the right of popular resistance, but he thought the circumstances that required it were extremely rare.) The imperial trust could be exercised in different ways, according to circumstances, and differently as those circumstances changed. In America, in the 1770s, the aim of the trust should have been to facilitate the growth of American prosperity, by exercising a minimal paternal guidance. Under the old policy of 'a wise and salutary neglect', America had prospered.[59] 'Salutary neglect', however, was not appropriate for Ireland or for India. Both required imperial intervention to reform misguided and oppressive local government, by the Irish Parliament and the East India Company.

Burke's Ireland and India were such different places, and Burke himself stood in such different relation to each, that to subsume both in a single category as sites of oppression may appear procrustean. Yet Burke himself linked them, if only casually.[60] In both cases, he perceived the problem in terms of a strong moral dichotomy between oppressors and oppressed; and in both case he demonized the oppressors. Since Burke habitually saw politics in terms of personalities, his doing so in these cases is hardly surprising. With regard to Ireland, Burke denied that the British connection was the cause of oppression. Instead, he attributed it to the 'jobbing Ascendancy' that had seized control of the Castle administration, and to the unwillingness of the British government to interfere.[61] Indeed, he demanded British intervention as the only way of destroying the Ascendancy. With his usual faith in 'men, not measures', he believed that Fitzwilliam's appointment as Lord Lieutenant was almost all that was needed. Even after Fitzwilliam's recall, he advocated his return, as the most probable means of quieting Irish discontents.[62] For India, likewise, his solution to the depredations of the Hastings regime was to transfer power to those who could be trusted to exercise it responsibly, and for the benefit of Indians.[63] In each case, the effect is to turn attention away from the political system, and from any systemic inequities, presuming that virtuous men will be able to rule justly and equitably. This enables Burke to be highly critical of the men who are, or have been in control, while evading the question of fundamental changes to the Irish constitution itself, or bringing into question the British presence in India.[64]

In the 1790s, Burke became increasingly furious with the Ascendancy for refusing concessions to the Catholics, and therefore (as he thought) driving them into the hands of the Jacobins. No words were too bad for the Castle and its clique. As with the atrocity stories, Burke's language is so violent as to render not entirely implausible the argument that he was affected by 'revolutionary tremors'.[65] Yet careful attention to what Burke actually advocated (discounting the abuse he heaped on his opponents) suggests that his ideas had changed little since the 1760s, when he drafted his 'Tract on the Popery Laws'. For Burke, the primary injustice of the Penal Laws was their exclusion of the Catholics from one of the fundamental 'real rights of men' in society, the acquisition and transmission of property.[66] For Burke, this meant primarily landed property. For him, property was the great grievance. When he advocated the admission of Catholics to the franchise, he did so not as a matter of a right denied, but as necessitated by the circumstances of the times. The Catholics needed to be conciliated. The concession would be symbolic rather than practical, for few Catholics would possess the necessary property qualification. It could therefore be made without endangering security of property, which would certainly be threatened by the universal franchise proposed by the United Irishmen.[67] Conversely, for all his hatred of the Protestant Ascendancy, Burke never contemplated except with horror any suggestion that the lands confiscated in the seventeenth century should be restored to their old owners. When he advocated the creation of 'an aristocratic interest', he meant more what today would be called a 'Catholic middle class', and he expected it to emerge gradually.[68] While he might excoriate the 'new' owners for absurdly drawing attention to the iniquitous origins of their titles, instead of allowing them to remain concealed under a 'politick, well-wrought veil', he never questioned that their titles were now valid, and should not be disturbed.

This was a victory of reason over emotional loyalty, for Burke's maternal relations, the Nagles, had lost much of their land in the seventeenth century. Burke's choice of argument is significant:

> If it were permitted to argue with power, might one not ask these gentlemen, whether it would not be more natural, instead of wantonly mooting those questions concerning their property as if it were an exercise in Law, to found it on the solid rock of prescription; the soundest, the most general, and the most recognized title between man and man that is known in municipal or in publick jurisprudence; a title, in which not arbitrary institutions [such as the Penal Laws], but the eternal order of things gives judgment; a title which is not the creature, but the master of positive Law; a title which, though not fixed in its term, is rooted in its principle, in the law of nature itself, and is indeed the original ground of all known property, for all property in soil will always be traced back to that source, and will rest there.[69]

This passage deserves as much attention as his atrocity stories in determining Burke's ultimate loyalties and values. Much as he disapproved of the confiscations on which the present landownership in Ireland was based, he was anxious to give them a more philosophical foundation than 'positive Law'. To do this, he appeals beyond the mere 'municipal' law to 'prescription', which he identifies as part of the 'the law of nature itself'. Such a claim would be difficult to sustain in strictly historical, legal or jurisprudential terms.[70] Burke, however, was always impatient of legal pedantry. He used 'prescription' in the enlarged moral sense, defined by Dr Johnson, 'Rules produced and authorized by long custom; custom continued till it has the force of law'.[71] Since he was prepared to allow its claims even on behalf of the hated Irish landlords, prescription in this moral sense was clearly of paramount importance to Burke. The appeal to prescription is in effect an appeal for national reconciliation: let the Protestants abandon the iniquitous legality of their titles, and let the Catholics accept that what they have lost cannot now be recovered. This is not a revolutionary speaking.

Prescription was likewise the basis of Burke's opposition to reform of the Irish Parliament. Admittedly, he had vigorously advocated extending the franchise to Catholics. But of this they had been formally deprived as recently as 1728, so that its restoration was not an innovation.[72] But the inequities of the parliamentary representation were as old as 1613, and had therefore acquired prescriptive validity. In any case, based on his English experience, Burke believed that apparent anomalies were often latent virtues. He had himself sat, for example, for Wendover, a 'pocket' borough of the kind that was the first target of reformers. In Britain, many distinguished statesmen (including both Pitts) had sat for such boroughs. Burke believed that the British system provided a 'virtual representation' of the people that was in many respects better than an actual representation. If the Catholics were readmitted to the franchise on a slightly higher property qualification than Protestants, the Irish Parliament would achieve a similar 'virtual representation'.[73]

Burke was not oblivious of the plight of the peasants. Indeed, the passage on prescription continues immediately, and in a more emotive vein, with the tart denial that 'the miserable natives, who ninety-nine in a hundred are tormented with quite other cares, and are bowed down to labour for the bread of the hour' are plotting for the restoration of estates lost 'centuries ago'. Whose side was Burke on? His sympathies were with the oppressed majority. Yet rational conviction told him that existing property rights, whatever their origin, could not now be questioned without undermining the entire fabric of Irish society. Reason triumphed over emotion.[74] Burke never wavered in his commitment to property. So far from succumbing to revolutionary impulses, then, Burke's first concern remained property, because he believed (as he had argued in 1768 at the time of the Nullum Tempus controversy) that all property enjoyed the same basis.[75] To call into question the title to any property, was tantamount to subverting all property (as the revolutionaries had done in France). In the 1790s, Burke saw every question in relation to the fight against Jacobinism, the enemy of everything he loved and valued in human society.[76]

In thus privileging the interests of property, Burke was influenced by his belief that all societies, inevitably, in the nature of things, would always consist of a small elite (the one in a hundred) supported by a vast mass of (mainly agricultural) workers destined to permanent subsistence living, even in Britain, where the social hierarchy was more gradated and the contrasts between rich and poor were less sharp than in Ireland or India. This view is starkly articulated in his *Thoughts and Details on Scarcity*.[77] Subsequent historical experience has shown that Burke was wrong. Though true of all societies he knew, this social divide is not part of 'the nature of things'. Nevertheless, Burke believed that the conditions of the poor could not be substantially ameliorated. The poor could, however, and should, be protected from oppressions of the kind that were endemic in Ireland under the Protestant Ascendancy and in India under the rule of the East India Company. Burke accepted that the rich were, in a sense, 'the pensioners of the poor'.[78] This was built into what he thought 'the nature of things'. With this privileged position came concomitant responsibilities. Burke's ideal legislators and administrators were drawn from the 'natural aristocracy', men whose assured fortunes and moral upbringing put them above temptation.[79] Burke viewed both the 'jobbing ascendancy' in Ireland and the cadre of East India Company officials led by Hastings as examples of administrations that were (in the phrase of Conrad's Marlow) 'merely a squeeze'.

Throughout his career, Burke was critical of the extent to which Irish politics was about patronage. By the 1790s, he was charging that the government of Ireland was indifferent to the threat of Jacobinism, attentive only to the patronage of its friends and cronies.[80] Burke was probably naive in supposing that Fitzwilliam would long have been able to maintain an administration in which appointments were based on personal qualifications rather than jobbery.[81] But his faith testifies to the importance he placed on the moral characters of individuals. By an ominous coincidence, Hastings was acquitted of bribery and oppression at about the same time that Fitzwilliam was recalled from Ireland (as Burke thought) for his attempt to end the system of jobbery. This insane reversal of the moral order prompted Burke to equate the House of Lords and the Cabinet with the arbitrary 'Revolutionary Tribunals' of France.[82] In India, Burke condemned the company's rule in even more dramatic terms than he did the regime of the jobbing Ascendancy, as a constant drain on the country's resources into the pockets of a few arch-villains. What made this worse was that the money, transmitted to Britain, was then used to corrupt politics there.[83]

Burke was certainly concerned with the injustices and oppressions inflicted on the poor under British rule in India. Even in India, however, his primary concern was with the protection of the propertied classes. A crucial difference from Ireland was that the British depredations were recent. Burke could therefore advocate a restoration of the status quo at about the time of British intervention. In Bengal, this would have meant primarily the restoration of the zemindars displaced by Hastings in his revenue reform of 1772, when 'the landed interest of a whole kingdom, of a kingdom to be compared to France, was set up to public auction'.[84] Burke shows no interest in interfering with the internal dynamics of the Indian system. He assumes that to restore the rightful possessors (as he saw the zemindars) will be enough. Burke could take this view because, in the idealized India of his imagination, rich and poor had lived in harmony. An hereditary elite, he believed, being able to take a long view, would exercise its powers and privileges responsibly, with due regard to the rights and interests of the peasants. He discounts the possibility that a native zemindar might be as oppressive as a Company collector. As in the case of Ireland, the rights of property are paramount to a concern for what are today regarded as 'human rights'. The role of the British administration would be protection, analogous to that (ideally) provided by the Mughal Empire before its collapse, and preferably exercised with more benevolent paternalism. How Burke expected this would operate in the longer term is not clear.

For Burke, the morality of empire was the responsible exercise of a trust. The central, superintending authority (in the British case, Parliament) acted as a providential vicegerent, assuring the protection and stability that were necessary preconditions for growth and prosperity. In return, the imperial centre enjoyed economic benefits, to be sure. But for Burke, these were opportunities for fair trade rather than exploitation. Indeed, he particularly denounced the large sums of money that he believed were flowing from India into Britain, where they were used for purposes of political corruption and social dislocation. This trust did not need to be validated by the consent of the governed. In India, there was no tradition of representative institutions, and Burke certainly never contemplated introducing them.

For all their differences in geography, history, politics and religion, Ireland and India presented Burke with comparable moral and rhetorical problems: how to justify the imposition, and the maintenance by force, of alien rule and economic exploitation. In solving these problems, in neither case was Burke entirely free. His room for manoeuvre was limited by his own position as an Irishman in England, by loyalty to his political associates, and by the ideas and prejudices of his day. Conor Cruise O'Brien has argued that, especially with regard to Ireland, these constraints mean that Burke's real opinions have to be inferred from his silences.[85] This view has some force, especially for the period before 1790. Yet after 1790, Burke spoke so often and so openly against both his old associates and his new that his sincerity is less easy to question. He was as ready to disagree with Pitt as with Fox. There seems, then, every reason to believe that, in justifying British rule in Ireland and India, Burke was expressing deeply held personal convictions. The consistency of the ideas and values to which he appeals is further evidence. In each country, he saw a mass of mankind needing protection, guidance and control. For this purpose, a heredi- tary landed elite, respected by the majority and exercising responsibility for (but not responsible to them) was his solution. In Ireland, the gentry class need- ed to be broadened, by the readmission of the Catholics into full membership, and by opening the elite to new Catholic recruits. In Bengal, the structure of landownership had been so damaged as to require a continuing British presence to restore and protect the hierarchy. The masses themselves needed the comfort and support of their traditional religion. In Ireland, therefore, all vestiges of anti-Catholicism needed to be suppressed. In India, Hindu practices and susceptibilities should be treated with respect. With the confidence that came naturally to a disciple of Montesquieu, Burke was sure that he knew best what was good for Ireland and what was best for India.

To acknowledge that Burke accepted the fact of empire is not to depreciate his concern for its victims. But neither should his concern for these victims be used to co-opt him into the anti-imperialist camp. Burke believed that the British Empire, however destructive its effects had been, in Ireland as well as in India, possessed the potential to govern beneficently the peoples it ruled. That such a belief may seem quaint or absurd today is no argument against Burke having held it. Some of his ideas are more alive than others. His *Philosophical Enquiry into the Origin of our Ideas of the Sublime and Beautiful* (1757), for example, after a long neglect, has enjoyed a remarkable revival of interest. But the search for a usable Burke should not be pursued at the expense of distorting his ideas to support such current shibboleths as anti-colonialism.[86] The divide in Burke is not a split between the official 'ideologue of empire' and a fellow feeling with the oppressed and the downtrodden, but a rationally sus- tained distinction between the theory and practice of empire. A firm believer in monarchy, Burke could be highly critical of kings; an ardent supporter of aris- tocracy, he could satirize rogue aristocrats so mordantly as to be accused of Jacobinism. In the same way, his acceptance of the providential nature of empire did not prevent his relentless exposure of the oppressions and corrup- tions incident to British rule in India.

NOTES

1. Thomas Moore, *Memoirs of the Life of the Right Honourable Richard Brinsley Sheridan* (London, 1825), pp.455, 454.
2. Isaac Kramnick, *The Rage of Edmund Burke: Portrait of an Ambivalent Conservative* (New York, Basic Books, 1977).
3. Conor Cruise O'Brien, *The Great Melody: a Thematic Biography and Commented Anthology of Edmund Burke* (Chicago, University of Chicago Press, 1992).
4. Ibid., pp.271–2.
5. Luke Gibbons, *Edmund Burke and Ireland: Aesthetics, Politics, and the Colonial Sublime* (Cambridge: Cambridge University Press, 2003).
6. Conor Cruise O'Brien, *The Suspecting Glance* (London: Faber, 1972). O'Brien took the phrase from an English translation of Nietzsche.
7. O'Brien, *The Great Melody*, pp.xxvi–xxvii, 1, 95, 178, 272.
8. Gibbons, *Edmund Burke and Ireland*, p.15.
9. William O'Brien, *Edmund Burke as an Irishman* (Dublin, 1924), pp.1–22; Conor Cruise O'Brien, *The Great Melody*, pp.15–23; Louis Cullen, 'Burke, Ireland, and Revolution', *Eighteenth-Century Life*, 16 (1992), pp.21–42, especially pp.23–5.
10. Reported in James Prior, *Memoir of the Life and Character of the Right Hon. Edmund Burke* (London, 1826, 2nd edn), vol.i, pp.8–10.
11. O'Brien, *The Great Melody*, pp.20–3.
12. Burke to Patrick Nagle (17 April 1759); to Richard Burke, Jr. (20 March 1792), *Correspondence*, vol.i, pp.125–6; vol.vii, p.106.
13. Burke to Shackleton (1 May 1768), *Correspondence*, vol.i, p.351.
14. Speech on Trade Concessions to Ireland (6 Dec. 1779), *Writings and speeches*, vol.ix, pp.541–2. Accepting John Keogh's compliment that he was a 'true Irishman', Burke added that every 'genuine Englishman' was also a 'true Irishman' (17 Nov. 1786; *Correspondence*, vol.ix, p.113). J.C. Beckett, 'Burke, Ireland, and Empire', in Oliver MacDonagh, W.F. Mandle and Patrick Travers (eds), *Irish Culture and Nationalism, 1750–1850* (London: Macmillan Press, 1983), pp.1–13, is unusual among recent writers in emphasizing Burke's Englishness.
15. Burke to Sir Charles Bingham (30 Oct. 1773); to Thomas Hussey (18 May 1795), *Correspondence*, vol.iii, pp.474–81; vol.viii, pp.246–7). Burke made another strong statement of British imperial supremacy in an unfinished semi-public letter of 1797 (*Writings and speeches*, vol.ix, pp.675–6).
16. A notable expression of this idea is the 'little platoon' image in *Reflections on the Revolution in France*, edited by J.C.D. Clark (Stanford: Stanford University Press, 2001), [pp.68–9]. Citations in square brackets refer to the pagination of the first edition, inserted by Clark in his text.
17. The cost of this was shared by his cousin William Burke. William L. Pressly, *The Life and Work of James Barry* (New Haven, Yale University Press, 1981), pp.6–16.
18. The rational and evidential basis of Burke's involvement with India is eloquently expressed in his letter to Mary Palmer of 19 Jan. 1786 (*Correspondence*, vol.v, pp.252–7).
19. *Thoughts on the Cause of the Present Discontents* (1770), in *Writings and speeches*, vol.ii, p.256.
20. *Thoughts and Details on Scarcity* (written in 1795, posthumously published in 1800), in *Writings and speeches*, vol.ix, p.129.
21. Reviews of 'Southey's Colloquies' (1830), in F.C. Montague (ed.), *Critical and Historical Essays Contributed to the 'Edinburgh Review'* (London, Methuen, 1903), vol.i, p.206.
22. Francis P. Canavan, *The Political Reason of Edmund Burke* (Durham, N.C., Duke University Press, 1960).
23. *Letter to Sir Hercules Langrishe* (1792), in *Writings and speeches*, vol.ix, p.621.
24. Daniel Ritchie, *Reconstructing Literature in an Ideological Age: a Biblical Poetics and Literary Studies from Milton to Burke* (Grand Rapids, Eerdmans, 1996), p.182.
25. F.P. Lock, *Edmund Burke: Volume I, 1730–1784* (Oxford: Clarendon Press, 1998), pp.488–9.
26. Canavan, *Political Reason*, p.26.
27. In his Speech on the Unitarian Petition (11 May 1792), Burke excepts the Quakers from his criticism of Protestant sects on the grounds that 'it is strict, methodical, in its nature highly aristocratic, and so regular that it has brought the whole community to the condition of one family'; Burke's *Works* (London: Bohn's British Classics, 1854–89), vol.vi, p.125.
28. Burke's rejection of the instrumental value of religion is expressed in an early essay, 'Religion of No Efficacy Considered as a State Engine', in *A Note-Book of Edmund Burke*, edited by H.V.F. Somerset (Cambridge, Cambridge University Press, 1957), pp.67–9. The same point is made in Clark (ed.), *Reflections on the Revolution in France*, [pp.150–1].
29. Speech on the Unitarian Petition, in *Works*, vol.vi, pp.114–16.
30. The charge was common in Burke's lifetime; witness the numerous caricatures in which he is portrayed

as a monk or a Jesuit. No modern scholar has actually identified Burke as a Catholic, though Conor Cruise O'Brien comes close, for example in repeating the anecdote about Burke's receiving Catholic last rites on his deathbed (*The Great Melody*, pp.590–1).

31. Burke to William Smith (29 Jan. 1795), *Correspondence*, viii. 130–2.

32. 'Letter to Richard Burke' (1792, unfinished), in *Writings and speeches*, vol.ix, pp.644–5.

33. W.J. McCormack, *From Burke to Beckett: Ascendancy, Tradition and Betrayal in Literary History* (1985; revised edn, Cork: Cork University Press, 1994), pp.58–78.

34. William Burke to William Dennis, 3, 6 April 1770 (reporting what Edmund said in the Commons on 2 April); *Correspondence*, vol.ii, p.128. *A Letter to a Noble Lord* (1796), in *Writings and Speeches*, vol.ix, p.159.

35. From *Observations on a Late State of the Nation* (1769) to the *Letters on a Regicide Peace* (1796–97). The density of statistical material in the *Third Letter*, however, which was completed after Burke's death by his executors, may not represent his intentions.

36. The two most important of Burke's Select Committee reports, the Ninth and the Eleventh, were print- ed with massive documentary appendices (394 and 253 double-column, folio pages respectively); *Reports from Committees of the House of Commons, 1715–1801* (London, 1803), vol.vi, pp.91–489, 593–854. The 98-page text of the *Speech on the Nabob of Arcot's Debts* (1785) is supported by a 93- page appendix.

37. Clark (ed.), *Reflections on the Revolution in France*, Introduction, pp.43–53.

38. Written about 1762–63; posthumously published in 1812 as 'Fragment of a Tract on the Popery Laws (*Writings and speeches*, vol.ix, pp.435–82). Parts of the 'Tract' circulated in manuscript in Burke's life- time.

39. Burke to Thomas Hussey (9 June 1795); to Edward Hay (26 June), *Correspondence*, vol.viii, pp.264, 272.

40. Aristotle, *Rhetoric*, 1.2.1 (1355b), my translation.

41. Uday Singh Mehta, *Liberalism and Empire: a Study in Nineteenth-Century British Liberal Thought* (Chicago, Chicago University Press, 1999), p.156.

42. Gibbons, *Edmund Burke and Ireland*, pp.113–16.

43. Mehta, *Liberalism and Empire*, pp.157–8. Gibbons likewise argues that his 'unapproved roads' provide a better guide to Burke than the 'main thoroughfares in his thought' (Gibbons, *Edmund Burke and Ireland*, p.15).

44. Gibbons, *Edmund Burke and Ireland*, pp.114, 185–9.

45. *Writings and speeches*, vol.v, p.386.

46. Lock, *Edmund Burke*, vol.i, pp.136–8.

47. In Burke's four-day opening speech at the trial of Warren Hastings, for example, the notorious Rangpur atrocity stories, told on the third day (18 Feb. 1788) probably occupied no more than twenty or twenty- five minutes in a speech that lasted over eleven hours.

48. 'History of England' (begun 1757, unfinished), in *Writings and speeches*, vol.i, p.399.

49. In his 'History of England', for example, Burke praises both Cnut and William the Conqueror (*Writings and speeches*, vol.i, pp.419, 476–7).

50. Mehta, *Liberalism and Empire*, p.155.

51. Debate on the Army Estimates (14 Dec. 1778), in *Writings and speeches*, vol.iii, p.394. As late as January 1777, Burke had hoped that his conciliation proposals of 1775 (which retained the Declaratory Act of 1766, the symbol of imperial supremacy) would provide a basis for peace (*Correspondence*, vol.iii, p.310). Only on 6 April 1778 did he reluctantly agree not to oppose the repeal of the Declaratory Act (*Writings and speeches*, vol.iii, p.313).

52. Burke to Fitzwilliam (20 Nov. 1796), *Correspondence*, vol.ix, p.122.

53. *Speech on Fox's India Bill*, in *Writings and speeches*, vol.v, p.403–4. Years of fighting against the abus- es of the Hastings regime did not diminish Burke's faith in 'the dominion of the glorious Empire given by an incomprehensible dispensation of the Divine Providence into our hands'. Letter to French Laurence (18 July 1796), *Correspondence*, vol.ix, p.62.

54. Gibbons, *Edmund Burke and Ireland*, pp.88, 113.

55. *Two Letters on the Prospect of a Regicide Peace* (1796), in *Writings and speeches*, vol.ix, pp.250–1, 237, 240, 249. Jennifer M. Welsh, *Edmund Burke and International Relations: the Commonwealth of Europe and the Crusade against the French Revolution* (New York: St Martin's Press, 1995).

56. Francis P. Canavan, *Edmund Burke: Prescription and Providence* (Durham, N.C., Carolina Academic Press, 1987), p.87.

57. In 'Burke and India: the Failure of the Theory of Trusteeship', *Political Research Quarterly*, 46 (1993), pp.291–309, James Conniff argues that Burke's theory is undermined by his unwillingness to accept 'the ultimate enforcement of that trust by some expression of popular will' as its 'logical corollary' (pp.306–7). For Burke, however, the 'popular will' was always subordinate to a higher moral law.

58. Clark (ed.), *Reflections on the Revolution in France*, [p.138] (trust), [pp.44–5] (prescription).

59. *Speech on Conciliation* (22 March 1775), in *Writings and speeches*, vol.iii, p.118.
60. *Letter to Sir Hercules Langrishe* (1792), in *Writings and speeches*, vol.ix, pp.635, 640.
61. Burke to Richard Burke, Jr. (2 Nov. 1792); to Thomas Hussey (18 May 1795), *Correspondence*, vol.vii, p.283; vol.viii, p.246.
62. Burke to the Duke of Devonshire (11 March 1795), *Correspondence*, vol.viii, p.184.
63. Holden Furber observes that, 'It sometimes seems as if he would have been satisfied with the transference of British power into hands which to him were virtuous' (Introduction to *Correspondence*, vol.v, p.xvi).
64. Burke 'flinched from the possibility that the colonial relation was of itself incompatible with any set of principles that could be said to be in accord with universal justice'; Seamus Deane, 'Factions and Fictions: Burke, Colonialism, and Revolution', *Bullán: an Irish Studies Review*, 4, 2 (2000), pp.5–26 (quotation from p.12).
65. A sample, mostly variations on the 'jobbing ascendancy' theme: Burke to Richard Burke, Jr. (*c.* 8 March, 20 March, 18 Nov., *post* 21 Nov. 1792); to William Windham (16 Oct. 1794); to Earl Fitzwilliam (7 May 1797); to French Laurence (5 June 1797), *Correspondence*, vol.vii, pp.94, 101, 290, 301; vol.viii, p.40; vol.ix, pp.330, 368). Gibbons, *Edmund Burke and Ireland*, pp.163–4.
66. Burke explains his idea of 'the real rights of men' in Clark (ed.), *Reflections on the Revolution in France*, [p.86].
67. Burke to Richard Burke, Jr. (26 Jan. 1792, 16 Dec. 1791), *Correspondence*, vol.vii, p.40, vol.vi, p.464).
68. *Letter to Sir Hercules Langrishe*, in *Writings and speeches*, vol.ix, p.597. The Catholic Committee's proposal would have allowed Catholic forty-shilling freeholders who also possessed, or bona-fide rented, land worth a further £20 a year to vote in county elections. Richard Burke, Jr. to Henry Dundas (*post* 16 Dec. 1791), *Correspondence*, vol.vi, p.467. Burke himself thought this 'far into the Aristocratick mode of Election', and suggested a simple qualification of £5 a year (*Correspondence*, vol.vi, p.464). This shows that what Burke meant by an 'aristocratic interest' was broader than the phrase is likely to suggest today.
69. 'Letter to Richard Burke', in *Writings and speeches*, vol.ix, p.657.
70 Paul Lucas, 'On Edmund Burke's Doctrine of Prescription; or, an Appeal from the New to the Old Lawyers', *Historical Journal*, 11 (1968), pp.35–63.
71. *Dictionary of the English Language* (London, 1755), s.v. 'prescription'.
72. Burke brands the disfranchisement 'the yoke of late prostitute Acts of an innovating Parliament, made within the Memory of some yet living'; to Richard Burke, Jr. (*post* 21 Nov. 1792), *Correspondence*, vol.vii, p.301. The significance of 'within the Memory of some yet living' is to deny them prescriptive force. An old legal maxim defined custom as usage so long 'that the memory of man runneth not to the contrary'; William Blackstone, *Commentaries on the Laws of England* (London, 1765–9), vol.i, p.76. The sixty-year rule prescribed by (for example) the Statute of Limitations of 1540, and more recently by the Nullum Tempus Act of 1768 (to which Burke refers), defined the term more exactly. By this principle, the boroughs created in 1613, and the seventeenth-century confiscations, had now acquired the protection of prescription.
73. *Letter to Sir Hercules Langrishe*, in *Writings and speeches*, vol.ix, p.629.
74. Conor Cruise O'Brien makes the same point in relation to Burke's refusal to break with Pitt, even after his betrayal (in Burke's opinion) of Fitzwilliam: 'one of the most remarkable examples in history of a great capacity for reason, managing to keep a torrent of emotions under control' (O'Brien, *The Great Melody*, p.516).
75. 'Memnon' to the *Public Advertiser*, 22 Feb. 1768, and draft for an unpublished letter, in *Writings and speeches*, vol.ii, pp.78, 85.
76. Burke to Lord Loughborough (19 Oct. 1794); to William Smith (29 Jan. 1795), *Correspondence*, vol.viii, pp.44, 129.
77. *Writings and speeches*, vol.ix, pp.121, 128–9. The same assumption is behind a passage in Clark (ed.), *Reflections on the Revolution in France*, [p.351].
78. *Thoughts and Details on Scarcity*, in *Writings and speeches*, vol.ix, p.121.
79. Clark (ed.), *Reflections on the Revolution in France*, [pp.74–6].
80. Burke to Fitzwilliam (20 Nov., *post* 9 Dec. 1796), *Correspondence*, vol.ix, pp.121, 158.
81. Burke to Fitzwilliam (*c.* 22 Nov. 1794), *Correspondence*, vol.viii, p.79.
82. Burke to Henry Grattan (20 March 1795), *Correspondence*, vol.viii, p.206.
83. *Speech on Fox's India Bill*, in *Writings and speeches*, vol.v, p.402.
84. Ibid., p.426.
85. O'Brien, *The Great Melody*, p.xxvi.
86. Thus Luke Gibbons argues that, the 'shelf life of many of his key political ideas' having passed, Burke can be recuperated through 'some of his more critical stances on the Enlightenment, colonialism and indigenous cultures'. Gibbons, *Edmund Burke and Ireland*, p.15

11

Burke, Ireland and the Counter-revolution, 1791–1801

TADGH O'SULLIVAN

Recent years have witnessed a flourishing of scholarship devoted to the defini-tion and exploration of British loyalism and the counter-revolution that followed in the wake of events in France. While Mark Philp has traced the emergence of a visceral lower class 'vulgar conservatism' not necessarily subject to control from above, Jennifer Mori has reconstructed a state-sponsored patriotism which incorporated 'the multiple identities and inclinations of Britons into acceptance of and active participation in the wars against revolutionary and Napoleonic France'.[1] Particularly prominent in the development of a unified anti-revolution-ary front during the 1790s were voluntary associations of loyal subjects, a common religious identification with High Church Anglicanism, the vigorous dissemination of conservative propaganda, and a sophisticated range of rhetori-cal and intellectual languages.[2] By way of contrast, Irish historiography has been slow to devote comparable attention to the issue of loyalism in Ireland during the 1790s, despite the wealth of recent scholarship dealing with the late eighteenth-century.[3] As Jim Smyth has acknowledged, the Irish historiographical 'master theme' of the 1790s has been the development of 'mass politicisation' and the extent to which this process superseded and transformed traditional modes of dissent.[4] In a provocative recent discussion, Tom Bartlett has suggested that the history of 1798 remains to be written, a remark bound to attract a certain amount of incredulity given the sheer weight of publication and commentary that accom-panied the bicentenary of the Rebellion.[5] Furthermore, Bartlett has correctly underlined the fact that we lack sufficient insight into the nature of counter-revolutionary Ireland, another reminder that the recent historiography has not been without its significant lacunae.

In an influential interpretation of conservative forces during the 1790s, Kevin Whelan has identified the sectarian state, as exemplified by the Ascendancy lead-ership of John Foster, Patrick Duigenan and John Fitzgibbon, as forming the prin-ciple counter-revolutionary bulwark against the secularizing challenge of the United Irishmen.[6] This reading, while capturing the defensive and confessional nature of the state, occludes a full examination of the range of alternative count-er-revolutionary positions that emerged during the period. It is in this context that I argue that – in the broadest sense – many of these alternatives are implicitly

'Burkean', in that they attempt to defend legal, social and political proprieties against the Jacobin challenge, while also displaying a reluctance to identify with the Irish Anglican *ancien régime*. While the general discussion pursued here will not describe any episode in particular detail, it will suggest a reading of the print culture of the period which underlines the varied character of Irish anti-radicalism during the 1790s. In turn, it also argues that Catholic and liberal anti-radical stances had a greater claim on Burkean authority than that available to Ascendancy loyalism.

If the work of R.B. McDowell, Louis Cullen and Eamonn O'Flaherty has underlined Burke's complex relationship to Ireland, particularly in relation to his well established position on Catholic inclusion in the Irish state, the publication of an Irish edition of his *Reflections on the Revolution in France* was to provide plenty of intellectual succour for conservative opinion, much of it ultra-Protestant.[7] Burke's *Reflections* went through eight reprintings in Dublin during 1791–93, and was also published in extracts in *The Hibernian Magazine* in the last two months of 1790, in addition to featuring in contemporary newspapers. His role as counter-revolutionary sage was underlined by the award in December 1790 of an honorary doctorate in law from the University of Dublin. However, as was the case in England, Burke inspired Whig retorts in Ireland, examples including Benjamin Bousfield's *Observations on the Right Hon. Edmund Burke's Pamphlet on the Subject of the French Revolution* and the anonymous *An Answer to the Right Hon. Edmund Burke's Reflections on the Revolution in France*.[8] Both texts are symptomatic of a Foxite Whig reaction to Burke's text, particularly in their attempt to refute his defence of hereditary right. Thomas Goold's *Vindication of the Right Honourable Edmund Burke's Reflections on the Revolution in France* on the other hand, was one Irish text that came out in explicit support of Burke. A family friend of the Burkes, Goold had, unlike most commentators, direct experience of early revolutionary France, as he had fled there to escape his creditors after squandering his landed estate. Goold's text focused on the prospect of the property-less acquiring political dominance, and in the aftermath of the abolition of feudalism and privileges in August 1789, he wrote that France 'offered the only instance I know of, where men assuming to themselves the sacred names of legislators, have reduced robbery to a system'.[9] Not explicitly dealing with Burke, but offering similar arguments relating to property and maintaining the principle of inequality, Sir Lawrence Parsons' *Thoughts on Liberty and Inequality*, defended 'natural diversity' against a 'sameness, a uniformity, a monotonous equality in situation, rank, wealth, possessions, powers, rights, [which] was never destined for us'.[10]

These examples included, the comprehensive and sustained discussions of *Reflections on the Revolution in France* that took place in England are missing from Ireland. There are a number of points to be made here. Firstly, Burke himself was reticent to push the distribution of the *Reflections* in Irish elite circles: as he wrote to Earl Charlemont, the leading Irish Whig and leader of the

Volunteers, he had neglected to send the work on to an obvious circle of influential Irish readers, including Charlemont himself.[11] Secondly, Burke's involvement in Catholic Committee politics through his son Richard's tenure as Secretary to the Committee, along with his strident advocacy of Catholic entitlement in his *Letter to Sir Hercules Langrishe* (1792), made it difficult for conservative Ascendancy opinion to deploy explicitly Burkean arguments in the propaganda wars of the 1790s.

In light of this, W.J. McCormack has stated that the 'battle to control public opinion shifted away from Burkean themes' for the remainder of the 1790s.[12] However, this underplays the crucial issue of the re-emergence of the Catholic question in an aggressive and innovatory manner. The formation of a 'Catholic Society' by Thomas Broughall, Theobald McKenna, a Scottish-educated medical doctor and member of the Royal Irish Academy, and some forty others, led to the publication of a *Declaration* which argued the case for Catholic admission to the electoral franchise as an act of political necessity.[13] To add to the growing sense of conservative dismay in Dublin, two weeks after the setting up of the Catholic Society, the Dublin Society of United Irishmen was formed, composed largely of the same body of men.

McKenna's *Declaration* deserves detailed discussion for a number of reasons. As Ian McBride has observed, 'The process by which Catholics learned to couch their demands in the terms of English Whiggery remains a mystery, but it was the necessary precondition for their participation in Irish radicalism in the 1790s'.[14] Bearing this in mind, McKenna offers the most forceful statement of Catholic grievances yet to appear in Ireland during the late-eighteenth century, and an understanding of reactions to the *Declaration* must be based on a recognition of how he had transformed the tradition of deferential applications for enfranchisement. Reflecting the influences of a generally 'enlightened' intellectual atmosphere, McKenna firmly disabused those who imagined that the traditional Catholic acquiescence had survived: 'In the present enlightened and improving period of Society, it is not for the IRISH ROMAN CATHOLICS alone to continue silent. Not accused of any crime; not conscious of any delinquency; they suffer a privation of rights and conveniences, the penalty reserved, in wise states, for offences of atrocious magnitude.'[15]

The key demand of McKenna's polemic was that the property amassed by a Catholic mercantile and commercial class be recognized as an entitlement to full political participation, any alternative interpretation leading to the conclusion that Roman Catholic property served only as revenue for the confessional state. A further remarkable feature of the *Declaration* is the manner in which it dealt with the post-Williamite property settlement, the safeguarding of which was obviously a central element of Ascendancy ideology. McKenna outlined the security of confiscated property as an essential aspect of the political *status quo*, and one which would not be overturned in the event of Catholic relief. The *Declaration* served as another reminder that the advancement of the Catholic middle class in the commercial sphere had resulted in a displacement of the aristocratic/clerical axis, which had previously controlled Catholic applications for political advancement.

However, the Catholic Society was to prove an ephemeral organization among the politics of the early 1790s. Soon after the passage of the Catholic Relief Act of 1793 it faded away, and Theobald McKenna was to take a decidedly reactionary turn, as evidenced by *An Address to the Roman Catholics of Ireland* (1792). The *Address* begins with a sustained refutation of the influence of 'French politics' on Irish Catholic appeals for political enfranchisement, which entails chastening remarks on both the United Irish and Presbyterian appeals for political radicalism. As McKenna stated, 'The whole tribe of pseudo philanthropists so common in Ireland, who, wrapt in the admiration of French or American liberty cannot spare a compassionate thought for their elevated brethren'.[16] Henceforth he became the most eloquent proponent of Catholic loyalty, a call for obedience to the state in the face of the Jacobin threat, which was combined with insistent calls for Catholic emancipation.

His reading of events in France is a clearly conservative one. Whatever the outcome of the revolutionary upheaval – and the assumption is that the political and constitutional 'innovation' will cease, and the despotic challenge from France will crumble. However, '*Despotism is subverted*' and 'even if the royalists succeed, there is a revolution in public opinion, which will prevent the possibility of restoring the former detestable domination'.[17] This reading of continental developments, and their implications for the Irish relationship to the British state, continued in his *An Essay on Parliamentary Reform* (1793).[18] The text appeared at a time when the Catholic Committee, having failed in its attempt to secure complete political enfranchisement, was about to disband. Furthermore the United Irishmen were reaching the end of their constitutionalist phase, and were to begin the transition into an underground secret society and eventual alliance with Defenderism. The *Essay's* declared intention was to refute 'the calumnies against the British Constitution, idolizing, as I have ever done, the fortunate institution, and censuring every measure, which inclines to alter it'.[19] McKenna continued by arguing that the Glorious Revolution was 'conformable to the universal wish, and produced of course (so far as related to that kingdom) little undeserved inconvenience'.[20]

The impression of gradual religious toleration, which many contemporary commentators had impressionistically traced from the dissemination of enlightened ideals, was shown by the reaction to Catholic Committee and Catholic Society agitation to be illusory. As mentioned earlier, 1791 was the starting point for a number of processes that can be discussed under the heading of a more general counter-revolutionary and loyalist ideology, a process only cemented by the drift towards war in 1792 and the execution of Louis XVI in 1793. The reinforcement of ultra-loyalist opinion was particularly evident in parliamentary debate on the Catholic Relief Bills. Likewise, parliamentary conservative opinion reverted to the constitutional conservatism offered by Patrick Duigenan's *An Address to the Nobility and Gentry of the Church of*

Ireland (1786) and the paper war that followed the Rightboy campaign of the mid-1780s.[21] A formative moment at the outset of this debate was the reiteration of Ascendancy offered by Dublin Corporation in September 1792, in turn a reaction to the decision to hold a representative Catholic Convention. While reaffirming the recent concessions offered to Catholics that enshrined their right to 'personal liberty', the Corporation's *Letter to the Protestants of Ireland* lamented the Catholic's decision to 'proceed upon the plan of the French democracy to elect a representation of their own'.[22] The Catholic 'Back Lane Parliament' with its uncomfortable echoes of a Catholic National Assembly within the heart of Dublin offered a dangerous precedent. Elsewhere, Grand Juries began drawing up objections to the renewed Catholic campaign and Protestant Volunteering corps in the north were revived.

In the aftermath of the fiasco of the Fitzwilliam viceroyalty and his recall in 1795, we can see the emergence of a fear of invasion in numerous commentators, inspiring in turn quite a range of responses. A particularly early commentary is the anonymous military guidebook, *On the Defense of Ireland* (1795). The author, keen to establish his counter-revolutionary credentials, outlined that 'In this slight sketch there is, at any rate, no wanderings of imagination, no abstract theories, no inapplicable speculations, none of those theoretical reveries, specious in the closet, but impracticable in the application'.[23] The text offers a detailed topographical and military survey of Ireland, going so far as to propose the raising of a yeomanry drawn from the peasantry, for which three illustrations are offered, displaying relevant arms, probable appearance, et cetera. Given the obviously widely disaffected state of the countryside, along with the doubtful loyalty of the Catholic rural poor, *On the Defense of Ireland* somewhat circumspectly offered the hope that the Irish peasantry could perform the same counter-revolutionary function as the *chouans* of western France.[24] Disregarding the fear of those who 'suspect every grey-coated fellow as a Defender', Sir Henry Sheehy proposed a liberal solution of Roman Catholic enfranchisement as a measure to cement an Irish version of the English yeomanry.[25]

In the aftermath of the failed French invasion attempt outside of Bantry Bay in December 1796, the initial dispersal of the fleet was acclaimed as a providential escape, a deliverance celebrated in numerous printed sermons and letters. However, invasion and the prospect of invasion fundamentally questioned all social, political and religious allegiances in as direct a manner as possible. As Fitzgibbon, Earl of Clare remarked, those who celebrated the fact that the peasantry in the fields surrounding Bantry town displayed no signs of anticipation at the sight of the invasion fleet missed the point: it was their reaction when the first French foot fell on Irish soil was what mattered. Implicit in his cynical, knowing comments was the reality that Irish counter-revolutionary opinion was not monolithic, and in contrast to much of its continental counterpart, did not enjoy a confessional cohesiveness and leadership due to the particularities of Irish religious identities.

This part of our discussion is bookended by two invasion scares: the very immediate threat of 1796, and the prospect of Napoleonic invasion after the breakdown of the peace of Amiens in 1803. In between these years the political structures of the Irish kingdom were to see drastic change. In the aftermath of the sustained campaign of 'White Terror' in 1796–98, and the outbreak of rebellion in the summer of 1798, the reality of a militarily vulnerable dependant neighbour under the direction of a self-serving and unreliable Irish Anglican oligarchy proved too much for a British state in the midst of a major war. The forced political and administrative amalgamation of the Irish Act of Union which was eventually voted into being at the second attempt in 1800, in effect fundamentally undermined Ascendancy leadership of Ireland, a fact perhaps not appreciated at the time given George III's refusal to countenance Catholic Emancipation, an essential feature of the new political dispensation as far as Pitt had envisaged. Thus the Burkean dream of Irish incorporation into the ways of English liberty and the resultant dissolving of Irish confessional differences failed to materialize.

That said, a particular feature of more liberal counter-revolutionary writings was the articulation of a rather idealized conception of the foundation and premise of Irish civil society. This was partly a necessity in the light of the challenge of United Irish radicalism, and its increasingly visceral call to arms and attempt to mobilize popular opinion on the basis of both historical and contemporary grievances. In discussing the intellectual achievement of bourgeois Irish radicalism during the late eighteenth-century, James Livesey has posed the question whether or not 'the Irish experience of revolution [was] uninformed by the transforming effects of the creation of new ideologies of politics? Should it be understood as the eruption of violence into a vacuum unpopulated by civil society or public sphere?'[26] Livesey answers his rhetorical question by citing the example of the United Irishman Arthur O'Connor's *State of Ireland* (1798), a text heavily influenced by the writings of Adam Smith and Condorcet, yet this is the only sustained example we have of an United Irish engagement with the new political economy.[27] However, the question usefully underlines some of the most significant lacunae in recent scholarship on the 1790s. To what extent can we speak of an established Irish 'civil society', in the sense that such a construct was understood and discussed by Irish contemporaries in public discourse, particularly if we take the term as meaning the relations of men, and their political and economic implications in a modern commercial society? The extent to which the United Irish project created a sustainable language of social and political protest, is difficult to maintain in light of the realities of the post-Rebellion, post-Union period.

In the light of this apparent failure, we should consider some conservative and anti-revolutionary attempts to deal with Irish socio-economic problems, which many commentators saw as motivating Catholic peasant restiveness. One testament to the effect that the prolonged and apparently irrepressible Defender campaign was having is demonstrated by the Rev. Michael Sandys' *Letter to Henry Grattan on the State of the Labouring Poor* (1796).[28] In common with other relatively liberal interpretations of the source of poverty, Sandy's solution revolved around a benevolent paternalism which included an implicit criticism of absenteeism. Such implicit criticisms were made a lot more explicit in *An Address to the Thinking Part of the Community* (1797) which argued that 'If the gentlemen of property in the country [did] not abandon their own strong position, and that conduct which mist ever insure to them respect and influence, it is not to be imagined that they [could] want power to repress the disorders of the lower classes'.[29] In Pratt Winter's *Reflections on the Best Means of Securing Tranquillity* (1796), he remarked that the combined effect of Defenderism and the repression of the lower orders had led to the complete retardation of 'the progress of industry and improvement', while the manner in which 'the most daring acts of violence were unceasingly renewed was equally surprising and alarming'.[30] Winter's remedy is a finely balanced mixture of security measures and social improvement, a combination that Whitley Stokes also advocated. Stokes, a fellow of Trinity College, might be a controversial inclusion in a discussion about the Irish counter-revolution during the 1790s. A United Irishman and outspoken radical for most of the 1790s, Stokes was thanked by the University of Dublin for his answer to Thomas Paine's deistical *Age of Reason*. By 1799 he had published *Projects for Re-establishing the Internal Tranquillity of the Country*, an extended pamphlet dealing with the necessity of different programmes of social improvement as a solution to Irish, particularly lower-class, disaffection, an example of the sometimes fluid categories of radical and conservative, particularly when it came to dealing with the difficult issue of the Catholic peasantry.[31]

It is the Act of Union that demands the tensions inherent in counter-revolutionary Irish opinion in the immediate post-rebellion period. Having just successfully defeated all the significant radical threats in open battle during the summer, Ascendancy, and ultra-Protestant opinion soon found itself faced with the very unwelcome prospect of fighting London's move to impose legislative and political union in the autumn of 1798. By January 1799 the first attempt to pass the measure had been effectively defeated in the Irish House of Commons, and was followed by an extensive paper war in which over 200 pamphlets, many in vast quantities, were published. Opposition included the mainstays of Anglican Ireland, including loyalist aldermen, bankers, merchants and Dublin Corporation, all under the political leadership of John Foster, the speaker of the Irish House of Commons. What should be emphasized here are the strains evident in Irish counter-revolutionary opinion, one example of which is provided by the Revd Dr Clarke's interventions during the Union debates. In *The Political, Commercial and Civil State of Ireland* (1799), he argued that Ireland's persistent civil strife had managed to stagnate the nation in an earlier state of economic and societal development. It proved a telling – if implicit – critique of Ascendancy leadership of Ireland, as well as the current state of Irish manners and commercial development. As he writes,

We do not say however that the people of Ireland were oppressed by the Government. We protest against the assertion. The barbarous spirit of feudal times looked *down* upon the cottage, and looked *above* the throne; therefore the government was governed, and the subjects were vassals. But as commerce enriched, and knowledge enlightened mankind, the lordly yoke of feudal tyranny has been broken throughout Europe, kings freed from slavery, and people from oppression. Thus, through *commerce*, will the barbarous spirit of feudal power finally depart from Ireland, and the old and corrupt body of civil defects find a sepulchre in the Union.[32]

Feudal power in this context means the dead hand of Ascendancy leadership. Economic improvement will follow Union, which in turn will cast aside deficiencies in Irish civil society.

In a different arena, the recent history of the Rebellion and its origins was also proving a highly contentious issue, particularly evident with the publication of Sir Richard Musgrave's vast and ultra-sectarian *Memoirs of the Various Rebellions in Ireland*, first published in Dublin in 1801. Musgrave, a member of the minor Protestant gentry from the lower Blackwater valley in west Waterford, was also the author of a number of loyalist commentaries during the 1790s, and the *Memoirs* are largely a compendium of evidence collected to prove the existence of a conscious conspiracy, informed from an early date by Catholic revanchism which in turn takes its place in a long chain of such Catholic behaviour dating from the Ulster rebellion of 1641.[33] Two issues deserve emphasis here: Musgrave's *Memoirs* are testament to the difficult reception of Burke, the intellectual leader of the Anglophone counter-revolution, in an Irish context. Burke, given his very public contribution to campaigns for Catholic enfranchisement, appears here as playing a shadowy part in a priestly cabal, fomenting Catholic resentfulness and thus implicated in rebellion.[34] In addition to this the first issue of the *Memoirs* included a dedication to the Lord Lieutenant, London's leading figure of authority in Ireland, for which permission had to be sought. Permission for the dedication was swiftly withdrawn once the potential divisiveness of Musgrave's text was fully appreciated. There is a certain irony here, given the fact that Burke, prophet of the counter-revolution, should be identified as the Jesuitical conspiratorial influence behind the outbreak of Irish rebellion.

Post-rebellion attempts to comprehend the Catholic populace – and in particular the peasantry which had participated so readily in the challenge to the Anglican state – made up a large part of post-union Irish surveys. Henceforth the emphasis on Irish manners or *moeurs* was clearly on show, particularly in volumes such as the Dublin Society's series of *Statistical Surveys* that sought to delineate the main features of each individual Irish county.[35] This is part of the longstanding tradition of 'improving' literature, which typically stressed civil accord and a social and confessional cohesiveness that was not easily assumed in late eighteenth-century Ireland. In the light of the more heightened sectarian atmosphere of the Second Reformation, the literature of improvement sought to promote economical efficiencies, primarily in agriculture, and shares much in common with the Burke of *Thoughts and Details on Scarcity*.[36] However, James Livesey has also argued that both radicals and conservatives shared a common vocabulary of 'the common good' and could 'express their own interests in terms of general utility'. Developing the argument that 'Smithean political economy was the backbone of this language', he goes on to question the use of such languages outside the central metropolitan countries, France and Britain. Crucially, for the Irish context, he asks, 'Could the language of political democracy and that of modern commercial relationships remain linked in a radical discourse [...], especially one in which the fundamental premises of inclusion of the community, let alone of political representation, were far from settled?'[37] The answer apparently is a negative one, or at the very least a heavily qualified one, and offers at least one explanation for the paucity of Irish 'Jacobin' political and economic theorizing. However, we should alter the terms of Livesey's question slightly: much of Irish conservative thinking during this period did attempt to come to terms with precisely this issue – the formation of a cohesive polity based on the manners and political organization of a modern commercial society, albeit one which existed under London's direct political control. While straightforwardly anti-Catholic and narrowly Ascendancy opinion is one aspect of conservative thinking, it should not be assumed that it marked the exact parameters of Irish counter-revolutionary thought during this period. It was this particular Irish context which allowed Theobald McKenna to sign off a counter-blast to Patrick Duigenan in 1800 by proclaiming himself a 'Catholic and Burkist'.[38] Taken in its broadest context, this Burkean pose allowed an entire sector of Irish anti-radical opinion to maintain a distance from the oligarchical rule of the Anglican state, while simultaneously letting it free to reject the Jacobin threat. The complexity of Irish reactions to Burke during the 1790s is a direct reflection of the dissonances evident in Irish counter-revolutionary opinion at the end of the eighteenth-century.

NOTES

1. See M. Philp, 'Vulgar Conservatism, 1792–3', *English Historical Review*, 110 (1995), pp.42–69, J. Mori, 'Languages of Loyalism: Patriotism, Nationhood and the State in the 1790s', *English Historical Review*, 118 (2003), pp.33–58 (p.58).
2. For a discussion of the intellectual resources which loyalist thought drew on during the 1790s, see T. P. Schofield, 'Conservative Political Thought in Britain in Response to the French Revolution', *Historical Journal*, 29, 3 (1986), pp.601–22.
3. Of the eight sections in the monumental volume bringing together the Dublin and Belfast 1998 commemorative conferences, only one (section 4) deals explicitly with Irish loyalism. See T. Bartlett, D. Dickson, D. Keogh, and K. Whelan (eds), *1798: A Bicentenary Perspective* (Dublin: Four Courts Press, 2003), pp.299–377.
4. J. Smyth, (ed.), *Revolution, Counter Revolution and Union: Ireland in the 1790s* (Cambridge: Cambridge University Press, 2000), p.6.
5. T. Bartlett, 'Why the History of the 1798 Rebellion has yet to be written', *Eighteenth-Century Ireland*, 15 (2000), pp.181–90.
6. See K. Whelan 'United and Disunited Irishmen: the State and Sectarianism in the 1790s', in *The*

Tree of Liberty: Radicalism, Catholicism and the Construction of Irish Identity, 1760–1830 (Cork: Cork University Press, 1996), pp.99–130.

7. See L.M. Cullen, 'Burke, Ireland and the Revolution', *Eighteenth-Century Life*, 16, 1 (1992), pp.22–42; R.B. McDowell, 'Burke and Ireland', in D. Dickson, D. Keogh and K. Whelan (eds), *The United Irishmen: Republicanism, Radicalism and Rebellion* (Dublin: Lilliput Press, 1993), pp.102–14; E. O'Flaherty, 'Burke and the Catholic Question', *Eighteenth-Century Ireland/Iris an dá chultúr*, 12 (1997), pp.7–27.

8. For an account of these two pamphlets, see R.B. McDowell, *Irish Public Opinion, 1750–1800* (London: Faber and Faber, 1944), pp. and P. Kelly, 'Irish Writers and the French Revolution', in *La Storia della Storiografia Europea sulla Rivoluzione Francese* (Roma: Istituto Storico Italiano per L'Età Moderna e Contemporanea, 1990), pp.327–49.

9. T. Goold, *A Vindication of the Right Hon. Edmund Burke's Reflections on the Revolution in France, in Answer to all his Opponents* (Dublin, 1791), pp.16–17.

10. Sir L. Parsons, *Thoughts on Liberty and Inequality. By a member of Parliament* (Dublin, 1793), p.4.

11. Burke to the Earl of Charlemont, 8 Aug. 1791, in A. Cobban and R.A. Smith (eds), *The Correspondence of Edmund Burke*, July 1789–December 1791 (Cambridge: Cambridge University Press, 1967), vol.6, pp.330–1.

12. See W.J. McCormack, 'Between Burke and the Union: Reflections on PRO: CO 904/2', in J. Whale (ed.), *Edmund Burke's Reflections on the Revolution in France: New Interdisciplinary Essays* (Manchester: Manchester University Press, 2000), pp.60–93 (p.62).

13. For a more detailed treatment of McKenna, see C.D.A. Leighton, 'Theobald McKenna and the Catholic Question' (unpublished M.A. thesis, St Patrick's College, Maynooth, 1985). For a discussion of the workings of impact of the Catholic Society, see T. Bartlett, *The Fall and Rise of the Irish Nation: the Catholic Question, 1690–1830* (Dublin: Gill & Macmillan, 1992), pp.129–31.

14. Ian McBride, *Scripture Politics: Ulster Presbyterians and Irish Radicalism in the Late Eighteenth-Century* (Oxford: Clarendon Press, 1998), p.25.

15. Theobald McKenna, *Declaration of the Catholic Society of Dublin* (Dublin, 1793), pp.2–3.

16. Theobald McKenna, *Address to the Roman Catholics of Ireland, Relative to the Late Proceedings, and on the Means and Practicability of a Tranquil Emancipation* (Dublin, 1792), p.12.

17. Ibid., pp.15–16.

18. *An Essay on Parliamentary Reform, and on the evils likely to ensue, from a republican constitution, in Ireland* (Dublin, 1793).

19. Ibid., pp.14–15.

20. Following the London publication of a substantial collection of McKenna's works in 1794, his next significant work was *The Interests and Present State of the Nation*, published in 1797. By the time of the Union he had been awarded a government pension, and was to continue publishing on the issue of Catholic Emancipation.

21. See W.J. McCormack, *The Dublin Paper War of 1786–88: A Bibliographic and Critical Enquiry* (Dublin: Lilliput Press, 1993); J. Kelly, 'The Genesis of "Protestant Ascendancy": the Rightboy Disturbances of the 1780s and their Impact upon Protestant Opinion', in G. O'Brien (ed.), *Parliament, Politics and People: Essays in Eighteenth-Century Irish History* (Dublin: Irish Academic Press, 1989), pp.93–127.

22. See J. Hill, *From Patriots to Unionists: Dublin Civic Politics and Irish Protestant Patriotism, 1660–1840* (Oxford: Clarendon Press, 1997), pp.212–13.

23. *On the Defence of Ireland: Including Observations on Some Other Subjects Connected Therewith* (Dublin, 1795), p.2. The pamphlet is variously ascribed to Sir Henry Sheehy Keating or Maurice Bagenal St Leger Keating of Narraghmore, the liberal Kildare MP. My thanks to Liam Chambers for a discussion of the contested authorship of the tract.

24. Ibid., illustrations depicting a mounted yeoman (p.52), an armed peasant with sword (p.55), and an armed peasant with musket (p.58).

25. Ibid., p.83.

26. J. Livesey, *Making Democracy in the French Revolution* (Cambridge, MA: Harvard University Press, 2001), p.79.

27. For an introduction to O'Connor's political economy see the introduction to A. O'Connor, *The State of Ireland*, edited by J. Livesey (Dublin: Lilliput Press, 1998), pp.1–26.

28. M. Sandys, *A Letter to the Rt. Hon. Henry Grattan, on the state of the labouring poor in Ireland. From the Rev. M. Sandys, A.M., Minister of Powerscourt with Mr. Grattan's Answer* (Dublin, 1796). Sandys' pamphlet is a defence of the Irish peasantry against accusations of indolence and restiveness, and cites authorities as diverse as Swift, Berkeley, Montesquieu and Smith.

29. Ibid., pp.20–1.

30. J.P. Winter, *Reflections on the Best Means of Securing Tranquillity. Submitted to the Consideration of Country Gentlemen* (Dublin, 1796), pp.8–9.

31. W. Stokes, *Projects for Re-establishing the Internal Peace and Tranquillity of Ireland* (Dublin, 1799). For a detailed treatment of Stokes, see chapter 7, 'Radical Politics in Trinity: the Faith and Politics of Whitley Stokes', in J. Liechty, 'Irish Evangelicalism, Trinity College Dublin, and the Mission of the Church of Ireland at the End of the Eighteenth-century' (unpublished PhD Thesis, St Patrick's College, Maynooth, 1987), pp.390–469.

32. There is some confusion over the precise identity of the Revd Dr Clarke. Irish born, Thomas Brooke Clarke, an Anglican clergyman, moved to Britain where he began publishing texts devoted to political economy. An interest in Smithean economics is evident from his pamphlet *The Crisis, or Immediate Concernments of the British Empire* (1785), an attack on the enervating effects of colonies, while celebrating the effects of trade and commerce. By the 1790s Clarke was generating a raft of texts such as *A Publicistical Survey of the Different Forms of Government* (1791), and *A Statistical View of Germany* (1790). However, an alternative Dr Clarke is presented in the form of James Stanier Clarke (1765?–1834), naval chaplain and eventually appointed by the Prince of Wales as his domestic chaplain and librarian. Authorship of letters and printed works is variously ascribed.

33. R. Musgrave, *Memoirs of the Different Rebellions in Ireland, from the Arrival of the English: also, a Particular Detail of that which broke out the 23rd of May, 1798* (Dublin, 1801).

34. See A. Hofman, 'Opinion, Illusion, and the Illusion of Opinion: Barruel's Theory of Conspiracy', *Eighteenth-Century Studies*, 27, 1 (Autumn 1993), pp.27–60, for an illuminating discussion of the trope of conspiracy as crucial to the counter-enlightenment writings of John Robison, the Abbé Barruel and others.

35. For an examination of the body from a later period, see Kevin Bright, *The Royal Dublin Society, 1815–45* (Dublin: Four Courts Press, 2004). To date the Dublin Society's *Statistical Surveys* have yet to find their historian.

36. Unpublished during his lifetime, *Thoughts and Details on Scarcity* was first printed in 1800. R.B. McDowell (ed.), *The Writings and Speeches of Edmund Burke. Vol. 9, 1: the Revolutionary War, 1794–1797, 2: Ireland* (Oxford: Clarendon Press, 1991), pp.119–45.

37. Livesey, *Making Democracy*, p.78.

38. Theobald McKenna, *An Argument against Extermination: Occasioned by Doctor Duigenan's "Representation of the Present Political State of Ireland". By a Catholic and Burkist* (Dublin, 1800).

12

Thomas Hussey, Edmund Burke
and the Irish Directory[1]

DÁIRE KEOGH

Edmund Burke's letter of 9 December 1796 to Reverend Thomas Hussey, president of the Catholic seminary at Maynooth, has been described by Conor Cruise O'Brien as 'Burke's political testament with regard to Ireland'.[2] While some might dispute such an appellation, few can deny the significance of this missive. For at once we are forced to confront the paradox of Burke: his opposition to reform in England, while advocating a radical reordering of society in Ireland. At the same time, this letter, which is reprinted in full below, reflects his alarm at Ireland's rapid descent into anarchy. He partially attributed the deteriorating conditions in Ireland to the influence of the French Revolution, what Hussey called the 'French Disease', the spread of Jacobin ideas that also identified a more sinister element propelling Ireland towards rebellion: the machinations of those whom he considered to be the real Jacobins in the country – the leaders of the Protestant Ascendancy. Burke eyed these unfolding events in his native land from his adopted home in England, but, as his letter to Hussey makes clear, this vantage point did not blur his vision.

I

From as early as 1779 Thomas Hussey was counted amongst Burke's most intimate friends.[3] As chaplain to the Spanish embassy in London, Hussey, a native of County Meath, was at the heart of a lively political and intellectual circle which included the Duke of Portland, Lord Chatham, the younger Pitt, Charles James Fox and Dr Johnson.[4] These social connections gave rise to various opportunities for Hussey. During the American Revolutionary War, a secret embassy under the leadership of Richard Cumberland, Secretary of the Board of Trade, was sent to Spain in an effort to break the Franco-Spanish alliance. At the special request of King George III, Dr Hussey joined the delegation and, despite its failure, he made an impression in the Spanish Court.[5]

But while Hussey rose to the top echelon of British society (in 1792 he was admitted a fellow of the Royal Society of London) he was despised by some. Just as John Wilkes, who represented Middlesex in parliament, had claimed that

Burke's oratory 'stank of whiskey and potatoes', William Drennan, the Belfast Presbyterian United Irishman, dismissed the 'native broadness and vulgarity' of Hussey's brogue, finding it 'strange that someone of the most ancient strain of Ireland and in foreign courts all his life should smack so strongly of the bogtrotter'.[6]

Undeterred, Hussey immersed himself in the affairs of the Catholics of England and Ireland. In 1790 he was requested to represent the committee of English Catholics in Rome in an effort to defuse the crisis produced by their 'Protestation', namely, their declaration of Catholic civil and religious principles that contained a repudiation of papal authority.[7] In spite of his commitment to the Catholic cause, Hussey declined this invitation. Nonetheless, exhibiting what Burke called 'a very rare union ... of the enlightened statesman with the ecclesiastic', he argued that full Catholic emancipation was not only desirable, but essential.[8] In 1790, as the prospect of conflict between Great Britain and Revolutionary France loomed on the horizon, Hussey wrote to Edmund Burke's son, Richard, asserting that 'should these kingdoms be involved in a war, a further toleration of the Catholics in Ireland will become unavoidable'.[9] It was absurd, he argued, to wait until necessity compelled what true policy should offer voluntarily:

> Hitherto, the Catholics of that Country have proceeded with proper deference and submission to the laws, in their application for redress ... Sublimated, however, as men's minds are by the French Disease ... one cannot foresee what a continuation of oppressive laws may work upon the minds of the people; and those of Irish Catholics are much altered within my own memory and they will not in future bear the lash of tyranny and oppression which I have seen inflicted upon them, without resisting or even complaining.

Such arguments reflected the unity of sentiment which existed between Hussey and Edmund Burke. As the decade progressed their relationship deepened, and the priest eventually became his principal Irish correspondent.

II

The bulk of Burke's writings on Ireland constitute a concerted attack against the Protestant Ascendancy. While the Glorious Revolution of 1688 had restored the Constitution of England, in Ireland it had proved an unmitigated disaster for Catholics. The revolution facilitated the establishment of a sectarian Protestant state buttressed by the provisions of the penal laws, which, in Burke's own words, has 'divided the nation into two distinct bodies'. 'One of these bodies was to possess *all* the franchises, *all* the property, *all* the education: the other was to be composed of drawers of water and cutters of turf for them.'[10] Burke attacked not only the injustice of the system, but its folly. The laws had failed to destroy Catholicism in Ireland; they had impoverished the island and were the root cause of the problems of government. The solution lay in gradual reform and the removal of the penal disabilities; such advances would be dependent on the goodwill of Irish Protestants and the English, but Burke constantly urged Irish Catholics to assert the justice of their case and to maintain pressure for reform.[11] When conditions demanded it, however, Burke counselled a more subtle approach. In 1779, for instance, the British government seemed disposed to playing the Catholic Card in order to counterbalance Irish Protestant sympathy for the American War of Independence, so Burke urged Catholics to keep themselves quiet, to show themselves dutiful to the crown.[12]

In the 1790s Burke's principal concern was the spread of Jacobinism; in Ireland this crusade was intimately related to his assault upon the Protestant Ascendancy, which he believed lay at the heart of Catholic disaffection. Hussey's writing reflects similar sentiments. More important, as Burke's principal Irish correspondent, the cleric's alarming reports on the condition of Ireland fuelled Burke's anxiety. Hussey sent one such warning in February 1795 when Henry Grattan introduced a Catholic Relief Bill into the Irish House of Commons. Hussey urged Burke to impress upon the British government that Grattan's measure, which proposed the abolition of the bar against Catholics sitting in Parliament, in reality involved 'another awful one – whether they mean to retain Ireland or abdicate it to a French government, or to a revolutionary system of its own intention'.[13]

The recall one month later of Burke's esteemed Lord Fitzwilliam, his replacement as Lord Lieutenant by the Earl of Camden and the consequent defeat of the Relief Bill astonished Hussey, who had recently arrived in Ireland to assist in the establishment of a proposed Catholic seminary. 'How in the name of God', he asked Burke, 'can the spirit of this nation bear [that] the most popular and virtuous viceroy that ever came to this country should be removed?'[14] He continued, with reference to the Irish House of Commons:

> The people begin to view the interference of the British cabinet in a hostile light … They will wish for a separation from Great Britain and the contemptible light in which they will view their own parliament will induce them to lay it in the dust and to erect a convention on the French scale in its place.

This was a defining moment in the political development in the 1790s.[15] Ireland was poised on the brink of civil war, constitutional reform channels were blocked and the new viceroy, the Earl of Camden, arrived with specific instructions to 'rally the friends of the Protestant interest'.[16]

Hussey intended to return to England, but remained in Ireland at the request of the Duke of Portland, the Home Secretary, to ensure the progress of the Catholic seminary, duly established in Maynooth in County Kildare. Hussey's satisfaction at being appointed the first president of the College was unquestionable: in November 1796 he assured Burke that Maynooth was his 'favourite spot, this *punctum saliens* of the salvation of Ireland from Jacobinism and anarchy'.[17] Yet Hussey's position became more complicated in August 1796 when Pope Pius VI granted him vicarial authority over the King's forces in Ireland. This appointment was controversially confirmed by William Pitt, who knew Hussey to be a staunch anti-Jacobin, in the hope that the cleric would help stamp out disaffection in the ranks.[18]

The folly of this ministerial appointment became immediately apparent once Hussey began to seek redress for what he regarded as a gross injustice: the practice of forcing Catholic soldiers to attend Protestant services. This problem was not new but it had become more acute in 1793 when the government established the Irish Militia, a second-line force, the rank and file of which were predominantly Catholic. The issue came to a head in 1795 with the case of Private James Hyland of the Irish Light Dragoons, who had been sentenced by a court martial at Carrick-on-Suir to 200 lashes for refusing, on the advice of his confessor, to attend Protestant services. Hussey complained to Burke about Hyland's treatment and also raised the question with Lord Fitzwilliam, whom he urged to issue a proclamation against such practices. Burke, in turn, warned Fitzwilliam that the French revolutionary war against religion could only benefit from a civil war in Ireland.[19]

In the autumn of 1796 there were further reports that the men of the Irish militia regiments stationed at Ardfinnan Camp in County Tipperary were being compelled to attend Protestant services. Hussey attempted in vain to meet the viceroy or his secretary; both he informed Burke in November, 'were too busy settling their bargains with the orators of College Green' to afford him a meeting.[20] This alienation from Dublin Castle alarmed Hussey, particularly as recent approaches from several military corps prompted him to describe for Burke the dire alternatives now facing Irish Catholics: 'the two evils of oppression, or Jacobinism'. If the consequences of the latter choice were alarming, the causes were clear. Hussey placed responsibility for the disturbed state of Ireland at the door of the so-called 'junto', the coterie of Ascendancy jobbers who surrounded the viceroy at the Castle:

> How little does His Majesty suspect, that those upon whom he heaps honours, and powers here, are his greatest enemies and the very men who are Jacobinising the country! They are urging these cursed sentiments throughout the country under ... he name of United Irishmen, this evil is extending beyond imagination ... I am terrified at what I foresee regarding my own unfortunate country, To pass by parliament, and break the connection with Great Britain, is I am informed the plan of the United Irishmen. The wretches never consider that their grievances are not from England but from a junto of their own countrymen.

It was actually this dire warning from Hussey in November 1796 that prompted Burke's letter of 9 December.[21] It is, indeed, an extraordinary missive that
openly expresses Burke's sympathy for the rebellious Irish Catholics.[22] As
Kevin Whelan has observed, Burke' arguments, 'conservative in a British
framework, became radical when transposed into Ireland.[23]

III

At the heart of all of Burke's great crusades was his opposition to the abuse of
power. How then was he to respond to Hussey's image of the Catholic soldier,
'with down cast head, and arms, whipped like a quadruped to a hostile church,
by a little Tyrranizing Officer'?[24] This ill-treatment of Catholic soldiers roused
Burke's emotions as had the horrors of the 'Munster Circuit' during the
Whiteboy disturbances of the 1760s, particularly the judicial murder of Father
Nicholas Sheehy at Clonmel in 1766. On that occasion he gathered material to
write about the case – just as Voltaire had exposed the murder of Calas in
France.[25] In December 1796, Burke expressed his anger in his extended letter to
Hussey and granted him permission to 'shew [it] to all those (and they are but
very few) who may be disposed to think well of my opinion'.

Motivated by his disgust at the spectre of the soldier called to church 'not by
the bell, but by the whip', Burke initiated a renewed assault on his favourite
enemy, the Protestant Ascendancy. In 1767 Burke had attributed the 'rottenness
of the country ... to the ill policy of government towards the body of the
subjects there' – referring, of course, to the deleterious effects of the penal laws.[26]
By the late 1790s circumstances had changed; it is true that the bulk of the penal
laws had been removed, but the manner in which Catholic relief had been
imposed by London upon an unwilling Irish parliament deprived these measures
of conciliatory effect in Ireland. For example, the response to the Relief Act of
1793, which extended the forty shilling county franchise to Catholics, reflected
the frustration of both parties – the Protestant Ascendancy and the Catholic
majority. John Foster, a pillar of the Ascendancy, was convinced that the Relief
Act would only whet the appetite of Catholics for further reform (more than this,
it was an admission of the justice of the Catholic cause). It was vain, he said, 'to
imagine that admission to the elective franchise does not draw with it the right
of representation'.[27] Theobold Wolf Tone aptly described Catholic anger when he
declared that if they deserved what had been granted, they also deserved that
which had been withheld.[28] Similarly, Fitzwilliam's great plan to bind Irish
Catholics to 'their' state had failed; they remained, according to Burke, 'public
Enemies' within society and were subjected to numerous informal impediments
that replaced the crumbling penal laws.[29]

As the 1790s progressed the forces of reaction at the disposal of the state –
regular forces, militia and yeomanry – proved insufficient in the face of revolutionary threats from Defenders, the United Irishmen and their French allies.[30]

Consequently, starting with the Carhampton campaign in north Leinster and Connacht in the summer of 1795, the Dublin Castle administration increasingly abandoned normal legal restraints, adopting instead measures that the French Terrorists had applied with such effect in the Vendée. This illegal campaign, described by Camden as 'a salutary system of severity', was retrospectively excused by the terms of an Indemnity Act (1796), while the tactics were enshrined in law by an accompanying Insurrection Act.[31] At an unofficial level, the Orange Order (Burke's 'Zealots in Armagh' in his letter to Hussey) inflicted horrors upon Catholics of mid-Ulster which James Coigly, the Armagh priest, compared to the 'tyranny of Robespierre'.[32] There was, however, no recourse to justice. Increasingly, Catholic Defenderism became the only restraint upon the Protestant Ascendancy since, as one victim concluded, 'every magistrate in Ulster, but one or two, was an Orangeman'.[33]

Such contingencies, Burke told Hussey in his December 1796 testament, presented Catholic subjects with the 'desperate alternative between a thankless acquiescence under grievous Oppression, or a refuge in Jacobinism with all its horrors and all it crimes' (thus echoing the priest's own words).[34] Burke understood the attraction of the latter, but had no doubt about its destructive potential in Ireland. It was, indeed, more dangerous than continental Jacobinism, which was 'Speculative in character' – 'the very levity of character which produces it may extinguish it'. Irish Jacobinism, on the other hand, arising from spurned loyalty, was a more intransigent phenomenon.[35] Still, since growing Catholic frustration could not be ignored, Burke warned Hussey of the dangers of preaching passivity to an 'irritated people' – thus revealing once again his sensitivity to particular political circumstances.

Burke was equally alarmed by the nature of government on Ireland. Throughout the eighteenth century the problem of political management had dogged successive administrations. Some stability had been achieved in the late 1760s by the replacement of the undertaker system with resident viceroys,[36] but the so-called 'Constitution of 1782' had made the problem of management more acute, because it had extended the powers of the Irish parliament. What's more the constitutional safeguards afforded by Poyning's Law and the Declaratory Act were now gone. As Burke put it in his epistle to Hussey, the English government had 'farmed out Ireland, without the reservation of a pepper Corn rent in Power or influence'.[37] In this way Ireland's Catholics were deprived of the protection previously afforded by the 'superintendency of the British parliament'. Burke lamented: 'If the people of Ireland were to be flayed alive by the predominant faction it would be the most critical of all attempts so much as to discuss the Subject in any public Assembly upon this side of the water.'[38] Catholics were prey to the 'junto', the die-hards of the Ascendancy, Ireland's 'Directory', which centred on John Beresford, John Fitzgibbon and John Foster, who were now working from within the Castle administration, not from without, as had been the case in Burke's earlier crusades.[39] Such considerations clearly illustrated the desirability of a union of the kingdoms; not a

Protestant union but one that would admit emancipated Catholics to the British state. Significantly, in the course of the Union debated three years later, in 1799, Thomas Hussey welcomed this proposal, declaring his preference for 'a union with the Beys and Mamelukes of Egypt to that of being under the iron rod of the Mamelukes of Ireland'.[40]

IV

In retrospect, Conor Cruise O'Brien's description of Burke's missive as his 'political testament with regard to Ireland' is justified. Certainly, Burkes letter 'To Unknown' written two months later addresses the many ills of Ireland, the reckless policy of the government and the injustice of the penal laws, but this correspondence lacks the vigour of his earlier assault.[41] The contrasts between the two are immediate. The former is addressed to his most intimate confidential correspondent, Hussey, who within months would administer spiritually to him in his last illness.[42] The latter document, which O'Brien believes might be marked 'for beginners', is directed towards an acquaintance, a contemporary of his son, Richard, and contains a more superficial analysis of Ireland.[43]

While composing the December letter, which he dictated from his home in England, Burke was conscious of his imminent demise; in this sense he *believed* this would be his testament and may have anticipated its publication. His mental powers had begun to decline, but the urgency of his task produced a rally that mirrored the vigour and ability of his prime. The consistency of his argument is immediately apparent – if the impact of the 'French Disease' had introduced a 'stridency and anger' into Burke's writings of the mid-1790s, his critical condition in December 1796 produced a red-hot assault on the Irish establishment.[44] Burke adopts a sarcastic tone to disparage the Dublin Castle junto, 'the little wise men of the West', 'snakes, whose *primum mobile* is their Belly'.

In Burke's view the threat to the security of the kingdom came not from the United Irishmen or the Defenders, but from this junto *within* the Castle. From this intellectual position Burke produced an ironic parody, one which measures the 'victories' of the Ascendancy against the accomplishments of its allies in Europe: the pathetic 'Glories of the Night expeditions in surprising the Cabin fortresses in Louth and Meath' – the harsh, illegal measures employed to suppress Defenderism in South Ulster and North Leinster – are sardonically compared to the substantial achievements of the 'Zealous Protestant Buonoparté' on the Plains of Lombardy. The cabal, Burke believed, were the real Jacobins of Ireland, the arrogant zealots of the Ascendancy who had abandoned the rule of law and violated the 'compact of human Society' in their 'Western crusade against Popery'. Yet, in the spirit of the Nagles, his revered Catholic cousins of the Blackwater valley, Burke urged Catholics to be assertive: not to imitate the Jacobinism of their oppressors, but rather to steer a middle course. 'There is nothing,' he concluded, 'which will not yield to perseverance and method'.

EDMUND BURKE TO THE REV THOMAS HUSSEY [*post* 9 December 1796][45]

My dear Sir,
This morning I received your Letter of the 30th November from Maynooth. I dictate my answer from my Couch, on which I am obliged to lie for a good part of the Day. I cannot conceal from you, much less can I conceal from myself, that, in all probability I am not long for this world. Indeed things are of such a Situation independently of the Domestic wound that I never could have less reason for regret than quitting the world than at this moment; and my End will be, by several, as little regretted.

I have no difficulty at all in communicating to you or, if it were of any use to mankind at large, my sentiments and feelings on the dismal state of things in Ireland; but I find it difficult indeed to give you the advice you are pleased to ask, as to your own conduct in your very critical Situation.

You state, what has long been but too obvious, that it seems the unfortunate policy of the Hour, to put to the far largest portion of the Kings Subjects in Ireland, the desperate alternative, between a thankless acquiescence under grievous Oppression, or a refuge in Jacobinism with all its horrors and all its crimes. You prefer the former dismal part of the choice. There is no doubt but that you would have reasons if the election of one of these Evils was at all a security against the other. But they are things very alliable and as closely connected as cause and effect. That Jacobinism, which is Speculative in its Origin, and which arises from Wantonness and fullness of bread, may possibly be kept under by firmness and prudence. The very levity of character which produces it may extinguish it; but the Jacobinism which arises from Penury and irritation, from scorned loyalty, and rejected Allegiance, has much deeper roots. They take their nourishment from the bottom of human Nature and the unalterable constitution of things, and not from humour and caprice or the opinions of the Day about privileges and Liberties. These roots will be shot into the Depths of Hell, and will at last raise up their proud Tops to Heaven itself. This radical evil may baffle the attempts of Heads much wiser than those are, who in the petulance and riot of their drunken power are neither ashamed nor afraid to insult and provoke those whom it is their duty and ought to be their glory to cherish and protect.

So then the little wise men of the West, with every hazard of this Evil, are resolved to persevere in their manly and well timed resolution of a War against Popery. In the principle and in all the proceedings it is perfectly suitable to their character. They begin this last series of their Offensive Operations by laying traps for the consciences of poor Foot-Soldiers. They call these wretches to their Church (empty of a Volunteer congregation) not by the Bell, but by the whip. This Ecclesiastic military discipline is happily taken up, in order to form an Army of well-scourged Papists into a firm Phalanx for the support of the Protestant Religion. I wish them Joy in this their valuable discovery in Theology, Politicks and the Art military. Fashion governs the world; and it is the fashion in the great French Empire of Pure and perfect Protestantism, as well as in the little busy meddling Province of servile imitators that apes, at an humble distance, the Tone of its Capital, to make a crusade against you poor Catholicks. But whatever may be thought in Ireland of its share of a war against the Pope in the outlying part of Europe, the Zealous Protestant Buonoparté has given his late Holiness far more deadly blows in the centre of his own power and in the nearest seats of his influence, than the Irish Directory can arrogate to itself within its own Jurisdiction from the utmost efforts of its political and military skill. I have my doubts, (they may arise from my ignorance) whether the Glories of the Night expeditions in surprising the Cabin fortresses in Louth and Meath[46] or whether the Slaughter and expulsion of the Catholic Weavers by another set of Zealots on Armagh,[47] or even the proud trophies of the late potato Field in that County,[48] are quite to be compared to the Protestant Victories on the Plains of Lombardy; or to the possession of the Fiat of Bologna,[49] or to the approaching Sack of Rome where even now the Protestant Commissaries give the Law. In all this Business, Great Britain, to us merely Secular politicians, makes no great figure; but let the glory of great Britain shift for itself as it may. All is well, provided Popery is crushed.

This war against Popery furnishes me with a Clue that leads me out of a Maze of perplexed politicks, which without it I could not in the least understand. I now can account for the whole. Lord Malmsbury[50] is sent to prostrate the dignity of the English Monarchy in Paris, that an Irish Popish common Soldier may be whipt in to give an appearance of habitation to a deserted Protestant Church in Ireland. Thus we balance the account. Defeat and dishonour abroad; Oppression at Home – We sneak to the Regicides, but we boldly trample on our poor felloe Citizens. But all is for the Protestant Cause.

The same ruling principle explains the Rest. We have abdicated the Crown of Corsica, which had been newly soldered to the Crown of Great Britain and to the Crown of Ireland, lest the British Diadem should look too like the Pope's triple Crown.[51] We have ran away from the People of Corsica, and abandonned them without Capitulation of any kind; in favour of those of them who might be our friends. But then, it was for their having Capitulated with us, for Popery, as a part of their Constitution. We make amends for our Sins by our Repentence, and for our Apostacy from Protestantism by a breach of faith from popery. We have fled, overspread with dirt and ashes but with hardly enough of Sack Cloath to cover or Nakedness. We recollected that this Island (together with its Yews and other salubrious productions) had given birth to the illustrious Champion of the Protestant World Buonoparté – It was therefore not fit (to use the favourite French expression) that the Cradle of his religious Hero should be polluted by the feet of the British Renegade Slaves, who had stipulated to support Popery in that Island whilst his friends and fellow Missionaries are so gloriously employed in extirpating it in another – Our policy is growing every day into more and more consistency. We have shewed our broad back to the Meditterranian. We have abandoned too the very hope of an alliance with Italy. We have relinquished the Levant to the Jacobins. We have considered our Trade as nothing – Our policy and out honour went along with it; but all these objects were well sacrificed to remove the very suspicion of giving any assistance to that Abomination, the Pope, in his insolent attempts to resist a truly protestant power resolved to humble the Papal Tiara, and to prevent his pardons and his dispensations from being any longer the standing terror of the wise and virtuous Directory of Ireland; who cannot sit down with any tolerable comfort to an innocent little Job, whilst his Bulls are thundering thro' the world. I ought to suppose that the arrival of General Hoche is eagerly expected in Ireland;[52] for He, too, is a most zealous Protestant; and he has given proof of it by the studied cruelties and insults by which He put to death the old Bishop of Dol;[53] whom, (but upon me) I should call a glorious martyr and should class him among the most venerable prelates that have appeared in this Century. It is to be feared, however, that the Zealots will be disappointed in their pious hopes by the Season of the Year, and the bad condition of the Jacobin Navy, which may hinder him this Winter from giving his Brother Protestants in Ireland his kind assistance in accomplishing with you, what the other friend of the cause, Buonoparté, is doing in Italy; and what the Masters of these two pious Men the Protestant Directory of France, have so thoroughly accomplished in that the most Popish, but unluckily whilst popish the [most] cultivated, the most populous and the most flourishing of all Countries the austrian Netherlands.

When I consider the narrowness of the views and the total want of human wisdom displayed in our Western Crusade against Popery, it is impossible to speak of it but with every mark of contempt and scorn – yet one cannot help shuddering with horror when one contemplates the terrible consequences that are frequently the results of craft united with Folly - placed in an unnatural elevation. Such ever win be the issue of things, when the mean vices attempt to mimick the grand passions – Great men will never do great mischief but for some great End. For this they must be in a state of inflammation and in a manner out of themselves – Among the nobler Animals whose blood is hot, the bite is never poisonous, except when the Creature is mad; but in the cold blooded reptile race, whose poison is exalted by the Chemistry of their icy complexion, their venom is the result of their health, and of the perfection of their Nature – Woe to the Country in which such snakes, whose primum, Mobile is their Belly, obtain wings and from Serpents become dragons. It is not that these people want natural Talents and even a good cultivation; on the contrary, they are the sharpest and most sagacious of mankind in the things to which they apply – But having wasted their faculties upon base and unworthy objects, in any thing of a higher order, they are far below the common rate of two legged animals.

I have nothing more to say, just now, upon the Directory in Ireland which indeed is alone worth any mention at all. As to the half dozen (or half score as it may be) of Gentleman, who, under various names of authority, are sent from hence to be the subordinate agents of that low order of beings, I consider them as wholly out of the question – Their virtues or their vices; their ability or their Weakness, are matters of no sort of consideration. You feel the thing very rightly – all the evils of Ireland originate within itself. That unwise body, the United Irishmen, have had the folly to represent those Evils as owing to this Country, when in truth its chief guilt is in its total neglect, its utter oblivion, its shameful indifference and its entire ignorance, of Ireland and of everything that relates to it, and not in any oppressive disposition towards that unknown region. No such disposition exists. English Government has farmed out Ireland, without the reservation of a pepper Corn rent in Power or influence, publick or individual, to the little narrow Faction that Domineers there. Thro' that alone they see, feel, hear or understand, anything relative to that Kingdom; nor do they any way interfere that I know of, except in giving their countenance and their sanction of their Names to whatever is done by that *Junto*.

Ireland had derived some advantage from its independence on Parliament of this Kingdom; or rather it did derive advantage from the arrangements that were made at the time of the establishment of that Independence.[54] But human blessings are mixed; and I cannot but think that even these great blessings were bought dearly enough, when along with the weight of the authority, they have totally lost all Benefit from the superintendency of the British Parliament. Our Pride is succeeded by fear. It is little less that a breach of Order, even to mention Ireland in the House of Commons of Great Britain. If the people of Ireland were to be flayed alive by the predominant faction it would be the most critical of all attempts so much as to discuss the Subject in any public Assembly upon this side of the Water. If such a faction should by its folly or iniquity or both, provoke disturbances in Ireland, the force paid by this Kingdom would infallibly be employed to repress them. This would be right enough, if our public Councils here at the same time possessed and employed the means of enquiry into the merits of that cause in which their blood and treasure were so laid out. By a strange inversion of the order of things not only the largest part of the Natives of Ireland are thus annihilated; but the Parliament of Great Britain itself is rendered no better that an instrument in the hands of an Irish faction – This is ascendancy with a Witness! In what all this will end it is not impossible to conjecture; tho' the exact time of the accomplishment cannot be [fixed] with the same certainty you can calculate an Eclipse.

As to your particular conduct it has undoubtedly been that of a good and faithful Subject, and of a man of integrity and honor – You went to Ireland this last time, as you did the first time, at the express desire of the English Minister of that Department[55] and at the request of the Lord Lieutenant himself.[56] You were fully aware of the difficulties that would attend your Mission; and I was equally Sensible of them – Yet you consented, and I advised that you should obey the voice of what we considered and indespensible duty. We regarded as the great Evil of the time the growth of Jacobinism, and we were very well assured that from a variety of causes no part of these Countries were more favourable to the growth and progress of that Evil than our unfortunate Country. I considered it as a tolerably good omen, that Government would do nothing further to foment and provoke the Jacobin malady, that they called upon you, a strenuous and steady Royalist, and an enlightened and exemplary Clergyman; A man of birth and respectable connexions in the Country; a man well informed and conversant in State Affairs, and in the general Politicks of the several Courts of Europe, and intimately and personally habituated in some of those Courts. I regretted indeed that the Ministry which had my most earnest good wishes declined to make any sort of use of the reiterated information you had given them of the Designs of the Enemies, and had taken no notice of the noble and disinterested Offers, which thro' me, were made for employing you to save Italy and Spain to the British Alliance. But this being past and Spain and Italy lost I was in hopes, that they were resolved to put themselves in the right at home by calling upon you that they would leave on their part no cause or pretext for Jacobinism except in the seditious disposition of Individuals; but I now see that instead of profiting by your advice and services, they will not so much take the least notice of your written representations or permit you to have access to them on the part of those who it was your Business to reconcile to the Government as well as to conciliate Government towards them. Having rejected your services as a friend of the Government, and in some sort of its employment, they will not even permit to you the natural expression of those sentiments which every man of sense and honesty must feel, and which every plain and sincere man must speak upon this vile plan of abusing Military discipline and perverting it into an instrument of religious persecution. You remember with what indignation I heard of the scourging of the Soldier at Carrick[57] for adhering to his religious Opinions – It was at the time when Lord Fitzwilliam[58] went to take possession of a short lived Government in Ireland – *Breves et infaustos populi Hibernia amores.*[59] He could not live long in power because he was a true Patriot, a true friend of both Countries a steady resister of Jacobinism in every part of the World. On this occasion he was not of my Opinion. He thought, indeed that the Sufferer ought to be relieved and discharged and I think he was so:[60] But as to punishments to be inflicted on the Offender, he thought more lenient measures comprehended in a general plan to prevent such Evils in future, would be the better course. My Judgement, such as it was, had been, that punishment ought to attach so far as the laws permitted, upon every evil action of subordinate power as it arose. That such acts ought at least to be marked with the displeasure of Government because general remedies are uncertain in their Operation when obtained, and that it is a matter of great uncertainty whether they can be obtained at all. For a time his appeared to be the better Option. Even after He was cruelly torn from the embraces of the people of Ireland, when the Militia and other Troops were encamped, (if I recollect it rightly, at Laughlinstown) you yourself with the knowledge and acquiescence of the succeeding Government publickly performed your function to the Catholicks then in Service.[61] I believe too that all the Irish who had composed the foreign Corps taken into British pay had their regular Chaplains.[62] But we see that things are returning fast to their old corrupted Channels. There they will continue to flow.

If any material Evil had been stated to have arisen from this Liberty that is, if Sedition Mutiny, or disobedience of any kind to Command, had been taught in their Chappels, there might have been a reason for not only forcing the Soldiers into Churches where better doctrines were taught, but for punishing the Teachers of disobedience and Sedition, – But I have never heard of any such Complaint. It is a pert therefore of the Systematic illtreatment of Catholicks – This System never will be abandoned as long as it brings advantage to those who adopt it – If the Country enjoys a momentary quiet it is pleaded as an argument in favour of the good effect of wholesome rigours – If, on the Contrary, the Country (grows) more discontented; and if riots and disorders multiply, new Arguments are furnished for giving a vigorous support to the authority of the Directory on account of the rebellious disposition of the people. So long therefore as disorders on the Country become pretexts for adding to the power and emolument of an odious junto, means will be found to keep one part of it or other in perpetual state of confusion or disorder. This is the old traditionary policy of that sort of men. The discontents which under them break out among the people become tenure by which they hold their situation.

I do not deny, that in these Contests the people however oppressed are frequently to blame, whether provoked to their excesses or not, undoubtedly the Law ought to look to nothing but the Offence and to punish it. The redress of grievances is not less necessary than the punishment of disorders; but it is of another resort. In punishing however, the Law ought to be the only rule – If it is not of sufficient force, a force, consistent with its general principles, ought to be added to it. The first duty of a State is to provide for its own conservation. Until that point is secured it can preserve and protect nothing else; but, if possible, it has a greater interest in acting according to strict Law, than event he Subject himself. For if the people see, that the Law is violated to crush them they will certainly despise the Law, They on their part will be easily Led to violate it whenever they can, by all the means in their power. Except in cases of direct War, whenever Government abandons Law, it proclaims Anarchy.

I am well aware, (if I cared one farthing for the few Days I have to live, whether the vain breath of men blow hot or cold about me) that they who censure any Oppressive proceeding of Government are exciting the people to Sedition and revolt. If there be no oppression it is very true or if there be nothing more than the lapses, which will happen to human infirmity at all times and in the exercise of all power, such complaints would be wicked indeed – These lapses are exceptions implied: an allowance for which is part of the understood covenant by which Power is delegated by fallible men to other men that are not infallible; but whenever a hostile spirit on the part of Government is shewn the Question assumes another form. – This is no casual Errour, no lapse, no sudden surprise. Nor [is] it a question of civil or political Liberty. What contemptible stuff it is to say, that a Man who is lashed to Church against his conscience would not discover that the whip is painful, or that He had a conscience to be violated, unless I told him so? Would not a penitent Offender confessing his Offence, lamenting it, and explaining it by his blood, when denied the consolation of Religion at his last moments, feel it as no injury to himself or that the rest of the world would feel so horrible and impious an oppression with no indignation, unless I happened to say it ought to be reckoned amongst the most barbarous acts of our barbarous time. Would the people consider their being taken our if their beds and transported from their family and friends to be an equitable and legal and charitable proceeding, unless I should say that it was a violation of justice, and a dissolution, 'pro tanto', of the very compact of human Society? If a House of Parliament whose Essence it is to be the Guardian of the Laws, and a Simpathetic protectior of the rights of the people (and eminently so of the most defenceless) should not only countenance but applaud this very violation of all Law, and refuse even to examine into the Grounds of the necessity upon the allegation of which Law was so violated, would this be taken for a tender Solicitude for the welfare of the poor, and a true proof of the representative Capacity of the House of Commons, unless I should happen to say (what I do say) that the House had not done its duty either in preserving the sacred rules of Law or in justifying the woeful and humiliating privilege of necessity. They may indemnify and reward others.[63] They might contrive, if I was within their grasp, to punish me, or if they thought it worth while to stigmatize me by their censures; but who will indemnify them for the disgrace of such an Act? Who will save them from the censures of Posterity? What act of Oblivion will cover them from the wakeful memory, from the Notices and issues of the Grand remembrancer, the God within? Would it pass with the people, who suffer from the abuse of lawful power when at the same time they suffer from the use of lawless violence of Jacobins amongst themselves that Government had done its duty and acted leniently in not animadverting on one of those Acts of violence? If I did not tell them, that the lenity with which Government passes by the Crimes and oppressions of a favourite faction, was itself guilty of the most atrocious of all Cruelties. If a Parliament should hear a declamation, attributing the Sufferings of those who are destroyed by these riotous proceedings to their misconduct and then to make them self-felonious, and should en effet refuse an enquiry into the fact, is no interference to be drawn from thence, unless I tell men in high places, that these proceedings taken together form not only an encouragement to the abuse of Power, but to riot sedition, and a rebellious Spirit which sooner or later will turn upon those that encourage it?

I say little of the business of the Potatoe field, because I am not yet acquainted with the particulars. If any persons were found in arms against the King., whether in a field of Potatoes, or of Flax, or of Turnips, they ought to be attacked by a military Power, and brought to condign Punishment by course of Law – If the Country in which the rebellion was raised, was not in a temper fit for the execution of Justice a Law ought to be made, such was made in regard to Scotland on the Suppression of the rebellion 45 to hang the Delinquents.[64] There could be no difficulty in convincing men who were found 'flagrante delicto'. But I hear nothing of all this. No Law, no trial, no punishment commensurate to Rebellion; nor of a known proportion to any lesser delinquency, nor of any discrimination of the more or the less guilty. Shall you and I find fault with the proceedings of France, and be totally indifferent to the proceedings of the Directories at home. You and I hate Jacobinism as we hate the Gates of Hell – Why? Because it is a system of oppression. What can make us in love with oppression because the Syllables Jacobin are not put before the *ism*. When the very same things are done under the *ism* preceded by another Name in the Directory of Ireland.

I have told you, at a great length for a Letter, very shortly for the Subject and for my feelings on it, my sentiments of the scene in which you have been called to act, – on being consulted you advised Sufferers to quiet and submission; and giving Government full credit for an attention to its duties you held out, as an inducement to that submission, some sort of hope of redress. You tried what your reasons and your credit could do to effect it. In consequence of this piece of Service to Government you have been excluded from all communication with the Castle; and perhaps you may thank yourself that you are not in Newgate. You have done a little more in your circumstances that I should have done. You are indeed very excusable from your motive; but it is very dangerous to hold out to an irritated people Any hopes that we are not pretty sure of being able to realize. The Doctrine of Passive obedience as a Doctrine, it is unquestionably right to teach; but to go beyond that is a sort of deceit; and the people who are provoked by their Oppressors do not readily forgive their friends, if whilst the first persecutes and the others appear to deceive them. These friends lose all power of being serviceable to that Government in whose favour they have taken an illconsidered Step. Therefore my Opinion is, that until the Castle shall shew a greater disposition to listen to its true friends than hitherto it has done, it would not be right in you any further to obtrude your services. In the mean time upon any new Application from the Catholics you ought to let them know simply and candidly how you stand.

The Duke of P[ortlan]d sent you to Ireland from a situation in this country of advantage, and comfort to yourself and of no small utility to others. You explained to him in the clearest manner the conduct you were resolved to hold. I do not know that your writing to him will be of the least advantage – I rather think not; yet I am far from sure, that you do not Owe it to him, and to yourself to represent to his Grace the matters which, in substance, you have stated to me.

If anything else should occur to me I shall, as you wish it, communicate my thoughts to you. In the mean time, I shall be happy to hear from you as often as you find it convenient. You never can neglect the great object of which you are so justly fond; and let me beg of you not to let slip out of your mind the Idea of the auxiliary studies and acquirements, which I recommend to you to add to the merely professional pursuits of your young Clergy; and above all, I hope that you will use the whole of your influence among the Catholics to persuade them to a greater indifference about the Political Objects which at present they have in view. It is not but that I am aware of their importance; or wish them to be abandond. But that they would follow opportunities and not to attempt to force anything. I doubt whether the privileges they now seek or have lately sought are compassable. The Struggle would, I am afraid only lead to some of Those very disorders which are made pretexts for further Oppression of the oppressed. I wish the leading people amongst them would give the most Systematic attention to prevent a frequent communication with their adversaries. There are a part of them proud, insulting, capricious, and tyrannical. These of Course will keep them at a distance. There are others of a seditious Temper who would make them at first the instruments and in the End the Victims of their factious Temper and purposes. Those that steer a middle course are truly respectable but are very few. Your friends ought to avoid all imitation of the Vices and their proud Lords. To many of these they are themselves sufficiently disposed. I should therefore recommend to the middle ranks of that description in which I include not only all merchants but all farmers and tradesmen, that they would change as much as possible those expensive modes of living and that dissipation to which our Countrymen in general are so addicted. It does not at all become men in a state of persecution. They ought to conform themselves to the circumstances of a people whom Government is resolved not to consider as upon a par with their fellow Subjects. Favour they will have none. They must aim at other resources to make themselves independent in fact before they aim at a nominal independence. Depend upon it, that with half the privileges of the others, joined to a different system of manners they would grow to a degree of importance to which, without it, no privileges could raise them; much less any intrigues or factious practices. I know very well, that such a discipline among so numerous a people is not easily introduced; but I am sure it is not impossible – If I had youth and strength, I would go myself over to Ireland to work on that plan, so certain I am, that the well being of all descriptions in the Kingdom, as well as of themselves depends upon a reformation among the Catholicks. The work will be very slow in its operation but it is certain in its effect. There is nothing which will not yield to perseverance and method. Adieu! My dear Sir – you have full liberty to shew this Letter to all those (and they are but very few) who may be disposed to think well of my Opinions. I did not care, so far as regards myself, whether it was read on the change; but with regard to you more reserve may be proper – But that you will best judge.

NOTES

1. An earlier version of this paper was published as 'Thomas Hussey, Edmund Burke and the Irish Directory', in J. Skelly(ed.), *Ideas Matter: Essays in Honour of Conor Cruise O'Brien*(Dublin: Poolbeg Press, 1998).
2. Conor Cruise O' Brien, *The Great Melody: A Thematic Biography and Commented Anthology of Edmund Burke* (London: Sinclair-Stevenson, 1992), p.572.
3. William Wardlaw to Lord Germain, 8 June 1779, Historical Manuscripts Commission, Report on Stopford Sackville MSS, I (1904), p.323; For Thomas Hussey, see Dáire Keogh, 'Thomas Hussey, Bishop of Waterford and Lismore 1797–1803 and the Rebellion of 1798', in W Nolan (ed.), *Waterford: History and Society* (Dublin: Geography Publications, 1992), pp.403–24; William Murphy, 'The Life of Dr Thomas Hussey (1746–1803), Bishop of Waterford and Lismore' (unpublished MA thesis, University College Cork, 1968).
4. C. Butler, *Historical Memoirs of the English, Irish and Scottish Catholics since the Reformation* (London, 1822), vol.iv, p.39.
5. R. Cumberland, *Memoirs* (London, 1806), p.139; S. Flagg Bemis, *The Hussey-Cumberland Mission and American Independence* (Princeton: Princeton University Press, 1931).
6. D.A. Chart (ed.), *The Drennan Letters* (Belfast: HMSO, 1931), p.228.
7. Butler, *Historical Memoirs of the English, Irish and Scottish Catholics*, vol.iv, p.43; Eamon O'Flaherty, 'The Catholic Convention and Anglo-Irish Politics, 1791–3', in *Archivium Hibernicum*, xi (1985), p.16; P. O'Donoghue, 'The Holy See and Ireland, 1780–1803', in *Archivium Hibernicum*, xxxiv (1977), pp.99–108.
8. Burke to Hussey (4 Feb. 1795), *Correspondence*, vol.viii, p.136.
9. Hussey to R Burke, 28 August 1790, *Correspondence*, vi, p.134.

10. Edmund Burke, 'Letter to Sir Hercules Langrishe on ... the Roman Catholics of Ireland', [1792], cited in R.B. McDowell, *Writings and speeches*, vol.ix, p.597.
11. See L.M. Cullen, 'Burkes Irish Views and Writings', in Ian Crowe (ed.), *Edmund Burke: His Life and Legacy* (Dublin: Four Courts Press, 1997), pp.62–75; Eamon O'Flaherty, 'Burke and the Catholic Question', *Eighteenth Century Ireland*, xii (1997), pp.7–27.
12. Burke to John Corry (14 Aug. 1779), *Correspondence*, vol.iv, p.119.
13. Hussey to Burke (19 Feb. 1795), *Correspondence*, vol.viii, p.152.
14. Hussey to Burke (3 March 1795), *Correspondence*, vol.viii, p.169.
15. Deirdre Lindsay, 'The Fitzwilliam Episode Revisited', in D. Dickson, D. Keogh and K. Whelan (eds), *The United Irishmen: Republicanism, Radicalism and Rebellion* (Dublin: Lilliput Press, 1993), pp.197–209.
16. Portland to Camden, 26 March 1795, London Public Records Office, Home Office, 100/56/455–6.
17. Hussey to Burke (30 Nov. 1796), *Correspondence*, vol.ix. p.141; P. Corish, *Maynooth College, 1795–1995* (Dublin: Gill and Macmillan, 1995).
18. Portland to Pelham (1 Nov. 1796), in W.J. Fitzpatrick, *Secret Service under Pitt* (London, 1892), p.285.
19. Burke to Fitzwilliam (10 Feb. 1795), *Correspondence*, vol.viii, p.145.
20. Hussey to Burke (30 Nov. 1796), *Correspondence*, vol.ix, p.141.
21. O' Brien, *The Great Melody*, p.572. For Thomas Hussey, see Keogh, 'Thomas Hussey, Bishop of Waterford and Lismore 1797 – 1803 and the Rebellion of 1798', pp.403–24; Murphy, 'The Life of Dr Thomas Hussey (1746–1803), Bishop of Waterford and Lismore'.
22. Conor Cruise O'Brien, 'Introduction', in Matthew Arnold (ed.), *Irish Affairs: Edmund Burke* (London: Crescent Library Edition, 1988), p.xxxvi.
23. Kevin Whelan, 'Introduction to Section I', in Thomas Bartlett, David Dickson, Dáire Keogh and Kevin Whelan (eds), *1798: A Bicentenary Perspective* (Dublin: Four Courts Press, 2003), p.4; Seamus Deane, 'Factions and Fictions; Burke, Colonialism and Revolution', in *Bullan*, iv (2000), pp.5–26.
24. Hussey to Burke (30 Nov. 1796), *Correspondence*, vol.ix, p.142.
25. I am grateful to Professor Thomas Bartlett for this suggestion. See F.P. Lock, *Edmund Burke; Volume I: 1730–1784* (Oxford: Clarendon Press, 1998), pp.192–5; Luke Gibbons, *Edmund Burke and Ireland* (Cambridge: Cambridge University Press, 2003), pp.9–11.
26. Burke to Charles O'Hara (27 Nov. 1767), *Correspondence*, vol.i, p.337.
27. *Report on the debates ... of 1793*, pp.310–11.
28. T.W. Tone, 'Statement of the light in which the late act for the partial repeal of the penal laws is considered by the Catholics of Ireland', in Thomas Bartlett (ed.), *Life of Theobald Wolfe Tone* (Dublin: Lilliput Press, 1998), pp.408–12.
29. Burke to Unknown Bishop [Hussey?] (6 June [1797]), *Correspondence*, vol.ix, p.369; K. Whelan, *The Tree of Liberty: Radicalism, Catholicism and the Construction of Irish Identity 1760–1830* (Cork: Cork University Press, 1996), p.115.
30. See Thomas Bartlett, 'Counter-insurgency and Rebellion: Ireland, 1793–1803', in T. Bartlett and K. Jeffery (eds), *A Military History or Ireland* (Cambridge: Cambridge University Press, 1996), pp.247–93.
31. Camden to Portland (17 June 1796), London Public Records Office, Home Office, 100/69/398.
32. See Dáire Keogh, *A Patriot Priest: The Life of James Coigly 1763–98* (Cork: Cork University Press, 1998).
33. Burke to Hussey (18 Jan. 1796), *Correspondence*, vol.viii, p.378; John Lennon, *The Irish Repealers Mountain Harp of the Triumphant Year 1843* (Dublin, 1843), v: cited in Whelan, *Tree of Liberty*, p.123.
34. Burke to Hussey (9 Dec. 1796), *Correspondence*, vol..ix, p.162.
35. O'Brien, *The Great Melody*, p.573.
36. See M.J. Powell, 'The Reform of the Undertaker System: Anglo-Irish Politics, 1750–67', *Irish Historical Studies*, xxxi, 121 (May 1998), pp.19–37.
37. Burke to Hussey (9 Dec. 1796), *Correspondence*, vol.ix, p.165.
38. Ibid., p.166; see James Conniff, 'Edmund Burke on the Coming Revolution in Ireland', *Journal of the History of Ideas*, 47 (1986), pp.37–59
39. Cullen, 'Burke's Irish Views and Writings', pp.73–4.
40. Hussey to J.B. Clinch (10 Jan. [1799]), Madden MS, Trinity College Dublin, 873/197.
41. Burke to Unknown (Feb. 1797), *Correspondence*, vol.ix, pp.253–63.
42. *Irish Magazine* (Feb. 1808). John Healy was more emphatic claiming that Hussey had received Burke into the Catholic Church: *Maynooth College, Its Centenary History* (Dublin, 1895), p.100.
43. O'Brien, *The Great Melody*, p.577.

44. Conniff, 'Edmund Burke on the Coming Revolution', pp.44–5.
45. Source: Draft (corrected by Burke) in Fitzwilliam MSS (Sheffield Archives); reprinted in *Correspondence*, vol.ix, pp.161–72.
46. Burke is referring to the harsh, illegal measures used in the suppression of Defenderism in South Ulster and North Leinster.
47. During the Armagh expulsions of 1795 and 1796, the Orange Order banished hundreds of Catholic families into Leinster and Connacht.
48. When United Irishmen were taken into custody, neighbours would dig their potatoes or reap their corn in solidarity – such assemblies could consist of between 500 and 2,000 people. After the diggers started marching in semi-military formations, the government banned such gatherings by an order of 6 November 1796, but this was largely ignored in the north: see A.T.Q. Stewart, *Summer Soldiers: The 1798 Rebellion in Antrim and Down* (Belfast: Blackstaff, 1995), pp.26–30.
49. In December 1796 the Senate of Bologna issued a proclamation announcing that the constitution of that new republic was complete and that it had been sent to Napoleon Buonoparte for his approval.
50. James Harris, first Earl of Malmsbury (1746–1820) went to Paris in October 1796 in an attempt to negotiate peace between Great Britain and France. His efforts proved unsuccessful due to his insistence that the Low Countries be restored to the Emperor of Austria.
51. The British had taken Corsica in February 1794, but retreated in haste in August 1796 just as a French force arrived from Italy.
52. Lazare Hoche (1768–97). As commander of the Army of the Ocean, he had brought the civil war in Brittany and the Vendée to an end, defeating an *émigré* royalist army at Quiberon Bay in July 1795. Commander of the ill-fated Bantry expedition of December 1796, he was the main hope of the United Irishmen in France until his early death in 1797.
53. Urbain-René de Hercé (1726–95), Bishop of Dol, was executed in the wake of Hoche's victory in Quiberon.
54. Burke here refers to the so-called 'Constitution of 1782'.
55. William Henry Cavendish Bentick, third Duke of Portland: Home Secretary; Lord Lieutenant of Ireland, 1782; twice Prime Minister, 1783 and 1807.
56. John Jeffreys Pratt, second Earl of Camden (1759–1840), Lord Lieutenant of Ireland, March 1795 to June 1798.
57. James Hyland.
58. William Wentworth Fitzwilliam (1748–1833), Lord Lieutenant of Ireland, December 1794 to March 1795.
59. 'Brief and unblest the loves of the Irish people': see Tacitus, *Annals*, II, 41.
60. It is not actually known what happened to James Hyland.
61. Apparently, in the summer of 1795, Hussey was able to secure the appointment of Catholic chaplains to a few Irish militia regiments then encamped at Loughlinstown, just outside of Dublin: *Hibernian Journal*, 6 July 1795.
62. In 1796 Catholic chaplains were appointed to regiments of the British Army, as opposed to regiments of the Irish militia: *Dublin Gazette*, 6–9 Aug. 1796.
63. As part of Camden's assault on sedition, the Irish Parliament passed an Indemnity Act in the spring of 1796 to prevent the prosecutions relating to the illegal methods used by the Crown forces in their suppression of Defenderism in Connacht and Ulster.
64. An act for the more easy and speedy trial of such persons as have levied, or shall levy War against His Majesty: 19 Geo. II, c. 9.

13

The National Identity of Edmund Burke*

MICHAEL BROWN

'Edmund Burke was pure Irish.'[1] So reads the opening sentence of Philip Magnus' 1939 biography. Yet, far from informing a full reading of his subject's life and work, Magnus does little more than acknowledge Burke's birth in Dublin before widening his gaze to events in Europe in 1729. Even in treating of Burke's education, in a 'hedge school' in Cork, in a dissenting academy in Ballitore, County Kildare, and at Trinity College, Dublin, Magnus' treatment never rises above the cursory. And when Burke leaves Ireland behind, for the twin attractions of London and the law, and begins his journey towards political activism, so too does Magnus leave the country to its fate, only offering a backward glance when his subject, late in his career, decides from patriotic affection to try to ameliorate the wretched circumstances of Irish Roman Catholics. This though, is seen as little more than a subplot in Burke's greater drama, for it is treated here as intertwined with his engagement with Revolutionary France.

Magnus' rendition of Burke's Irish elements is in many ways typical of much of the scholarship that surrounds him. His Irish origins are always recognized and his Irish character often asserted, but it remains little more than a truism, and is rarely investigated. Stanley Ayling, for example, in his study of 1988 paid some lip service to Burke's Irish dimension, but did little to explore the consequences of such a political origin.[2] So too, more recently, F.P. Lock in his authoritative biography has accepted Burke's origins while ascribing to the view that it had little formative influence on the young man's mind, beyond developing some awareness of the poverty in the bleak climate of mid-eighteenth-century Dublin. Yet his response was not simplistic or even, necessarily, wholly humanitarian:

> In a naturally fertile country, people were starving … The experience might have turned him into an ardent nationalist, or into a revolutionary. Instead he became his generation's most eloquent spokesman for the rights of property. He would never concede that the people had a 'right' to more than the charity of the rich. This apparent paradox illustrates the complexity and ambivalence of Burke's Irish heritage. He left Ireland in

1750, at the age of twenty. During the remaining forty-seven years of his life, he returned to Ireland only four times, for a total of about eighteen months. Yet his Irish upbringing conditioned in important ways the development of his mind and ideas. Growing up in Ireland his earliest impressions of human life and society were far removed from those he would have absorbed in England or in Scotland. Just as he never lost his Irish accent, he never forgot his Irishness.[3]

Certainly, some interpreters have underplayed, or disregarded Burke's early life, viewing it as essentially unrelated to his subsequent reasoning. According to J.C.D. Clark, for example,

> Edmund Burke was an Irishman, born in Dublin but in an age before 'Celtic nationalism' had been constructed to make Irishness and Englishness incompatible: he was therefore free also to describe himself, without misrepresentation, as an 'Englishman' to denote his membership of the wider polity. He never attempted to disguise his Irishness ... Yet Burke's personal ambition from the 1750s or 1760s was to assimilate to the English landed elite, not to return in triumph to Ireland as its political deliverer ... His Irishness had its limits: he was no Jonathan Swift, no Wolfe Tone, no Daniel O'Connell.[4]

This line of interpretation finds its most eloquent exponent in the Anglo-Irish historian R.B. Mc Dowell, who perceived in Burke the need to re-invent himself as an establishment man. For McDowell, it is imperative to recollect throughout one's dealings with the vexed relationship between Burke and Ireland that he had left the country largely behind and 'reliance on memory (that defective, highly selective instrument) had its dangers'.[5] Indeed, Burke's views of Irish issues 'reflected his metropolitan attitude, the outlook of a man who lived in London and was very proud of his Westminster seat'.[6]

From a very different perspective, Elizabeth Lambert concurs. In her intimate portrait, *Edmund Burke of Beaconsfield*, she documents how Burke left Ireland behind and created for himself the persona of a Ciceronian *novus homo*, or New Man.[7] Integral to this was Burke's purchase of a landed estate – in pursuit of which he took great financial risks – and his submerging of his origins among Ireland's middling sort. However, Lambert contends that Burke's drive to position himself at the head of a landed family, which explains something of his starry-eyed compliance when dealing with the British aristocracy and his petition for a title in the 1790s, was actually grounded in his Irish childhood. For Lambert, it was Burke's years in Cork where he witnessed his extended family, who were Catholic, struggle with the impact of the penal code that supplies the explanation for this overweening need for security of tenure.[8]

Whatever the truth of this assessment, Burke's Irish origins and connections help to make sense of his involvement, and sympathy for some of the protagonists, in the country's politics, or, in less generous treatments, explain his servility to British nobility and his anxieties over political and social status. That was the treatment he received from the cartoonists of his day, who regularly depicted him as a Jesuit to highlight his Catholic connections. They disparaged Burke for his perceived Irishness, finding in his humble, foreign origins, a source of bemusement and belittlement.[9]

But it has been clear since the nigh on comprehensive treatment of Burke's Irish connection, compiled by Thomas H.D. Mahoney in 1960, that Burke never fully left the country behind. As Mahoney pertinently wrote:

> This was because his concern for Ireland had deeper roots in his personality than could be accounted for by political theory, practical politics or indeed any merely rational or practical causes. Like every other responsible and intelligent Irishman with sufficient heart from his day to this, Burke carried Ireland around with him as his personal 'old man of the sea', often, certainly, to the detriment of his own interests.[10]

Certainly, Burke remained informed about, and engaged in, developments in the country, and although he only ever returned for two sustained visits, his Irish concerns ran alongside his political commitments in England.

While *Edmund Burke and Ireland* successfully rendered Burke's Irish interests across his career and placed them within his wider political activity, it remains a moot question whether these endeavours were more than the sum of their multiple parts. Put succinctly, what is the significance of the material Mahoney has collated? Is it anything more than the occasional efforts of a native son to help the land of his birth as and when the opportunity arises? Or are the Irish connections of a piece with his other campaigns, fitting snugly in beside his hounding of Warren Hastings, or his rhetorical warfare with Jacobins in France and their fellow travellers in England? Or is there, in this composite, evidence of an Irish Burke; a Burke who's Irish background and concerns serve as the foundations of his other pursuits? Across the twentieth century a school of thought has slowly emerged which, for a variety of reasons, has taken Burke's origins in Ireland to be an essential source of his political insight and intelligence.

DEFINING THE QUESTION

How Irish was Edmund Burke? It should be noted that in dealing with an Irish identity, one is already staking a series of related claims about the nature of political culture in the period in which Burke was active. First, the question presumes that some version of national identity was both extant and politically meaningful in the second half of the eighteenth century. This is itself a highly contentious claim.

So too, one is assuming that an idea of Ireland in particular, not merely nationhood in general, has some purchase on the political culture of the country. It is these assumptions that provide Burke's Irishness with its interpretative power. To merely assert that Irish conditions, such as the country's economic underdevelopment, produced in Burke's thought an Irish character or component is not sufficient. These conditions could be, and were, met just as abrasively in the British Isles, and more widely in Europe. The status of Burke's Irishness, however related to these conditions it may be, is dependent on the assertion of a quality to the national experience that was not to be found elsewhere.

That being so, it remains the case that the Irish materials collected by Mahoney require assessment. Three major interpretative schools have emerged since Mahoney's publication and will be considered briefly here.[11] The intention is to highlight both the accuracy of some of their insights and to reassess the fundamental question of Burke's Irishness.

THE GAELIC THESIS

The origins of this thesis reside in Burke's childhood, namely his five-year sojourn in County Cork from the age of six under the care of his Catholic relatives, the Nagles. L.M. Cullen has done most to reconstruct the political, religious and familial context of Burke's Cork connections, tracing out the interconnections between the Burkes, the Nagles and the Hennesys.[12] Notably, the Blackwater valley in which these families resided was one of the few remaining strongholds of Catholic landed gentry in the country, albeit surrounded by the landholding of staunch members of the Protestant interest. For Burke, as Cullen recognizes, the region 'nourished the loyalty which is one of Burke's most attractive features'.[13] It was also the site of his earliest education, which took place at a hedge school run by an itinerant Catholic schoolmaster named O'Halloran. Burke may also have studied at the feet of Liam Inglis, who went on to become a Catholic priest, and a celebrated Gaelic poet.[14]

The Nagle family in particular were a notable power in the region, and, while this attracted the venom of the local Protestant establishment, it also ensured that they were able to sustain a modicum of cultural patronage which was unusual among minor Catholic gentry. The childhood experience in north Cork, Cullen suggests, had interesting and long-lasting ramifications for Burke, for,

> Burke's writing too is in many ways a product of the region, not only indi-
> rectly, but directly because of the political events of the 1760s: it is not an
> exaggeration to claim that his Irish politics and his writings on the penal
> laws all grew out of his stay on the banks of the Blackwater and happenings
> there.[15]

Building on this insight, Katherine O'Donnell has suggested that the Gaelic culture he encountered in Nagle country was to be embedded in Burke's writings. Indeed, in the light of his childhood amidst this culture, she 'proposes that one fruitful way of interpreting Burke's work is to hear in his voice the modulations of the genres and conventions of Irish poetic and literary composition as practised in eighteenth-century Gaelic Ireland'.[16] It is these echoes that account for the 'strangeness of his compositions' when heard by English ears, providing Burke with a subtle rhetorical undercurrent which informs some of his most noted orations; paradoxically, particularly those speeches in defence of the British constitution.[17]

The political implications of this echo were, for O'Donnell, to affiliate Burke, at least linguistically, with the Jacobite literary tradition. According to O'Donnell, 'Jacobitism infused Irish poetry with memories of greatness and the promise of restoration and renewal. Jacobitism also provided an alternative lexicon of political concepts and ideas of social order to the English parliament and commercial metropolis. This alternative lexicon might be described as "genealogical politics".'[18] It was this inheritance that enabled Burke to articulate so fluently ideas about the sanctity of tradition, the legitimacy of inheritance and defence of rights.[19] In particular,

> The practice of 'genealogical politics' encapsulated in [the idea of] Ceart [Right] is echoed in Burke's description of the immemorial practice of claiming liberties. He claims that the British constitution which safeguards British liberty is an 'entailed inheritance derived to us from our forefathers, and to be transmitted by us to our posterity'.[20]

In treating of the constitution in this fashion, Burke was driven to perceive the Glorious Revolution as a Reformation, not a making anew; a policy which while derived from his Jacobite origins, enabled him at once to confront the threat of Jacobin politics and defend the legitimacy of the British sovereign.

In assessing the extent and import of Gaelic culture as an influence on his thought, Burke bears some comparison with his great Irish forebear, Jonathan Swift. Like the dean of St Patrick's Cathedral, Burke may well have had an awareness of, and taken some delight in, the Gaelic culture which he occasionally encountered. However, it is actually Swift, for whom the experience of Gaelic culture clearly extended into adulthood, in which the influences are most easily delineated. His poem, 'The Description of an Irish Feast' was, as the text itself acknowledged, 'translated almost literally out of the original Irish'.[21]

As for Burke having Jacobite leanings, again Swift serves as a useful comparator. Ian Higgins has made the claim that Swift's Tory tendencies tipped over into outright, if guarded, support for the Stuart Pretender.[22] Again, the evidence for this political attachment, although contested, is stronger for Swift than for Burke. After all, Swift was politically sympathetic to the Tory party, while Burke held firmly Whig credentials until the last decade of his life, when the threat came, not from any court-in-exile, but from Republicanism. For Burke, the evidence for Jacobite sympathies emerges primarily as literary echoes in his works. However, the suspicion was voiced by contemporaries primarily because of his actions on behalf of Catholics charged with treason in the 1760s. This activity was, however, a consequence of the complex political configurations in which Burke found himself while aiding the Halifax administration in Dublin.

Under Halifax's watch a series of agrarian outrages spread across north Munster and south Leinster, enacted by a secretive society of tenant farmers known as the Whiteboys.[23] Their actions, which seem to have been prompted primarily by economic malaise in the region and in protest at the tithe payment, were set against the background of the Seven Years War (1756–63) between Britain and France. Given the political circumstance, the Whiteboys were understood by the local Protestant interest as rebels, who feared the possibility that, with French aid, the agrarian unrest might provoke a rising aimed at re-establishing the Stuart pretender upon the throne.

How far the Whiteboys were committed to the Jacobite cause is still a matter of academic dispute, and it appears that Protestant fears concerning the extent and venom of the movement were exaggerated.[24] However, as Thomas Power has documented, the outrages were interpreted within the framework of a narrative of Catholic barbarity and violence that dated back to the 1641 Rising in Ulster, and the massacre myth that ensued. This mythic landscape was recalled with the issuing of an edition of Sir John Temple's *Irish Rebellion* by the Cork publishing family, the Bagwells, with the extensive support of the middling ranks of Cork Protestant society.[25] Indeed, it is possible that Burke's patronage of the historians John Curry and Thomas Leland, which dates from this period, arose from a desire to offer a second, less damaging, if equally polemical, narrative of 1641 to counter the impact of the Cork edition.[26]

The Cork ascendancy was primarily responsible for bringing the Whiteboy insurgency to national attention. As L.M. Cullen has shown, the Lord Shannon interest in parliament pushed to create a committee to investigate the outrages, and were significantly disappointed with the initial judicial response to the perceived threat. In the summer of 1762, John Aston, a government appointment and the son of a convert, gained a reputation for leniency in dealing with Whiteboy offences.[27] Burke, although not a formal member of Halifax's Irish administration, was closely involved in shaping the government's response to these events, going so far as to enable a search in Cork city for Catholic firearms, which, predictably, had an insignificant return for their efforts.[28] However, this, and Aston's progress, did little to allay Protestant fears.

While Burke was convinced that the Whiteboy phenomenon was economically, rather than politically, motivated, and held no serious threat to the Protestant interest, much has been made of his family ties to some of the victims of the judicial reprisals which followed Aston's return from the region. In 1763–64, Halifax lost control over the House of Lords and a new committee was pressed into service in the pursuit of Whiteboys. By the time of the 1765–66 session, the backlash against the Whiteboys was in full flood. Caught up in this were a number of Burke's maternal relatives. Of the Nagle clan, James Nagle was arrested in Tipperary, while both Garret Nagle and Robert Nagle conformed to the Church of Ireland in this period, doubtless to forestall rumours of political disaffection. Burke was further implicated in the Whiteboy agitation during his visit to Ireland in late 1766, which he undertook to organize the legal defence of the Whiteboys.[29]

In this Burke was eminently successful. But retribution had already been exacted. Indeed, his actions may well have been prompted by the execution of three minor Catholic gentry and, notoriously, a Catholic priest, Fr Nicholas Sheehy, in the spring of 1766. This has long been seen as an act of judicial murder, emblematic of the mal-administration of the country by the Protestant community.[30] What is certain is that Sheehy was the victim of Protestant paranoia and over-reaction, and his death highlights how questions of political loyalty got entangled with religious affiliation.[31]

Yet, while the Jacobite tenor of Whiteboy activity remains circumstantial, and other motives, including simple support for the court party in parliament in the face of opposition from the Munster coterie around Lord Shannon, can be attributed to Burke, the assertion of Jacobite sympathies on his part is implausible. One of his few direct expressions of support for the Whiteboys – in contrast with his efforts to deflect the Munster Protestants or to protect his Nagle relatives from their ire – comes in a letter of April 1763. He wrote to a friend, John Ridge, of the trial of a man named Dwyer at Clonmel, 'for God's sake let me know a little of this matter, and of the history of these new levellers. I see that you have but one way of relieving the poor in Ireland. They call for bread, and you give them not a stone, but the gallows.'[32] This actually suggests that Burke's understanding of the protest was primarily economic, and that his sympathies were driven in the main by simple humanity. It is noticeable that his phrase 'not a stone' was later used in a debate on the rights and wrongs of American taxation, suggesting a fusion in his mind of the two expressions of grievance.[33]

More striking is his defence of the Catholic community's integrity, for it was at this time he wrote the devastating critique of the penal code, *Tracts Relative to the Laws against Popery in Ireland*, and he certainly informed the Irish administration's calm estimate of the Catholic threat in the period.[34] Such direct evidence of familial attachment to, and intellectual advocacy of, the Roman Catholic community's circumstance has led some commentators to develop the second of our interpretive strands, perceiving a Catholic Burke hidden in his Irish writings.

THE CATHOLIC THESIS

At the epicentre of the Catholic thesis is the highly contentious claim that

Richard Burke, Edmund's father, was a convert from Roman Catholicism to the Church of Ireland. The assertion rests on two distinct, if complementary pieces of evidence. First of all, there is the presence in the 1722 listing of a Richard Burke on the *Convert Rolls*, which were kept by the Irish authorities as an official record of those who had undergone the complex legal and religious procedure of conversion.[35] Secondly, there is the circumstantial evidence, that Richard Burke was a lawyer of some standing in Dublin whose practice may have included some high profile cases with Catholic interests at their heart, particularly that of the Jacobite James Cotter.[36] While the Richard Burke named on the rolls cannot be definitely identified as Edmund's father, it is certainly the case that lawyers were one of the largest categories of professional conversions, as nominal membership of the Church of Ireland was a legal requirement for practicing the law.[37]

However, the identification of Richard Burke as a convert, while it would be of some interest in rethinking Burke's religious origins, might have had little influence upon his subsequent thought. He was, after all raised as a member of the Church of Ireland, while his mother was a Roman Catholic. This interesting aside has, however, been raised to a higher standing in the interpretation of Burke's career and thought by the commentator Conor Cruise O'Brien.[38]

For O'Brien, Richard Burke's apparent conversion was a central explanatory factor in Edmund Burke's political actions throughout his career. He even posits the suggestion, briefly and with a degree of scepticism expressed, that Edmund secretly returned to the Roman fold when a student in Middle Temple.[39] Whether this is the case or not, it is O'Brien's assessment that 'for adequate reasons, he did his best to cover his tracks over Ireland. The student of Burke must uncover those tracks as best he may, often relying on cryptic remarks, strained silences, perceived constraints, together with a scrutiny of the actual Irish context of positions that he took up, or avoided, over Ireland.'[40] Indeed,

> he was always secretive about his Irish origins and Catholic connexions, which his enemies used against him, and he is known to have destroyed many of his papers ... Detachment and even dissimulation were desirable, both in the interests of his personal career and in order to help Ireland, and specifically the Catholics ... in the persona of a disinterested and liberal observer of the Irish scene.[41]

So deep did this anxiety run that it could be traced, as O'Brien attempts to do in *The Great Melody*, in Burke's adoption of reformist policies over America and India, while it also shaped his response to the French Revolution in that he increasingly feared the possibility that Jacobin politics might destroy the relationship with Britain he spent his life serving.[42] It even impinged upon his personal relations, causing a cooling in his friendship with his childhood companion, Richard Shackleton when he wrote in 1770 of Burke's background for the *London Evening Post*.[43] So too O'Brien observes in dealing with Burke's correspondence with Charles O'Hara:

> As we shall see throughout this study, he [Burke] was almost always on his guard where Ireland was concerned, not only in public, but, until his later years, in private letters. The copious correspondence ... is unique in the insight it affords into Burke's thinking and feeling about Ireland. But it is coded; it needs to be read with a key ... The key to the correspondence is the unspoken bond between the two men. The bond is that both belonged to a special and suspect category – old Catholic gentry conforming to the Established Church.[44]

The real purchase of this reading of Burke as a kind of crypto-Catholic resides in Burke's familial connections. As O'Brien rightly writes: 'The clan at whose head Burke marched was shot through with Catholicism ... His family background was such – and his family feeling so strong – that he could not possibly contemplate attacks on the Church of Rome with any of the feeling of a proper Englishman.'[45] This emotional attachment led, in O'Brien's view, to a crisis of loyalty that Burke repeatedly struggled to resolve. This tension, what Michel Fuchs describes as 'a choice between treasons', was embedded in, and gave energy to, Burke's political orations.[46] O'Brien notes: 'Burke was not English, although he often wrote and spoke in the character of an Englishman'.[47] For O'Brien the adoption of just such a persona was a kind of willed false consciousness, evident in the convolutions Burke had to complete in articulating some of his most famous statements of policy. For example, in Burke's extraordinary intervention into imperial affairs, *Conciliation with America*, O'Brien argues that Burke's adoption of the stance of an English Whig oligarch is so complete that he 'temporarily talks himself out of existence'.[48] Picking up on Burke's celebration of 'the wisdom of our ancestors' O'Brien ironically inquires whether, given 'some copies must have found their way into the Nagle country in the Blackwater valley of County Cork, did anyone smile, I wonder, at the phrase...? Such Whiggish ancestors as Richard Nagle of Carrigacunna, James II's Attorney General?'[49]

Paradoxically, this tension between Burke's willed persona and his actual origins was creative, yet it failed him when he turned his powers of oratory to Ireland. According to O'Brien:

> Burke attains his highest level of eloquence only in those conjunctures when he feels fully free to speak what he thinks and feels ... Burke never feels free over Ireland. During most of his life, with one startling exception, Burke's public statements over Ireland were few, guarded, cryptic, sometimes evasive. The startling exception is supplied by a passage in the Bristol Guildhall speech (1780) in which, at a moment of great stress, his real feelings about the penal laws gush out in almost a trance-like manner.

Ireland, in the Great Melody, is a brooding presence, expressed in haunted silences and transferred passions.[50]

This dialectic between acculturation and resentful and truculent resistance found its apogee in the 1790s when confronted with the crisis of the French Revolution. What Burke discovered, according to O'Brien, was how anti-Catholic England remained, and how deeply problematic any celebration of the Glorious Revolution actually was, given the horrific cost the ensuing war in Ireland had inflicted on his native country. Thus, O'Brien contends:

> This intruding vision had to be exorcised: much of the argument – and the most forced part of the argument – both of the *Reflections* and the *Appeal from the New to the Old Whigs* – consists of an attempt to show that the English Revolution, unlike the French one, had not really been revolutionary at all … It is as if the words and actions of Price had awakened within that reasonable elderly Whig, a slumbering Jacobite.[51]

Whatever the strength of this assessment, O'Brien is surely on firmer ground in his contention that it was Burke's Irish background that gave him such deep insight into the Jacobin politics of the Revolution and such cause for concern that it might find a fruitful environment in disaffected Irish communities. As Burke was well aware, the increasingly radicalized United Irishmen seriously threatened the Irish administration and Burke remained haunted by the possibility that dissenters and Roman Catholics might combine in revolutionary violence. In this, as O'Brien asserts: 'The author of the *Reflections* wrote in the persona of an Englishman … but was in fact Irish to the marrow of his bones'.[52]

However, the argument that Burke repressed his Irish identity in favour of reconstituting himself as an Englishman is not wholly persuasive. It is certainly true that, as we have already noted, he envisioned himself as founding a noble line, which would serve the greater good of the community, and in pursuit of this sought to purchase a landed estate in England. Equally, Burke did write at times as an English parliamentarian, which to a certain extent, given he represented a series of English constituencies and attended the British parliament at Westminster and not its Dublin-based Irish counterpart, he was. But he was not, as O'Brien suggests, silent about his Irish roots and interests.

The truth is that Burke wrote and spoke repeatedly, persistently and publicly about the Irish Catholic question.[53] As early as his sojourn in Ireland as private secretary to his patron Chief Secretary Hamilton during the Halifax administration of 1761–62, he was composing a denunciation of the anti-Catholic penal code, which he later described as: 'machine of wise and elaborate contrivance, and as well fitted for the oppression, impoverishment and degradation of a people, and the debasement in them of human nature itself, as ever proceeded from the perverted ingenuity of man'.[54] He was even actively involved in subverting the penal code's implementation on behalf of his Nagle relatives. He was engaged in a complex property transfer with regard to a small property in Clogher, County Cork. Upon his death in 1765, Burke's elder brother Garret bequeathed the estate to Edmund; an estate which Garret appears may have had title to as a result of a collusive arrangement with Catholic relatives; Garret acting as the Protestant underwriter for the property holding, required under penal legislation.[55]

Moreover, Burke was damning in his criticism of the penal code's upholders, the Irish Protestant community. So economically damaging was their mismanagement of the country – it should be emphasized that much of Burke's criticism of the penal code was economic in content – and so destructive to the ancient communal structures of the Catholic community, that Burke drew a comparison between their levelling tendencies and the devastation wrought by the Jacobin administration in France:

> By the use that is so frequently made of the term, and the policy that is engrafted on it, the name Protestant becomes nothing more or better than the name of a persecuting faction, with a relation of some sort of theological hostility to others, but without any sort of ascertained tenets of its own, upon the ground of which it persecutes other men; for the patrons of this Protestant ascendancy, neither do nor can by anything positive, define or describe what they mean by the word Protestant ... This makes such persecutions ten times worse than any of that description that hitherto have been known in the world. The old persecutors, whether Pagan or Christian, whether Arian or orthodox, whether Catholics, Anglicans or Calvinists, actually were, or at least had the decorum to pretend to be, strong dogmatists. They pretended that their religious maxims were clear and ascertained, and so useful, that they were bound, for the eternal benefit of mankind, to defend or diffuse them.[56]

But we should not confuse Burke's antipathy for the jobbing ascendancy for a hidden affiliation with the religious belief system offered by Roman Catholicism. To be sympathetic to the plight of the Roman Catholic community does not imply any intellectual assent to their foundational assumptions. This simply does not follow, for individuals are fully capable, as Burke was, of criticizing both sides of an argument, however vitriolic or polarized that contention has become. But, by focusing on the theme of Ireland and Burke's familial ties with Roman Catholicism, O'Brien does raise, by default, an important question about the significance of Burke's Catholic sympathies. What do his writings against the penal code and in favour of Catholic relief tell us about his life and thought if it does not imply closet affiliation to the Roman Catholic faith? One answer to that question, which has been articulated by interpreters of a post-colonial bent, is that Burke was consistently, and for reasons to do with his Irish origins, temperamentally on the side of the victim. Or as Michel

Fuchs explains it:

> To attribute this passion to Burke to a burning sympathy for Catholicism, or even for Christianity in general, is to miss the main point of his arguments in favour of his countrymen. Men are perhaps made to live in society, but they also have individual rights, among them being happy here on earth.[57]

THE POST-COLONIAL THESIS

Fuchs' study of the pre-parliamentary life and career of Edmund Burke draws a striking portrait of an emerging man of letters, tormented and haunted by the condition of his country. He grew up aware of the economic and legal uncertainties that bore down on his extended, Catholic, family. According to Fuchs, Burke was also given a brusque education in the politics of religion when his childhood friend, the Quaker Richard Shackleton, had to forego entry into Trinity College, Dublin because of the requirement to take a series of oaths upon entry – whether this was the problem or whether Quakers had any inclination to attend an Anglican educational establishment is something which Fuchs fails to discuss.[58] In Fuchs' reading, Burke began a subtle campaign of undermining the consequences of this iniquity. Through his letters to Shackleton, and then in founding a debating society in which his friend could openly participate, Burke tried to incorporate the Quaker into the institutional life of the college.[59] This policy of internal protest, Fuchs suggests in a subtle reading of Burke's early prose, infested Burke's literary experimentation. His style became an ironic form of parody, making mock of the high, effusive and decorative quality of much aristocratic writings.[60] In doing so Burke also ingested much of their manner, which was to serve him well upon entry in parliament, allowing him at once to speak the language of the caste with whom he now frequented, while subtly deprecating its form and content.

This internal protest was ultimately driven by an awareness that, due to the accident of birth, Burke would always remain on the fringes of social life. In England, this was to be a consequence of his Irish origins, but it was also true in Ireland. Paradoxically this was because of the way his Anglican identity empowered him. As Fuchs observes:

> Burke realised that, wherever he was and whatever he did, he belonged to a minority, an obvious truth that he later admitted to Boswell: 'I believe that in any body of men in England, I should have been in the minority.' Burke, of course, belonged to the privileged Irish minority and had enjoyed some of its most important advantages. But this minority was also part of the exploited people of Ireland, which means that Burke belonged to that minority of people who are unable to be an integral part

of any group, sect or class, adopting all its prejudices and all its hatreds. He has therefore to be considered as belonging to that minority of social, religious and political 'cross-breeds' who, excluded or excluding themselves, in part at least, from all the communities which they could claim as theirs, are condemned to a succession of precarious alliances and to sacrificing all their dreams of social integration as utopian.[61]

Burke was, in this light, a 'cultural mulatto' who was 'too English for the Irish and too Irish for the English'.[62]

This awareness might have remained inarticulate, driven under for fear that his Irish identity might degrade his protest on the country's behalf, but for his intellectual excursus into colonial history. It was in writing the early *An Account of the European Settlements in America* with his kinsman, William Burke, that Edmund perceived the wider implications of the Irish situation. As Fuchs contends, it was

> while working on the book [that] Burke discovered the universality of violence. He had first experienced violence in Ireland, where he had condemned it as a peculiar, anomalous and therefore intolerable local phenomenon; but the moment violence assumes the aspect of a universal reality, it raises many more problems.[63]

What this awareness gave Burke was an understanding of the moral ambiguities involved in imperial expansion. For Burke, colonial contact was complicit with the corrupting of local cultures and the imposition of hardship on the colonized. Thus, slavery was perceived by Burke to rest at the moral core of the experience of empire. However, as *European Settlements* also made clear, the economics of slavery were advantageous to the colonizer, and the English culture Burke participated in and celebrated rested upon this truth. Thus 'to colonial harpies correspond metropolitan bloodsuckers, and between them there is a difference of degree, but not in kind'.[64]

It was this increasing comprehension of the moral deficiency of the imperial structure, Fuchs argues, coupled with the personal experience that Burke had garnered in the Irish colony, which produced a deep undercurrent of anger in his prose. Building on an observation of Mary Wollstonecraft, that 'had you [Burke] been a Frenchman, you would have been, in spite of your respect for rank and antiquity, a violent revolutionist ... your imagination would have taken fire', Fuchs contends there is an anarchic, Jacobin, levelling edge to much of Burke's excoriations of empire:

> This European world seen in the colonial mirror could lead Burke to some kind of anarchic revolt. It is not easy for an educated Irishman, that is to say for a citizen of a colonised colony, to reconcile himself to an immoral reality. In Burke's case, the contradiction between his craving for justice

and the spectacle of injustice offered by the world was so powerful that he was strongly tempted by anarchism, as both the *Vindication* [*of Natural Society*] and his attacks in parliament against English rapacity in India show. These reactions may be considered an oblique and indirect way of liberating a suppressed revolutionary passion, forged in Ireland and with the repeated tragedies of Irish history in mind.[65]

Thus, for Fuchs, Burke's career can be read as a lengthy and complex series of protests against the moral degradation implicit in colonial rule, produced by his Irish experience and fuelled by his perception of the archetypal status of that case. In arguing this case, Ireland becomes for Fuchs, 'the most ancient and systematically exploited of the British colonies'; a 'perverted country, and therefore a perverting influence, a country tortured by contradictions and, therefore, a country breeding contradiction'.[66] In this, Fuchs simplifies the country's history to a tale of 'six centuries of English domination, punctuated by innumerable massacres' in a manner which, ironically, underestimates the ambiguities and contradictions which he finds so clearly embedded in the mind of the youthful Burke.[67]

It should be recognized that Fuchs' focus is, quite explicitly, on Burke's pre-parliamentary career and writings, for, as he writes:

> too often considered as 'false starts' or unfulfilled promises, these writings have not received the attention they deserve. Yet analysing this group of works as a whole reveals their seminal importance. Such an approach is necessary if we really want to understand Burke as he lived the experience of his century – torn as he was between Ireland and England and finally confronting the mighty challenge of the French Revolution.[68]

Yet, despite some hints and suggestions strewn through the book, and the assertion that Ireland is not 'just another of those political or economic themes that were to engage the attention of Burke throughout his life, for his country occupied a place in his affective and intellectual life on quite a different level. It was an all-pervading existential structure', Fuchs does little to tease out the influence of this, his most clearly Irish phase, on his later work.[69] Indeed, he openly disowns the project as it 'would mean believing that, in all its essentials, the real Burke is to be found in his parliamentary work' whereas Fuchs suggests his relationship to political patrons actually muted his critical voice.[70] Thus, despite the fact that Irish concerns repeatedly forced themselves onto Burke's agenda throughout his parliamentary career, and it is in giving voice to his opinions in parliament that he was to become known, Fuchs' decision ensures that the consequence of his Irish formation for his subsequent thought is still an open question.

In contrast to the narrow remit adopted by Fuchs, Luke Gibbons' study, *Edmund Burke and Ireland* supplies a wide-ranging set of meditations that are actually often tangential to Burke and more concerned with the Irish condition. The second chapter, for example, 'Philoctetes and Colonial Ireland' treats not of Burke, but his acquaintance, the artist James Barry.[71] Gibbons proposes here that Barry's painting of the Greek hero was actually an allegory of Ireland, for just as Philoctetes was eternally wounded, so Ireland was a political injured body, wounded by the horror of British imperialism and Catholic suffering. This may be stretching the limits of allegorical interpretation. Barry, after all, was on the Grand Tour at the time of the painting's execution, gifting it to a learned Academy in Bologna, and was to enter the Royal Academy upon his return to London, suggesting that the painting was perhaps more an academic exercise in the sublime than a fully achieved political allegory. More personally, the study in suffering may just as fruitfully be read as a premonition of the psychological turmoil that would see Barry withdraw from society in a paranoid retreat at the end of his life. Yet it important to note the polemical charge which the political reading supplies, for it allows Gibbons to postulate a relationship with Burke's *Philosophical Enquiry* (itself read by Gibbons as a sublimation of political concerns) and hence supplies supporting evidence for the thesis of an Irish school of the sublime. First mooted in a footnote to the introduction, Gibbons writes of how 'Burke was the most influential Irish figure to deal in a systematic fashion with the sublime, but was by no means the only Irish writer to explore this dark side of the aesthetic landscape. Among other important contributions to what might be termed the "Irish sublime" [are] John Lawson ... James Usher ... James Barry ... Richard Stack ... [and] George Milner.'[72]

For Gibbons this Irish school of the sublime was transmuting political ruptures into aesthetic reflection, allegorising the dilemmas and conflicts of Irish society into philosophical concepts. This he then places in tension with the aesthetic sensibilities of the Scottish writer, Adam Smith, who provides Gibbons with a foil with which to identify the distinctly Irish characteristics of Burke's aesthetic mediation. And it is here where problems emerge.

For Gibbons, Smith is best read as an imperial stoic. His moral philosophy, which advocates a submission to suffering, is read as an argument for colonial subjection. Smith becomes a compliant victim of empire and a willing participant in its exploitative actions, and

> in this, it is possible to see in microcosm the dilemma of Scottish culture in the mid-eighteenth century: it has to adjust itself and curb excesses so as not to give offence to its more temperate, civilised neighbour. It is fitting that *The Theory of Moral Sentiments* opens with a section 'On Propriety', for Smith was to be at the forefront of that anxious strain of Scottish patriotic sentiment which sought to remove the impurities of their own native culture in order to present a more acceptable face to English polite society.[73]

In contrast, Burke's aesthetics, which has at its heart the concept of sympathy between individuals, is read as a kind of colonial Christianity, which at once offers charity and assistance to the subjects of imperial dominion and, in a similar fashion to Fuchs' reading of Burke as tinged with Jacobin rage, advocates a moral resistance to imperial cultivation.

There are two problems with this contrast that suggest that it is actually a false dichotomy.[74] First of all, even if one follows Gibbons' logic that the interest in the sublime may emerge from the tensions implicit in Irish society in the eighteenth century, it does not follow that the school of the sublime were necessarily on the side of the victimized. Instead, aesthetic reification of colonial conflict could take the shape of the fear of the repressed, and of the potential for violence such a community held. The nightmares of the sublime might emanate, not from an awareness of the colonial repression of a community but from a terror of the possibilities of their retribution. That Gibbons is aware of that possibility can be evidenced in his reading of an Irish subtext to Gothic literature.[75] Hence aesthetics could contain an anti-Catholic agenda, related to the paranoia that kept alive the memory of the 1641 massacres and the dramatic narrative of Catholic perfidy and native barbarism. Indeed, the theme is later explored by Gibbons himself, but not in relation to his pamphlet *Gaelic Gothic*.[76]

Secondly, Gibbons' rendering of Adam Smith's *Theory of Moral Sentiments* is problematic. Smith's system proposes, to a certain, if important extent, a brand of situationalist ethics, in that moral behaviour is determined by the social context in which it occurs. The *Theory of Moral Sentiments* is an attempt to explore a sufficient range of possible contexts in order to develop a general theory of moral responses. Gibbons is right to notice that, for Smith, moral responses are prioritised over moral action, hence making Smith's moral philosophy akin to the spectatorial nature of aesthetic theory. However, for Smith this is only one element within a reflexive system in which moral sentiments and action interact. The role of the sentiments are to inform the actor as to how to respond to the circumstances which present themselves, and they do so by imaginatively placing the actor into the vantage point of a potential observer: Smith's impartial spectator.[77] The outcome of this leap of the moral imagination is that the actor will endeavour to do what the society would expect a morally righteous individual to do, placing least stress on the social fabric. The situationalist aspect emerges because different people have different vantage points and so the same circumstance can make different demands of different individuals.

Smith offers as an example the vision of a man stretched out upon the rack, undergoing the agonies of torture.[78] For Smith, there are two significant perspectives to be taken. The first, which is from where Gibbons derives his reading of Smith, is that of the victim. Smith argues that the individual's moral responsibility is to minimize the extent of the pain that they are undergoing, so as not to discommode any observer of their torment. They should, in effect, adhere to the Stoic system of ethics in which life is an endurance test and the passions and the sentiments lead only to unhappiness. However, there is a second perspective on the scene, and one that complicates Gibbons' contrast between Burke and Smith. Smith contends that although the man on the rack should remain Stoic about his suffering – a compliant victim – that is not the demand made upon an observer of the horror. For them, it is necessary to adopt a Christian ethic that involves an imaginative leap into the place of the victim, the expression of sympathy and an emotional engagement with their travails. Thus, while the victim is not to burden the observer with the true depth of their torment it is incumbent on the Christian observer to act to alleviate the suffering to which he is witness.

Indeed, it was Burke, not Smith, who argued that the sensibility of the sublime involves a degree of emotional distance from the trauma. In the *Philosophical Enquiry* he rightly noted that terror, if immediate, was simply terror: 'when danger or pain press too nearly, they are incapable of giving any delight, and are simply terrible; but at certain distances, and with certain modifications, they may be, and they are delightful'.[79] However acute Burke may be about the nature of the sublime sensibility – one thinks of the extraordinary purchase horror inflicted on others has on the imagination – the distance from the victim his thesis required complicates Gibbons' assertion that Burke was on the side of the victim, as much as Smith's defence of Christian charity in his *Theory of Moral Sentiments* problematizes Gibbons' reading of Smith as an imperial apologist.

Ultimately, the dilemma for Gibbons is that no one or no community has a monopoly over suffering and no person's suffering has a priority over someone else's. As Conor Cruise O'Brien's aphorism from a different context reminds us 'the blood shed is real blood' whether it is that of a colonial agent or a colonized resister.[80] As Linda Colley's recent volume documents at length, imperialists could be victims too, for the edges of imperial power were blurred and the hegemony of the British Empire over its holdings was insecure and contested.[81] In linking concern for victim-hood with the Irish experience of colonialism, Gibbons has offered up a provocative thesis but one that is undermined by an essentialist understanding of national identity which draws him close to an openly nationalist line of interpretation. The contrast between Scottish and Irish aesthetics is surely not reducible to a series of binary oppositions between colonizer and colonized; morally cold and emotionally generous.

NATIONHOOD IN THE EIGHTEENTH CENTURY

In assessing the array of related versions of Burke's Irish identity, one can find embedded in each a belief in some form of essential Irishness. As noted above, this relies upon the twin assumption that national identities had some purchase on political culture in the last half of the eighteenth century, and that Ireland was one such developed national identity. Yet, can we take these assumptions for granted? Take the specific case of Ireland first.

To what extent can Ireland in the eighteenth century be considered a fully-fledged nation? Predictably, the answer depends heavily on your formulation of what constitutes a nation, which we will come to, but some clarifications can at least eliminate some senses of the word. Ireland was not a fully independent nation-state at any time before 1922. Indeed, the final outcome of political debate and discord in the eighteenth century was not independence but rather the fuller incorporation of the country into the political life of its dominant neighbour, through the mechanism of the Anglo-Irish Act of Union of 1800.[82] Even in the century before this event, Ireland was at best a dependent kingdom, which shared a monarch with the United Kingdom of England and Scotland, and whose political activities were, until 1782, further delimited by a cluster of legislative barriers to parliamentary and judicial autonomy.[83]

The political culture more generally was also deeply indebted to British languages of identity. Neither of the two prevalent discourses of politics – Hanoverian loyalism and Jacobite resistance – were to any great extent nationally-minded. Neither Tory nor Whig Hanoverians were determined on removing the monarch – who was of German birth or descent – while those who were committed to just such an upheaval were equally determined to place a Scot onto the combined thrones of England, Scotland and Ireland. Only with the emergence of the United Irishmen in the 1790s was room given in the political discussion to ideas of Irish national sovereignty and self-determination, and even here it is unclear that outcome was widely desired even amongst that revolutionary movement. Instead, many of its main protagonists were content to rely militarily on Jacobin France, or aimed to spawn a pan-British revolution in which all three kingdoms would be replaced with a republican regime.

Even if one accepts that the United Irishmen were, in fact, espousing a brand of republican nationalists and endeavouring to break the ties with Britain and inaugurate an independent, egalitarian polity, it is unclear whether this can be availed of to supply Edmund Burke with a national dimension.[84] Burke notoriously, and vociferously, opposed the political programme of the United Irishmen, spending his final days in fear of an impending revolutionary upheaval in the country – which actualised only ten months after his death on 9 July 1797. If anything, this suggests that Burke was consciously opposed to the emergence of the Irish nation and disparaging of any closet Irishness in his make-up.

Yet this is not the end of the issue, for we need to explore more broadly the potential resonance of nationhood in the eighteenth century. As recent literature has made clear, the modernist equation of nationhood with the nation-state was not made until the saddle-period between the eighteenth and nineteenth centuries.[85] The language of nationhood, however, was older and subtler than that. It depended in part on a biblical language of tribes and of faiths.[86] This biblical, tribal language of nationhood fitted into an understanding of politics which did not accord with the fraternal equality that underpins modern nation states, and which was forged in the republican fires of the French Revolution. Rather eighteenth-century politics was arranged through systems of hierarchy and of privilege. The nation was a tribe in the sense that it relied on its relationship to a chieftain, or monarch, for its meaning and its borders. And its limits were often also conceived of as religious. Thus, English Presbyterians and Catholics found themselves proscribed by a self-consciously Anglican state, while in Scotland Episcopalians struggled in the face of Presbyterian hegemony. In Ireland the Anglican State actively sought to demarcate politics on religious grounds and sporadically attempted to undermine and eradicate the Roman Catholic faith of the majority.

Nationhood, in other words, was a vision of divinely inspired order, which accommodated both hierarchy and privilege. And it was this church-state settlement that Edmund Burke entered the lists to defend. Indeed, his counter-revolutionary campaigns of the 1790s can be understood as a defence of this older formulation of political nationhood against the modern conceptualization of a fraternal community, defined by geographic origins, co-existing under a single polity and equal under law.

BURKE'S NATIONAL IDENTITY

So what was the national identity of Edmund Burke? Certainly it was complex, and easy formulations of its impact on his general political thought are difficult to sustain. But, the first thing to recognize is that Burke was a life-long communicant of the Anglican Church. In that, he was in accordance with the primary entry requirements for the British state, although whether his allegiance was simply pragmatic and strictly functional is not to be determined here.[87] Irish scholars have, rightly, highlighted his familial ties with Roman Catholics, although the import of these connections is, however, impossible to determine with any precision. Burke's pleas for leniency towards Irish Roman Catholics were, after all, just that: petitions for tolerance and patience. Where he did propose the inclusion of Catholics into political life, it was on the basis that property qualifications would maintain hierarchical relations and that those who gained access to the political life of the country would remain loyal to the crown and defend the established order. This view led him to inquire of Hercules Langrishe:

> Are we to be astonished that when, by the efforts of so much violence in conquest, and so much policy in regulation, continued without intermission for near an hundred years, we had reduced them to a mob; that whenever they came to act at all, many of them would act exactly like a mob, without temper, measure or foresight? ... If the disorder you speak of be real and considerable you ought to raise an aristocratic interest; that is, an interest in property and education amongst them, and strengthen by every prudent means, the authority and influence of men of that description.[88]

Secondly, as the solution proffered here makes clear, Burke remained wedded to a politics of privilege: a commitment that profoundly shaped his politi-

cal intelligence. It was the traditions of social deference and of authority that
ensured the survival of the government and the flourishing of the community
beneath it. It was this that explains why he defended Roman Catholicism so
vociferously in the *Reflections on the Revolution in France,* for it was a central
pillar of the system of governance that had emerged in France, and its degradation and destruction implied a systemic collapse in the lines of authority in the
country. Indeed, as he explicitly argued, it was corporate identity that defined
the nation and ensured the welfare of the community it served: 'Corporate
bodies are immortal for the good of the members, but not for their punishment.
Nations themselves are such corporations.'[89]

The outcome of this is a realization that one can have more than one national identity, for one could participate in more than one patronage structure. In
Burke's case there was clearly a layering of identities onto each other. Burke's
Irish birth and education placed him within that nation, defined through religious affiliation and political circumstance as well as geographic origins.
However, his career also supplied him with an English and a British political
identity, which both complicated and problematized his Irishness. Burke was,
after all, an English landlord, an MP in the parliament at Westminster and a proponent of reform of the British Empire. The first two of these elements placed
him within an English web of political privilege and duties, and supplied him
with a set of commitments to the English nation. The third element, Britishness
– which spanned not only the British Isles but evolved into a world-wide
identity, – both comprehended the other two facets of his political identity and
articulated the relationship between them.

CONCLUSION

Was Edmund Burke Irish? Yes, but only in a limited and highly specific sense.
To focus attention on this component of his identity can be rewarding, and
informative, but care must always be taken to evade the temptress of reduction.
Burke's national identity was multiple, polyphonic and integrative. It was pli-
able enough to allow him access to Westminster and to condemn the government in their treatment of the American colonists, yet stable enough for him to
denounce the treatment of the Irish Catholics by the Protestant Ascendancy and
to wage a war of rhetoric upon the Jacobin republic of France. It made Burke
both a reformer of the state and of the empire, and a defender of the establishment.

How then do we make sense of the evidence of his Irish aspect? Crucially
we need to supply an answer to the three lines of interpretation outlined above,
the Gaelic; the Roman Catholic and the post-colonial. All three lines of analysis raise a significant question about Burke, which deserve consideration. The
Gaelic line asks readers to assess the import of Burke's ongoing and intimate
concern with Irish affairs. Mahoney has clearly adduced that Burke did not

leave Irish issues behind when he left for England, and the Gaelic interpretation posits the possibility that there is something specific to, and particular about, Irish experience that needs to be comprehended in any analysis of Burke's career. The Roman Catholic interpretation offers one way to make the nature of that specificity clear. It contends that it was the unusual confessional circumstances which prevailed in Ireland, with the established church only having the affiliation of a small, if powerful, minority, that colours any form of Irishness in the century. In Burke's case, this line further argues, this resulted in the articulation of Roman Catholic sympathies, grounded on familial and emotional ties to that community. What is clear is that these sympathetic outpourings, and the political engagements which resulted, do require explanation, even if Richard Burke was not a convert and the emotional ties less close than some of this interpretation's advocates believe. Finally, and in a similar vein, the postcolonial reading of Burke raises the question of where Burke's ultimate sympathies lay. Although he was a Member of Parliament, his denunciation of the mechanics of British rule in America and India suggest he was no simple-minded apologist for British imperial expansion. And, this critique, the post-colonial line proposes, derives from his personal experience of imperial mismanagement in the land of his birth. One does not have to read Burke as a mirror of the Jacobins, or as a fifth columnist intent on destroying the imperial claim to moral and political authority to see that the post-colonial interpretation raises serious questions about the origins and intent of Burke's profound critique of imperial practice.

The answer to how these issues might be resolved, and how Burke's Irish identity fused with his other concerns is, predictably, interrelated. What his response to the penal code and the Protestant ascendancy makes plain is that Burke perceived Ireland as poorly run and maliciously managed. In that, however, it did not provide Burke with sufficient reason for removing Ireland from the British imperium. Rather it remained simply what he said it was, an example of a country being badly run by imperial administrators, although it is important to keep in the mind that it was not the imperial connection that was at fault but the jobbing ascendancy. It was people not structures that were to blame. The Roman Catholic question was, for Burke, an indication of the depth of the problem, for without solving the issue of religious relations, the country would remain mired in the economic doldrums and people would be driven by political frustration to extreme, and even violent protest. The Roman Catholic question did not just arise, therefore from emotional ties with the community, but from an intellectual understanding that the issue of religious discrimination was the powder keg that might destroy the ties between Ireland and Britain, and hence generate a crisis in the empire as a whole. Burke's vision was of a morally righteous empire be it in America, India, France or Ireland. It was this vision of an efficiently run, virtuously led civilization that made sense of his critique of the grubby actualities of British rule across the globe. Ireland was, in this light, one of the most extreme cases, and geographically the closest example to home, and hence worthy of intense examination. Although paradoxical to modern eyes, it was Burke's stance as an imperial legislator that makes sense of the role Ireland was to play in his thinking, and enabled him to bring insight drawn from his particular national identity to bear on a series of apparently unrelated concerns. It was his understanding of how Ireland exemplified the British failure to live up to the moral responsibilities and civilizing agenda of empire-building that ensured that his experience of his native country under-pinned all the campaigns that defined his life, career and thought.

NOTES

* I would like to thank Professor F.P. Lock for commenting on a draft of this article.

1. Philip Magnus, *Edmund Burke: A Life* (London, John Murray, 1939), p.1.
2. Stanley Ayling, *Edmund Burke: His Life and Opinions* (London, Cassell, 1988).
3. F.P. Lock, *Edmund Burke, Volume 1, 1730–1784* (Oxford: Clarendon Press, 1998), pp.1–2.
4. J.C.D. Clark, 'Introduction', in Edmund Burke, *Reflections on the Revolution in France: A Critical Edition*, edited by J.C.D. Clark (Stanford: Stanford University Press, 2001), p.25. It might be noted that Swift, Tone and O'Connell are themselves reified here into a brand of colonial nationalist tradition that much recent Irish scholarship has been at pains to deconstruct. For a recent re-reading of this tradition see S.J. Connolly, 'Precedent and Principle: The Patriots and their Critics', in S.J. Connolly (ed.), *Political Ideas in Eighteenth-Century Ireland* (Dublin, Four Courts Press, 2000), pp.130–58.
5. R.B. McDowell, 'Burke and Ireland', in David Dickson, Dáire Keogh and Kevin Whelan (eds), *The United Irishmen: Republicanism, Radicalism and Rebellion* (Dublin, Lilliput, 1993), p.103.
6. Ibid., p.106. This description arises in a discussion of Burke's views of Grattan's parliament, but has a more general pertinence within McDowell's reading of Burke.
7. Elizabeth R. Lambert, *Edmund Burke of Beaconsfield* (Newark: University of Delaware Press, 2003), pp.50–2.
8. Ibid., pp.46–50.
9. See Nicholas K. Robinson, *Edmund Burke: A Life in Caricature* (New Haven: Yale University Press, 1996).
10. Thomas H.D. Mahoney, *Edmund Burke and Ireland* (Cambridge MA, 1960), p.ix.
11. It should be noted that the Irish nationalist William O'Brien did write a study that endeavoured to reclaim interpretive power for Burke's Irish origins. Written during the Irish civil war, it offers a more traditionally nationalist analysis than any of the trends in recent scholarship would evince: William O'Brien, *Edmund Burke as an Irishman* (Dublin, 1924).
12. See in particular, L.M. Cullen, 'The Blackwater Catholics and County Cork Society and Politics in the Eighteenth Century', in Patrick O'Flanagan and Cornelius G. Buttimer (eds), *Cork, History and Society: Interdisciplinary Essays on the History of an Irish County* (Dublin: Geography Publications, 1993b), pp.535–85.
13. Ibid., p.537.
14. Katherine O'Donnell, 'The Image of a Relationship in Blood: *Párliament na mBan* and Burke's Jacobite Politics', *Eighteenth-Century Ireland*, 15 (2000), p.103. On Inglis, see Éamonn Ó Ciardha, 'A Voice from the Jacobite Underground: Liam Inglis (1709–1778)', in Gerard Moran (ed.), *Radical Irish Priests, 1660–1970* (Dublin, Four Courts Press, 1998), pp.16–38.
15. Cullen, 'The Blackwater Catholics', p.537.
16. O'Donnell, 'The Image of a Relationship in Blood', p.98. Later in this article she offers evidence suggesting that Burke remained competent in the Gaelic language into his adulthood. Ibid., p.107.
17. Ibid., p.99.
18. Ibid., p.110.
19. Ibid., pp.117–18.
20. Ibid., p.118.
21. Jonathan Swift, *Selected Poems* (Schull, 1997), pp.95–7.
22. Ian Higgins, *Swift's Politics: A Study in Disaffection* (Cambridge: Cambridge University Press, 1994).
23. On this episode, see J.S. Donnelly, 'The Whiteboy Movement, 1761–5', *Irish Historical Studies*, 21 (1978), pp.20–54.
24. See Vincent Morley, '"Tá an Cruatan ar Sheoirse" – Folklore or Politics?', *Eighteenth-Century*

Ireland, 13 (1998), pp.112–20; idem, 'Queen Sadhbh and the Historians', *Eighteenth-Century Ireland*, 17 (2002), pp.112–20; S.J. Connolly, 'Jacobites, Whiteboys and Republicans: Varieties of Disaffection in Eighteenth-Century Ireland', *Eighteenth-Century Ireland*, 18 (2003), pp.63–79.

25. Thomas P. Power, 'Publishing and Sectarian Tension in South Munster in the 1760s', *Eighteenth-Century Ireland*, 19 (2004), pp. 83–91. William King's *State of the Protestants* which the Bagwells also reprinted in this period, also fits into the massacre myth, narrating the events of 1688–91 as the repercussion of a Catholic plot.

26. W. D. Love, 'Charles O'Connor of Belanagare and Thomas Leland's " Philosophical" History of Ireland', Irish Historical Studies, 13 (1962), pp. 1–25.

27. L.M. Cullen, 'Burke's Irish Views and Writings', in Ian Crowe (ed.), *Edmund Burke: His Life and Legacy* (Dublin: Four Courts Press, 1997), pp.65–6.

28. Ibid., p.66.

29. This is documented in ibid., pp.66–7 and Cullen, 'The Blackwater Catholics', pp.565–75.

30. W.E.H. Lecky, *Ireland in the Eighteenth Century* (London, 1892, 5 vols), vol.ii, p.43: 'The trial appears to have been one of most scandalous ever known in Ireland'. More recently Éamonn Ó Ciardha, *Ireland and the Jacobite Cause, 1685–1766: A Fatal Attachment* (Dublin: Four Courts Press, 2002), p.332: 'Sheehy's execution on a trumped up charge of murder in 1766 was a witch-hunt'.

31. The best recent account is Thomas Power, 'Father Nicholas Sheehy (c.1728–1766)' in Moran (ed.), *Radical Irish Priests*, pp.62–78.

32. Cited in Conor Cruise O'Brien, *The Great Melody: A Thematic Biography and Commented Anthology of Edmund Burke* (London: Sinclair-Stevenson, 1992), pp.60–1.

33. In replying to the marquis of Carmarthen, who had asked how the American child could revolt against the British parent, Burke responded: 'They are our children, but when children ask for bread, we are not to give a stone'. Cited ibid., p.143.

34. Cullen, 'Burke's Irish Views', p.64 suggests that Burke actually drafted Hamilton's speech on the military augmentation bill in 1762, in which he attacked the penal code as unnecessary and damaging to the national interest.

35. See Thomas P. Power, 'The Theology and Liturgy of Conversion from Roman Catholicism to Anglicanism', and Charles Ivar McGrath, 'The Provisions for Conversion in the Penal Laws, 1695–1750', both in Michael Brown, Charles Ivar McGrath and Thomas P. Power (eds), *Converts and Conversion in Ireland, 1650–1850* (Dublin: Four Courts Press, 2005), pp. 60–78, 35–59.

36. On the significance of this trial more generally see Ó Ciardha, *Ireland and the Jacobite Cause*, pp.192–3. For a treatment suggesting this trial was the outcome of local political infighting, rather than high political ideological strife, see Neal Garnham, 'The Trials of James Cotter and Henry, Baron Barry of Santry: Two Case Studies in the Administration of Criminal Justice in Early Eighteenth-Century Ireland', *Irish Historical Studies*, 31 (1999), pp.328–42. Luke Gibbons also accepts the identification of the Richard Burke of the Cotter case with Burke's father. See Luke Gibbons, *Edmund Burke and Ireland: Aesthetics, Politics and the Colonial Sublime* (Cambridge: Cambridge University Press, 2003), p.24.

37. Thomas P. Power, 'Conversions among the Legal Profession in Ireland in the Eighteenth Century', in Dáire Hogan and W.N. Osborough (eds), *Brehons, Serjeants and Attorneys: Studies in the History of the Irish Legal Profession* (Dublin: Irish Academic Press, 1990), pp.153–74.

38. For his rendition of the circumstantial evidence surrounding this question, see O'Brien, *The Great Melody*, pp.4–11, where the debate moves from assertions of possible identification through probability, to where no further provisos need to be recalled: 'five years after Richard Burke's conforming'. Ibid., p.11. For a rather more sceptical treatment see Lock, *Edmund Burke, Volume I*, pp.4–5.

39. O'Brien, *The Great Melody*, pp.37–8. See also the challenge to this suggestion by Elizabeth R. Lambert, and Cruise O'Brien's subsequent defence of his reading of the evidence in Conor Cruise O'Brien, 'The Great Melody: Discordant Notes', *History-Ireland*, 1, 2 (1993), pp.24–5. Lambert revisits the issue in Lambert, *Edmund Burke of Beaconsfield*, p.33.

40. O'Brien, *The Great Melody*, p.xxvii.

41. Ibid., p.68.

42. Indeed as Eamon O'Flaherty wrote of the study, 'Another positive aspect of the book is its emphasis on the importance of Burke's Irish background, and the degree to which his involvement with Irish politics, particularly the Catholic question, are consistent with the positions he adopted on the other central themes of his career – the rights of the American colonies, the British government of India, and his opposition to the French Revolution.' However, O'Flaherty tempers this with the observation that while 'the roots of Burke's Irishness are properly traced to the minor recusant gentry of the Blackwater valley in Munster, the consequences of this fact tend to dominate, and to some extent, to consume the remainder of the book'. Eamon O'Flaherty, 'Review of Cruise O'Brien, *The Great Melody*', *Irish Historical Studies*, 30 (1996), p.134.

43. See O'Brien, *The Great Melody*, pp.63–7.
44. Ibid., p.56. O'Brien continues by recognizing that the O'Hara family had converted as far back as 1616 but asserts that while 'a stranger would have seen O'Hara, in the mid-eighteenth century, as a secure member of the Protestant oligarchy. Yet he was not fully accepted as such, even after more than a century of conformity on the part of his family.' Ibid.
45. Conor Cruise O'Brien, 'Introduction', in Edmund Burke, *Reflections on the Revolution in France* (London: Penguin Books, 1968), p.30.
46. Michel Fuchs, *Edmund Burke, Ireland and the Fashioning of Self* (Oxford: Voltaire Foundation, 1996), p.10.
47. O'Brien, 'Introduction', p.28.
48. O'Brien, *The Great Melody*, p.152.
49. Ibid., p.152. O'Brien does recognize that Burke was here speaking on behalf of the Rockingham party as a whole and this may have induced a greater distancing than normal on his part.
50. Ibid., p.xxvi.
51. O'Brien, 'Introduction', pp.37–8.
52. Ibid., p.41.
53. For a thoughtful overview of Burke's views of the issue, see Eamon O'Flaherty, 'Burke and the Catholic Question', *Eighteenth-Century Ireland*, 12 (1987), pp.7–27.
54. 'Tracts on the Popery Laws', in *Writings and Speeches*, vol.ix, pp.434–81; 'Letter to Hercules Langrishe', in *Writings and Speeches*, vol.ix, p.637. Although Burke did not publish the 'Tracts', it would seem likely that it was circulated, at least within the Irish administration, and thus constitutes a kind of manuscript publication.
55. See Magnus, *Edmund Burke*, pp.336–7; Cullen, 'The Blackwater Catholics', pp.553–5. Lock, *Edmund Burke: Volume I*, pp.232–3. Burke eventually transferred the holding to a Nagle in 1790.
56. Edmund Burke, 'Letter to Richard Burke', in *Writings and Speeches*, vol.ix, pp.644–5.
57. Fuchs, *Edmund Burke, Ireland and the Fashioning of Self*, p.306.
58. Ibid., p.28.
59. Ibid., p.31. In later life this found a strange echo when Burke again undermined the religious bar by ensuring the Roman Catholic Charles O'Conor gained access to the College library holdings.
60. Ibid., pp.49–54.
61. Ibid., p.39. The contrast with Lambert's reading of Burke's motivations is striking. It might be noted that Burke is not commonly associated with valuing the views of the majority.
62. Ibid., pp.313, 311.
63. Ibid., p.97.
64. Ibid., p.104.
65. Ibid., pp.12, 104. Conor Cruise O'Brien foreshadowed this assessment in 1958. Writing of the emotional intensity which Burke brought to bear in his counter-revolutionary crusade, O'Brien remarked: 'I should like to offer here a conjectural answer which seems to me to be in full accord with what we know of Burke's life and writings. This is that Burke, in his counter-revolutionary writings, is partially liberating – in a permissible way – a suppressed revolutionary part of his own personality.' Cruise O'Brien, 'Introduction', p.34.
66. Fuchs, *Edmund Burke, Ireland and the Fashioning of Self*, pp.63, 85.
67. Ibid., p.10.
68. Ibid., p.10.
69. Ibid., p.312.
70. Ibid., p.305.
71. Gibbons, *Edmund Burke and Ireland*.
72. Ibid., pp.240–1.
73. Ibid., p.95.
74. Other problems are offered by F.P. Lock in his review of Gibbons' work in *Eighteenth-Century Ireland*, 19 (2004), pp. 211–16.
75. Luke Gibbons, *Race, Colonization and Irish Culture* (Galway: Arlen House, 2004).
76. Ibid.
77. Adam Smith, *The Theory of Moral Sentiments*, edited by D.D. Raphael and A.L. Macfie (Indianapolis: Liberty Fund, 1982), p.82.
78. Ibid., p. 9.
79. Edmund Burke, *A Philosophical Enquiry into the Origin of our Ideas of the Sublime and the Beautiful*, edited by Adam Phillips (Oxford: Oxford University Press 1990), p.36.
80. Conor Cruise O'Brien, 'The Ferocious Wisdom of Machiavelli', in O'Brien, *The Suspecting Glance* (London: Faber, 1972), p.15. This is followed by an essay entitled, 'An Anti-Machiavel: Edmund Burke', ibid., pp.33–50.

81. Linda Colley, *Captives: Britain, Empire and the World, 1600–1850* (London: Jonathan Cape 2002).

82. See Patrick Geoghegan, *The Irish Act of Union: A Study in High Politics* (Dublin: Gill & Macmillan, 1999); Dáire Keogh and Kevin Whelan (eds), *Acts of Union: The Causes, Contexts and Consequences of the Act of Union* (Dublin: Four Courts Press, 2001); Michael Brown, Patrick Geoghegan and James Kelly (eds), *The Irish Act of Union, 1800: Bicentennial Essays* (Dublin: Irish Academic Press, 2003).

83. See, for example, James Kelly, 'Monitoring the Constitution: The Operation of Poynings' Law in the 1760s', in David W. Hayton (ed.), *The Irish Parliament in the Eighteenth Century: The Long Apprenticeship* (Edinburgh: Edinburgh University Press, 2001), pp.87–106.

84. This reading has predominated in the reassessments made surrounding the bicentenary of the rebellion. See, in particular, Dáire Keogh and Kevin Whelan (eds), *The Mighty Wave: The 1798 rebellion in Wexford* (Dublin: Four Courts Press, 1996); Kevin Whelan, *The Tree of Liberty: Radicalism, Catholicism and the Construction of National Identity 1760–1830* (Cork: Cork University Press, 1996). Thomas Bartlett, David Dickson, Dáire Keogh and Kevin Whelan (eds), *1798: A Bicentennial Perspective* (Dublin: Four Courts Press, 2004) contains a wide-ranging overview of recent scholarship, including much that differs from any neo-nationalist line.

85. Elie Kedourie, *Nationalism* (London, 1960 rev edn, Oxford: Blackwell, 1983); Ernest Gellner, *Nations and Nationalism* (Oxford: Blackwell, 1983); Benedict Anderson, *Imagined Communities: Reflections on the Origins and Spread of Nationalism* (London: Verso, 1983); E.J. Hobsbawn, *Nations and Nationalism since 1780* (Cambridge: Cambridge University Press, 1990).

86. Adrian Hastings, *The Construction of Nationhood: Ethnicity, Religion and Nationalism* (Cambridge: Cambridge University Press, 1997); Anthony D. Smith, *Chosen Peoples: The Sacred Origins of Nationalism* (Oxford: Oxford University Press, 2002). On the eighteenth-century use of the biblical language of tribes see Colin Kidd, *British Identities before Nationalism: Ethnicity and Nationhood in the Atlantic World* (Cambridge: Cambridge University Press, 1999).

87. This is in fact a matter of some interpretative controversy. See Fredrick Dreyer, 'Burke's Religion', *Studies in Burke and his Time*, 17 (1976), pp.199–212; Nigel Aston, 'A "Lay Divine": Burke, Christianity and the Preservation of the British State, 1790–1797' in Nigel Aston (ed.), *Religious Change in Europe, 1650–1914: Essays for John McManners* (Oxford: Clarendon, 1997), pp.185–212; Fuchs, *Edmund Burke, Ireland and the Fashioning of Self*, pp.76–81.

88. Edmund Burke, 'Letter to Hercules Langrishe', in *Writings and Speeches*, vol.ix, p.597.

89. Edmund Burke, *Reflections on the Revolution in France*, edited by Conor Cruise O'Brien (London: Penguin Books, 1968), p.247.

14

Edmund Burke, Yeats and Frobenius: 'The State a tree' ?

W. J. Mc CORMACK

> The pride of people that were
> Bound neither to Cause nor to State,
> Neither to slaves that were spat on
> Nor to the tyrants that spat,
> The people of Burke and of Grattan
> That gave, though free to refuse –
> ('The Tower', 1928)

In Arthur Conan Doyle's novel, *A Study in Scarlet* (1887), detection of the plot is frustrated by the failure of all but Sherlock Holmes to recognize that certain scrawled letters constitute a sign in the German language as distinct from the English. The tendency to substitute a familiar code, where a different one is either present or required, could be taken as exemplary for readers of Edmund Burke. Too often he is pronounced one of *us*, and hence not one of *you*. A more open, or Holmesian, treatment would allow the possibility of both, while also investigating the covert links (even negative identifications) existing between the allegedly distinct parties.

I

More particularly, the paradox of Edmund Burke turns on the manner in which this least systematic of politicians became after his death the author of a veritable doctrine. Or, rather, from the Romantic generation onwards, he was revered for a cluster of doctrinal positions various followers plundered for what each needed to secure his creed. In this way, Burke becomes tradition in the Early Church sense of *traditio* as improper appropriation, the theft of sacred objects or texts. The religious metaphor is deliberately chosen because the posthumous contentions usually involved an element of credal belief or a defence of revealed religion against sceptical philosophy and revolution in the state.

Virtually synchronic with this desperate para-theology of the Victorian era comes a de-sacralization, or secularization, by which literature is invested with hope as a bulwark against a receding tide of faith.[1] Matthew Arnold on Dover Beach (also on Ireland) provides briefly canonical textual fragments even as the aridity of the new shorelines is painted into semi-permanence, by (for a disturbing example) William Dyce (1806–64) in his 'Pegwell Bay: a Recollection of 5 October 1858'.[2] Here, rather than in any Irish political forum, Burke and Yeats meet in a ghastly depersonalized Sublime. Drawing on the implications of a dissident Pre-Raphaelitism such as Dyce's, while shoring up Sligo Bay into the bargain, W.B. Yeats will become one of the most notable twentieth-century advocates of a Burkean politics in this sense. Yet, as we shall see, Burke for him was not a life-long preoccupation, while the best-known of Yeats's invocation of Burke may turn out to be, in part at least, a translation from the German.

John Butler Yeats (1839–1922) served an indolent apprenticeship to the Pre-Raphaelite movement, but fashion has removed him and his heirs from the contexts of any United-Kingdom-wide assessment. Similar tunnel visions frame the inheritance of his eldest son, in politics as in literature. Thanks to the selective efforts of the Irish Studies movement, Burke's views on Protestant Ascendancy have been widely broadcast in recent years, the interpretations offered being no less wide of the mark laid down by Burke himself. Yeats too had things to say about Protestant Ascendancy, and to some it has seemed justifiable to assume that Burke and Yeats were at one on the topic. Not so. How could it be so, across more than a century? Indeed, it might be proposed as an initial thesis for debate whether it is at all possible to reconcile Burke on Ascendancy with Yeats's view of Burke. In time, this *aporia* might come to acquire a representative value in the larger context of epochal historic changes occurring between the 1790s and the 1930s, specifically with regard to politics in Ireland.

By politics, of course, is meant something more than the contestation of parties and the formulation of programmes and manifestos. Bearing in mind the specific condition of Irish debate, we should acknowledge in politics a very specific enactment of culture (including literature) just as it also remains a rhetoric of economic activity and contestation. In Burke's world, the elements known as England and Ireland (or, if you like, Britain and Ireland) were not in any absolute sense distinct. Constitutionally, the two islands had separate arrangements, linked at the top by a coincidence in the crown. Politically, the smaller island was ever affected by powerful influences from the larger, virtually on a day-to-day basis. Yet it would be wrong to conclude that no traffic occurred in the opposite direction or that Ireland was a wholly passive figure. For the last fifteen years of Burke's life, the Dublin parliament was a factor no London government could take for granted. From 1789 onwards, the alphabet of Irish grievances seeped into the algebra of Reform±Repression. Linguistically, both islands shared the English language, while other far less widely spoken (Celtic) languages constituted a secondary bridge-cum-barrier on the Irish Sea and North Channel. Northern Ireland and the West of Scotland were, in many important economic and (even) cultural matters linked, not

divided, by the Channel. In religious practice, and in the relations between affiliation and the law, there were similar structures of resemblance and difference.
These structures, it need hardly be said, were registered experientially as
tension and, at certain moments, as violence. But the violence – for example,
the Gordon Riots (1780), the Battle of the Diamond (1795), Scullabogue
(1798), the death of Lord Kilwarden (1803), Dolly's Brae (1849) – cannot be
isolated as a purism, to indict this faction or that, this confession or that, this
idea of politics or its rival.[3] That is to say, the violence (which Burke in his last
years apprehended with striking eloquence) is not separable from either literature or the economy, though it yet may be examined without a prompt capitulation into either of those.

Before proceeding to relate Edmund Burke and W.B. Yeats in a way that
inevitably prefers the latter, we should take note of vast changes occurring in
society between 1797 and 1939. In global terms, there were the Napoleonic
Wars, the rise of the United States of America, the revolutions of 1848–49,
Marxism and the Communist movement, competition in Africa and China, the
growth of nationalism, the unification of Germany, the Great War, mechaniza-
tion of travel and communications, the development of fascism. These cannot
be listed in any strict chronological order because they impinge on each other
and on factors left unnamed. The scramble for Africa can be narrated in terms
of Christian missions or Leninist theories of imperialism, in Napoleonic (historical) terms or those of aggressive trade. Yet behind this difficulty of presentation, the list surely confirms our sense of colossal and profound historical
change registered through the passage of time. The near-invisible comet in
Dyce's 'Pegwell Bay 1858' may serve as a figure for these vast intrusions into
a cosmic and metaphysical realm previously conceived on infinitely smaller
scales.

A similar list of events occurring in (or to) Ireland is more easily drawn up
– the United Irishmen's rebellion, the Union, the campaign for Catholic
Emancipation, consciousness of land, the Famine, urban industrialization round
Belfast, American-Irish agitation, Home Rule and Unionism, Trade Unionism,
sectarian tension, IRB conspiracy and 1916, partition, domestic parliaments,
and limited independence. That's not all. Consideration of the United Kingdom
as a whole, and not any anachronistic exclusive focus on Ireland alone, would
require additional acknowledgement of electoral reform in 1832, 1867 and
1884. Conversely, necessary attempts to define *Ireland as such* would involve
admission of a massively growing population, a seemingly empirical observation not (however) to be isolated without reference to Malthusian theories of
scarcity and supply, especially as refined in the second edition (1803) of *An
Essay on the Principle of Population*. Necessary attempts are not automatical-
ly sufficient ones.

To these basically politico-social developments one must add a significant
cultural component, for which the emergence of the Abbey Theatre (1904)
can serve for short-hand. At its most pervasive (or diffuse) level, this cultural

factor is early observed in the eclipse of the secondary Gaelic language and the growth of communications in English through educational systems, newspapers and political organization. In its most concentrated (or hermetic) form, it is the system of belief propagated by Yeats through poetry, drama, discursive prose and – occasionally – political action, up to what Patrick Kavanagh termed 'the Munich bother' of 1938.

The name of Edmund Burke features as a sign in this broad Yeatsian discourse. It is one of the more recognizable signatures in a list including Mrs French, Blind Raftery, and O'Leary's noble head, not to mention Berkeley, Goldsmith, Grattan and Swift. Do we read it aright? Can we learn anything from the manner in which Holmes finally read the scrawled letters RACHE in *A Study in Scarlet*, not as the immediately recognizable if incomplete English name, Rachel, but as German VENGEANCE? The tendency to see a personal name, even an incomplete one, where an abstraction is more fully inscribed, may be attributed to that well-known yet anonymous abstraction, common sense.

II

Burke for Yeats was the author of *Reflections on the Revolution in France* (1790), and related polemics on the issue of Jacobinism. Any interest in Burke's earlier career was subordinated to a high-frequency transmission of arguments against radical change, of defences provided for tradition, of justifications of custom against calculation. Though the 'Speech on America' was widely studied as an example of English prose and/or parliamentary rhetoric, Yeats remained largely unmoved by Burkean proposals of conciliation, temperamentally or ideologically unsuited to his appetite.[4] When he and Edward Dowden clashed in 1895 over the former's favouring a boycott of English literature, the professor's list of acceptable Irish texts included Burke on the American War, a list Yeats icily found 'admirable' if clearly not part of the 'racial tradition'.[5] Three years later and speaking amid disputatious centennial commemorations of the United Irishmen's rebellion, Yeats declared:

> She [that is, Ireland] is turning to the great men of her past – to Emmet and Wolfe Tone, to Grattan and to Burke, to Davis and to Mitchel, and asking their guidance (cheers). She is turning, too, to subtler sources of national feeling than are in politics.[6]

Superficially, this looks like a straightforward set of liturgical binaries – discrete heroes dressed as twins. To this end, Parnell remains an absence, for with whom might one twin an uncrowned king? O'Connell is also omitted, and Yeats will proceed systematically to deprecate the Liberator's influence and achievement. Here we note how Yeats places O'Connell and Parnell in opposition to each other, even when both are excluded as names unwelcome at the specific gathering that Yeats is addressing. There is scarcely any acknowledgment of Richard Brinsley Sheridan in these historical pronouncements, more nearly a Gael than any of the commended eighteenth-century heroes, MP for several constituencies in succession, and a sympathizer with radical Irish causes.[7] By his own time (Yeats avers) the parliamentary movement is rotting hay, through which new grass (great men of the past) is springing up (Phoenix-like). The coming force is something other than political – it will be a Sinn Féin (or Do It Yourself) necromancy. Wherever Wolfe Tone stands in the Yeatsian sweet by-and-by, he for one must wonder at this turn of events.

The character of Yeats's placing of Burke in 1898 should be recalled as we review other, more familiar and negative citations from the poet's early critical utterances. For example, in 1904 he rebuked Clement Shorter for his praise of 'Swift, Berkeley and Goldsmith, who hardly seem to me to have come out of Ireland at all'.[8] To 'come out of Ireland' is a deeply ambiguous phrase, suggestive of taking the fight to an enemy and/or abandoning the folks back home. In a simpler world Shorter, Yeats says, *naturally* prefers these writers; here the adverb is perhaps more important than the verb. An implication is that an Englishman would choose from the lists of Irish literature figures who have somehow conformed to an English model, or who at least acted upon an English stage. In the light of the necromantic predictions of 1895, Yeatsian distaste for a *natural* preference deserves consideration. Edmund Burke, it seems, will triumph in the struggle between natural and supernatural auspices, even to the point where temporal sequence is reversed or dissolved. The most occultic of these divinations will be traced under the battlements of 'The Tower'.

Readers newly admitted to the CD-ROM riches of Yeats's correspondence must wait almost two decades to discover a sequel to the early, basically hostile characterization of Burke as writer or thinker.[9] Replying to an American student, and imagining himself for a moment her professor – a sort of Yankee Dowden Dandy – Yeats speculated that if he

> were compelled to choose examples of fine prose for an Irish reading book, I would take some passages from Swift, some from Burke, one perhaps from Mitchell [*sic*] (unless his mimicry of Carlyle should put me off), and from that on find no comparable passages till [Augusta Gregory's] 'The Gaol Gate' and the last act of [J. M. Synge's] 'Deirdre of the Sorrows'.[10]

The hypothetical role as academic anthologist helps Yeats to avoid the tricky business of choosing from his own very fine prose, but it can hardly be offered as explanation of a drastic separation of eighteenth-century discursive prose and early twentieth-century drama. If Mitchel is finally excluded, an entire century disappears. As Goldsmith is already out – and Sheridan, we said, black-balled as a radical Whig – drama becomes exclusively a 'peasant' matter. No Shaw, no Wilde, no O'Casey. Indeed this fundamentally rural priority is indicated in the following sentence, in which Yeats would direct his pupils 'to show that this strange English, born in the country cottages, is a true speech, with as old a history as the English of Shakespeare, and that it takes its vocabulary from Tudor England and its construction from the Gaelic'.[11] Burke finds no place in a neo-archaism designed neither to serve nor ennoble, but to control, a new polity in its cultural and educational domains.

Though Yeats had sixteen stridently political years to live, recipients of his letters heard little of Edmund Burke. In 1930, he read much biography but avoided lives of Swift or Burke because anything Irish was 'too exciting'. Here perhaps we touch on the subterranean quality of Burke's influence on Yeats during these years. Burke is a volcanic force best surveyed at a distance even though it has shaped the very landscape one stands in. With his political valet, Joseph Hone, Yeats was less guarded: 'I want Protestant Ireland to base some vital part of its culture on Burke, Swift & Berkley [sic] ... Gentile & other Italian philosophers found themselves on Berkeley'.[12]

The years immediately following publication of *The Tower* (1928) have been identified with a 'turn' in the poet's ideological orientation.[13] Until that point, he had been (let us say) an Irish political thinker primarily, more Irish than political, more poet than thinker. His role in the Senate had its practical effects, but membership was as much a tribute to the part he had played in the growth of cultural nationalism. From 1928 onwards, he attended increasingly to practical politics, albeit at the distance recommended by vulcanists. British, German, Irish, Italian, Spanish affairs each claimed a share. No neat calculation of days spent on this task or that can be attempted; anticipating Theodore Roethke's definition of a poet, Yeats was incapable of doing one thing at a time. Behind the public spectacle of the senator chairing his committees and haranguing his colleagues, there had been a secret politics, decidedly anti-democratic in its objectives and Italian fascist in some of its sources. In 1925 Hone became secretary to a small cabal in Dublin; when on holiday with Yeats on Capri, he took part in the formulation of policy for a new National Unionist Party. Little came of this, in practical Irish terms, just as little in the philosophy of Giovanni Gentile (1875–1944) can be attributed to the influence of George Berkeley. Yeats may well have believed in the reviving powers of idealism, tar-water and the theory of vision; in Mario Rossi he found a useful student of eighteenth-century Irish thought who was also a citizen of Mussolini's republic. Far more than mere citizen, Gentile was the activist philosopher of Italian fascism, minister for public instruction and (later) president of the National Fascist Institute of Culture, sufficiently identified with the regime before and after the outbreak of war to be killed by partisans after the Duce's fall in 1944.

If Berkeley was a code word for the desired relationship between 'Protestant Ireland' and continental fascism in its more intellectual manifestations, what did Burke mean for Yeats? To some extent, he signified the difficulties inherent in any conception of 'Protestant Ireland' for the eighteenth century. Born and brought up in the Church of Ireland, Burke was never wholly free of associations with a society lying outside the Establishment in church and state. It was an extensive community, by no means impoverished though hard pressed, especially in its lower reaches. His consciousness of a Catholic ancestry rooted in this extra-official world has (I think) been exaggerated in some recent commentary. Certainly, the marginalized Gaelic culture to which part of this community looked back for sustenance was not his immediate patrimony. In his lifetime, pre-romantic and antiquarian enquiry quickened interest in Gaelic Ireland, in tandem with a relaxation of hostility towards Catholicism in the latter third of the eighteenth century. It is unquestionably true, however, that Burke in his last years was derided as a quasi-lay-Jesuit. His support for the resumption of Catholic clerical education in Ireland lent credence to the caricature, while his opposition to the French Revolution was grounded in views of monarchical authority that were, in essence, theological.

Burke's influence did not take the form of apostolic succession. Writers as totally different as S.T. Coleridge, Benjamin Disraeli and Maria Edgeworth adopted elements of his thought. Karl Marx, inevitably hostile, was none the less well-informed. The apparent paradox of Burke the reformer in Irish terms being a defender of the British *status quo* is less blinding if considered in two distinct aspects. First, the notion of the 'little platoon' as the focus of loyalty was central to a more comprehensive, if implied, romantic philosophy of particularism: if this has been sometimes crudely reduced to regionalism, or apologetics, the fault is not Burke's. Second, Burke's emphasis on circumstances as a vital factor in assessing policy contributed a similar nuanced sensitivity to historico-temporal experience. What Marx dismissed as the calculated opportunism of a bourgeois had been a complex, tentative but innovative romantic politics.[14]

Yeats stands at the latter end of the romantic tradition, placing himself (with Douglas Hyde, J.M. Synge and other Irish post-Protestants) among 'the last Romantics'. It is richly ironic that Burke and he should have so profoundly differed in their approach to the concept of 'Protestant ascendancy'. The problems were inherent in the concept itself, and began with its introduction in the 1780s. (They persist even today.[15]) In short, Protestant ascendancy arose in heated debates about the relationship between church and state. While the new term gradually replaced 'the Protestant interest', it cannot be taken simply as a synonym. The lexical register from which the noun ascendancy emerged was not that of economic or political relations (cf. 'the landed interest') but of astrology ('the ascendancy of Mars' et cetera). Here, already in the Irish pamphlet and pulpit wars of the late 1780s, one encounters a register and a pressure of new modes of apprehension. If 'the Protestant interest' denoted an economic or political state of affairs, it did so by using codes that presented themselves as rational, enlightened discourses of human interaction and ideological justification. Ascendancy, in contrast, invoked the super-human and non-rational discourse of planetary influence, pagan or wholly non-religious. More exactly, 'ascendancy' (unlike 'interest') connotes a temporary state of affairs, preceded by a rising of the (now) ascendant power and to be followed by the decline of that power and its replacement by a new ascendancy of something else. The shift from 'interest' to 'ascendancy' marked at one level the recognition of a more active, changing and even turbulent structure in affairs of the state; at another, proleptic level, it acknowledged the coming eclipse of the Protestant aspect and its replacement by some other.

Yeats's discussions of Protestant ascendancy are limited to public occasions or to prose publications where the hortatory character of the term can be readily endorsed. It finds no place in his private correspondence. This distinction serves to underline the manner in which he practiced a multi-layered rhetoric – the term is used neutrally – according to which specific hearers or readers are addressed in different registers. Protestant ascendancy was not for the quiet ears of Olivia Shakespear, John Quinn or other intimates. There had been some early uses of the phrase while Standish O'Grady fulminated against the mental and moral blankness of Irish landlordism, but Protestant ascendancy for Yeats only comes into its own in the 1920s.

It is hard to resist the conclusion that he adopted it partly at least in reaction to the campaign of mockery organized through *The Catholic Bulletin*, mockery directed at his own origins, at his family links with the mercantile Pollexfens of Sligo, and at the attitudes of the Royal Irish Academy. Yeats, together with Oliver St John Gogarty and the National Library of Ireland, was regarded as representative of 'the New Ascendancy'. This editorial re-deployment of an eighteenth-century terminology was not casual. During the Treaty debates in late 1921 and early 1922, *The Catholic Bulletin* dramatized its incipient republicanism through mock-puzzlement at the 'dominion' status conferred on Ireland; this mystery (the *Bulletin* ironically argued) 'is not the same status which Molyneux, Swift and Lucas interpreted as being hers, and which they had not the slightest difficulty in lucidly defining in their time'.[16] What is striking in the editor's politicized historiography is the distinction, valid in itself, that he makes between early-to-mid-eighteenth-century Ireland and the later world epitomized in 'the Town Houses' of a 'colonial ascendancy', a world of 'ascendancy bashaws'. In its 1790s, Irish, application this last, Indian, detail is directly traceable to Edmund Burke's influence.[17]

Father Timothy Corcoran, SJ, editor of *The Catholic Bulletin,* may have been a philistine, and a zealous 'Die-Hard', but he was no fool. In response to, or more certainly, in the aftermath of, these mockeries Yeats chose to close the temporal gap between William Molyneux (1656–98) and Edmund Burke by applying the term Protestant Ascendancy to cover the 'long' eighteenth century. He was by no means the first to make this assumption, but unquestionably he has been the most suasive for students of cultural debate. The task was no easy one. In a *Letter to Richard Burke* (1792) Burke made scornfully plain his contempt for the neologistic phrase and the invention thus masked, the bigotry and pretensions of its sponsors. Its adoption in the exclusively Protestant Dublin guilds was in turn signalled in his use of 'striking' or 'minting' as metaphors for the new 'coinage', with the implication that (as with Wood's

Halfpence for Swift) this was a debased (verbal) currency. Though 'new ascendancy is the old mastership', the newness was what required emphasis as Burke proceeded to parallel commercially motivated Protestant ascendancy with Jacobinism in France and with the regime of Warren Hastings in India. Nowhere in Burke's commentary is it possible to find any justification for assuming that Protestant ascendancy had a venerable or dignified pedigree in the days of Molyneux or even Swift.

Yeats's most extended statement is found in a prose commentary, published in 1934 to accompany the poem 'Parnell's Funeral', but whose sentiments can be traced back to an earlier lecture delivered on tour in the United States of America. Speaking of tapestries in the Irish House of Lords, he declared that their Huguenot designers had celebrated 'the establishment of a Protestant Ascendancy which was to impose on Catholic Ireland, an oppression copied in all details from that imposed upon the French Protestants'. As the relationship between visual image and (supposed) constitutional concept must remain vague and unattached, Yeats energetically associates his own line with a Huguenot name (that of Marie Voisin) just as he can rely on Yeats family history to produce evidence of an engagement in the textile business. This fabricated early eighteenth-century Protestant ascendancy is then sketched without sentiment – 'armed with this new power, they were to modernize the social structure, with great cruelty but effectively, and to establish our [*sic*] political nationality by quarrelling with England over the wool trade, a Protestant monopoly'.[18]

The next step in Yeats's account of old Protestant ascendancy brings him precisely to the years of Burke's commentary upon its newness. 'The influence of the French revolution woke the peasantry from the mediaeval sleep, gave them ideas of social justice and equality, but prepared for a century disastrous to the national intellect.' Entirely forgetting the great cruelty and the modernization, Yeats now pits 'the Protestant Ascendancy with its sense of responsibility' against nineteenth-century decline, 'the Garrison, a political party of Protestant and Catholic landowners, merchants and officials'. The sleight-of-hand is at once dexterous and sinister. Whereas 'the Protestant ascendancy' had no provenance as a phrase describing the ruling elite in eighteenth-century Ireland – though it would achieve that usage in the mid-to-late Victorian period – Yeats first associates it with necessary oppression, then with social responsibility, and finally with defeat at the hands of a vulgar alliance including officials and merchants. The strangely convenient mediaeval sleep, during which peasants dozed collectively through cruel modernization, assists in the dehistoricising process.[19] In Burke's account of 1792, it was precisely the officials and the merchants who were propagating their own (Protestant) ascendancy. In Burke's account, *unnecessary* oppression – for example, of Catholic soldiers in the army – emerged in tandem with the new idiom of Protestant ascendancy. His focus on individual soldiers, flogged when in conscience they refused to attend Protestant church services, is a good example of particularism in moral argument and political analysis.

III

Yeats the poet explicitly addressed these historic matters on only two or three occasions. In 'The Seven Sages' (written January 1931) he inscribed the names of selected eighteenth-century heroes in a brief dramatic exchange, its opening lines reading:

> *The first*:   My great-grandfather spoke to Edmund Burke
> In Grattan's house.
> *The second*:   My great-grandfather shared
> A pothouse bench with Oliver Goldsmith once.

The genealogical wisdom of this second sage can hardly be challenged, as it is likely the great-grandfathers of many men (and women) often joined Nol in a pub. That of the first sage is more open to question. The encyclopaedic late editor of Burke's correspondence, John Woods, pointed out some years ago that, in Burke's lifetime, Grattan had no house except in Dublin, a city which Burke did not frequent during his political career, the last brief visit occurring in October 1786. In the letters surviving from these weeks, no reference to Grattan is found.[20] These minute but imprecise observations are (I hope) in keeping with the strategy adopted in the poem itself, which contrasts markedly with 'Blood and the Moon', first published in the spring of 1928.

The earlier poem dates from the year of the great *Tower* volume, though it was not collected until *The Winding Stair* (1929); consequently it occupies a position central to the 'turn' in Yeats's political orientation. Here too we meet Swift, Berkeley, Goldsmith and Burke (but not Grattan). For students of Burke, the crucial moment arises in the second stanza of the poem's second section:

> And haughtier-headed Burke that proved the State a tree,
> That this unconquerable labyrinth of the birds, century after century,
> Cast but dead leaves to mathematical equality.

Viewed even in strictly stylistic terms, these lines pose problems.

> QUESTION ONE: why should Burke be assigned the neuter relative 'that' in line 1 instead of the personal 'who'?
> Possible (but hardly flattering) ANSWER: Yeats had to avoid an unhelpful vowel repetition in 'who proved...'
> QUESTION TWO: is the 'that' of line 2 an awkward parallel to 'that' of line 1; or is it a purposive or consequential 'that', i.e. the equivalent of 'so that...' or 'with the result that...'?

These points are very different from the one raised by John Woods about 'The

Seven Sages', because they open up divergent interpretations of the State, whether by Burke or by Yeats-reading-Burke.

With this, we reach the crux of the matter. Again, a questioning approach may be helpful. In what text or speech did Yeats find Burke proving that the state was [like] a tree or indeed, proving that this labyrinth cast[s] leaves? Is the evidence as elusive as the evidence establishing Burke's visit to Grattan's house for 'The Seven Sages'? To the best of my knowledge none of the diligent editors and annotators of the poetry has provided a source.[21] Nor can I find scholars of Burke drawing attention to any passage in which so organicist a metaphor is employed to characterize the State. (Note Yeats's fondness for the capital initial in this noun.) Marx and his editors seem to cleave more closely to the original in their mockery of it that the Yeatsians do in veneration. The nearest one comes to a claim may be found in A.N. Jeffares who annotates the compacted phrase 'the State a tree' with the following: – 'Yeats thought Burke the first to say (in *Reflections*, *Works*, II, 357) that a nation is a tree.'

The passage Jeffares refers us to is well known, though for reasons additional to any theory of state or nation:

> I have often been astonished, considering that we are divided from you but by a slender dyke of about twenty-four miles, and that the mutual intercourse between the two countries has lately been very great, to find how little you seem to know of us. I suspect that this is owing to your forming a judgment of this nation from certain publications, which do, very erroneously, if they do at all, represent the opinions and dispositions generally prevalent in England. The vanity, restlessness, petulance, and spirit of intrigue, of several petty cabals, who attempt to hide their total want of consequence in bustle and noise, and puffing, and mutual quotation of each other, makes you imagine that our contemptuous neglect of their abilities is a mark of great acquiescence in their opinions. No such thing, I assure you. Because half a dozen grasshoppers under a fern make the field ring with their importunate chink, whilst thousands of great cattle, reposed beneath the shadow of the British oak, chew the cud and are silent, pray do not imagine that those who make the noise are the only inhabitants of the field; that, of course, they are many in number; or that, after all, they are other than the little shriveled, meagre, hopping, though loud and troublesome, insects of the hour.[22]

A careful reading of this passage by Burke certainly assists us to clarify the business of annotating Yeats. Quoted at length to remove any suspicion that relevant material has been suppressed, these sentences reach their climax in a metaphor which clearly juxtaposes the behaviour of grasshoppers under a fern with that of cattle under 'the British oak'.[23] The point, however, is to read this particular figure of speech clearly. Comparing the insects and the beasts, one notes a complex of well-integrated implication – the insects are small, noisy and highly mobile ('hoppers'); the cattle are large, silent and 'reposed'; the insects are small in number as well as scale; the cattle large in every sense – thousands of them. If we are allowed to understand that the insects are 'your literary men, and your politicians' (p.359), then the cattle are contented, quintessentially passive dwellers in an essentially rural civilization. Like milch- or beef-cattle they are creatures at once natural and domestic, bountiful uncomplaining well-fed givers. The image has various sources, one being the style of English landscaping practiced by Lancelot 'Capability' Brown (1716–83) in which agricultural activity was incorporated as a view, but not a presence, for denizens of the great house. Denizens not *citoyens*; if thousands of bovine subjects repose under the British oak, it must have been a mighty growth.

As indeed it was. The oak has played a prominent and consistent role in the imagery of English historical consciousness from at least the time of the Norman Conquest. In Windsor Great Park stands a specimen that afforded shelter (not concealment) to William I. Another, in the same park, is named after Herne the Hunter. Sherwood Forest's Parliament Oak was the tree under which Edward I held a parliament in 1282. These and a dozen other instances would have been familiar to Burke. Foremost in his thoughts was surely the Royal Oak at Boscobel where Charles II hid after the Battle of Worcester in 1651. As the paragraph, immediately following those sentences of Burke's just quoted, opens with remarks about the humiliated king and queen of France, the deeper juxtaposition in his figure is that between a restored English monarchy (1660) and an endangered French one (*now*). At the visual centre and discursive conclusion of this figure, he places a shade-providing British oak. The latter is British rather than plain English, perhaps because he wishes to assure his French correspondent that the Scots are also on side. (For Burke in the 1790s, the Irish of all sorts are quite another problem.) Just as there is a visual structure and a discursive progress, so too do we attend to lexical shifts and doublings. The passage moves from 'English' to 'British', from 'kingdom' to 'country' to 'nation'; these are rhetorical variations, sometimes for variation's sake. Burke's tree is an age-old emblem, its association with Charles II uppermost in his mind.[24]

Other details of the larger metaphor might be examined minutely. The fern has certain folkloric associations with invisibility that, for Burke, may associate with conspiracy; ancestor to this, Voltaire to whom he shortly refers (p.358) was sometimes called the philosopher of *Ferne*y (though not here, of course). The oak grows slowly, massively; then becoming the material of warships, it is doubly protective in this final condition. Cattle are ruminant (like conservative philosophers) et cetera. We are still a long way from finding anything that approximates to Burke proving the State a tree. But Professor Jeffares has been helpful, if unconvinced and unconvincing, where other editors are silent (or cud-chewing).

IV

'Cast but dead leaves...'

There may be other sources for Yeats's well-known lines, provided we are willing (like Sherlock Holmes) to think in German and to follow the poet as far as
Rapallo. The date is April 1929, the poet writes breathlessly to the English
designer, Thomas Sturge Moore, conveying the excitement of his Italian
surroundings, the renewal of an old friendship, and the discovery of a new,
ancient authority:

> Ezra Pound has just been in. He says 'Spengler is a Wells who has found-
> ed himself on German scholourship instead of English journalism'. He is
> sunk in Frobenius, Spengler's German source & finds him a most inter-
> esting person. Frobenius originated the idea that cultures (including arts
> & sciences) arise out of races, express those races as if they were fruit &
> leaves in a pre-ordained order & perish with them; & the two main sym-
> bols that of the Cavern & that of the Boundless. He proved from his logic
> – some German told Ezra – that a certain civilization must have once
> existed at a certain spot in Africa & then went and dug it up. He proves
> his case all through by African research. I cannot read German & so must
> get him second hand. He has confirmed a conception I have had for years,
> a conception that has freed me from British liberalism & all its dreams.[25]

Once adjustments are made for Yeats's casual punctuation and systematic
dyslexia, the reader can establish the German Africanist, Leo Frobenius
(1873–1938), as cause of the excitement. There is good reason for responding
with caution to the impression of Yeats's sudden happy encounter with an unexpected endorsement of ideas long cherished uncertainly. The impression given
by the letter, that Frobenius was just some new thing being read (and, consequently, discussed) in the poet's presence, is too blurred to stand unchallenged.
Yeats possessed at least one book of the great Africanist's – *Paiduma,* published
in Munich in 1921.[26] It was still in his library when he died, annotated by Ezra
Pound with a view to underscoring pernicious Jewish influence in America. In
itself, this evidence is inscrutable, as we cannot say for certain when the book
came into Yeats's possession. Before the Great War, some of Frobenius' work
had been translated and published in London, at a time when Yeats and Pound
were sharing a house in Sussex.[27] Donald Torchiana has pointed out Yeats's
admiration of a sentence from Frobenius' *The Voice of Africa* (in English,
1913), yet caution must be advised in assuming that the poet read the book on
publication or shortly afterwards.[28] August 1914 re-classified the Africanist
among the enemy, delaying his rediscovery outside Germany. Did Yeats know
of Frobenius' propensity to stimulate anti-Semitism (at least in Pound) early in
the 1920s, and did Yeats admirably resist the temptation (at least until the mid-

1930s), nonetheless recalling Frobenius when he came to write 'Blood and the Moon' in August 1927?

Alternative schedules suggest themselves. Perhaps Yeats acquired *Paiduma* as late as 1929, even hearing of its author for the first time in Rapallo? If the latter timetable proves the more likely, then Frobenius becomes a small-part player in 'the turn' with which Yeats moved inexorably (for this and other reasons) into the closer embrace of fascism? For evidence of this last, we have only to note the city of Frankfurt's Goethe-Plakette presented to Yeats in 1934, the German press's extensive celebration of his seventieth birthday in 1935, and his own wholly voluntary public approval of the Nuremburg Laws in 1938?

These are matters the dedicated Burke scholar, and the eager Burke reader, may regard as superfluous to need. Yet at the heart of Yeats's account of his brief encounter with Frobenius there lies an unmistakable paraphrase of Burke's view of the State as versed by Yeats himself. Drawing presumably on Pound's synopsis of the Africanist's ideas, Yeats tells Sturge Moore of Frobenius' theory 'that cultures ... arise out of races, express those races as if they were fruit & leaves in a pre-ordained order & perish with them'. In 'Blood and the Moon', he attributed to Burke the theory that the State was a tree:

> That this unconquerable labyrinth of the birds, century after century,
> Cast but dead leaves to mathematical equality.

In this possible equation, Frobenius-through-Yeats speaks of leaves which perish, Burke-through-Yeats speaks of leaves cast [in]to a mere mathematical equality. The latter clearly parallels the poet's contemptuous definition of equality as 'muck in the yard' (a phrase finally dropped from 'Three Marching Songs') and generally conforms to his ever-growing hatred of democracy. Frobenius has been described as 'the pace-setter' of fascism, a description too exclusive and too metaphorical to be helpful. Yet, as ethnologist or paleo-anthropologist, he served Carl Gustav Jung, Ezra Pound, Oswald Spengler, and (however fleetingly) Yeats well. Thus, one interpretation of the Burke advanced in 'Blood and the Moon' would propose him as a code for a quasi-racialism, a reading encouraged by Yeats's final tribute to Frobenius as someone who freed him from British [*sic*] liberalism and all its dreams. Other Burkes endure. Through Disraeli, who took his title Earl of Beaconsfield from Burke's last place of residence, Edmund Burke had been transformed into the founder of a 'liberal', concessive or 'one-nation' conservatism, of which Yeats's 1930s publisher, Harold Macmillan, was to be the last successful practitioner. That the poet in Rapallo should conclude his rhapsody on a theme from Frobenius with a grateful farewell to British liberalism encourages the notion that Disraeli's mentor lurks in the background.

Before accepting the proposed reading of Burke as sometimes part of a code for Yeats's keen interest in racial theory, we should give the same degree of attention to the letter of April 1929 as we did to the passage from *The*

Reflections. Five elements deserve comment – Germany, Africa, race, leaves and British liberalism.

1) Yeats never visited Germany, and neither read nor spoke the language. His acquaintance with the literature was limited to the mystic Jakob Boehme, Goethe (as author of *Faust*) and Gerhard Hauptmann, a prolific and distinguished playwright. He also had some contact with the plays of Ernst Toller, a communist whom he disliked. The month before writing to Sturge Moore, Yeats had met Hauptmann in Rome, and became impressed by the older man's capacity for champagne. At all times, he needed mediators in dealing with German culture; in Rapallo he had access to Hauptmann (who certainly was no racist) but this access depended on Ezra Pound's linguistic grass-hoppery. It strikes me as unlikely that the unnamed 'some German', who told Pound about Frobenius' deductive powers in choosing a site for excavation, was Hauptmann, for Yeats had already met and liked the ageing dramatist whose name it would have been pleasing to drop into a letter.

2) Yeats the post-colonialist, anti-imperialist and Kiberdian paragon is a recent invention. The topic of Africa usefully permits a synopsis of his views on what we now call the third world. Here Yeats was principally concerned with Asia, especially the ancient and literate civilizations of India, China and (somewhat later) Japan. Indian independence he approved without, however, so much as mentioning the name of Mahatma Gandhi or the Congress. Black men, or Negroes, were assumed to be inferior to Indians, and in this Yeats concurred with Queen Victoria's own assessment. Burke's prosecution of Warren Hastings met with Yeats's approval for it seemed that the ancient dignity and present wealth of Indian royalty were at stake. (Again, Sheridan's part in the impeachment is never mentioned.) Africa is of strictly limited interest, in its northern and southern extremities, the first because of the learned Arab presence, the second because of the Boers and their aggressive attitude towards the British. (As with so many pro-Boers, the fate of native Africans was not a concern.) In the 1930s Yeats listened to 'astonishing stories of North Africa [*sic*] Negroes' told to him by the profoundly unreliable Dermot MacManus.[29] These appear to have had a sexual content, and may (I suspect) derive from fieldwork research by Frobenius for his *Schwarze Dekameron* (Berlin 1910). In *On the Boiler* (1939), Yeats recalled a black girl who lived in county Sligo during his childhood, noting that she was one of 'those our civilization must reject'.[30] The coolness of this is in harmony with his indifference to the revelations of extreme cruelty practiced by the Belgians in Africa, as revealed by Roger Casement in 1904. In none of Yeats's subsequent engagements with Casement's fate – in 1916, and again in 1936 with the controversy over allegedly forged diaries – did he allude even passingly to the treatment of Negroes or blacks documented so damningly by his fellow Irish patriot and Anglo-Irish knight. The point in this digression of mine is simply to demonstrate that Frobenius' one great subject – Black Africa – had little attraction for Yeats, though the German's theoretical assumptions about race, culture and the shedding of 'leaves' certainly did.

3) Yeats on race is conventionally regarded as a less deplorable record than Pound or Eliot on the same topic. And this remains true, though with modifications and admissions far from negligible. As the late recollection of a black girl in Sligo demonstrates, the mature Yeats confidently classified peoples into an implicit hierarchy of racial characteristics. The brighter parts of suburbia, from Aberdeen to Penzance, did likewise, nor could ducal palace nor proletarian cell nurture seeds of positive discrimination. Frankly, Yeatsian racial preferences were standard issue in his generation, rendered extraordinary by the imaginative strength with which he occasionally mobilized them.

The literary *avant garde* was not suburban. Compared with Pound, Yeats was almost innocent of anti-Semitic prejudice. Nevertheless, in a few letters to friends, and in his behaviour when awarded the Goethe Plakette, he manifested attitudes that were expressly (in the first case) and effectively (in the second) hostile to Jews at the time of their greatest vulnerability. A letter to Dorothy Wellesley of 19 May 1937 gleefully reports Gogarty's difficulties over a story alleging child-molestation by a Dublin Jewish individual, and using the shorthand 'chicken-butcher' for 'one who makes love to the immature'. All that can be said in mitigation is that Yeats is not known to have repeated the offence, though the poem 'John Kinsella's Lament for Mrs Mary Moore' (written July 1938) sails close to the whirlwind. Yeats's inactivity when European Jews were seeking a refuge and a sponsor has, to date, inspired a matching incuriosity among biographers. One charitable summary of Yeats's attitude on this issue has been built around a phrase attributed to Edmund Burke – all that is needed for evil to triumph is that good men do nothing.[31]

Yeats's recourse to the language of race can be traced much earlier than the period of fascism, and its focus carefully observed not to be *different races now* but instead *we as racial continuity*. This is a nineteenth-century usage in essence, developed from earlier and less thoroughly formulated expressions. Even during the high Victorian period, race was often intertwined with the pursuit of family history, with genealogy and antiquarianism. In a discourse of this kind, it remained relatively untouched by biologist theories, doctrines of ethnicity, and xenophobic nationalism. Burke's interest in those writers who had provided 'an interior History of Ireland, the genuine voice of its records and monuments' was ignited as early as 1765, and he contrasted it with the seventeenth-century work of Clarendon and Sir John Temple.[32] Here one meets in Burke not so much a proto-nationalist as a pre-romantic, whose concerns are paralleled in those of poets like Thomas Grey and William Collins. In time, of course, the political implications of such a double history were touched in the *Letter to Richard Burke* of 1792. Yeats in turn was aware of Burke's sensitivity to 'interior history'.[33]

Between the moment of Burke's great jeremiad against the French Revolution and Yeats's public endorsement of the Nuremberg Laws, so much had changed in discourses on race that careful reading of every utterance is required. Nowhere is this caution more advisable than in the undertaking to

disinter Burke's 'Gaelic background', or to posit his association with 'the possibility of a more grounded, ethnographic Enlightenment'.[34] Race, language,
and groundedness are notions that have passed through successive funnels,
sieves and mills, from the generation of Herder and Coleridge to that of T.S.
Eliot and Heidegger.

For present purposes, and keeping in mind Yeats's sudden enthusiasm for
Frobenius, what needs to be emphasized is this: – in an age of rapidly transforming population patterns, of revolutionized transport and general cultural
disillusion after unprecedented slaughter, the maintenance of a settled Victorian
idiom gave no guarantee of clear and mutual understanding on each side of a
verbal exchange. For an old example, what Burke meant by Protestant ascendancy and what Yeats meant by the identical phrase differed greatly. 'A very
great part of the mischiefs that vex the world, arises from words.' If this was
true when Burke said so in 1792, it had become more true *and* more problem-
atically true by the 1920s when Yeats was writing 'The Tower', 'Blood and the
Moon' and 'The Seven Sages'. The problematic of truth and language cannot
be tackled here.

4) That leaves leaves – and British Liberalism – to be examined as the
significant *topoi* in Yeats's brief account of Frobenius. By leaves I mean, of
course, a wider network of metaphor with the tree at its centre, with branches
reaching outwards, and with leaves budding, flourishing and falling. In his
annotated edition of the *Poems*, Daniel Albright appends to 'Blood and the
Moon' a veritable woodman's tour of related texts:

> In 'Vacillation' VI there is a tree sprung from human blood, and Burke's
> tree, in this context, almost seems to grow from the blood of Swift. Yeats
> often cited Burke's figure of the state as a tree: 'Feed the immature imag-
> ination upon that old folk life, and the mature intellect upon Berkeley ...
> upon Burke who restored to political thought its sense of history, and
> Ireland is reborn, potent, armed and wise. Berkeley proved that the world
> was a vision, and Burke that the State was a tree, no mechanism to be
> pulled to pieces and put up again, but an oak tree that had grown through
> centuries' (*SS Y*, p.172; *UP* II, p.459).
> See also Yeats's 1930 Diary: 'A State is organic and has its childhood and
> maturity and, as Swift saw and Burke did not, its decline' (*Ex*, p.318); a
> speech on education (1925), which urges school teachers to teach religion
> as 'a part of history and of life itself, a part, as it were, of the foliage of
> Burke's tree (*UP* II, p.459); and a speech on Emmet (1904), which con-
> joins blood and moon: 'A nation is like a great tree and it must lift up its
> boughs towards the cold moon of noble hate no less than to the sun of
> love, if its leaves are to be thick enough to shelter the birds of heaven'
> (*UP* II, p.323). The decline of the state-tree is suggested in 'Three
> Marching Songs' II 23: 'What tears down a tree that has nothing within
> it?'[35]

Here indeed is a fine example of editorial genius, with all its accomplishments and limitations. Behind the multiple reverberations allegedly springing from 'Burke's figure of the state as a tree', there remains a silence or at best an undiscovered original locus; undaunted, the editor systematizes what remains a theme-less set of variations. Nothing is hazarded on the question of assessing what Burke's opinion of Emmet might have been and, in that silence (not peculiar to Albright), Yeats's tendency to associate irreconcilables goes unchallenged. To some, he is a poet adapting discrete material to his central purpose; to a few others, he is a muddled thinker confusing state and nation, Swift and Burke, when it suits him. One could point to other trees – the liberty tree of the American Revolution, transplanted to France; or, by way of contrast, the transcendental symbol of the second section in 'Vacillation'. In short, western culture employs the tree in a wide range of figurative ways, and so does Yeats. What Albright avoids is any correlation of Yeats's Burkean tree with the hate, violence, irrationalism, and (to put it mildly) authoritarianism of his writings after *The Tower*.[36]

5) Yeats's attitude to British liberalism needs little comment. His rejection of its moral earnestness, its complicity in empire, its consequent hypocrisy, and its groundless optimism can be verified through any of a dozen major texts in prose and poetry. In their very different ways Marx, Nietzsche and Freud had all detected crumbling foundations under the western edifice. What does require more than comment, however, is Yeats's serial persistence in rejecting again and again what he has already rejected many times. The last flickering of a liberalism based more on a desired class identification than any loyalty to Britain had surely been heard in 'Easter 1916' with the ambiguous lines

> For England may keep faith
> For all that is done and said...

Ambiguous grammatically or semantically, because the second of these lines may suggest that the English will keep faith EITHER *because of* what has been done and said, OR *despite* what has been done and said. Less ambiguous stylistically, because 'faith' is rhymed with 'death' (two lines up) and 'said' with 'dead' (two lines down). After the passage of thirteen years, the Treaty and the Civil War, April 1929 will strike some readers of his work as a rather late moment at which to express gratitude for the German ethnologist's – anyone's – having 'confirmed a conception I have had for years, a conception that has freed me from British liberalism & all its dreams'. The writer of these words was sixty-three, two years older than Burke was when writing the *Reflections*.

Quite what the 'conception' is remains veiled. But those dreams, are they not plausibly identified with the 'mere dreams, mere dreams' of Yeats's very fine poem, 'Meditations in Time of Civil War'? In the opening stanzas, the poet delineates a cultured society in which architect has transmuted his patron's bitterness into a lasting symbol, into more than symbol, into a landscape at once

244 EDMUND BURKE'S IRISH IDENTITIES

civilized and natural, a place of cut-stone and water. However, greatness and bitterness remain interdependent, the former unable to spring from the stone, the latter ever eroding its own origin and source.

One could find other instances. There are earlier acute and profoundly expressed insights into the inadequacy of Whig historiography and of a benign belief in political stability – progress and the *status quo* in mystic union. Equally, there are later iterations of relief at Yeats's liberation from a delusive idea of human nature. If one tabulated these counterpointing textual moments, Yeats would appear as a man of great intelligence, insight, sensitivity and commitment, who nevertheless felt compelled to go on (and on) announcing a constitutive break which had already been achieved. Perhaps there was some aspect of what is here loosely termed 'British liberalism' which he thought or suspected as yet surviving in his own psyche, despite repeated announcements to the contrary. And perhaps only repeated verbal acts of exorcism could bring comfort. That aspect might itself be tentatively and loosely termed 'the heart', a conception of human emotion hardly compatible with some of the strong doctrines, occultic or political, evident even before the outbreak of the Great War.

We find Yeats opening 'The Tower' with exactly such an image:

> What shall I do with this absurdity –
> O heart, O troubled heart – this caricature,
> Decrepid age that has been tied to me
> As to a dog's tail?

The surface grammar of these lines reveals old age to be the substantive concern, with 'heart' addressed quaintly in the vocative. But an underground reading is not out of the sight, in which Yeats rages at his old age because the heart (or 'the bourgeois individual subject' as the centre of emotional coherence) doggedly remains, despite the strong doctrines. The canine detail vividly conveys the dilemma of a man who cannot turn round far enough to confirm what it is that still remains attached to him, despite all his shaking and barking. What is forever behind is a past from which one is/has imperfectly cut free.

Yeats never cut free from John Butler Yeats, partly because the exasperating old painter and conversationalist never played the tyrant role. He was a decidedly Irish version of the British Liberal, an enthusiast for John Stuart Mill and later for Walt Whitman, a debunker of Nietzsche and, in some highly personalized sense, a humanist. He threw books at his eldest son as a form of chastisement, and refused to earn his living. Oedipal revolt came to naught in his relaxed impoverished domain. The poet Yeats was still fighting with his dead father in 1939, as drafts for *On the Boiler* reveal. There is a Burkean parallel here though, in a figure to which I am too much addicted, the parallel lines run in opposite directions. The ageing Burke grieved inconsolably for his son, Richard, who died in 1794 with a consequent cancellation of the father's hopes for continuance of his campaigns after his own death. This particularly struck

Burke in his attitudes towards Ireland where Richard had occasionally acted as an envoy. Yeats's keen sense of the terminal, his enthusiasm for continuity through 'the best bred of the best' is part and parcel of his racial discourse. The family, which had been a potent image in Burke's *Reflections*, becomes an ideological obsession for Yeats. Decrepid age mocks his ambitions for a perpetual philosophy, son and daughter fail to measure up to his poetic manifestoes, and so eugenics is called in as bulwark against a liberalism which is now (in the 1930s) espousing an even wider participatory democracy, for example through Popular Fronts.

These extrapolations from the letter to Sturge Moore should now face-about to address the more precise phrase that echoes Yeats's lines about Edmund Burke. The words were 'cultures ... arise out of races, express those races as if they were fruit & leaves in a pre-ordained order & perish with them'. It is perhaps not entirely clear to which noun the pronoun 'they' relates – cultures or races – but the point is academic as both referents perish together. Here the ancient, perhaps even pre-historic, material of Frobenius' African researches is made specific: or rather, Yeats is not concerned with any hypothesis about continuity between a culture excavated and a culture observed going about its business alongside the archaeologists' trench. Races become extinct, cultures die, and that is as natural as the falling of leaves and fruit from a tree. Naturalists would protest that trees don't die after this fashion, nor does it make sense to say that fruit dies. But Yeats will not wait for an answer.

Explored to this extent, Yeats's summary-theory begins to look gimcrack. Pressed further, it does not relate convincingly to release from the grip of British liberalism – if by this last term the generally accepted political nostrums are meant – freedom of conscience for the individual, rule of law, market capitalism, government by consent. Yeats's idea of (a hated) liberalism may derive from a period later that J.S. Mill's classic statement, *On Liberty* (1859), may indeed owe more to social reform and even municipal socialism as attempted by Joseph Chamberlain in Birmingham. In a myopic Irish version of UK politics, Chamberlain is a please-none villain, a Liberal Unionist. What Frobenius apparently 'proved' universally was that even progress must eventually come to extinction. This endorsement of cultural entropy, useful for Yeats in revising *A Vision*, had both historical and contemporary applications. In his diary for 1930, he observed that 'a State is organic and has its childhood and maturity and, as Swift saw and Burke did not, its decline', this following a renewal of interest in Frobenius. What Swift saw was a tree, an elm which prompted him to reflect on his own mental condition and fears for his sanity, 'I shall be like that tree. I shall die at the top.'[37] Soon Swift is displacing Burke in Yeats's citation statistics, because the older man can (it seems) be related to contemporary Italian thought. The contemporary applications of Entropy Theory were soon pursued in Frobenius' homeland where an end to non-Aryan cultures was to be industrialized. If Yeats lies outside that episode of unprecedented human depravity, his insouciant attitude to the extinction of ancient races and cultures did little to avert the catastrophe. In his own sphere, the issue of genocide had arisen earlier in the twentieth century when Roger Casement reported the brutal, and inevitably extinguishing, exploitation of small native populations in South America. Whatever the role of British liberalism in the economic policy that drove the exploitation, or in the moral revulsion which followed, Yeats had as little to say on this Third World tragedy as he had on Casement's earlier African discoveries. Like the little black girl in Sligo, some races are doomed.

V

A very great deal of the mischiefs that vex the academic world arise from words. The instance of Protestant ascendancy, to be found in the discourses of Burke and Yeats, remains a case in point. To be sure there are others, evident within the present argument. Does Yeats use the words Nation, Race, State et cetera with any kind of consistency or measurable breadth of connotation? Does the metaphoric phrase 'the state a tree' depend on such widely differing notions of growing, reproducing, sustaining, dying as to make the metaphor an obstacle to understanding, rather than a vehicle? Here, we should note two differing kinds of differing. Inside Yeats's poem, there is a metaphoric statement relating the state and the tree; metaphors may be thought to be forms of comparison, bringing out likeness, or emphasizing a particular element of likeness; more fundamentally, metaphor is based on unlikeness, contrast, what is now covered by the cliché of difference.

Let me illustrate this. I want to create a literary figure about a yacht in a storm. There is no point in saying that the yacht moved like a ship or a canoe, a barge or a barque: all these things are too alike to provide a simile or a metaphor of any worth. So I say, 'it went forward like an arrow ... it was a knife in the water'. Coming back to Yeats ('paraphrasing' Burke), we now see that 'the State a tree' is a true metaphor because it is also untrue – non-true is better – at some level. The point is nicely made by Yeats himself when he continues, referring to 'this pragmatical pig of a world' – none of us think reality, even sub-lunary reality, is porcine. Metaphor, we should note again, requires unlikeness in its two parts.

The second kind of differing is not structural but historical; or, if you prefer Saussure's terminology, not syntagmatic but paradigmatic. Here we need other illustrations. Words change their meanings over the years and centuries, so that 'knave' now means something different from its meaning before Shakespeare's day; the difference can be traced, partly because the length of time involved is great. Words also have shades of different meaning depending on geographical region or social class. 'The dogs in the street' of the colourful phrase are not urban, but only in certain districts does 'street' retain its rural meaning of (farm)yard, cobbled enclosure et cetera. Finally, words are affected by the development of concepts, relatively closely defined, for specific discourses.[38]

Yeats's account of Protestant ascendancy does not tally with Burke's, partly because the poet is engaged in an ideological tussle in which he wishes to re-deploy a term which has (in the interim) achieved the status of a concept or hard descriptor. When James Kelly and I tussled on this question some years ago, each of us claimed the victory because we were in practice fighting different battles. Professor Kelly was concerned with a term and its (for him) synonyms; I was concerned with the same term, the method and moment of its conceptualization. He regarded 'interest' and 'ascendancy' as the equivalent of cup and mug in which the same coffee went on being served, even if mug had displaced cup. I held that, when 'ascendancy' arrived (in the 1780s), some *thing* (for example, concept or ideological construct, not just some word) different from 'interest' had arrived.

Let us take two examples, one from the 1780s, one from Yeats's period. Janet Todd, who is Francis Hutcheson Professor of English at the University of Glasgow, has recently published 'Ascendancy: Lady Mount Cashell, Lady Moira, Mary Wollstonecraft and the Union Pamphlets'. As this valuable and entertaining article opens up the real possibility of attributing three anonymous anti-Union pamphlets to Margaret King (the countess Mount Cashell), its appearance is particularly welcome.[39] But why call it 'Ascendancy'? Burke's examination of the new phrase makes no contact with the titled classes exemplified here by Mount Cashell and Moira, nor with radicals of the Wollstonecraft cut. If Margaret King's ultra-Protestant family origins go some way to explaining the article's title, they still fall short of justifying it.

There is, however, one moment of poignant textual convergence. Discussing Wollstonecraft's experience in the King family's County Cork establishment, Professor Todd notes that the only man who attracted the young English governess was a visitor, George Ogle (1742–1814), a minor poet and an MP for Wexford. In February 1786, Ogle had assured the Irish House of Commons that he rarely intervened in debates on economic matters: 'but when the landed property of the kingdom, when the Protestant ascendancy is at stake, I cannot remain silent ... it is the business of the representatives of the people to guard the Protestant interest of Ireland'.[40] Ever hard-pressed financially, the speaker defends the landed property of Ireland and the '*de facto* principle' (my conceit) of restricting control of it to members of the established church. Ogle gives no indication that he uses the phrase 'Protestant ascendancy' to denote a social group, whether elite or otherwise, and Edmund Burke six years later will concur on this point, while deploring the usage generally. Yet, in Todd's 'Ascendancy' we read that Ogle's opinions 'found favour with many in the Ascendancy, including his friends the Kingsboroughs'.[41] Part of the problem lies in Professor Todd's acceptance of the view that 'the Protestant ascendancy' already named such a group even while she dealt with one of the first users of the phrase in its very different early usage. Another part of it turns on the distinction between *naming now* and *naming then*.

This latter point can be illustrated through my second example. In its 2004 issue, *Irish Economic and Social History* published an article about Roger Casement's humanitarian relief work in Connemara during the years 1913–14.

Reference was therein made to the appointment of non-Irish-speaking doctors to dispensaries in the Gaeltacht. *Now*, the term 'Gaeltacht' denotes an area official-ly recognized as one where the predominant vernacular language is Irish (or Gaelic) and where distinctive policy applies or results; *then*, in 1913, no such term existed because no such official policy of recognition – no native government even – existed.[42] As for the notion that east Galway in 1780 was a Gaeltacht, such an expression would betray total misunderstanding of the conceptual structure, as distinct from meaning, of the term. To write in 2004 about a Gaeltacht of 1913 may provide adequate geographical bearings for latter-day readers, but other issues are occluded. The word (not term) 'Gaeltacht' existed before the legisla-tion of a Dublin parliament proposing the concept of officially recognized Gaelic-speaking districts. The first (1904) edition of Patrick Dinneen's dictionary defines it primarily as 'the state of being Irish or Scotch'; only in 1927 do we find refer-ence to the meaning 'Irish speaking district or districts' – with the attached hybrid usage 'the Gaeltacht' (cf 'le weekend' in Franglais). Similarly, the word 'ascen-dancy' was used to connote the state of affairs relative to Protestantism in Ireland during the last two decades of the eighteenth century, long prior to any emergence of 'the Protestant ascendancy' as a social group/class/constituency Ogle or Mount Cashell might have been a member of.

Doubtless, other instances of concept-formation, and its retrospective appli-cation, could be charted. It is likely that these will differ in some respects, even while they conform to the pattern just outlined. 'Ascendancy' and 'Gaeltacht', however, share a further characteristic. Each may be described as a compensa-tory imaginative construct, mobilized with reference to an unverifiable past or a programme for the future that defies implementation.[43] Legislation establish-ing 'Gaeltacht' districts indirectly acknowledged that the Irish Free State would never be predominantly Gaelic-speaking, while at the same time establishing the primacy of Gaelic in the state's self-image. Gaelic had been – at some notional moment in the past – the national language, which is to say it was the criterion by which filiation by individuals or groups would now be retrospec-tively measured. Yeats, in old age, made a clumsy token effort to fall in line but the Gaeltacht Commission of 1926 had little impact on him, despite his membership of the Senate at the time. Unlike Augusta Gregory or J.M. Synge, he had little or no knowledge of the language. As a concept 'the Gaeltacht' had only a limited application to the past; one might say that Patrick Pearse spend his holidays in the Galway Gaeltacht, but no one seriously declared that Raftery or Mary Hynes (cf. 'The Tower' Section II) were inhabitants of that district, *so conceived*. Ideologically, as distinct from formally, invocation of 'the Gaeltacht' served to persuade (or *re*-mind) people that the whole island had been at some notional time Irish-speaking. Quite where the time-frontier lay, between a period to which the concept might be applied and one in which it would anachronistic, is a question further vexed by the implication in the very term 'the Gaeltacht' itself that not all inhabitants of such places spoke Gaelic.[44]

VI

The question of twentieth-century language policy is relevant to a discussion of Yeats's relationship with Edmund Burke because those 'inner histories' of Ireland to which he referred in the 1760s steadily increased in number and influence as Romanticism in the arts lead into a national movement which invoked and encouraged historiography. The antiquarians Charles O'Conor (1710–91) and Sylvester O'Halloran (1728–1807) had corresponded with Burke who was familiar with earlier work by Geoffrey Keating (c. 1570–1644) and Roderick O'Flaherty (1629–1718). He in turn had made a point of visiting Sir John Sebright whose valuable collection of ancient Irish manuscripts was consequently presented to the library in Trinity College, Dublin. The more fanciful Charles Vallencey (1721–1812) sent copies of his publications to Burke, whose qualified approval of them was used further to discredit their author. These highly contested areas of debate and research form one level of structural allusion in Maria Edgeworth's *The Absentee* (1812), a novel in which the model land-agent is significantly named Burke.

John Woods's index-volume to the Cambridge/Chicago edition of Burke's *Correspondence* includes a valuable and succinct guide to his subject's engagement with the writing of history generally and of Irish history in particular. His influence on Thomas Leland (1722–85) was evident in the latter's *History of Ireland from the Invasion of Henry II* (1773), even though Leland's account of the 1641 rebellion dismayed liberal Catholic writers, a point grievous to Burke who had assisted John Curry in preparing his *Historical Memoirs of the Irish Rebellion* (London edn, 1765).

Burke's own efforts at history-writing were circumscribed by his political commitments. Nevertheless, he constantly encouraged the publication of documents, assisted in the transfer of the Sebright manuscripts to his *alma mater*, and corresponded vigorously with more active workers in the field. His contemptuous dismissal of Sir John Temple's account of 1641 was based in part at least on his negative assessment of the Depositions collected from Protestant victims and claimants – 'the rascally collection in the College relative to the pretended Massacre'.[45] It would be misguided, however, to regard Burke as a historian *manqué*, who (but for pressures of other business) would have produced his own balanced, even objective, account of the Irish past. Even while being fair-minded, Burke had partisan priorities, and Irish Catholic inherited grievances ranked high on his list from the 1760s until his death. He was also prone in his last years to a devastating sense of personal anguish that could sweep aside balance and measured reflection. Imaging the impact of his son's death in August 1794, Burke resorted to a simile which decisively re-works the protective royal symbol of *Reflections*:

> The storm has gone over me; and I lie like one of those old oaks which the late hurricane has scattered about me. I am stripped of all my honours;

I am torn up by the roots, and lie prostrate on the earth![46]

I have not conducted an inquiry into the weather conditions of the period (very late 1795 to February 1796) during which Burke composed these sentences for his pamphlet, *Letter to a Noble Lord*, defending his reputation (and his pension). But it seems clear that the hurricane had been an actual recent occurrence in England, whereas the storm had been the freak-of-nature violence depriving an ageing man of his son and successor. From the hurricane and the damage it has caused in parks and woodlands, the reader is allowed to move on to the metaphorical storm which, besides laying low the son (in his grave), had prostrated the father (with grief). If Burke as fallen (British) oak inspires awe, the effect is intensified by the implication that honours have been stripped from him, as they were stripped from the fallen (French) king before he was executed in 1793. This complex passage combines pathos with presumption to a degree deserving recognition of its literary artfulness. Burke's personal career, even his bereavement, is inscribed in a metaphorical history that is itself enhanced by allusion to his own best-known writing.

Yeats's literary achievements are, nonetheless, of another order. In due course, we cannot only measure these as they bear upon the question of influence but we can also consider his formidable rhetoric of historical citation. Imbued in a nineteenth-century debate which constantly invoked Strongbow or Kinsale, the broken treaty and bribery for the Union, Yeats readily threw off the superficiality of such thought while retaining its liturgical patterns, at least in part. Behind the familiar names and dates, he practiced something very different from the historical discipline we know today founded as it is on the efforts of young scholars coming to maturity in Yeats's last decade. To an eminent editor of Swift's works, he wrote in 1933 about the third book of *Gulliver's Travels*,

> thinking how much Swifts passion for political justice resembles that of Burke. The un-completed conquest & completed suffering of Ireland seems to have created this passion ... He was certainly thinking of Ireland (Burke would have thought of America or India) when he makes the Flying Island destroy the enemies of its government by crushing them with its adamantine bottom – not an active tyranny but a tyranny of insensibility or indifference.[47]

A habitual tendency to think of Burke and Swift as contemporaries – they were separated by more than half a century – is only one example of Yeats's decidedly unhistorical way of considering the past. With the fusion of the 1720s and the 1790s goes a kind of confusion – that of the objective (conquest of Ireland) with the subjective (suffering of Ireland) genitive. In both these instances what accrues to Yeats is a form of argument – more rhetoric than logic – by which the invader and the native may be temporarily identified, and by which again

the solitary may be regarded as a symbol of his age. Yeats is not greatly interested in authentic ancient documents, nor in modern 'scientific' history. His
source for Mrs French in 'The Tower' is – to put it brutally – a corrupt judge,
an embezzler writing his memoirs in well-chosen exile.

The claims of Jonah Barrington (1760–1834) to authority in this or any
other historical matter rest mainly on kinship, comradeship, and *esprit de corps.*
Sir Jonah – he was knighted in 1807 – was the third son of an MP father and
his wife Sibella (daughter of Patrick French of County Galway). In marriage he
chose Catherine Grogan, a Dublin silk-merchant's heiress about whose working knowledge of shops catty gossip persisted. Yeats's own ancestry depended
on an earlier generation of Dublin textile merchants (including one termed a
pedlar). Yet his interest in Barrington ignores the urban and commercial worlds
their families shared, to concentrate instead on vignettes of country or parliamentary matters. In these ranks, or their lower tiers, Burke located the bigoted
advocates of 1790s 'ascendancy'.

Another line of Yeats's ancestry touched awkwardly on Barrington's secret
relations with authority; the poet's great-grandfather married the daughter
of William Taylor (1747–1817), whose duties in Dublin Castle centred on the
payment of secret service money to spies, informers and turncoats. Barrington
was a political careerist, unremarkable in eighteenth-century Ireland apart from
his talents as an embellisher of his own experience. Quite apart from peculation
or bribery, Yeats was not perturbed by any suspicion that *Personal Sketches of
His Own Times* (1827), or Barrington's other recollections, were crafted for
lucrative English consumption with suitably exotic scenes of Bacchanalian
devastation.[48] One such provided 'The Tower' with Mrs French with whom
Barrington claimed kinship. What results from Yeats's reading of these pages is
uncanny evidence of his willingness to take on 'great cruelty' as the twin
of 'responsibility' in cultural and social contexts from which the actuality of
historical time has been evacuated.[49]

                                VII

The rhyme schemes employed by Yeats in his poem, 'The Tower' (1925) rarely
concern readers of Edmund Burke. Nevertheless, as Burke cannot be wholly
extricated from the places and procedures of interpretation he has endured, and
as Yeats has been a strong interpreter, it may be advisable for even the most lit-
eralist reader to pause over such details. Together with 'The Seven Sages',
and 'Blood and the Moon', the title-piece of the great collection of 1928
constitutes a major poetic statement of Yeats's engagement with the Irish eighteenth century.

The poem falls into three contrasting sections. The first (and shortest) is thematically focused on old age. Its sixteen lines basically rhyme ABAB in four
successive instances, without stanza division. On the surface, this would seem

to provide eight sonar elements of rhyme, but in practice Yeats rhymes eye/fly in lines 5/7 and eye/by in lines 13/15 which reduces the range and variety of his effects. As he also employs the weak (or 'feminine') rhyme absurdity/me in lines 1/3 – a rhyme close to those already instanced – the range is further and deliberately limited. One could say this opening section renders in terms of rhyme its official theme of poetic resignation, bidding the Muse go pack et cetera.

The second section is strongly formal, thirteen stanzas of eight lines, each rhyming AABBCDDC in a complex music of rapid succession (AA) and delay (CDDC). For the most part, each pair of rhyme-words rings clear and true, though there are strategic variations (for example, half-rhymes) which need not concern us here. We are bent on reaching the third section where Burke emerges. In it, the uneven number (seventy-five) of lines makes for either an end-word left unrhymed, or a break in the pattern whereby a sonar element is rhymed with two (or perhaps more) words in the same sub-set. In the conclud-ing lines, we find Yeats's insistent yet resigned solution – to rhyme eye/sky/cry, thus echoing the first section and its dominant rhyme element.

I inflict these nuances because Yeats's incorporation of Burke in lines 7–13 involves some unexpected (and largely unnoted) crudities of expression and (perhaps related) obscurities of implication. The crucial lines appear at the head of this paper, and so are not repeated here. The local thematic emphasis falls on pride, and an inheritance of the speaker's own pride by people whom he choos-es. Ostensibly, these are 'upstanding men / That climb the streams' (line 3). However, by a recurrence of the streams (line 18), a second, less clear-cut, interpretation of the will becomes a possibility. According to this more occult reading, Yeats and/or his inheritors are bound 'neither to Cause nor to State'. This interpretation is neither logical nor legalistic; it takes its force from the manner in which Yeats inscribes names – 'The people of Burke and of Grattan' – as if naming beneficiaries, rather than mere exemplaries. By this admittedly strong interpretation, the late eighteenth century inherits from the mid-twenti-eth. Here not only history but also temporary succession would be dissolved just as (in the physical domain) streams have been conceived as upward-rising and solid. The speaker conjures the dead so that they inherit from the living.

If this must remain a speculation, it is encouraged by some odd technical effects. The first dissonance in this passage occurs when 'State' (again with the initial capital already noted in 'Blood and the Moon') is made to rhyme. The capital initials dignify cause and state, or perhaps mock them. Certainly there is ambiguity, for those who will inherit are chosen because they are not bound to such loyalties. 'State' is particularly sullied by its close resemblance (two of three consonants repeated) to the word 'spat' with which it (however) imper-fectly rhymes. More of the same follows immediately. 'Spat' is duplicated in 'spat on' which is inflicted on Henry Grattan as a scarcely complimentary rhyme for his surname. These are lines of lofty, but unstable, contempt for the political experience. The very act of declaring Burke and Grattan to be unbound by the moils of enslavement or of tyrannic power contaminates them, as if the speaker himself spat. Moreover, the initial and discretionary capitals of Cause and State pair up with the inevitable initial capitals in the two surnames, so that the four words constitute an actual visible quartet of similitude whereas Burke and Grattan are ostensibly employed *in contrast* to exemplify freedom from the other two as loyalties. The effect is best illustrated by bringing lines 9 and 11 together:

> Bound neither to Cause nor to State
> The people of Burke and of Grattan

so that the replication of the surnames in the same positions (fourth and seventh words) becomes unmistakable.

Fortunately for Burke, he occupies a mid-line position where the dangers (as they must now seem) of rhyme are held at arm's length. (Available rhymes scarcely exceed lurk, murk, Turk and work, though there is also the perfect rhyme in burke, 'to murder by suffocation'.) His privileged obscurity in the poem is partly accomplished by the strange manner in which Yeats extends 'the pride of people' through 'pride like that of the morn ... or that of the fabulous horn' into the quite unexpected and puzzling

> Or that of the sudden shower
> When all streams are dry

Though I admire 'The Tower' greatly in its final fifteen lines (from which Samuel Beckett derived a play-title), I cannot say that the 'pride' passage just examined reveal Yeats at his rigorous best. How can a shower possess pride? Or, to make the question more sympathetic to a symbolist poet's activities, in what ways does the image of a sudden shower illuminate the idea of pride? If one reads down to line 24, it emerges that all these instantiations of 'pride like that ... or that of...' are stages of a landscaped progression towards the site of a lone swan's death, that is, the speaker's swan-song. The sudden shower 'when all streams are dry' is (I think) to be regarded as an instance of unforced benev-olence in Nature, like the liberality of those who give 'though free to refuse'. Others might think it an instance of the pathetic fallacy.

As with the less than eight rhyme sounds of Section I, so the imagery of admirable pride in Section III serves an integrated, but not always perceivable, purpose. Metonymically, the shower is the stream upon which the dying swan floats out (and the verb to 'float' already implies that the bird is dead or is an insensate thing like the boat upon which the dying king is conveyed in Tennyson's poem:

> So said he, and the barge with oar and sail
> Moved from the brink, like some full-breasted swan

> That, fluting a wild carol ere her death,
> Ruffles her pure cold plume, and takes the flood
> With swarthy webs. Long stood Sir Bedivere
> Revolving many memories, till the hull
> Looked one black dot against the verge of dawn,
> And on the mere the wailing died away.[50]

Whereas, in 'Morte d'Arthur', the boat becomes animated through association in simile with a swan, and this animation counters (and compensates for) the death of its human freight, 'The Tower' offers a tougher, less complete, and frankly contradictory perspective on human mortality. Perhaps distorting or echoing 'What the Thunder Said' in Eliot's *The Waste Land* (1922), the shower comes 'when all streams are dry', suggesting a condition at once extreme and paradoxical. If the shower revives the stream to the point where it expands into a swan-bearing 'long / Last reach', it is the terminality of the transformation which is emphasized.

The Yeatsian metonymy is a good deal less dignified than Tennyson's. Underscored by a rhyme which does Grattan little honour, it moves upon ladder-like streams, across spittle, dry river-beds, sudden rain, and the re-emergent final 'glittering stream' (line 23) where the adjective matches 'fading' two lines above. These discordant juxtapositions, marshalled into a snap-shot sublimity, connote *accidie*, or a sinful dryness of soul. This is often taken to be the seventh deadly sin of sloth, but from Dante onwards we associate it with desiccation of the spirit. Maybe Swift lies deeply concealed behind this aspect of the poem, for Yeats asks later in relation to his 'historical phase' – 'Is not Swift the human soul in that dryness, is not that his tragedy & his genius[?]'.[51] Swift will soon succeed Burke in Yeats's thought, as if to mimic the anti-sequentiality of the occult will in 'The Tower' Section III.

According to the first section, the speaker resigns himself to 'be content with argument and deal / In abstract things'. The poem thereafter seeks redemption from this premature surrender, and the path trodden is a *via dolorosa* intermittently. What might be sought in place of abstraction is a renewal of words. Language is traditionally associated with water (cf. fluency, torrents of abuse et cetera) and something really shocking happens when the great orator of eighteenth-century Ireland is embroiled in an imagery of spitting, of the most contemptuous misuse of the organ of speech. He who is spat on is treated with contempt, but he who spits is no better. *A Tale of a Tub* hints that speech is close to expectoration, voluntary or otherwise, and the central act of human culture might be reduced to meaningless oral projection. From this looming gutter or last ditch, the poem laboriously and grandly renews efforts to resurrect itself. Burke remains in reserve as the poet finally resolves to 'make my soul'.

Yeats's high reputation, and the high reputation which the Irish eighteenth-century inherited from him, deserves the corrective implied in the preceding paragraphs. 'The Tower' cannot be summarized through quotation of its striking first image or its de-tumescent resolution. Section II surveys the past, from the invading Normans who erected the tower to the poet's own careful constructions from the materials of local folklore. In stanzas 2 and 10 we meet Mrs French who, by virtue of her silver candlestick and mahogany table, we can assign to the eighteenth century, the 'one Irish century that escaped from darkness and confusion'.[52] In practice, Yeats found the details in Sir Jonah Barrington's self-serving memoirs.

The story is too familiar:

> A serving man, that could divine
> That most respected lady's every wish,
> Ran and with the garden shears
> Clipped an insolent farmer's ears
> And brought them in a little covered dish.

The eager-to-please servant is of course a victim of debased language, unable to distinguish the metaphorical use of words – I wish someone would clip his ears – from a crudely literal or mechanical implementation. It is fitting that the effect is to deprive another of the means of apprehending spoken language and this, together with the effectively deployed rhyme-scheme, makes the stanza. Yeats himself could be accused of aiding and abetting the effect by choosing the verb 'to divine' for the servant's violent understanding. It rhymes with the wine that has lubricated the conversation, the lady's wish, and the table's loud applause. The ears are uncannily assimilated to these dining-room furnishings by being conveyed to their patroness like devilled kidneys 'in a little covered dish'. Swift's ironic metaphor for Irish 'ascendancy' attitudes towards the poor – *cordon bleu* cannibalism – is nowhere to be heard, not Berkeley's description of Mrs French's class as 'vultures with iron bowels'. The second section of 'The Tower' can be reconciled with Yeats's proclaimed Protestant ascendancy only if we attend well to the parts he ceases to reach – the great cruelty. And the mutilation of an insolent – rather say, independent – neighbour of a lower economic class – stands in for an entire penal code of punishment and humiliation by which this retrospective ascendancy maintained itself, a code which provided for branding and disfigurement and which even contemplated castration as a means of disciplining a famously celibate priesthood. Even in her name, Mrs French neatly recalls the legislation of Louis XIV imitated to repress Catholicism in Ireland; Burke's local instance was the Catholic soldier flogged for devotion to his devotions.

There is no point in chastising Yeats for indulging a moral sense which retained few devotees outside the Kildare Street Club. Apart from other considerations, the passage quoted should be read in its structural context within 'The Tower' as a completed poem. Stanza 10 resolutely implicates the poet himself where figures from the past, historical and literary-fictional, are called up. Among these is 'Mrs French, / Gifted with so fine an ear'. Thus aligned with a sensitivity towards music and the aural arts (including poetry, oratory and the recitation of genealogical dignities), Mrs French is the very model of a modern major poet. The summer before 'The Tower' was finished Yeats had been preoccupied with two interrelated political schemes. In Capri, and in cahoots with Joseph Hone, he drew up plans for a National Unionist Party, decidedly anti-democratic in its objectives and openly indebted to Mussolini's experiments. Back home, he intrigued to have Henry Grattan's remains disinterred from Westminster Abbey for repatriation in a triumph of the recent Roman kind.[53] Dual monarchy, recognition of George V as King of Ireland, connivance with a few National Army officers salted these Italian recipes.

Burke and Frobenius lie wholly out of view. Grattan is temporarily useful because he was essentially a gestural, performative figure – not an original or substantial one. Fascism might elide this distinction but it still held some validity in Yeats's thought. Besides, the real consequences of summer 1925 were poetic, not anti-parliamentarian. The poetry, as we have seen, was deeply political even as Yeats gradually withdrew from the Senate and betook himself increasingly to the Mediterranean. In January 1931, 'The Seven Sages' returned to Grattan, Burke and the others, but the poem's title does not refer to these. On the contrary, sagacity is the prerogative of the seven old men who utter their childish boasts and gnomic diagnoses to the great satisfaction of Yeats's commenders. As with the rhyme of Grattan / spat on, little dignity is conferred upon Burke through the phrase 'great melody'. A sardonic tone runs through these ancestral loose associative virtues – 'mine saw Stella once'.

If there is a substantial point to 'The Seven Sages' it is the conclusive assertion that 'wisdom comes of beggary.' This is not a new doctrine in the Yeatsian credo. Beggars have long featured in the poems and plays, encouraged by the example of J.M. Synge's Wicklow tramps and tinkers. As with the refined listing of Irish dramatists for the Californian students in 1923, Yeats's beggars are invariably rural figures – no contamination from Brecht's *Threepenny Opera* (1928), despite the German's use of an eighteenth-century model and an epic theatrical style. In 1929 one reviewer of Brecht's own gramophone recordings of songs from the opera observed that the speaking or singing poet 'has the chance to reanimate deadened worlds' and noted a 'hint of mediaeval Bavaria' in Brecht's broadcasting voice. The wireless was a technical innovation Yeats would only take up years later, when the divergence between his cultural politics and the German's was unambiguously clear. As Yeats's editor, Daniel Albright, observes in this (lack of) connection, radio had the potential to restore poetry 'carnally, as Homer's audience perhaps felt the *Iliad*.[54] Yeats's attitude to Homer stresses a tragic dimension which really belongs to quite a different and later phase of Greek culture, not Attic but Hellenic. His primitivism led him away from the newly proclaimed Gaeltacht and the oral traditions of Kerry, West Cork, Connemara and Donegal immediately to hand; instead he chose to flit at Leo Frobenius, to invoke Nordic myths by way of William Morris, and to cultivate *race* as distinct from *language*.

VIII

As a child of the Irish nineteenth-century, Yeats inherited a rhetoric of personal invocation in which saints, historical personages, dates and folkloric names were regularly advanced as a species of argument in themselves. In his poetry, this legacy is best known through the strings of names which provide an inky chorus in 'September 1913' and 'Easter 1916'. The name of Edmund Burke instanced this tradition in a curiously rich but problematic way; Burke was himself a rhetorician who wrote, a speaker in ink; he also occupied a political position at once exposed and entrenched, and his views on the great issues – America, France, and (as a poor third, surely) Ireland – have been amply analysed for their paradoxical character.[55] In Yeats's refined practice of this inherited rhetoric, Burke becomes a highly nuanced but multivalent term.

This practice had been honed in the innumerable cabals, committees, covens and limited liability companies through which Yeats made his tortuous way from the twilight 1880s right up to the year of resumed World War. He possessed a ready political dexterity which none of his fellow poets – even the arch-ideologue, Ezra Pound – could rival. A lesser Irish poet, Austin Clarke, noted with jealous admiration how Yeats cunningly drew patriotic attention to himself during the Great War by invoking Nietzsche in public, then seen as the arch-priest of hunnish barbarism. Beyond *Beyond Good and Evil*'s author, there were even more *outré* names whom Yeats regularly, if not publicly, invoked – the denizens of *séance* and the Instructors through Automatic Writing.

The relation between Yeats's occultic and poetic languages has been considered principally in terms of their shared lexical elements – gyre, tincture, emanation et cetera – together, of course, with the greater themes of which these words are signs. Less attention has been given to the *grammar* of these languages or discourses of his, the occultic and poetic, and through a deeper understanding of this one might find the two are closely-related dialects of a central language. By grammar, I would more particularly mean the grammatical mood of conjugated verbs – for example, Yeats's increasing fondness for the imperative in his late poems, his use of the vocative ('O heart, O troubled heart') at a time when the demotic English language had virtually lost that faculty. I have argued elsewhere that the imperatives of Yeats's late poems should be considered as part of a literary style, which so early a commentator as George Orwell diagnosed as fascistic.[56]

Here, we concentrate briefly on the vocative. As to figures (of speech), it relates closely to personification; as to (literary) genres it relates especially to drama. These in turn are essential, constitutive components of the wider discourse of history especially for the romantic movement in literature and philosophy for which Burke was an ageing, well-shaved John the Baptist, a late precursor, a *vox clamens* with a wilderness as its message. One of the most

renowned instances of parliamentary invocation of persons comes in the accepted text of Henry Grattan's speech on Irish legislative independence (1782),
'Spirit of Swift, Spirit of Molyneux!' A cunning aspect of Yeats's historical
imagination recognized that Grattan had a low recognition factor outside Ireland;
Burke, by comparison, was international and intercontinental; he also possessed
that chameleon ability of appearing to be native Irish Catholic sometimes and
Anglo-Irish Whig on other occasions. Grattan one might, for a spell, plot to disinter from Westminister for reburial amid Green Legionaries at Saint Patrick's
cathedral. Burke was not to be disturbed in this fashion.

In any case, both Grattan and Burke are replaced by Swift as the dominant
eighteenth-century figure in Yeats's imagination. Part of this can be attributed
to the work of Joseph Hone, Yeats's sometime political secretary, who published a stylish and intelligent, if eccentric, life of the dean in 1934. A better
part of it can be attributed to allegedly dramatic qualities in Swift's life – his
relationship with women, his fear of madness, his bitter attachment to the place
of his birth. A play, 'The Words Upon the Window-pane' (1934), powerfully
dramatizes Swift's voice as it announces a veritable philosophy of history and
'the ruin to come'. Nothing so grand in Yeats's 1930s repertory employs Burke.

There are surviving lines from a private journal of March 1934 that indicate
how nearly Burke joined other historical names in Yeats's Blue Shirt ballads.
Employing the figure of growth-rings in the timber of felled trees, these trial
pieces indicate also how Yeats's symbol of the tree was coming to separate
itself from any conception of the state:

> A hollow heart hides in a withered oak tree
> Strength to the heart is the song that I sing
> Wisdom to the heart, & the whole state enlightened
> Beauty to the heart, then to ring after ring
> Swift, Grattan, Burke
> Began – finish the work.
> These fanatics etc.[57]

Growth-rings measure the age of trees in a way unimaginable in Burke's day.
In outwardly expanding succession, Swift and Grattan and Burke are seen
as stages in the growth of the tree which cannot *be* the state if they are also the
theoretical phases of its 'evolution'. The confusion of physical growth (getting
wider and older) with structural complexity is only one of the problems Yeats
wisely abandons, though – unwisely – he adopts instead an uncritical approval
of 'these fanatics'.

The lines quoted were written in March 1934. Two months earlier Yeats's
'Countess Cathleen' had been produced in German translation by SS-
Sturmbahnfuhrer Friedrich Bethge at the Frankfurter Schauspielhaus; two
months later Yeats was waiting impatiently for Hitler's Oberburgermeister in
Frankfurt to send him a Goethe-Plakette from the 1934 batch whose recipients

would also include Josef Goebbels.[58] During this period, the new Nazi authorities in Frankfurt's university decided to honour Leo Frobenius with an ethnographical Institute bearing his name.

Edmund Burke had a narrow squeak.

NOTES

1. Not for the first time, I draw on Fredric Jameson's brilliant analysis of the Weberian 'protestant ethic'; see Fredric Jameson, 'The Vanishing Mediator' in his *The Ideologies of Theory; Essays 1971–1986; vol 2, Syntax of History* (London: Routledge, 1988), pp.3–34. There is not room here to discuss a further and central aspect of Weber's theory peculiarly appropriate to the Irish transition from eighteenth-century dependent parliament to conditional neutrality in the late 1930s; that is, the aspect of charisma and the charismatic leader. Popularization of the term in certain contemporary religious contexts should not blind us to Weber's insight, nor should we ignore the way Yeats sets up O'Connell and Parnell as Bad Charisma and Good Charisma in his own account of the nineteenth century.

2. See Quentin Bell and Marcia Pointon, *William Dyce 1806–1864, A Critical Biography* (Oxford: Oxford University Press, 1979). Dyce's image of the Kent coast should be considered alongside Holman Hunt's 'Our English Shores' (1852), painted when invasion from France was once again feared. As the likely invader was a Napoleon (the nephew, subject of Marx's excoriation in 'The 18th Brumaire'), a parallel with Burke's period was consciously felt.

3. It is important to stress that the incidents listed are only visible and temporary symptoms of a condition perpetuating a less easily summarized violence. The list, one might add, could readily be extended into the twentieth century.

4. For a recent selection concentrating on this period see Ian Harris (ed.), *Edmund Burke; Pre-Revolutionary Writings* (Cambridge: Cambridge University Press, 1993).

5. W.B. Yeats to the Editor of the *Daily Express* (Dublin), 8 March 1895. Mary King has discussed a similar discourse in Oscar Wilde's writings of this period; see her 'Digging for Darwin: Bitter Wisdom in *The Picture of Dorian Gray* and "The Critic as Artist"', *Irish Studies Review*, 12, 3 (2004), pp.315–27.

6. Speaking at the Holborn Restaurant, London, 13 April 1898. See Yeats, *Collected Letters*, edited by John Kelly *et al.* (Oxford: Oxford University Press, 1986) vol.1, p.702.

7. On Sheridan's relationship with the United Irishmen, see Fintan O'Toole, *A Traitor's Kiss; The Life of Richard Brinsley Sheridan* (London: Granta, 1997).

8. W.B. Yeats to the Editor of the *Daily News* (London), 11 May 1904. See also related remarks reprinted in W.B. Yeats, *Explorations* (London: Macmillan, 1962), p.159.

9. The Intelex CD-ROM database reproduces the first three richly annotated volumes of Yeats's collected correspondence as published by Oxford University Press under the general editorship of John Kelly, together with typewritten and unannotated copies of the remaining (as yet unpublished) letters. All quotations from the letters are in practice taken from this searchable source, with the Access Number cited where appropriate.

10. 'A Letter to the Students of a Californian School', 1923. Access No.4243.

11. Idem. For a little noted commentary by a political philosopher, see Alisdair MacIntyre, 'Poetry as Political Philosophy: Notes on Burke and Yeats' in Vereen Bell and Laurence Lerner (eds.), *On Modern Poetry; Essays Presented to Donald Davie* (Nashville: Vanderbilt University Press, 1988) pp.145–157.

12. W.B. Yeats to Joseph Hone, 20 Nov. 1930. Access No.5409.

13. See W.J. Mc Cormack, *Blood Kindred; W.B. Yeats, the Life, the Death of Politics* (London: Pimlico, 2005), *passim*. I had hoped that this biography of the poet/politician would have been in print before the present article was completed.

14. Comments in the first volume of *Capital* suggest a close reading of the 'famous sophist and sychophant'. The best-known observation comes near the close, when Marx executes a Burkean rhetorical inversion at Burke's own expense. Calling the latter an 'execrable political cantmonger', he glosses this by pointing out that Burke thought ideas of the labouring poor just 'execrable political cant'. In the present context, the most relevant is Marx's first gibe – Burke 'goes so far as to make the following assertion, based on his practical observations as a farmer: that "in so small a platoon" as that of five farm labourers, all individual differences in the labour vanish, and that consequently any given five adult farm labourers taken together will do as much work in the same time as any

other five.' What is of interest here, in terms of Burke's influence on his detractors as much as his followers, is the recurrence of the 'platoon' imagery made famous in the *Reflections*, a point Marx misses. See Karl Marx, *Capital, a Critique of Political Economy* (trans. Ben Fowkes) (Harmondsworth: Penguin, 1976), esp. p.440. The platoon passage can be found in Burke's *Thoughts on Scarcity* (1795).

15. From 1987 to 1990, the journal *Eighteenth-Century Ireland/Iris an Dhá Chultúir* hosted an exchange between the present writer and James Kelly; see also W.J. Mc Cormack, *The Dublin Paper War 1786–1788; A Bibliographical and Critical Inquiry Including an Account of the Origins of Protestant Ascendancy and its 'Baptism' in 1792* (Dublin: Irish Academic Press, 1993).

16. See W.J. Mc Cormack, *From Burke to Beckett; Ascendancy, Tradition and Betrayal in Literary History* (Cork: Cork University Press, 1994), pp.312–19 for an extended account of *The Catholic Bulletin* and Yeats.

17. Burke enjoyed denouncing his enemies by ironically clothing them in the verbal garb of *their* enemies or opposites – thus the Dublin Castle cabal is described as a Directory (after the French); likewise the petty officials and guild-merchants who proclaim protestant ascendancy are Nabobs. The ironical use of the term 'bashaw' (deriving from Turkic) can be found in Henry Fielding, and in such semi-fictional titles as *Memoirs of the Bashaw Count Bonneva ... Written by Himself*, (1736). For an exact match of Fr Corcoran's phrase, cf the following from *The Dublin Morning Post* of 1792 – 'the ignorance and bigotry of those ascendancy Bashaws, who infest society...'

18. W.B. Ycats, *The King of the Great Clock Tower; Commentaries and Poems* (Churchtown: Cuala Press, 1934), pp.23–4. See Mc Cormack, *From Burke to Beckett*, pp.123–8 for further discussion which did not, however, adequately identify Yeats's debt to Burke for the comparison between Irish and French religious legislation; cf. 'Tracts Relating to Popery Laws' (chapter 3, part 1), in *Writings and speeches*, vol.ix, p.459.

19. The belief, or pretence, that reform and revolution at the beginning of the twentieth century would overturn a many-centuries-old oppression in Ireland, is a widespread phenomenon. In part it is constructed within a nineteenth-century historiography that sees the sequence of events from the Norman Invasion in the twelfth century through to the Act of Union as at one and the same time a unitary total subjugation and a cumulative one. Yeats's invocation of a mediaeval sleep, apparently prevalent up to the 1780s and then rudely interrupted, is not wholly dissimilar to the emotive title of Michael Davitt's *The Fall of Feudalism* (1904) which relates the collapse of a comparatively modern landlord system. Indeed, Yeats's phrase may be a glancing rebuke to Davitt, whose preferred solution to the land question was a form of comprehensive nationalization, and not the tenant-proprietorship now tacitly approved in Yeats's reply to the American students cited above.

20. Woods's comment was made in casual conversation when we were both attached to the University of Leeds in the 1980s, and is here recorded from memory. Confirmation, or modification, of his statement would be welcome.

21. For a still indispensable introduction to this topic, see Donald T. Torchiana, *W.B. Yeats & Georgian Ireland* (Evanstown: Northwestern University Press, 1966). See for recent commentary, Vereen M. Bell, *Yeats and the Logic of Formalism*. Columbia, London: University of Missouri Press, 2006. esp. pp.70–108 'History and Politics'.

22. Edmund Burke, *Works* (London: Bell, 1901), vol.2, p.357.

23. Clearly Burke was unfamiliar with cud-chewing cattle and the noises they make.

24. Luke Gibbons works the accepted metaphor to an unusual or, at least, undocumented end. 'Transplanted from the venerable oak of the ancient constitution in Britain onto the tree of liberty in late eighteenth-century Ireland, Burke's concept of tradition – in this case, the subaltern culture of his Gaelic, Catholic background – bore fruit in a grafting of a radical strain of Romanticism onto Enlightenment thought.' Gibbons, *Edmund Burke and Ireland* (Cambridge: Cambridge University Press, 2003), p.xiii.

25. W.B. Yeats to T. Sturge Moore, 17 April [1929]. Access No.5238. I have regularized a few details of punctuation for the sake of clarity. Later in the year, comment by Frobenius on 'Zimbabwe; Centre of Ancient Civilisation?' appeared in English (*African World*, 31 Aug. 1929). It is possible that the discussion between Yeats and Pound arose during the passage of his opinion. Yeats may also have heard of the German's theories through Wilfred Scawen Blunt (1840–1922).

26. The year 1922 marked a watershed in British anthropology, through the work of Malinowski and Radcliffe-Brown; thereafter Frobenius' chances of reinstatement (after the political prejudice attendant on the Great War) were seriously reduced. None of this would have swayed Yeats's opinion, merely underscoring his preference for non-British, unfashionable and academically unapproved authorities. I am grateful to Seamas O Siocháin, of the Department of Anthropology, National University of Ireland (Maynooth), for clarifying this chronology.

27. For example, *The Childhood of Man* (1909; 504pp) and *The Voice of Africa; being an Account of*

the Travels of the German Inner African Exploration Expedition ... 1910–1912 (2 vols, 1913). Yeats subsequently mentioned Frobenius in his diary for 9 August 1930 (see Yeats, *Explorations*, p.313) and in the 1937 (revised) edition of *A Vision* (London: Macmillan, 1962), pp.204, 258–61. I am grateful to Warwick Gould for his assistance in this regard. One relevant example of Frobenius' citation in support of the Nazi position can be found in Georg Ahlemann, *Das Heilige Nein*. Berlin: Esler, 1934 (see pp.291, 304.), relevant because Ahlemann was the father-in-law of the German diplomatic representative in Dublin from whom Yeats sought an 'objective' account of Nazism.

28. The sentence remarked on read: 'The great ages of universal history are not measured by the duration of their years, but by their style.' (Frobenius, *The Voice of Africa*, trans. Rudolf Blind [London, 1913], vol.1 pp.337–8.) See Torchiana, *W.B. Yeats and Georgian Ireland*, p.95.

29. W.B. Yeats to Margot Collis, 26 Nov. [1934]. Access No.6136. Much in this account is confused. North Africans are not usually termed Negroes, and the black peoples of Sudan, Ethiopia, et cetera are not usually termed North Africans. MacManus had been discussing his sexual problems with Yeats – both men suffered from impotence, for which the ex-soldier recommended the use of mirrors. It was in this reflective context that the African anecdotes arose. Frobenius' work related folk-wit and prowess in the larger sphere of the erotic, his research having been conducted in 'Inner Africa'. MacManus's post-war correspondence with Kathleen Raine makes explicit his virulently racist outlook.

30. See *On the Boiler* in W. B. Yeats, *Later Essays*, edited by W.H. O'Donnell (New York: Scribner's, 1994).

31. The phrase, though generally attributed to Burke in dictionaries of quotations, has never been established within the Burkean canon; see Mc Cormack, *Blood Kindred*.

32. See Chapter 7, 'Burke as Historian' in Michel Fuchs, *Edmund Burke, Ireland, and the Fashioning of Self* (Oxford: Voltaire Foundation, 1996) for a recent consideration of this topic.

33. See 'Tracts Relating to Popery Laws', *Writings and speeches*, vol.ix, p.479.

34. Gibbons, idem.

35. Daniel Albright (ed.), *W.B. Yeats, the Poems* (London: Dent, 1990), p.702. The references are to Yeats's posthumously collected *The Senate Speeches* (SS Y), *Uncollected Prose* vol.2 (UP II), *Explorations* (Ex).

36. The culmination of this imagery is the blasted tree, strangely restored to leafage, in the play 'Purgatory' (1938) and the pillar (or ossified trunk) in the final play 'The Death of Cuchulain' (1939).

37. See Yeats, *Explorations*, pp.313, 318; the Swift anecdote is incorporated by Joseph Hone and Mario Rossi in their *Swift; or The Egoist* (London: Gollancz, 1934), p.36.

38. This paragraph is only the roughest summary of a complex topic.

39. Janet Todd, 'Ascendancy: Lady Mount Cashell, Lady Moira, Mary Wollstonecraft and the Union Pamphlets', *Eighteenth-Century Ireland/Iris an Dá Chultúr*, 18 (2003), pp.98–117.

40. George Ogle, speaking on 16 Feb. 1786, quoted in W.J. Mc Cormack, 'Eighteenth-Century Ascendancy; Yeats and the Historians', *Eighteenth-Century Ireland/Iris an Dá Chultúr*, 4 (1989), p.165.

41. Todd, 'Ascendancy', p.101.

42. Angus Mitchell, '"An Irish Putumayo": Roger Casement's Humanitarian Relief Campaign Among the Connemara Islanders 1913–14', *Irish Economic and Social History* 31 (2004), pp.41–60.

43. I (largely) resist the possibility of applying a Lacanian term, 'the Imaginary' here, though there are certain features of the neo-psycho-analytical concept that appear relevant – the aspects of aggression and disappointment, for example.

44. For a stimulating if, for some, controversial discussion, see Reg Hindley, *The Death of the Irish Language; A Qualified Obituary* (London: Routledge, 1990).

45. Edmund Burke to Richard Burke Jr (20 March 1792), *Correspondence*, vol.vii, p.104.

46. *Writings and speeches*, vol.9, p.171.

47. W.B. Yeats to Harold Williams, 7 July [1933]. Access No.5912.

48. Edith M. Johnston, *History of the Irish Parliament 1692–1800* (Belfast: Ulster Historical Foundation, 2002), vol.3, pp.135–7.

49. For details of the source in Barrington's *Personal Sketches of His Own Times* (1827), see A. Norman Jeffares, *A New Commentary on the Poems of W.B. Yeats* (London: Macmillan, 1984), pp.217–18. The utensil employed was (according to Barrington) a snuff-box, though none of the few snuff-boxes I have seen were big enough to accommodate a pair of ears. An uncanny metonymy of nose and ear may have governed the author's preferred vessel.

50. Christopher Ricks (ed.), *The Poems of Tennyson* (London: Longmans, 1969), pp.596–7. Like Yeats, Tennyson is concerned with the absence of faith, authority and direction in the modern world; the well known poem, 'Morte d'Arthur', was equipped with a prologue and epilogue in which a fretful

Victorian conversation on these themes provides a framing justification for the Homeric law-di-daw.

51. W.B. Yeats to Mario Rossi, 9 February [1932]. Access No.5596.
52. W.B. Yeats, *Wheels and Butterflies* (London: Macmillan, 1934), p.7.
53. A suitably moderate version of this scheme was recalled in an article Yeats later published in the London-based *Spectator* (30 Jan. 1932), p.137. By this time, Grattan and Burke are being replaced in his thought by Swift. The theme of intellectual/political progeny develops in keeping with this replacement, and the repatriation of Grattan is described in 1932 as something Yeats might do if he were a young man.
54. Daniel Albright, *Beckett and Aesthetics* (Cambridge: Cambridge University Press, 2003), p.97. Referring to Brecht, Breton, Magritte, Marinetti and other 'continental' artists of the time, Albright (while concerned principally with the emergence of Beckett's late modernism) illustrates the relative isolation of Yeats (not to mention his thorough-going retrospection) in the late 1920s and 1930s. For Albright's work on Yeats, see his edition of the collected poems *W.B. Yeats, the Poems* (London: Dent, 1990).
55. In this context, Conor Cruise O'Brien's introduction to the Penguin edition of Burke's *Reflections* still rewards study.
56. See Mc Cormack, *Blood Kindred*.
57. See Torchiana, *W.B. Yeats and Georgian Ireland*, p.163.
58. For the general background, see Bettina Schültke, *Theater oder Propaganda? Die Städtischen Bühnen Frankfurt am Main 1933–1945* (Frankfurt: Waldemar Kramer, 1997), pp.125, 230, 417, 443 etc.

Select Bibliography

This bibliography is intended only as an aid to research. It is not comprehensive.

Arnold, M., *Letters, Speeches and Tracts on Irish Affairs* (London: Macmillan, 1881).

Barden, G., 'Discovering a Constitution', in T. Murphy and P. Twomey (eds), *Ireland's Evolving Constitution, 1937–97: Collected Essays* (Oxford: Hart Publications, 1998).

Barry, L., *Our Legacy from Burke: A survey of some of his Works; and a broad analysis from the literary aspect* (Cork: Cork University Press, 1952).

Beckett, J.C., 'Burke, Ireland and the Empire', in O. MacDonagh, W.F. Mandle and P. Travers (eds), *Irish Culture and Nationalism, 1750–1950* (London: Macmillan Press, 1983), pp.1–13.

Berman, D., 'The Irish Counter-enlightenment', in Richard Kearney (ed.), *The Irish Mind: Exploring Intellectual Traditions* (Dublin: Wolfhound Press, 1985).

Bourke, R.,'Liberty, Authority, and Trust in Burke's Idea of Empire', *Journal of the History of Ideas*, 61 (2000), pp.453–41.

Brooke, J., 'Burke in the 1760s', *South Atlantic Quarterly*, 58 (1959), pp.548–55.

Brown, M., 'J.C.D. Clark's *Reflections* and Edmund Burke's Irish Society', *Studies in Burke and His Time*, 20 (2005) (n.s.), pp.127–44.

Budd D. and R. Hines, *The Hist and Edmund Burke's Club: an anthology of the College Historical Society, the student debating society of Trinity College, Dublin, from its origins in Edmund Burke's Club 1747–1997* (Dublin: Lilliput Press, 1997).

Burke, H., *Riotous Performances: The Struggle for Hegemony in the Irish Theater, 1714–1784* (South Bend, IN: University of Notre Dame Press, 2003).

Burke, J., *Speeches of the Rt. Hon. Edmund Burke with Memoirs and Historical Introduction* (Dublin: Duffy, 1853).

Burke, P. *The public and domestic life of the Right Honourable Edmund Burke* (London: N. Cooke, 1854).

Chetwood Eustace, Rev. J., *An elergy to the memory of the Right Honourable Edmund Burke* (1798).

Clifford, B., *Edmund Burke and the United Irishmen: Their Relevance in Ireland Today* (Aubane: Aubane Historical Society, 1994).

Colum, P., 'An Irish constitutionalist and an Irish revolutionalist', *The Dublin Magazine*, 9 (1934) pp.57–67.

Conniff, J., 'Edmund Burke's Reflections on the Coming Revolution in Ireland', *Journal of the History of Ideas*, xlviii (1986), pp.37–59.

Connolly, C., 'Reflections on the Act of Union', in J. Whale (ed.), *Edmund Burke's Reflections on the Revolution in France: New Interdisciplinary Essays* (Manchester: Manchester University Press, 2000), pp.168–92.

Cullen, L.M., 'Burke, Ireland, and Revolution', *Eighteenth-Century Life*, 16 (1992), p.21.

——, 'Review of C.C. O'Brien, *The Great Melody: A Thematic Biography and Commented Anthology of Edmund Burke*', *Eighteenth-Century Ireland/Iris an dá chultúr*, 8 (1993a), pp.150–5.

——, 'The Blackwater Catholics and County Cork Society and Politics in the Eighteenth Century', in P. O'Flanagan and C.G. Buttimer (eds), *Cork History and Society: Interdisciplinary Essays on the History of an Irish County* (Dublin: Geography Publications, 1993b).

——, 'Burke's Irish views and writings', in I. Crowe, *Edmund Burke: His Life and Legacy* (Dublin: Four Courts Press, 1997).

Deane, S., 'Burke and the French Philosophes', *Studies in Burke and His Time*, 10 (1968–69), pp.1113–37.

——, 'Lord Acton and Edmund Burke', *Journal of the History of Ideas*, 33 (1972), pp.325–35.

——, 'An Example of Tradition', *Crane Bag*, 3 (1979), pp.373–9.

——, 'Edmund Burke and the Ideology of British liberalism', in R. Kearney (ed.), *The Irish Mind: Exploring Intellectual Traditions* (Dublin: Wolfhound Press, 1985a), pp.141–56.

——, *Celtic Revivals: Essays in Modern Irish Literature 1880–1980* (London: Faber, 1985b).

——, 'Swift and the Anglo-Irish intellect', *Eighteenth-Century Ireland/Iris an dá chultúr*, 1 (1987a), pp.9–22.

——, 'Irish National Character: 1700–1900', in T. Dunne (ed.), *The Writer as Witness: Literature as Historical Evidence* (Cork: Cork University Press, 1987b), pp.90–113.

——, *The French Revolution and Enlightenment in England 1789–1832* (Cambridge, MA: Harvard University Press, 1988).

——, Introduction to the 'Edmund Burke (1729–97)' entry in Deane (ed.), *Field Day Anthology of Irish Writing* (Derry: Field Day Publications, 1991).

——, 'Montesquieu and Burke', in B. Hayley and C. Murphy (eds), *Ireland and France – A Bountiful Friendship: Essays in Honour of Patrick Rafroidi*

(Gerrards Cross: Colin Smythe, 1992), pp.17–29.

——, *Strange Country: Modernity and Nationhood in Irish Writing since 1790* (Oxford: Clarendon Press, 1997).

——, 'Montesquieu and Burke', in G. Gargett and G. Sheridan (eds), *Ireland and the French Enlightenment, 1700–1800* (Houndmills: Macmillan Press Ltd., 1999).

——, 'Factions and Fictions: Burke, Colonialism and Revolution', *Bullán*, 4 (2000), pp.1–26.

——, 'Burke and Tocqueville: New Worlds, New Beings', in R. Savage Jr (ed.), *Ireland in the Century* (Dublin: Four Courts, 2003), pp.130–50 and *boundary 2* 31 (2004), pp.1–23.

——, 'Freedom Betrayed: Acton, Burke and Ireland', *Irish Review*, 30 (2003), pp.13–56.

——, *Foreign Affections: Essays on Edmund Burke* (Cork: Cork University Press, 2005).

Donlan, S.P., '"Beneficence Acting by a Rule": Edmund Burke on Law, History, and Manners', *Irish Jurist*, 36 (2001) (n.s.), pp.227–64.

——, '"Language is the Eye of Society": Edmund Burke on the Origins of the Polite and the Civil', *Eighteenth-Century Ireland/Iris an dá chultúr*, 18 (2003a), pp.80–97.

——, 'An Active Intelligent People: Edmund Burke's Scottish Enlightenment', *History-Scotland*, 3, 4 (2003b), pp.32–8.

——, 'Little Better than Cannibals: Property and Progress in Sir John Davies and Edmund Burke', *Northern Ireland Legal Quarterly*, 54 (2003c), pp.1–24.

——, '"A Very Mixed and Heterogeneous Mass": Edmund Burke and English Jurisprudence, 1757–62', *University of Limerick Law Review*, 4 (2003d), pp.79–88.

——, 'The Reformer?: Edmund Burke, "scorned loyalty, and rejected Allegiance"', *History-Ireland*, (2004), pp.21–25.

——, '"Our Barr does not Abound in General Erudition": Edmund Burke's Scottish Enlightenment', *Studies in Burke and his Times*, 20 (2005) (n.s.), pp.38–65.

Duddy, T., *A History of Irish Thought* (London: Routledge, 2002).

Eagleton, T., 'Aesthetics and Politics in Edmund Burke', in M. Kenneally (ed.), *Irish Literature and Culture* (Gerrards Cross: Colin Smythe 1992), pp.25–34.

——, *Heathcliff and the Great Hunger: Studies in Irish Culture* (London: Verso, 1995).

Fabricant, C., 'Colonial Sublimities and Sublimations: Swift, Burke, and Ireland', *English Literary History*, 72 (2005), pp.309–37.

Fuchs, M., *Edmund Burke, Ireland, and the Fashioning of Self* (Oxford: Voltaire Foundation, 1996).

Gaffney, C.C., Rev. J., 'Edmund Burke: his life and times', *Irish Ecclesiastical Record*, 9 (1872) pp.97–115, 10 (1873) pp.145–66.

Gibbons, L., 'Edmund Burke and our Present Discontents', *History-Ireland*, 5 (1997), pp.21–5.

——, *Edmund Burke and Ireland: Aesthetics, Politics, and the Colonial Sublime* (Cambridge: Cambridge University Press, 2003).

Gwynn, D., 'Dr Hussey and Edmund Burke', *Studies* 17 (1928) pp.529–46.

Hoffman, R.J.S., *Edmund Burke: New York Agent, with his Letters to the New York Assembly and Intimate Correspondence with Charles O'Hara* (Philadelphia: American Philosophical Society, 1956).

Keogh, D. '"Burke's Political Testament": Thomas Hussey and the Irish Directory', in R. English and J. Morrison Skelly (eds), *Ideas Matter: Essays in Honour of Conor Cruise O'Brien* (Dublin: Poolbeg, 1998), pp.211–30

Kiberd, D., 'Burke, Ireland and Revolution', in *Irish Classics* (London: Granta 2000), pp.203–20.

Lambert, E., 'Edmund Burke's Religion', *English Language Notes*, 32 (1994), p.19.

——, *Edmund Burke of Beaconsfield* (Newark: University of Delaware Press, 2003).

——, 'The Law, the Nun, and Edmund Burke', in I. Crowe, *An Imaginative Whig; Reaccessing the Life and Thought of Edmund Burke* (Columia, MO: University of Missouri Press, 2005).

Lecky, W.E.H., *A History of Ireland in the Eighteenth Century* (1892–96).

Lock, F.P., *Edmund Burke: Volume I, 1730–1784* (Oxford: Clarendon Press, 1998).

Love, W.D., 'Edmund Burke, Charles Vallancey and the Sebright Manuscripts', *Hermathena*, 95 (1961), p.21.

——, 'Charles O'Conor of Belanagare and Thomas Leland's 'Philosophical' History of Ireland', *Irish Historical Studies*, 13 (1962), p.1.

——, 'Edmund Burke and an Irish Historiographical Controversy', *History and Theory*, 2 (1962–63), p.180.

McCormack, W.J., 'Romantic Union: Burke, Ireland, and Wordsworth', *Éire-Ireland*, (1985), p.73.

——, *From Burke to Beckett: Ascendancy, Tradition and Betrayal in Literary History* (revised and enlarged edition of *Ascendancy and Tradition* [1985]) (Cork: Cork University Press, 1996).

——, 'Between Burke and the Union: Reflections on PRO: CO 904/2', in J. Whale (ed.), *Edmund Burke's Reflections on the Revolution in France: New Interdisciplinary Essays* (Manchester: Manchester University Press, 2000), pp.60–93.

McCormick, C. *Memoirs of the Right Honourable Edmund Burke; or, an impartial review of his private life, his public conduct, his speeches in Parliament, and the different productions of his pen …* (London: Printed by the author, 1797).

McDowell, R.B., 'Burke's Dualistic Vision in the *Tracts on the Popery Laws*', *Études Anglaises*, 34 (1981), p.180.

——, 'The Contexts of Edmund Burke's *Reformer'*, *Eighteenth-Century Ireland/Iris an dá chultúr*, 2 (1987), p.43.

—— (ed.), *The Writings and Speeches of Edmund Burke: Volume nine – The Revolutionary War, 1794–1797 and Ireland* (Oxford: Clarendon Press, 1990a – W.B. Todd, textual ed.; P. Langford, gen. ed.).

——, 'Edmund Burke's *Abridgement of English History'*, *Eighteenth-Century Ireland/Iris an dá chultúr*, 5 (1990b), p.45.

——, 'Did Burke write *The Reformer?'*, *Notes and Queries*, (1992), p.474.

——, 'Burke and Ireland', in D. Dickson, D. Keogh and K. Whelan (eds), *The United Irishmen: Republicanism, Radicalism and Rebellion* (Dublin, 1993).

——, 'Edmund Burke: The Divided Irishman', in *Contesting Ireland: Irish voices against England in the eighteenth century* (Dublin: Four Courts Press, 1999).

MacKnight, T., *History of the Life and Times of Edmund Burke*, 3 vols (London: Chapman and Hall, 1858–60).

MacSweeney, J.J., 'Edmund Burke', *Irish Ecclesiastical Record* (5th Series), 14 (1919) pp.231–41, 299–307.

Mahoney, T.H.D., 'Mr Burke's Imperial Mentality and the Proposed Irish Absentee Tax of 1773', *Canadian Historical Review*, 37 (1956), pp.158–66.

——, *Edmund Burke and Ireland* (Cambridge, MA: 1960).

Merriman, P.J., 'Edmund Burke and Ireland', *Journal of the Ivernian Society*, 2 (1910) pp.129–42.

Murphy, S., 'Burke and Lucas: An Authorship Problem Re-examined', *Eighteenth-Century Ireland/Iris an dá chultúr*, 1 (1986), pp.143–56.

O'Brien, C.C., 'Introduction' in *Reflections on the Revolution in France ...* (New York: Penguin Books, 1968).

——, *The Suspecting Glance: The T. S. Eliot Memorial Lectures Delivered at Eliot College in the University of Kent at Canterbury, November 1969* (London: Faber, 1972).

——, 'Introduction', to M. Arnold (ed.), *Irish Affairs: Edmund Burke* (London: Crescent Library Edition, 1988 – reprint of Arnold's *Letters, speeches and tracts on Irish affairs* [1881]).

——, *The Great Melody: A Thematic Biography and Commented Anthology of Edmund Burke* (London: Sinclair-Stevenson, 1992).

——, 'The Great Melody: Discordant Notes', *History-Ireland*, 1/2 (1993), pp.23–5.

——, *Edmund Burke* (London: Sinclair-Stevenson, 1997a – abridged version of *The Great melody* by Jim McCue).

——, '"Setting People on Thinking": Burke's Legacy in the Debate on Irish Affairs', in I. Crowe, *Edmund Burke: His Life and Legacy* (Dublin: Four Courts Press, 1997b – adapted from the 'Introduction' to the Arnold reprint).

O'Brien, W., *Edmund Burke as an Irishman* (Dublin, 1926 [2nd edn]).

O'Connell, B., 'The Rt. Hon. Edmund Burke (1729–97): A Basis for a

Pedigree', *Journal of the Cork Historical and Archaeological Society*, 60 (1955), p.69.

——, 'The Rt. Hon. Edmund Burke (1729–97): A Basis for a Pedigree (Part II)', *Journal of the Cork Historical and Archaeological Society*, 61 (1956), p.115.

——, 'Edmund Burke: Gaps in the Family Record', *Studies in Burke and His Time*, 9, 3 (1968), p.946.

O'Donnell, K., 'The Image of a Relationship in Blood: *Párliament na mBan* and Burke's Jacobite Politics', *Eighteenth-Century Ireland/Iris an dá chultúr*, 15 (2000), p.98.

——, '"Whether the White People like it or not": Edmund Burke's Speeches on India – *Caoineadh's Cáinte*', *Éire–Ireland*, (2002), pp.187–206.

O'Flaherty, E., 'Review of C.C. O'Brien, *The Great Melody*', *Irish Historical Studies*, 30 (1996), p.134.

——, 'Burke and the Catholic Question', *Eighteenth-Century Ireland/Iris an dá chultúr*, 12 (1997), p.7.

O'Hanlon, T. 'The Catholic instincts of Edmund Burke', *Irish Ecclesiastical Record* (5th Series), 8 (1916) pp.401–9.

Prior, J. *Memoir of the Life and Character of Edmund Burke* (London: Baldwin, Cradock and Joy, 1824).

Reynolds, L., 'Edmund Burke: A Voice Crying in the Wilderness', in O. Kamesu and M. Sekine (eds), *Irish Writers and Politics* (Gerrards Cross: Colin Smythe, 1989), pp.47–61.

Robertson, J.B., *Lectures on the Life, Writings, and Times of Edmund Burke* (London: John Philip, 1869).

Robinson, N., *Edmund Burke: A Life in Caricature* (New Haven: Yale University Press, 1996).

Samuels, A.P.I., *The Early Life Correspondence and Writings of the Rt. Hon. Edmund Burke: with a transcript of the minute book of the debating 'Club' founded by him in the Trinity College, Dublin* (with an introduction and supplementary chapters on Burke's contributions to the *Reformer* and his part in the Lucas controversy, by the Rt. Hon. Arthur Warren Samuels) (Cambridge: Cambridge University Press, 1923).

Weston, Jr, J.C., 'Edmund Burke's Irish History: A Hypothesis', *Proceedings of the Modern Language*, 77 (1962), p.397.

[?], 'The life and times of Edmund Burke', *Dublin University Magazine*, 55 (1860) pp.116–28, 275–97.

Index